ADVANCE PRAISE

"In *The Decency Wars*, Frederick Lane has written a fascinating and well-researched history of the battle over media decency in American culture. It is a provocative and compelling contribution to the essential debate over the proper balance between personal responsibility and government regulation. Lane's book is essential reading for anyone concerned about the growing role of religious fundamentalism in American politics."
> —Sharon Lamb, author of *Packaging Girlhood: Rescuing Our Daughters from Marketers' Schemes* and professor of psychology, Saint Michael's College

"This is a book that badly needed to be written; and America needs to read. It does an excellent job of demonstrating how a remarkably small number of people with an obsession can shape government policy in contravention of both fundamental notions of individual liberty and prevailing culture. It is well researched, well written, and fascinating. I was particularly amused reading about the ongoing controversy about sex education, which everyone knows is the only subject taught in public schools about which the students begin the course more familiar with the subject matter than the teachers. And don't miss the last chapter, where 'decency' is properly analyzed. Great reading!"
> —Clyde DeWitt, attorney, thirty-five-year veteran of defending adult entertainment, and legal columnist for *Adult Video News* (trade publication of the adult entertainment industry) since 1990

"The best and most detailed revelations about how the corporate-generated media spectacle is symbiotically allied with both the prurient sell and with the purveyors of 'family friendly' moral indignation."
> —Jay A. Gertzman, author of *Bookleggers and Smuthounds: The Trade in Erotica, 1920–1940*

"Frederick Lane's book starts with a 'wardrobe malfunction' but that is only the beginning. In a book about a controversial topic such as 'decency,' readers expect to get both sides of the story. But Lane gives us much more, presenting multiple and often surprising perspectives, a rich backstory, and his own incisive analysis. Lane has written a rich and important book."
> —David T. Z. Mindich, author of *Tuned Out: Why Americans Under 40 Don't Follow the News* and professor and chair, Journalism and Mass Communication, Saint Michael's College

"*The Decency Wars* is a balanced, meticulously researched, and frightening book detailing the insidious erosion of free expression in America. Frederick Lane has made a major contribution toward understanding the true agenda of the religious conservatives who are gaining power within our government at a chilling pace."
> —Barbara Nitke, author of *Kiss of Fire: A Romantic View of Sadomasochism* and plaintiff with the National Coalition for Sexual Freedom in *Nitke v. Gonzalez* against the Communications Decency Act

"*The Decency Wars* will fascinate anyone who is seeking to understand how a small minority has politicized sexuality in order to control what Americans see, read, and hear, despite the protections of the First Amendment."
> —Jeff Haig, Department of Sociology, University of Vermont

the decency wars

the campaign to
CLEANSE
american culture

frederick s. lane

Prometheus Books
59 John Glenn Drive
Amherst, New York 14228—2197

Published 2006 by Prometheus Books

Inquiries should be addressed to
Prometheus Books
59 John Glenn Drive
Amherst, New York 14228–2197
VOICE: 716–691–0133, ext. 207
FAX: 716–564–2711
WWW.PROMETHEUSBOOKS.COM

10 09 08 07 06   5 4 3 2 1

Library of Congress Cataloging-in-Publication Data

Lane, Frederick S., 1942–
    The decency wars : the campaign to cleanse American culture / by Frederick S. Lane.
        p. cm.
    Includes bibliographical references and index.
    ISBN 13: 978–1–59102–427–9 (hardcover : alk. paper)
    ISBN 10: 1–59102–427–7 (hardcover : alk. paper)
    1. United States—Social policy. 2. United States—Politics and government—
1945–1989. 3. United States—Politics and government—1918– . 4. Conservatism—
United States. 5. United States—Moral conditions. 6. Culture conflict—United States.
7. Social values—United States. 8. Social control—United States. 9. Sexual ethics—
United States. 10. Deviant behavior—United States. I. Title.

HN59.2.L37 2006
305.0973'09045—dc22

                                                                                        2006012125

Printed in the United States of America on acid-free paper

To my beloved Amy,
with whom I am unsundered

Contents

Acknowledgments

> Writing is a solitary occupation. Family, friends, and society
> are the natural enemies of the writer.
> He must be alone, uninterrupted, and slightly savage if he
> is to sustain and complete an undertaking.
> —Jessamyn West, 1902–1984

Throughout the past year, I have been tremendously fortunate to be surrounded by family and friends who not only demonstrated (or at least credibly feigned) interest in this project but who also tolerated with remarkable grace the writing process itself. My love and heartfelt thanks to my sons, Peter (eleven) and Ben (thirteen) Lane, and to my companion and partner, Amy Werbel. This book is vastly better for her thoughtful suggestions, thorough critique, and steadfast support.

It has been a particular pleasure over the past year to work with Linda Greenspan Regan at Prometheus Books. From the start, Linda has been an enthusiastic supporter of this project and, even more important, a superb editor. I am grateful for the time and care that she took in reviewing my text; that is an increasingly rare commodity in publishing these days, and I have learned a lot while working with her. Although I am just beginning to work with other members of the Prometheus community, it is clear that they bring a dedication to publishing and writers that is very gratifying.

This book, like most, has benefited from comments, suggestions, ideas, and

9

conversations that I've had with myriad people over the past several months. The following is a partial list of the people whose interest and helpfulness are woven into these pages: Warren and Anne Lane; Jonathan Lane and Alison Quinn; Elizabeth Lane and Jeremy Murdock; Kate Lane; Harvey and Glenda Werbel; Gale Golden (with a special nod for referring me to Prometheus); Professor Jeff Haig; Professor Will Mentor; Professor Bret Findlay; Professor Lance Richbourg; Professor Gregg Blasdel and Jennifer Koch; Professor Sharon Lamb and Paul Orgel; Anthony Lewis and the Honorable Margaret Marshall; Eliza Lewis and Neil Miller; Dr. Marc and Dana Lim vanderHeyden; Adam Snyder and Sue Buckingham; Professor Philip Baruth; Professor Roger Cooke; Laurel Neme; Josh Brown and Zoe Richards; Fritz and Maria Sentfleber; Adam Bluestein; Brian Goetz; Amy Johnston; Meg Jones; Tifani Niehaus; Jim Lantz; Cat Lubin; Ken Picard; Cathy Resmer; Jim Lowder; Chris McVeigh; Liana H. Zhou, head of the library, Kinsey Institute for Research in Sex, Gender, and Reproduction; Professor Haven Hawley; Professor Jay Gertzman; Carlos Monroy at *Genre*; and Seth Zimmerman.

One of the real pleasures of this project was the opportunity to speak to some fascinating people with personal knowledge of many of the recent decency battles. My thanks to the following individuals for taking the time to talk with me and share their experience and insights: Tommy Smothers, Bob Peters, Paul Weyrich, Emily Tarradash, Bob Kunst, Nicholas Johnson, and Scott Adams.

This is the first book I've written that has included illustrations, which has added an interesting new dimension to the writing process. Again, I have been very fortunate to have the help and encouragement of a number of different people. At the usual exchange rate (one picture for a thousand words), these people have collectively helped to make this book at least one-third better. My thanks to: Jordan S. Douglas, for his trips around Vermont to fill the eclectic photo requests I handed him; Karen Pike, for her lovely photos of a Vermont civil union; Heide J. Schaffner at the Associated Press, for her patient and relentless searches for just the right photo, and for her enthusiasm about this project in general; Edward Wirth, National Park Service, for his help in obtaining a copy of Thomas Edison's 1896 short film *The Kiss*; Dorinda Hartmann, Wisconsin Center for Film and Television Research, for tracking down the evocative photo of Faye Emerson; Melanie Clark, *Broadcasting & Cable*, and Mike Henry, University of Maryland, for their help in obtaining various broadcast-related images; and Tony Lovett and Jesse Dena, *Adult Video News*, for putting together a group photo of mobile devices capable of storing and viewing content.

I would like to offer a special acknowledgment to William Crowe and

Becky Schulte at the Spencer Research Library at Kansas University for their willingness to offer me a grant to travel to Kansas to use their materials. The time needed to make the trip to Kansas from Vermont never quite materialized, but I hope to have the opportunity to explore their resources for a future project. Thanks also to Laird Wilcox for establishing the Wilcox Collection on the Christian Right at the Spencer Research Library, and for underwriting the travel grants offered by the institution. Such support is invaluable to researchers and is much appreciated.

Lastly, I believe that environment plays an important role in any creative project. I've been fortunate to have the chance to write this book in a number of different locations, some of which provided much-needed social interaction and caffeine replacement, and others that provided both intellectual and architectural inspiration. My thanks to Jeannie Vento and Jessica Workman, the owners of Speeder & Earl's (and Jeannie's husband, Arthur) for their year-long support; to Carrie and Mark McKillop, the owners of Muddy Waters; and to the staffs at both, for their interest and thoughtful questions.

It was a particular privilege to spend several days with Amy working in Cambridge at Harvard's Widener Library, with its seemingly endless resources and pin-drop silence. Much of this book was also written at the Durick Library at St. Michael's College in Colchester, Vermont. I would like to extend my thanks to the staff there for their assistance in obtaining numerous books through interlibrary loan.

Finally, a few words on hardware and software. Much of my writing, at one level or another, is about the interplay between technology and society, and it is interesting to see how changes in technology affect the process of writing. The most significant development is in the amount of research material that is available on the Internet. This project was vastly easier due to the fact that over a century's worth of newspapers can be accessed anywhere there is an Internet connection. (It's a remarkable thing, really, to be sitting in a coffeehouse and viewing actual copies of newspaper articles from the 1870s.) And although the best-known media outlets are the first ones online, they are rapidly being joined by a nearly infinite variety of other resources, many of them in the category of primary sources. As usual, a tip of the hat to Google for its phenomenal search capabilities; to its subsidiary site, Google News, for breaking events; and to Gmail for its organizational capabilities and vast capacity. I also benefited from the resources of the online library Highbeam .com, and the archives maintained by ProQuest and Loislaw. On the software end, my stubborn resistance to giving up WordPerfect continues (version 12 and still counting); I have, however, abandoned Netscape for Firefox and have happily moved from Adelphia's PowerLink to a new fiber-optic service operated by Burlington Telecom. And every month, the database storage program InfoSelect proves more and more valuable (fifteen thousand articles and counting), particularly in helping me to see connections between seemingly disparate events or people. With each project, my respect for all those authors who scratched out books in longhand, or pounded away on an old Underwood, continues to grow.

A Few Words on Terminology

And the LORD God called unto Adam, and said unto him,
Where art thou?
And he said, I heard thy voice in the garden, and I was
afraid, because I was naked; and I hid myself.
—Genesis 3:9–10

GENESIS

The idea for this book predates its opening scene. Well before the startling
conclusion of the 2004 Super Bowl halftime show, it was abundantly clear
that a "decency war" had been well under way in this country. The names for
this phenomenon—"the culture wars," "moral values," and so on—may
change, but the core issue is clear: there is an ongoing struggle over the values
that guide our daily lives and the course of this nation. As I watched the furor
unfold following the Janet Jackson/Justin Timberlake incident (the infamous
end of the 2004 Super Bowl halftime show, when Timberlake ripped off part of
Jackson's costume and revealed her right breast), I wanted to learn more about
the roots of the conflict and to better understand the effects that the decency
wars have on our politics and our policies.

The central challenge in studying the decency wars is determining what is
in fact "decent." A quick review of the standard definitions turns up a variety

of meanings, most associated with a sense of propriety, virtue, and sexual modesty (although a common subsidiary meaning is "adequate," as in a "decent income"). The inverse of decent—"indecent"—is no more specifically defined: "not in keeping with accepted standards of what is right or proper in polite society" or "offending against sexual mores in conduct or appearance."

Clearly, much of the decency wars has to do with individual or cultural expectations of proper behavior. That makes "decency" a particularly slippery concept. We learn appropriate behavior from a bewildering array of sources, including parents, family, neighborhood, community, religion, media, custom, law. There is typically some overlap in standards among the various sources, but not infrequently there is conflict as well. In a steadily growing, determinedly pluralist nation like the United States, it should hardly be surprising that there is little unanimity on such a vague concept as "decency."

In the end, "decency" is little more than a vague sense of "appropriateness" in a given time, place, and group. That does not by any means make it a useless or unworthy concept, but it is a thin foundation for sweeping cultural pronouncements. There are simply too many possible permutations of "decency" or "appropriateness" for any one group to claim a preeminent understanding of the concept, let alone to claim sufficient moral authority to impose that understanding on everyone else.

JUDGES

The vagueness of the concept of "decency," however, has not stopped various groups and individuals from trying to incorporate it into our state and federal laws. The most common examples (detailed in various parts of this book) are the efforts by some federal legislators (most notably Senator Jesse Helms [R-NC]) to criminalize various types of "indecent" speech. Without exception, those efforts have been struck down by the federal courts on the grounds that bans on mere indecency are an unconstitutional restriction of free speech under the First Amendment.

The courts have based their decisions on the distinction between the concepts of "indecency" and "obscenity." For the better part of a half century, the United States Supreme Court has made it clear that any speech (which includes movies, music, photography, etc.) that is considered obscene is *not* entitled to protection under the First Amendment. The current test for determining whether a work of art is obscene was set out by the Supreme Court in *Miller v. California*, 413 U.S. 15 (1973). The Court ruled that in order for a work to be found obscene: (1) the average person, applying contemporary community standards, must find that the work, taken as a whole, appeals to the prurient interest; (2) the work must depict or describe, in a patently offensive way, "sexual conduct" as that term is specifically defined by applicable state law; and (3) the work, taken as a whole, must lack serious literary, artistic, political, or scientific value.

Clearly, a work of art that is not legally obscene can still be indecent, that is, not appropriate for a given place and time. It would be difficult to find a judge or jury in this country that would conclude that *Playboy* magazine is obscene under the *Miller* test, but it would not be difficult to find a fairly large number of people who would describe it as indecent. Again, time and place are a factor; most people in the United States would agree that it is indecent to flip through the magazine in a public space, but fewer would object to an adult reading the magazine in private. The problem, as most courts have observed, is that the term "indecent" (and by extension, "decent") is too vague to offer a realistic and predictable guide for conduct, particularly when the consequences of violating an "indecency" statute include a possible prison sentence.

REVELATION

There is a tendency to lump most conservatives together, but as my research progressed, it became increasingly clear that there is in American conservatism a trinity: the neoconservatives, committed primarily to the defeat of communism and the projection of American influence overseas; the economic conservatives, committed to the exaltation of Adam Smith (ca. 1723–1790) and a quasi-libertarian view of government; and the religious conservatives, committed to the cleansing of American society, primarily through the imposition of their moral code on the rest of the nation.

None of these three divisions of conservatism is monolithic; far from it. Religious conservatives in particular are a roiling hodge-podge of theologies and sects, each with its own particular view of decency, governmental authority, and religious doctrine. Not one page of this book is intended to suggest that there is unanimity among the faithful; not all evangelicals agree with fundamentalists, nor are Baptists identical to Neopentacostals. The myriad permutations of American religious belief, and Protestantism in particular, are fascinating in their diversity.

From a historical and political perspective, however, it is both fair and useful to identify a movement that has waxed and waned over the last century and a half under the banner of "religious conservatism." It is a movement that has typically been composed, to varying degrees, of the more conservative members of various American religious faiths, including Catholicism, Protestantism, and Judaism. With the exception of the brief period of Catholic preeminence in the decency wars in the 1930s, the bulk of this book addresses the social and political implications of the Protestant variant of the religious conservative movement. Some may chafe at being swept up into the same dustpan of history, but to the limited extent that religious conservatives have experienced political success, it is because they have managed to sell the idea of masked differences and monolithic political power to both the media and Capitol Hill. Truly, the variations among Protestant religious groups and conservative organizations fade in importance when the leaders purposely gather under a single banner (see the discussion of the Arlington Group in the conclusion of this book) to fight together on a particular issue, such as their opposition to gay marriage.

The other revelation that resulted from this work is in fact just how little the religious conservative movement has gotten for its three decades of vibrant activism. Having slogged through snow and bitter temperatures myself to hand out candidate brochures, ring doorbells, and get signatures on electoral petitions, I am empathetic to religious conservatives who question the results of their work and the commitment of their erstwhile allies.

Some may argue perfidy, and there may be some truth to that argument. It can be said that religious conservatives have been victimized by a "con" game run by the other two-thirds of American conservatism, the neocons and the economic conservatives. Repeatedly, religious conservatives are seduced by candidates promising a more "decent" America. Those same candidates, however, know full well that both public opinion and the Constitution prevent the adoption of much, if not most, of the religious conservative agenda.

But the uproar and confusion associated with the decency wars is useful cover for other aspects of the conservative policy agenda; it helps explain, for instance, how the most powerful nation on earth, in the midst of war, under the threat of terrorist attack, with a sputtering economy, failing infrastructure, underfunded education, and inadequate healthcare, can spend so much time obsessed with a single-second glimpse of one woman's exposed breast.

The tragedy is not that millions of people saw a brief flash of nudity; the tragedy is that we have allowed a debate about one type of "decency"—sexual mores—to distract us from what really makes this country decent: its commitment to human rights, its living example as a proud and functioning democracy, its commitment to the well-being of all its citizens, its early leadership in environmentalism. This is the story of how that happened.

Prologue

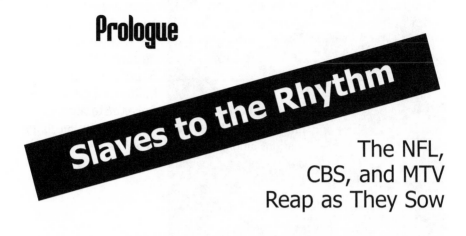

Slaves to the Rhythm

The NFL, CBS, and MTV Reap as They Sow

> We were shocked, to say the least. We immediately looked at the tape and tried to uncover what happened.
> —Van Toffler, president of MTV[1]

Janet Jackson was not the first member of her family to cause a stir during a Super Bowl halftime show. That honor goes to her brother Michael, who was persuaded in late 1992 by NBC to perform at Super Bowl XXVII in a show called "Heal the World." National Football League commissioner Paul Tagliabue said at the time that it was "a unique opportunity for both the NFL and Michael Jackson to send a message of hope and encouragement to people around the world, including the citizens of the Los Angeles area, where the game will be played."[2]

But—surprise—things did not go exactly as planned. Jackson was supposed to remove his sunglasses as the signal to start the music, but instead, for two long minutes, he stood motionless on the darkened stage. Michael T. Fiur, who worked on the show for Radio City Productions, described the scene in the control truck: "He just stood there, and our director was in the truck screaming at Michael, 'Take off your glasses!' which was the signal to begin the music. We learned that year to never allow for a break in pre-recorded tracks."[3]

Once the show started, however, Jackson's statuelike silence didn't look so bad. While sharing the stage with several thousand children, the "King of Pop" performed a series of sexually suggestive dance moves and on a few occasions

Janet Jackson and Justin Timberlake at the conclusion of their performance at the Super Bowl XXXVIII halftime show at Reliant Stadium in Houston, on February 1, 2004. (AP photo/ David Phillip)

blatantly grabbed at his crotch. A month later, when asked by talk show host Oprah Winfrey why he always grabbed his crotch, a giggling Jackson replied: "It happens subliminally. . . . It's the music that compels me to do it. I'm a slave to the rhythm."[4]

He's not the only one. The National Football League (NFL) and the broadcast networks are "slaves to rhythms" as well: the steady drumbeats of Nielsen ratings and advertising dollars. When ACNielsen released its findings on the ratings for the 1992 Super Bowl in mid-February, the company reported that 133.4 million people watched Michael Jackson's halftime concert (5 million more than watched the game itself).[5] On the basis of bodies-in-Barcaloungers alone, both the NFL and NBC declared the Jackson halftime show a rousing success, and from that point on, every broadcast network and halftime production company engaged in a game of musical celebrity one-upsmanship: the Judd sisters in 1994 (NBC), Diana Ross in 1996 (NBC), James Brown and ZZ Top in 1997 (Fox), Boyz II Men, Smokey Robinson, the Temptations, and the Four Tops in 1998 (NBC), Aerosmith and *NSYNC in 2001 (CBS), U2 in 2002 (Fox), and eventually, of course, Janet Jackson and Justin Timberlake in 2004 (CBS). Over the course of three decades, the halftime show had evolved into a blend of music video and infomercial fueled by the synergy of corporate cross-promotion.

The pressure each year to create a twelve-minute halftime show capable of keeping millions of television viewers from wandering off to the kitchen, bathroom, workshop, and so on—or at least to bring them back fairly quickly—is intensified by the implicit demand by fickle viewers for something bigger and better than the year before. A fascinating collection of social and economic forces drove the Super Bowl halftime show, once the province of college marching bands, swiftly and inexorably toward the Jackson/Timberlake "flash"-dance in Houston's Reliant Stadium.

SUPER BOWL SUNDAY: (CORPORATE) CHRISTMAS ALL OVER AGAIN

By any reasonable measure, the National Football League's championship game, the Super Bowl, has become the leading secular holiday in the United States. Each year, nearly one-third of the US population watches some or all of the game (just under ninety million in 2004)[6] and 26 percent of all viewers attend or host a party with six or more people; in fact, the *average* number of people at a Super Bowl party is seventeen.[7]

All those people, of course, are not merely watching the game. In their own inimitable fashion, Americans have turned Super Bowl Sunday into a festival of capitalism of Caligulan proportions:

- As a motivator for consumer purchases in certain categories—particularly loungers, couches, high-end electronics, grills, team logo clothing, and the all-important minifridges—the Super Bowl is second only to Santa Claus (before the 2004 Super Bowl, Americans bought an estimated 1.5 million new TVs, many of which were in the high-end HDTV category).[8]
- According to the American Institute of Food Distribution, Super Bowl Sunday is second only to Thanksgiving in terms of the amount of food consumed in a single day.[9]
- The Snack Food Association claims that during the game (roughly four hours), Americans eat between thirty and thirty-five million pounds of

snacks, including twelve million pounds of chips and four million pounds each of popcorn, pretzels, and nuts.[10]

- The sale of antacids rises by 20 percent on the Monday after the Super Bowl, and 6 percent of the US workforce call in sick.[11]

In the midst of all the hoopla and chip-dipping, it is easy to lose sight of the fact that at the center of it all is a football game, supposedly between the two best professional teams in the country. But ironically, the game itself is often considered to be something less than "super"; the Super Bowl has a well-deserved reputation for quickly decided blowouts and boring defensive struggles.

But football fans had little reason to complain about the 2004 Super Bowl—it was an exciting game that offered ample material for analysis and Monday-morning quarterbacking. On the morning of February 2, 2004, the lead story on the sports pages across the United States should have been that the New England Patriots, still fondly known to their long-suffering fans as the "Patsies," defeated a resilient Carolina Panther team 32–29, on a dramatic, last-second field goal by Adam Vinatieri (his second of the postseason). In virtually every major media outlet except Boston, however, the dominant story on Monday morning was not gridiron glory but instead the startling conclusion of the game's halftime show.

How the Tail Came to Wag the Dog

The whole concept of a halftime show is a uniquely American addition to a uniquely American game. In the rest of the world, where the term "football" refers to the "Beautiful Game" that we stubbornly insist on calling "soccer," there's no tradition of midgame entertainment (apart from drunken chants and occasional brawls in the stands). While other major US sports have adopted their own versions of fan entertainment, ranging from the overtly sexual (LA's Laker Girls) to the simply silly (Boston's Wally the Green Monster), only in American football has the game's intermission taken on an identity of its own.

When the National Football Conference and the American Football League agreed to play their first championship game in 1967 (the game did not actually become known as the Super Bowl until 1969), they continued the long-standing collegiate tradition of having marching bands entertain the crowd. The first championship halftime show featured squads from the universities of Arizona and Michigan. Over the next decade, shows featured marching units from Grambling State University (1968, 1975), Florida A&M

(1969, 1971), the US Marine Corps Drill Team (1972), the University of Michigan (1973), and the University of Texas (1974).

In 1977 the NFL and NBC initiated the corporate feeding frenzy by hiring Walt Disney Company to produce the halftime show for Super Bowl XI. The first six of the Mouse's stints in charge of the midgame entertainment were relatively unremarkable. But in 1991, to help the NFL celebrate its twenty-fifth anniversary, Disney asked the teen pop sensation New Kids on the Block to perform with two thousand children in a show titled "A Small World Salute to 25 Years of the Super Bowl."[12]

At first blush, inviting New Kids on the Block to their Super Bowl shindig seemed an odd choice for Disney and the NFL; the mostly female preteens and teens swooning over the New Kids on the Block were hardly the NFL's target audience. But by 1991, the Super Bowl was no longer just about post patterns and naked bootlegs. The far more important terms were "corporate synergy" and "cross-promotion." For Disney, showcasing the New Kids on the Block was a chance to play to the company's target audience—the teens who had purchased $73.8 million in New Kids concert tickets (making the band the top-grossing act of 1990).[13] Those concert tickets were merely a fraction of the $1 *billion* spent that same year on New Kids music, paraphernalia, and pay-per-view broadcasts (the New Kids marketed two concerts on the Disney Channel).[14] Like so many other kid-oriented companies, Disney was discovering just how powerful teen consumers could be; in January 1991, economists estimated that children either influenced or directly controlled $50 billion in spending each year.[15] And ABC, the network broadcasting the 1991 Super Bowl, was in on the fun as well. It was gearing up to launch a *New Kids on the Block* animated show during the fall season. Mercifully short-lived, the New Kids Saturday morning show joined the more than seventy toy- and brand-based shows that aired during the decade following the Reagan administration's deregulation of children's television.[16]

How Fox Network Is Really Responsible for the 2004 Halftime Show

There was one final reason why the selection of New Kids on the Block made sense. Thanks to a lack of serious competition from the other networks, Disney could indulge its corporate target audience without having to worry about losing the NFL's own preferred demographic, eighteen- to thirty-four-year-old males. The sedate offerings by the other major networks during the Super Bowl were something of a tradition because, as one media analyst put it, the three major networks "have deals with the N.F.L. and broadcast the Super Bowl on a rotating basis, so each has a vested interest in not seeing the games' halftime ratings diminished."[17]

Not everybody, however, was ready to play by the same rules. In 1986 Australian-born media magnate Rupert Murdoch launched Fox Television Network in an effort to compete with the so-called Big Three: ABC, CBS, and NBC. It looked at first like a dubious venture; Fox's initial lineup in the spring of 1987 consisted of a single evening of badly rated shows. But within six years, Fox was the number one choice of viewers in the coveted eighteen- to thirty-four-year-old age group, and its three most popular shows—*Beverly Hills 90210*, *The Simpsons*, and *In Living Color*—were among the leaders in their time slots.

In late 1991, Fox announced that it planned to spend some of its growing audience capital by offering the first serious counterprogramming to a Super Bowl halftime show. At that time, there seemed little prospect that the network would ever broadcast the Super Bowl, so it had little motivation to honor the informal agreement observed by the other networks. Jay Coleman, president of the advertising agency Entertainment Marketing and Communications International, came up with the idea of offering Super Bowl viewers the chance to join a "Fox-style party"—and still get back for the second half. Coleman also persuaded Frito-Lay to buy the bulk of the show's advertising time in exchange for the naming rights to the special broadcast. Frito-Lay agreed to call the event the "Doritos Zaptime/The 'In Living Color' Super Halftime Party" and to use it to launch a special bite-sized version of its Doritos brand.[18]

Both Fox and Keenan Ivory Wayans, producer and host of *In Living Color*, agreed with Coleman and Frito-Lay that the experiment was worth trying. Given the fact that Wayans's occasionally raunchy show was scheduled to air live in the eastern and central time zones, Wayans joked to reporters that Fox would have "snipers planted throughout the set."

"There will be," he explained, "[seven-second] delay buttons all around."[19]

Even without the competition from Fox Television (which was enjoying a tremendous publicity blitz), CBS might have had a hard time keeping people in their seats during the Super Bowl XXVI halftime show. The NFL and the network hired a Disney spin-off, Timberline Productions, which designed a program titled "Winter Magic." A homage to the game's location in wintry Minnesota and the upcoming Winter Olympics (which were being broadcast, not so coincidentally, a month later on CBS), the show featured a tribute to the 1980 Olympic "Miracle on Ice" hockey team, skating performances by Brian Boitano and Dorothy Hamill, and a thirty-foot inflatable snowman. Somewhat inexplicably, however, the main musical number for "Winter Magic" was performed by singer Gloria Estefan, a Cuban-born resident of Miami, Florida.

Many football aficionados considered the 1992 halftime show a low point for Super Bowl entertainment. In all likelihood, "Winter Magic" would have proven the obvious all by itself, that there is little common ground between the audiences for football and ice skating. But thanks to the perceived success of the *In Living Color* experiment, the entire concept of Super Bowl halftime shows—which Jay Coleman derisively dismissed as "video wallpaper"[20]—was called into question.

By traditional measurements, CBS had little reason to be concerned by Fox's audaciousness. The regular halftime show clobbered its competition in the ratings. "Winter Magic" had a 38.1 Nielsen rating, compared to an 18.3 rating for the special *In Living Color* episode.[21] And although *In Living Color* had hyped the fact that its halftime special would be aired live, beginning as soon as the teams headed to the locker rooms, it still relied primarily on canned comedy segments.

Nonetheless, the perception at Fox (and the other networks as well) was that the bold counterprogramming move had been a success. The year before, Fox had earned a mere 6.0 rating for its broadcast opposite the Super Bowl, which meant that the *In Living Color* stunt tripled the network's audience. Twenty-nine million people—roughly a quarter of CBS's estimated 120 million viewers—switched at halftime to watch the Fox broadcast.

More important, the upstart network provided its advertisers with tremendous value for their dollar. Not only did PepsiCo and Frito-Lay reach a significant number of households for a fraction of the cost of a Super Bowl ad (they paid Fox 0.4 cents per household, compared to advertisers who paid CBS 2.2 cents per household), but, more important, they also had the playing field to themselves. In anticipation of the potential audience drain by the Fox halftime show, CBS shifted all of its national ads to other slots in its Super Bowl broadcast.

Another significant aspect of the Fox experiment was what didn't happen. During the broadcast, the show's performers not only pushed the envelope, they generally ripped it up and set it on fire. In one of the broadcast's live sketches, for instance, a character ad-libbed a remark about the sexual use of rodents in Hollywood, and later questioned the sexual orientation of a well-known track star. But however tempted they may have been, the network's censors left their fingers off the delay button and the Federal Communications Commission (FCC) never came calling.

After the *In Living Color* stunt demonstrated the vulnerability of the halftime show, it is not particularly surprising that the NFL, NBC, and Radio City Music Hall Productions spent much of 1992 trying to persuade pop superstar Michael Jackson to headline the halftime show for Super Bowl XVII. At the time, Jackson was one the top performers in the world, if not *the* top live performer, and his most recent album, *Dangerous*, was the highest-selling album in 1992. Moreover, his somewhat bizarre personal life and unpredictable behavior undoubtedly cranked up the curiosity factor—there's no telling how many people tuned in to the halftime show that night to see if something outrageous might happen. It did, but once again, the government's decency watchdog did not bark. Jackson's act resulted in a couple of softball questions by Oprah, but thanks to some highly favorable Nielsen ratings, all was forgiven.

Final proof of the seductive power of both ratings and dollar signs came just a year later, when the NFL announced that it was awarding four years of broadcast rights to the National Football Conference and the 1997 Super Bowl to Fox Television, which reportedly outbid CBS by more than $100 million.[22] Despite its initial outrage over Fox's stunt in 1992, and despite the fact that CBS had been broadcasting National Football Conference games continuously since the 1950s, the NFL leaped at the chance to work with the enormously popular (and enormously well-funded) Fox network.

THE AOL TOP-SPEED SUPER BOWL XXXVIII HALFTIME SHOW

Given the obvious seductive power of well-funded corporations and the steadily increasing importance of younger consumers, there was a certain inevitability to MTV's eventual involvement in the Super Bowl halftime show. There's the "family" connection, of course: MTV is owned by Viacom, the media conglomerate that also owns CBS. There's the music industry angle: since its inception in 1981, MTV has become the premier distribution channel for music videos, one of the most powerful tools for developing and maintaining a fan base, and for selling music. And then there's the demographic angle: MTV is enormously popular in the lower half of the eighteen- to thirty-four-year-old age group, which also happens to be the demographic most desired by both the NFL and its advertisers.

In 2001 CBS reentered the rotation to broadcast the Super Bowl, and the network invited MTV to produce the halftime show for the telecast. Alex Coletti, producer of the halftime show (as well as MTV shows like *MTV Unplugged* and the *MTV Video Music Awards*) promised viewers an exciting event.

"Our goal," Coletti said, "is to transform the stadium, make you forget you're at a football game for 10 minutes and throw you into the middle of the best rock show you've ever been to."

Coletti recognized, however, that the audience of the game was somewhat different from the audience that normally tuned in for MTV's *Spring Break*.

"It's certainly a wider demographic than we've ever had to consider [at

MTV]," he said. "This isn't 18- to 24-year-olds. This is 8 to 80, truly. We have to take that into consideration."[23]

It's hard to find evidence of MTV's "consideration" of the Super Bowl's wider audience, however. Pairing boy band *NSYNC with rock band Aerosmith was perhaps an effort to appeal to different segments of the audience, but the issue of family-friendliness hardly seems to have registered. One of the promotional ads for the halftime show, for instance, featured the five singers of *NSYNC standing at stadium urinals. When the other men in the bathroom tell them they're due on stage, the band members each shake, zip up, and head out to the performance.[24] As for the show itself, MTV president Van Toffler told USA Today, "We'd like to try total nudity, but they won't let us."[25] The assumption was that he was joking.

Once again, the results were an apparent ratification of corporate synergy: more than 130 million people watched both the game and the halftime rock fest, making it one of the most watched evenings not just in 2001 but in all of television history.[26]

Three years later, CBS and MTV teamed up again to produce the halftime show for the 2004 Super Bowl in Reliant Stadium in Houston, Texas. At the same time, America Online announced that it would be the sole sponsor of the AOL Top-Speed Super Bowl XXXVIII Halftime Show. The online company planned to use the halftime show to help launch an ad campaign aimed at buttressing its sagging subscriber base. Exclusive sponsorship of the Super Bowl halftime cost AOL $10 million (in addition to the $12 million that the online company spent for five thirty-second Super Bowl commercial spots). AOL, however, hoped to recoup some or all of the cost with new member sign-ups and the sale of streaming video of the halftime show.[27]

MTV's goal was clearly to jam as many celebrities as possible into the brief program. The show opened with a public service announcement produced by MTV's Rock the Vote campaign. Titled "Choose or Lose," the segment featured various celebrities—Chris Rock, Julia Roberts, Muhammad Ali, Jay-Z, Beyoncé, Tom Cruise, and others—who reminded members of the audience (and particularly MTV's core demographic of eighteen- to thirty-year-olds) of their obligation to vote as citizens of a free country.

In homage to early halftime shows, actress and singer Jessica Simpson (star of MTV's Newlyweds) opened the live performance portion of the program by leading marching bands from the University of Houston and Texas Southern University onto the field. Clad in a glittering majorette uniform, Simpson promptly undercut the seriousness of the Rock the Vote message with her one line of the evening: "Houston, choose to p-a-a-r-rty!" which is, of course, one of the main reasons that MTV's core demographic doesn't vote in the first place.

From there, the rest of the entertainment raced straight downhill. The twelve-minute halftime show opened with three popular artists, rock-country-hip hop star Kid Rock, and hip-hop sensations P. Diddy and Nelly, performing master mixes of their hit songs. From the start, it was clear that this was not your father's marching band. Both P. Diddy and Nelly performed sexually suggestive dance moves that included crotch grabs, and Kid Rock pulled off a floor-length fur coat to reveal a poncho he had made by cutting a slit in an American flag. To the dismay and anger of the Veterans of Foreign Wars (among others), Rock closed his act by pulling off his poncho and throwing it into the crowd.[28]

In any other year, those antics alone would have been enough to dominate the next day's headlines and generate some complaints to the FCC, but the halftime show's jaw-dropping main act left them all but forgotten. Janet Jackson's performance began with her standing spotlighted on a hydraulic platform in a gauze-wrapped column above the center of the stage. As the music began for her first number (a condensed version of her 2001 hit "All for You"), the gauze dropped away (apart from one stubborn panel), and Jackson rode the platform down through the center of the column to the stage floor. As she marched toward the edge of the stage, Jackson was joined by a troupe of male and female dancers, all dressed (or undressed) in variations of her opening costume: high-heeled boots, black pants, a black leather bustier with hints of red lace peeking over the edge and metal snaps running around each bra cup, a studded black leather collar—running up from the bustier and around her neck—attached to white sleeves, and a floor-length white feather bustle. The provocative dance number, set against lyrics describing a woman at a party enticing a shy man to make a move, ended with Jackson standing center stage, doing a little shimmy with her hands over her breasts.

As the music ended, the cameras pulled back to give Jackson time to leave the stage. For the next minute and a half or so, CBS alternated between rooftop shots of the darkened stage and close-ups of scantily clad dancers lying prone or dangling like acrobats from the stage's curving tusks. Suddenly, the music died away, and Jackson rode up on the hydraulic platform from under the stage. Her white sleeves had been replaced with a pair of tight-fitting black leather sleeves, and her white feather bustle had been swapped for a black leather overskirt, cut and decorated like a samurai tunic. From makeup to outfits to stage lighting, it was a dark and almost Gothic-like design, with noticeable overtones of the type of bondage paraphernalia more typically found in upscale S&M boutiques.

Jackson and the dance troupe next performed a robot-inspired routine to her 1989 hit "Rhythm Nation." In the final chorus of the song, Jackson was surrounded by five female dancers. In a series of tightly choreographed moves, the dancer on Jackson's right reached over and put her spread hand over Jackson's right breast. Jackson lifted up her arm and theatrically thrust the hand away, carefully stepped over another dancer who had crawled through her legs, and sashayed to the edge of the stage, where she dramatically pointed to her left and said, "Go!" As drummers from the Houston and Texas Southern marching bands beat out a rippling cadence, Jackson strode to the right side of the stage, pointing to enormous words projected onto walls of gray balloons dangling from the ceiling. "Prejudice!" she cried, pointing to the balloons. "No!" shouted the crowd in response, carefully reading the word projected on the wall at the other end of the stage. Each word shouted by Jackson—"Ignorance!" "Bigotry!" "Illiteracy!"—elicited the same obedient roar from the crowd.

Having exhausted her list of the world's ills (or having simply run out of time), Jackson climbed the steps to the center stage and struck a closing pose. This could easily have been the end of her act, but for weeks MTV had been hinting at the possibility of a surprise guest. Just five seconds later, the hydraulic lift again rose up from under the stage, this time carrying Justin Timberlake. Unlike Jackson, he was dressed casually: sneakers, baggy khaki pants, a green T-shirt, and a black jacket with the collar turned up.

Pairing Timberlake, the former lead singer for *NSYNC, and Jackson in the halftime show finale was hardly a random choice. In 2002 the two had hooked up for a duet on Timberlake's debut solo album *Justified* (and were rumored to have hooked up outside the studio as well). The song they performed together, "(And She Said) Take Me Now," was described by MTV reporter Jon Wiederhorn as "easily the most sexually graphic song Timberlake has ever recorded, and Jackson's breathy vocals make the track sizzle with extra sensuality."[29]

An appearance by Timberlake at the Super Bowl also gave CBS some classic entertainment synergy for the upcoming Grammy Awards, scheduled to be broadcast by CBS on February 8, 2004. Jackson had been invited to help present an award to R&B legend Luther Vandross (1951–2005), and Timberlake had been nominated in five categories, including Best Pop Vocal Album for *Justified*. The "surprise" appearance by Timberlake at the Super Bowl, then, was essentially intended to be a live commercial for CBS's upcoming awards show broadcast.

When Timberlake joined Jackson on the Super Bowl stage, the other dancers swirled around them and then left. Jackson moved across the stage to join Timberlake, and the two performed a hump-'n'-grind duet of "Rock Your Body" from Timberlake's *Justified* album. The choreography for their number was uncomplicated, consisting largely of Timberlake pursuing Jackson around the stage and Jackson periodically pausing to bend forward and push her rear end into Timberlake's crotch.

As they began the final lines of the song, the two climbed the stairs to the center part of the stage. As Jackson stood straddle-legged in front of the central column, Timberlake carefully circled around to her left side, paused for fraction of a second, and then with his left hand reached across Jackson and pulled the right breast cup off of her bustier.

For a handful of heartbeats, Jackson stood on the spotlighted stage, her right breast exposed and covered only slightly by a silver brooch in the shape of a sun pierced through her nipple. As the two performers looked down, apparently in some confusion, CBS quickly cut to a distance shot showing fireworks going off at the back of the stage, and then without comment went straight to commercial. Ironically, the first advertisement was a cleavage-filled promotional spot for Jackson's scheduled appearance at the upcoming Grammy Awards on February 8. Across the country, jaws could be heard hitting the floor, and Tivo owners hit "replay" literally hundreds of thousands of times.[30]

Was the exposure of Jackson's breast a planned publicity stunt or simply an embarrassing but unintentional accident? Certainly, an argument can be made that both Jackson and Timberlake looked somewhat startled to see Jackson's breast exposed. And, of course, there's no question that unplanned "wardrobe malfunctions" do occur; among only recent examples, the elegant actress Sophie Marceau accidentally exposed her left breast on the red carpet at the Cannes Film Festival in May 2005 when her dress slipped, and actress Tara Reid suffered a similar fate during a paparazzi photo shoot at P. Diddy's thirty-fifth birthday party on November 4, 2004.

Malfunctions occurred even during the much more tightly scripted early days of television. At the 1957 Oscars, for instance, actress Jayne Mansfield was presenting one of the awards when her low-cut gown exposed more than she intended. Even earlier, Faye Emerson, affectionately known as "Television's First Lady," in part for her engaging personality and in part for her marriage to President Franklin Roosevelt's son Elliott, was widely known for the low-cut dresses she wore on the air.[31] (As one wag put it, Emerson put the "V" in TV.) During a 1950 broadcast, she moved the wrong way and accidentally exposed her breasts to the television audience. There was so much discussion about the propriety of her neckline that she put it to a vote of her audience, and no doubt was gratified when 85 percent (evenly split between men and women) voted for her clothing to remain unchanged.[32]

But given all of the circumstances of the 2004 halftime show, it's hard to come to any other conclusion than one of premeditation. The cup of Jackson's bustier was clearly designed with snaps so that it could be pulled off. Close-ups of the so-called costume reveal show that she wasn't wearing a bra or red lace camisole, and there are no torn bits of red lace remaining where her bra cup was. The edge of her costume forms a clean, straight line, and there's no obvious place where the lace could have been attached. Moreover, as a number of commentators pointed out, her breast itself seemed dressed for a show—the large piece of nipple-piercing jewelry could not have been particularly comfortable to wear on an everyday basis.

Add to all that the overtly sexual nature of the Jackson/Timberlake duet, the careful timing of the choreography at the end to match the lyrics of the song, and Timberlake's own fondness for provocative public displays (at the 2003 Brit Awards, he sang an entire duet with Kylie Minogue with his hand planted firmly on her rear end). It is not difficult to agree with the majority of Americans who openly scoffed at the idea that it was an accident.

Regardless of whether or not the event was planned, it was certainly one of the defining moments of 2004. That brief flash of one woman's breast had a tremendous impact on the culture of the United States in the days, weeks, and months that followed. Powerful corporate and media figures were dragged before Congress to answer hostile questions; various entertainment companies were fined nearly $8 million for indecency violations (including $550,000 assessed against CBS as the broadcaster of the halftime show); the course of that year's presidential election was influenced; one of the nation's most popular radio talk show hosts, Howard Stern, was driven off the air and into the welcoming arms of Satellite radio; and an additional impetus was given to Congress to increase broadcast indecency fines by more than tenfold.

By any reasonable measure, the end of the Super Bowl XXXVIII halftime show has proven to be the most costly second in network television history.

Mark Roberts, a self-described professional streaker, performing unofficially at the 2004 Super Bowl on February 1, 2004, prior to the start of the second half. (AP photo/Amy Sancetta)

Chapter One

A Nip in the Air

The Chilling Effects of the 2004 Super Bowl Halftime Show

Janet Jackson isn't the type of person you would think would be doing that. So yes, we were surprised, but such is the nature of what live TV can be.
— Tom Freston, chairman and CEO of MTV Networks[1]

The 2004 Super Bowl was a tough night for CBS. Unbeknownst to television viewers, Janet Jackson wasn't the only person to flash some skin during halftime. Despite the event's massive security, Englishman Mark Roberts, a self-described "professional streaker," ran out onto the field just before the second-half kickoff. As the two teams stared at him, he tugged away his fake referee uniform, leaving only a baseball cap on his head and a plastic football in front of his genitals. Roberts later described the scene to a reporter for the United Kingdom's Press Association:

> I was there, naked, apart from a plastic American football over my nether regions held on with Sellotape, doing a Riverdance in the middle of the Super Bowl, and nobody was coming after me.
>
> The two teams were looking at each other, trying to work out what was going on, so I started to Moonwalk.
>
> Then I started doing crazy body poses—and that's when the whole of the Houston police department came chasing on the field.
>
> I took off on the chase. One player tried to tackle me and I dodged him

and a second [Patriots linebacker Matt Chatham] ran into me and gave me a shoulder charge. He was huge. I spun like a top.

The morning after the Super Bowl, Roberts was ordered to appear in court to face charges of trespassing. His chief complaint was that his stunt was being over-looked after the Jackson/Timberlake incident. "She took my thunder," Roberts griped. "If she hadn't done that I would have been front page material."[2]

CBS made sure that Roberts, whose body was painted with the name of an Internet gambling site, never made it on to the airwaves; the network filled the time with additional ads and commentator chitchat.[3] When it was finally safe for CBS to show the football field again, announcers Greg Gumbel and Phil Simms made no direct reference to the incidents that had so memorably closed out the halftime show, although Gumbel did joke on air that the second half of the Patriots-Panthers game would feature "raw, naked football."[4]

The writers for late-night talk show hosts Jay Leno, David Letterman, and Jon Stewart arguably had the easiest job in America for much of the following week:

Leno: "It was quite a show, wasn't it—there was a streaker, Janet Jackson's breast was exposed and Kid Rock wore an American flag as a poncho. I was surprised that John Ashcroft's head didn't explode during that thing."[5]

Letterman: "This is important. Janet Jackson is being very contrite. She's pretending to apologize to everybody who is pretending to be offended. So, I think that works out."[6]

Stewart: "On the investigative urgency meter: Total breakdown of U.S. intelligence— 'Let's get together and form a panel and try to figure something out.' Janet Jackson bares a teat—six hours later the FCC launches an investigation. Someone will pay."[7]

SCRAMBLING FOR COVER, PART I

Any hopes in the respective headquarters of the National Football League, MTV, CBS, and Viacom that both halftime incidents would simply blow over with a few other inevitably raunchy jokes on late-night talk shows were quickly and thoroughly dashed. Despite the brevity of Jackson's exposure, enough of the ninety or so million viewers in the United States were sufficiently outraged to flood the switchboards of CBS and the NFL with angry phone calls. Other angry viewers clicked onto Jackson's Web site to send e-mails protesting the incident. Virtually overnight, the Parents and Grandparents Alliance[8] took out full-page advertisements in various newspapers, protesting the show and "urging readers to petition members of Congress to 'demand they act.'"[9]

Quickly recognizing the potential fallout from Jackson's on-air nudity, MTV issued a brief statement after the game, saying that "[t]he tearing of Janet Jackson's costume was unrehearsed, unplanned, completely unintentional and was inconsistent with assurances we had about the content of the performance. MTV regrets this incident occurred and we apologize to anyone who was offended by it."[10]

CBS's statement followed shortly thereafter, disclaiming any prior knowledge of the "costume reveal": "CBS deeply regrets the incident that occurred during the Super Bowl halftime show. We attended all rehearsals throughout the week and there was no indication that any such thing would happen. The moment did not conform to CBS broadcast standards and we would like to apologize to anyone who was offended."[11] Given the fact that CBS's "broadcast standards" permitted the airing of advertisements during the 2004 Super Bowl that featured, among other things, a flatulent horse, a crotch-biting dog, an implied sexual tryst between Kermit the Frog and Jessica Simpson, and three different cures for erectile dysfunction (along with dire warnings of possible four-hour erections), the network's disavowal of the breast-baring incident rang a little hollow. The somewhat inevitable conclusion is that a $2.3 million payment for a thirty-second advertisement buys a certain easing of "broadcast standards," particularly for a network struggling to shore up its popularity with eighteen- to thirty-year-old males, the demographic so favored by advertisers.

NFL commissioner Paul Tagliabue also expressed regret for the incident, saying that "[t]he show was offensive, inappropriate and embarrassing to us and our fans. We will change our policy, our people and our processes for managing the halftime entertainment in the future in order to deal far more effectively with the quality of this aspect of the Super Bowl."[12]

The performers themselves had strikingly different reactions to what happened onstage. Before the nation's Tivo systems had even cooled off, the entertainment news program *Access Hollywood* caught up to Justin Timberlake. He cheerfully described the show for cohosts Pat O'Brien and Nancy O'Dell: "It was fun. It was quick, slick, to the point."

"You guys were getting pretty hot and steamy up there," O'Brien pointed out to Timberlake.

"Hey man, we love giving you all something to talk about," Timberlake laughed.[13]

Someone in Timberlake's entourage undoubtedly realized that the situation called for a less flippant response. By the end of the evening, Timberlake was circulating a much more contrite statement, well outside the range of any cameras: "I am sorry if anyone was offended by the wardrobe malfunction during the halftime performance at the Super Bowl. It was not intentional and is regrettable."[14]

Janet Jackson did not issue a statement immediately after the game, but an apology was relayed to MTV News by her representatives.[15]

Across the nation, there was immediate and widespread skepticism that the baring of Jackson's breast was in fact accidental or unplanned. Numerous Web sites ran unscientific surveys of their visitors on the subject; a typical example is this survey run by WSB-TV in Atlanta, Georgia, which posed the following question:

> Janet Jackson's spokeswoman says a red lace garment was supposed to remain when Justin Timberlake tore off Jackson's top. Do you believe her?
> Yes. ___ I think she was shocked when the lace wasn't there.
> No. ___ I think they knew there would be no lace.

The station received more than 150,000 votes, and nearly 80 percent voted no.[16]

Predictably, at least two lawsuits were filed seeking damages for injuries allegedly caused by the one-second glimpse of Jackson's uncovered breast. *Rolling Stone* reported that a Tennessee bank employee sued Janet Jackson, Justin Timberlake, MTV, CBS, and Viacom. The plaintiff asked the court to certify a class action including the millions of Americans who watched the Super Bowl, claiming that the unexpected sight of Jackson's breast caused viewers to suffer "outrage, anger, embarrassment and serious injury." She asked the court to award compensatory and punitive damages equal to the amount earned by the corporate defendants over the last three years.[17] The plaintiff withdrew her lawsuit just four days later.

In Salt Lake City, Utah, an attorney sued Viacom for $5,000 in small claims court, alleging that the media giant was guilty of "false advertising." In court documents, the plaintiff claimed that Viacom's promotion for the Super Bowl led him to believe that he would see "marching bands, balloons and a patriotic celebration" during the halftime show. Instead, the lawyer argued, he and his family were exposed to nudity, simulated sex acts, and the desecration of the American flag. After a hearing in late May 2005, however, the judge dismissed the case, saying that the plaintiff should either have filed in federal court or complained to the FCC.[18]

The vast majority of Americans seemed to take the incident in stride. An Associated Press (AP) poll taken shortly after the Super Bowl found that just over half of those polled (54 percent) considered the stunt to be in "bad taste," but only 18 percent thought that it was an illegal act. In a Time/CNN poll taken a few days later, 47 percent agreed with the statement that the breast-baring marked "a new low in bad taste." However, a full 80 percent of those surveyed by the AP said that it would be a waste of time and money for the Federal Communications Commission to investigate the incident. Similarly,

Harris Interactive reported that 68 percent of the one thousand people it surveyed felt that the FCC should not fine CBS.[19]

SCRAMBLING FOR COVER, PART II

There were plenty of things to keep Congress and the Bush administration
occupied in early 2004, but few of them were pleasant. The International Mon-
etary Fund had expressed alarm about the potential impact of the rising budget
deficits in the United States. Levi Strauss closed its last United States manufacturing plant, marking the end of 130 years of "Made in the U.S.A." jeans.
The Iowa caucus results gave a boost to Senator John Kerry's campaign to
replace Bush, a trend that was confirmed by Kerry's victory over Dr. Howard
Dean in New Hampshire. And on January 28, just three days before the Super
Bowl, American scientist David Kay testified before the US Senate that there
were no weapons of mass destruction in Iraq and that the United States had
acted on faulty intelligence.

Given everything else that was going on in the world, it seems a little disproportionate (to put it mildly) that within hours of the "wardrobe malfunction," the awesome power of the federal government was mobilizing to prevent
any cover-ups over the exposure of Jackson's right breast. The opening salvo
was fired by Michael Powell, the chairman of the Federal Communications
Commission, who issued a blistering press statement when he got to his office
on the morning after the Super Bowl.

"I am outraged at what I saw during the halftime show of the Super Bowl,"
Powell said. "Like millions of Americans, my family and I gathered around the
television for a celebration. Instead, that celebration was tainted by a classless,
crass and deplorable stunt. Our nation's children, parents and citizens deserve
better. I have instructed the Commission to open an immediate investigation
into last night's broadcast. Our investigation will be thorough and swift."[20]

Powell was joined in his outrage by Rep. Fred Upton (R-MI), chairman of
the House Energy and Commerce Subcommittee on Telecommunications and
the Internet, who said that he was "appalled" by the "shameless stunt." "This
is a sad commentary, as the race to the bottom continues," Upton added. "How
low can we go?"[21]

The remarks by the conservative Upton did not come as a terrible surprise,
given the fact that he was already working on legislation to increase broadcast
indecency fines. But Powell's statement was remarkable, both for its rapidity
and for the announcement that he had ordered "an immediate investigation."

Normally, the FCC—which can punish stations that broadcast "indecent" material during certain times of the day—does not actively monitor television or radio shows but instead waits for complaints from aggrieved viewers. The FCC would not have had to wait long in this case, however. In the week following the Super Bowl, the commission received over two hundred thousand complaints about the halftime show in general and the Jackson/Timberlake duet in particular;[22] by the end of the year, the total number of complaints exceeded five hundred thousand.[23] (Based on the estimates of ninety million viewers, the FCC received complaints from just over one-half of 1 percent of the US audience.) Nonetheless, even before the deluge began, Chairman Powell made it clear that the FCC intended to push ahead with an investigation on its own initiative.

In addition, Powell did not think that the investigation should be limited to just the Jackson/Timberlake duet. On ABC's *Good Morning America*, Powell said the entire halftime show would be reviewed. "I think everybody's focusing on the finale, but a lot of what we've heard in terms of complaints and the breadth of the investigation is a little broader than just that incident," Powell said. "I personally was offended by the entire production."[24]

The apologies offered the day before by the corporations and individuals involved did little to assuage the FCC chairman's anger. "If the standard were you could do whatever you want and apologize the next day, then there would be no consequences, I think we would see even a worsening of television," Powell said during his CBS interview. "I'm very appreciative that they're regretful. I'm certainly saddened and regretful as well."[25]

Why was Chairman Powell so eager to bring the full power of the FCC to bear on Jackson's wardrobe malfunction and the other halftime improprieties? Part of it may have been genuine anger at the injection, accidental or otherwise, of admittedly gratuitous nudity and crude gestures into America's semiofficial sports holiday. As Powell told CBS News's *Early Show* on the morning after the Super Bowl, "I think our investigation has to determine whether it legally violates the definition of indecency or obscenity. But it is classless and deplorable and really a juvenile form of entertainment. I think we have always wanted to be careful about that kind of content being available at a time where there is a high probability of children watching. I really think that line was crossed"[26]

But regardless of how genuinely angry Chairman Powell was about the 2004 halftime show, it is also undeniably true that he was a man eagerly in search of a deep political foxhole. For much of the year prior to Jackson's partial disrobing, Powell had come under fire on two major issues: his efforts to ease the FCC's regulatory restraints on media ownership and (ironically) his seemingly cavalier attitude toward broadcast indecency. The Jackson/Timberlake incident gave Powell the perfect opportunity to not only divert attention from those more troublesome issues but also to placate some of the most aggressive critics of his leadership. For Powell (and many others in the Bush administration and in Congress), the flap over Janet Jackson's breast exposure turned out to be the perfect weapon of mass distraction.[27]

POWELL'S BEST-LAID DEREGULATION PLANS GO AWRY

Sitting as it does at the nexus of business, technology, and free speech, the Federal Communications Commission is often asked to tackle the difficult task of understanding and resolving complex public policy issues in terms of constitutional principles. Ironically, this often puts the FCC in the awkward position of promoting speech on the one hand (aiding the development of new media) and discouraging it on the other (indecency). Few issues are more central to the FCC's role in that debate than determining how many media outlets can be owned by a single individual or business entity, or whether a television or radio station should be allowed to own a newspaper in the same community. As FCC chairman (from 1997 to 2001) William Kennard wrote in 2000:

> For more than a half century, the Commission's regulation of broadcast service has been guided by the goals of promoting competition and diversity. These goals are separate and distinct, yet also related. . . . Competition is an important part of the Commission's public interest mandate, because it promotes consumer welfare and the efficient use of resources and is a necessary component of diversity. Diversity of ownership fosters diversity of viewpoints, and thus advances core First Amendment principles. . . . Promoting diversity in the number of separately owned outlets has contributed to our goal of viewpoint diversity by assuring that the programming and views available to the public are disseminated by a wide variety of speakers.[28]

The precise amount of "diversity of ownership" required to promote "viewpoint diversity," however, is not fixed, and has been the subject of considerable debate.

Over the years, the FCC has adjusted its limits on the number of outlets that may be owned by a single entity; the modifications were made in response to both changes in technology and the overall growth of the broadcast industry. When the limits were first introduced in the 1940s, a single owner was limited to three stations; in 1954, the limit was increased to seven. Thirty years later, during the Reagan administration, the FCC replaced the flat cap with a "12-12-12" rule (a single entity could not own more than twelve AM stations, twelve FM stations, and twelve TV stations, with the additional requirement that the total audience served not exceed 25 percent of the national audience).[29]

In 1975 the commission also adopted a regulation that prohibited the issuance of an AM, FM, or TV license to anyone who "owns, operates, or controls a daily newspaper" in the same community. "The newspaper/broadcast cross-ownership rule," the commission said, "rests on 'the twin goals of promoting diversity of viewpoints and economic competition.' . . . [G]ranting a broadcast license to an entity in the same community in which the entity also publishes a newspaper would harm local diversity, and should be prohibited."[30]

Despite the lofty goals behind the ownership cap and cross-ownership ban, business-owners interests and conservative theorists have challenged the rules for decades, and have often called for their outright abolition. The general arguments were summarized succinctly by James Gattuso for the conservative think tank the Heritage Foundation: "The case for changing the FCC's ownership rules is clear. They were written in a different era, and don't reflect the diversity and competitiveness in today's media marketplace. And, they are likely hurting consumers, by limiting the ability of media outlets to use resources as effectively as possible. The best course would be for the FCC to eliminate the rules entirely (in which case competition would still be covered by antitrust regulation, as it is for most other businesses)."[31]

Although this was precisely the type of regulatory reform championed by President Ronald Reagan (1911–2004) during his administration, Republicans were unable to make any headway on the ownership restrictions until after 1994, when the party took control of both the House and the Senate. Two years later, Congress adopted the sweeping Telecommunications Act (the same legislation that enacted the questionable Communications Decency Act). Among other things, it mandated that the FCC relax the ownership rules by increasing the cap on national television audience reach from 25 to 35 percent, and by increasing the number of radio stations that could be owned by a single entity in a given market. In addition, Congress ordered the FCC to conduct a biennial review of its regulations governing broadcast ownership to determine if any of the rules "are necessary in the public interest as the result of competition."[32]

When Michael Powell was first appointed in 1997 to the FCC by President Bill Clinton, he added an enthusiastic deregulatory voice to the commission's debates.[33] Powell had originally followed his father, General Colin Powell, into the military, but a near-fatal jeep accident in Germany cut his military career short. After his discharge, Powell enrolled at Georgetown University Law School, clerked for the US Court of Appeals for the DC Circuit, and then joined the Justice Department as a telecommunications lawyer. At the time of his appointment to the FCC, Powell was serving as chief of staff for Joel Klein, head of the department's antitrust division.

Regardless of his enthusiasm for deregulation, however, there was little

Powell could do about it at first. The commission, under the leadership of Clinton appointee William Kennard, was firmly supportive of ownership limits. When the FCC handed in its first biennial review on June 20, 2000 (more than two years late), it agreed that some of the more minor ownership rules should be changed, but voted 3–2 along party lines to uphold the existing regulations, which imposed limitations on national TV ownership and cross-ownership of a newspaper and television station in a single market.[34] The two Republican members of the commission, Powell and Harold Furchtgott-Roth, both dissented strenuously from the decision. Among other things, Powell argued that more analysis should have been done to determine if technological changes had eliminated the need for the ownership rules.

It would not be long before Powell was given an opportunity to put his own stamp on the commission. Chairman Kennard resigned on January 19, 2001, and two days after being sworn in, President George W. Bush nominated Michael Powell to replace him.

For someone generally opposed to excessive media regulations, Powell took over the FCC at a highly promising time. In May 2000, the US Court of Appeals for the DC Circuit struck down the FCC's rule that a single cable system may not reach more than 30 percent of all pay-TV subscribers.[35] On February 19, 2002, the same court of appeals also voided an FCC prohibition against the simultaneous ownership of a television station and a cable system in the same market, and, in the same opinion, ordered the FCC to either justify or abandon its rule prohibiting a single television station owner from reaching more than 35 percent of the national audience.[36] With the White House in the hands of a conservative Republican and Congress firmly under Republican control, Powell seemed to have all the tools in place to quickly and substantially rewrite the FCC's ownership rules.

Despite some grumbling from impatient media companies and deregulation-minded congressmen, however, the politically savvy Powell announced that the FCC's review would not be completed until the spring of 2003. This would give the new chairman time to assess which way the congressional winds were blowing after the November 2002 midterm elections. On September 12, 2002, the commission unanimously approved a Notice of Proposed Rulemaking, in which the commission announced its intention to review four of its ownership rules: "the national television multiple ownership rule; the local television multiple ownership rule; the radio-television cross-ownership rule; and the dual network rule."[37]

"This is the most comprehensive undertaking in the area of media ownership, I believe, in the commission's history," Powell told the *Chicago Tribune*. "It is ambitious, but I submit it is long overdue."[38]

The weather report following the midterm elections certainly seemed favorable for Powell's assault on the media ownership rules. The Republican Party solidified its hold on the House of Representatives and regained control of the Senate (which it had temporarily lost following the defection of Jim Jeffords [I-VT] from the Republican Party on June 5, 2001). Even more important, Powell's chief ally in the Senate, John McCain (R-AZ), took over the chairmanship of the Senate Commerce Committee, the committee directly responsible for overseeing the FCC.

With remarkable rapidity, however, a broad and ideologically diverse coalition formed to oppose any changes to the media ownership rules. Not surprisingly, the initial objections were raised by consumer advocacy and public interest groups. Gene Kimmelman, director of the Consumers Union, expressed a common concern when he spoke to the *Chicago Tribune* the day after the FCC's proposed review was announced. "I'm very concerned that [Powell has] embarked on a very dangerous course of favoring elimination of rules with selective review of facts in the marketplace."[39] Over the next several months, Kimmelman's remarks were echoed by labor organizations, the owners of some independent newspapers and radio stations, conservative interest groups like the National Rifle Association and the Parents Television Council (PTC), and, surprisingly, even some conservative members of Congress, including Senators Ted Stevens (R-AK), Mike DeWine (R-OH), Olympia Snowe (R-ME), Susan Collins (R-ME), and Wayne Allard (R-WY).

At the same time that Powell was under a near-constant barrage in the media, he began taking serious flak from other members of the commission. Early on, Democratic commissioner Michael Copps pushed Powell to schedule town hall–style meetings around the country to get input from the public on the media ownership rules. Powell initially resisted the suggestion, saying that the FCC's limited budget and the tight review schedule made it impossible to hold public hearings. As resistance to media deregulation intensified, however, Powell partially relented and agreed to hold a February public hearing in Richmond, Virginia.[40] Dissatisfied with Powell's lukewarm response to their suggestion, Copps and fellow commission Democrat Jonathan Adelstein organized additional rump meetings in Chicago; Durham, North Carolina; and Seattle, Washington; all of which had a distinctly antideregulation tone.[41]

No doubt particularly frustrating to Powell, however, was the steady sniping from his fellow Republican commissioner, Kevin Martin. A former White House economic aide to President George W. Bush, he was nominated to an open seat on the FCC by Bush in April 2001 and began serving on July 3. Just over a year later, Martin made it explicitly clear that Powell could not take his vote for granted. On a relatively minor vote over a proposed extension of program access rules for direct broadcast satellites, Martin spent five minutes offering tantalizing comments that seemed to suggest that he had broken with Powell and torpedoed the chairman's support of the extension. Although Martin ultimately voted with Powell, his overt display of independence was Topic A among Washington's telecommunications lawyers and lobbyists for weeks.[42]

In the months that followed, the growing animosity between the two commissioners was at best an ill-kept secret. The persistent threat that Martin would vote with Democrats Copps and Adelstein brought a not-so-subtle shift to the power balance in the commission, one that was confirmed in February 2003 when Martin's vote helped defeat a Powell proposal to eliminate the rules requiring telephone companies to lease their lines to competitors. Martin's action received a chilly reception on Capitol Hill. Rep. Billy Tauzin (R-LA), a big fan of deregulation, said that "regulatory reform had been stabbed in the back," and Senator Sam Brownback (R-KS) sternly declared that "[i]n future considerations of FCC nominees, I will examine carefully their interpretations of current telecommunications law."[43]

Despite the grumblings from Congress, however, Martin succeeded in positioning himself as the swing vote on the commission. To avoid the possibility of another embarrassing setback, Powell was forced to spend much of the spring negotiating with Martin over the final shape of the revised ownership regulations. When the final package was put to a vote of the commission on June 2, 2003, none of the proposals went as far as Powell originally intended; nonetheless, they still represented a significant loosening of the long-standing restraints on media ownership. By a 3–2 vote along party lines, the commission voted to abolish the cross-ownership rule, increase the audience cap for media conglomerates from 35 percent to 45 percent, and to allow companies to own as many as three television and eight radio stations in the same market.[44]

Following the FCC vote, the public protest shifted to Capitol Hill. Despite the opposition of both Republican and Democratic leaders in the House, a rebellious group of legislators (led by Maurice Hinchey [D-NY], David Price [D-NC], and Bernie Sanders [I-VT]) staged a floor fight that in July resulted in an overwhelming rejection (400–21) of the FCC's proposed 45 percent national audience cap. Members of Congress reported that they were receiving as many as one hundred calls per hour in support of the Hinchey amendment.[45]

On the Senate side, Trent Lott (R-MS) and Byron Dorgan (D-ND) spearheaded the adoption of a resolution to roll back all of the FCC's proposed changes. After President Bush announced his intention to veto any legislation challenging the FCC rules, however, the Republican leadership worked out a compromise that would allow an increase in the national audience cap from 35 percent to 39 percent. In a specific slap at the FCC, however, the compromise also included language designed to remove the FCC's ability to make any further adjustments to the cap.[46] Congress approved the revised 39 percent national audience cap on January 22, 2004, just one week before Super Bowl XXXVIII.

Needless to say, federal legislators did not pick the 39 percent figure out of a hat. The two media conglomerates lobbying most strenuously to get rid of the 35 percent audience cap restriction were Viacom and Rupert Murdoch's News Corporation, both of which had separately merged their way to a national audience of—*quelle surprise!*—just under 39 percent. Following their respective mergers, the two corporations were granted temporary waivers by the FCC to operate above the 35 percent audience cap. Without a loosening of the audience cap restriction, each would have been forced to sell off television stations, which neither wanted to do. To help promote their positions, the two corporations spent a combined $5.5 million in lobbying efforts in the eighteen months between January 1, 2002, and June 30, 2003, and donated an additional $2.3 million in campaign contributions in 2002 and 2004, including $153,300 to President Bush's reelection war chest.[47]

The start of 2004, then, found Powell's multiyear effort to deregulate media ownership in near-total disarray. Congress—a Republican Congress, no less—had rebuffed the chairman's efforts to roll the audience cap up to 45 percent, and the remainder of the rules languished in judicial limbo, subject to a stay issued by the US Court of Appeals for the Third Circuit on September 3, 2003.[48] And, remarkably, given the typical public disinterest in complex telecommunications issues, Powell had managed to awaken a significant portion of the country to the fact that in the balancing of interests of consumers and conglomerates, the chairman of the FCC had his thumb squarely on the side of Big Business.

THE TWELFTH COMMANDMENT—A REPUBLICAN FCC CHAIRMAN SHALL NOT IGNORE INDECENCY[49]

The other issue about which Powell was receiving considerable grief from conservatives, not so coincidentally, was decency. Religious conservatives in particular had always had suspicions about Powell's commitment to the goal of stamping out indecency at the FCC, much as neoconservatives harbored doubts about Powell's father, Secretary of State Colin Powell's passion for US global hegemony. Such doubts were justified, since Michael Powell's attitude toward government suppression of broadcast indecency was completely consistent with his overall regulatory philosophy. In public comments made prior to his appointment to the commission and then to the chairmanship, Powell made it clear that when it came to the regulation of content, he favored a light governmental touch.

In 1999, for instance, during a speech accepting the Media Institute's Freedom of Speech Award, Powell said: "We should think twice before allowing the government the discretion to filter information to us as they see fit."[50] Similarly, during his initial press conference as commission chair in February 2001, Powell told his audience, "I don't think my government is my nanny. I still have never understood why something as simple as turning it off is not part of the answer."[51]

Nonetheless, Powell demonstrated that he could tack to the prevailing political winds when necessary. The hearings for his reappointment to the commission followed not long after his appointment by President Bush as chairman, during which Powell received some mildly antagonistic questioning from the Senate Commerce Committee regarding the issue of decency. Powell promised that the FCC would not abandon its obligation to respond to complaints about broadcast indecency: "I don't believe [the First Amendment] is some cynical 'Get out of jail free' card for broadcasters."[52]

It does not seem entirely a coincidence, then, that within days of Powell's confirmation hearing, the FCC's Enforcement Bureau announced the assessment of a $7,000 indecency fine against two different radio stations: KKMG in Colorado Springs, Colorado, for playing a (mostly) bowdlerized version of rapper Eminem's song "The Real Slim Shady"; and KBOO, a Portland, Oregon, station for airing "Your Revolution" by feminist and African American performance artist Sarah Jones.

The fines came as a shock to most radio broadcasters, who had grown used to the FCC's seeming indifference to what they played. But despite the oft-repeated requests of decency watchdog groups like Morality in Media and the Parents Television Council, the radio station fines were not the start of a more intense FCC campaign against indecency. In fact, just six months later, in January 2002, the Enforcement Bureau quietly withdrew its fine against KKMG, saying that its initial analysis of the incident was incorrect and that it had since concluded that Eminem's song "is not patently offensive." In an editorial, the *Denver Rocky Mountain News* applauded the correction, if not the reasoning: "Well, it is offensive, actually, even in the bleeped version; we wouldn't print it. But that's beside the point; the FCC is no better equipped to judge the standards of the community than the people who live in it, and it should get out of the decency-policing business entirely."[53]

The amount of indecency fines assessed by the FCC over the past few years illustrates the tepidness of Powell's enthusiasm for indecency "enforcement." According to a CNN/Money survey, in the five years prior to the Jackson/Timberlake incident, the FCC assessed fines in the following total annual amounts:

1999 — $49,000
2000 — $48,000
2001 — $90,000
2002 — $100,000
2003 — $440,000[54]

Under Powell's leadership, the amount of indecency fines assessed by the FCC certainly rose, but the bulk of the rather significant increase in fines in 2003 did not come until October, not long after the US House, the Senate, and the DC Court of Appeals each rejected some or all of the FCC's proposed ownership changes. By that time, rumors were already circulating that Powell was planning on resigning in the fall, a suggestion strenuously denied by an FCC spokesperson.[55]

The FCC released two separate Notices of Apparent Liability on October 2: one in the amount of $55,000 against Clear Channel's WWDC-FM for an explicit on-air interview with two high school girls about oral sex in the hallways of Washington, DC's Bishop O'Connell High School, and one in the amount of $357,500 against Infinity Broadcasting for its series of broadcasts by hosts Opie and Anthony about a listener contest to have sex in as many public places as possible, "including St. Patrick's Cathedral, a zoo, Rockefeller Center, the Disney Store, and the FAO Schwartz toy store."[56] Morality in Media president Bob Peters praised the commission in a press release, saying that "[h]opefully, this is the start of a new era at the FCC, when broadcasters—and, in particular, broadcasters who air programming on a national or regional network of stations—will no longer be able to count on sporadic and small-in-amount indecency fines as a readily affordable cost of doing business."[57]

The following day, however, any goodwill Powell and the FCC had established with indecency activists by fining Clear Channel and Infinity promptly vanished. During the 2003 Golden Globe Awards, which were broadcast on Fox Television on January 25, 2003, the rock band U2 received the award for Best Original Song, "The Hands that Built America" (written for Martin Scorcese's film *Gangs of America*). Lead singer Bono, obviously excited by the award, exclaimed, "Ah, this is really, really, fucking brilliant!"

At the time, Bono's exuberant outburst caused relatively little comment. Out of an audience of 20.1 million people, the FCC, however, received just 234 complaints (roughly one one-thousandth of a percent), 217 of which came from a single source, the Parents Television Council.[58] The FCC, however, is required to investigate broadcasts when it receives even a single complaint, so the commission's Enforcement Bureau opened a review of the Golden Globes show. Ten months later, on October 3, 2003, the Enforcement Bureau concluded that neither Bono nor NBC violated federal decency laws with the outburst. David Solomon, chief of the Enforcement Bureau, explained his reasoning in a Memorandum Opinion and Order: "The word 'fucking' may be crude and offensive, but, in the context presented here, did not describe sexual or excretory organs or activities. Rather, the performer used the word 'fucking' as an adjective or expletive to emphasize an exclamation. . . . Moreover, we have previously found that fleeting and isolated remarks of this nature do not warrant Commission action."[59]

Solomon's opinion was well written and, more important, perfectly reasonable. But it brought a swift and predictably outraged response from L. Brent Bozell, president and founder of the Parents Television Council, who issued a press release stating that "I cannot imagine a ruling that could make a bigger mockery of an organization charged with serving the public interest."[60] The PTC filed an Application for Review on November 6, asking the commission to reconsider the decision of the Enforcement Bureau. In a reply to the PTC, Chairman Powell wrote that "[p]ersonally, I find the use of the 'F-word' on programming accessible to children reprehensible," and said that the commission would review Solomon's order.[61]

But the damage to Powell's perceived leadership had already been done. Much like the FCC's efforts to rewrite the media ownership rules, the "Bono" memorandum sparked a flurry of speeches and legislation by angry federal legislators. In the House, for instance, Rep. Jo Ann Davis (R-VA) rose on November 20 "to express my disappointment and outrage with the recent ruling by the Federal Communications Commission deeming the use of obscene language acceptable on television."

"Mr. Speaker," she added, "why do we even have an FCC if they are not going to uphold rules of decency? Why do we even as a society even make laws if they are not going to be followed? Turning a blind eye to this assault on decency will do a great disservice to America and damage the integrity of our airwaves."[62]

Two weeks later, on December 8, 2003, Rep. Phil Gingrey (R-GA) introduced a resolution that declared in part that "the House of Representatives does not support the which of standards or the weakening of the rules of the Federal Communications Commission prohibiting obscene and indecent broadcasts to allow network or other communications to use language that is indecent or vulgar," and added that "the House of Representatives will not allow the Federal Communications Commission to permit intrusion upon the family's ability to raise their children in an environment that is not inundated with indecent or profane language on our public airwaves."[63] The resolution was referred to the subcommittee on telecommunications and the Internet of the House Energy and Commerce Committee, where it quietly died.

Joining Gingrey's resolution in the subcommittee graveyard was the Clean Airwaves Act, a bill proposed the same day by Rep. Doug Ose (R-CA) to ban certain "profane" words from the airwaves. In the text of his bill, Ose thoughtfully listed the terms that should be forbidden: "shit," "piss," "fuck," "cunt," "asshole," and the phrases "cock sucker," "mother fucker," and "ass hole." When questioned about the bill's explicit language, Ose said that he had been advised by legislative counsel (the staff attorneys who assist Congress in the drafting of legislation) that "the only way to effectively accomplish what we were trying to do was to put the words in the legislation."[64]

Ose's bill raised the tantalizing prospect of a surge in expert witness work for grammarians across the country, since it also proposed outlawing the "compound use (including hyphenated compounds) of such words and phrases with each other or with other words or phrases, and other grammatical forms of such words and phrases (including verb, adjective, gerund, participle, and infinitive forms)."[65] Ironically, as *Washington Post* columnist Gene Weingarten gleefully pointed out, Ose's bill would not have criminalized Bono's acceptance speech at the Golden Globes, since Solomon mischaracterized the word's usage: Bono actually used "fucking" as an adverb—a part of speech not listed in the legislation.[66]

On the other side of the Capitol building, Senator Jeff Sessions (R-AL) introduced a somewhat belated resolution that called on the FCC to reconsider the Enforcement Bureau's decision and to compel more stringent compliance with its own indecency standards. The resolution passed the Senate on December 9, 2003, by unanimous consent.[67]

THE FCC USHERS IN THE ERA OF NOT-QUITE-LIVE TELEVISION

In the week following the 2004 Super Bowl, with storm clouds gathering at the FCC and on Capitol Hill, and with religious conservatives in full cry, the various parties involved in the halftime show did their best to control the damage. It quickly became apparent, however, that the incident was one of those events in American cultural history that defied control.

Even though they were not directly affected by the events at the Super Bowl, other media and entertainment organizations demonstrated that they could heed regulatory storm warnings just as quickly as CBS. Three days after the Super Bowl, the NFL announced that Justin Timberlake's former *NSYNC bandmate JC Chasez had been dropped from the halftime show for the Pro Bowl, scheduled to be played in Honolulu on February 8. Despite the fact that the Pro Bowl was being broadcast on the cable network ESPN (and thus out of the direct reach of FCC regulators), the NFL decided to take no chances with the lyrics or choreography of Chasez's song, "Blowin' Me Up (With Her Love)."[68] The singer was replaced with an innocuous and presumably safer lineup of local singers, hula dancers, and conch shell blowers.[69]

Initially, Chasez conceded that the Jackson/Timberlake performance had changed the environment for public performances: "No one could be more disappointed than I that the NFL has cancelled my Halftime performance at the Pro Bowl this coming Sunday. I've told the NFL I understand the pressure that they are under since the Super Bowl."[70]

The next day, however, he angrily rejected the league's offer to sing the "Star-Spangled Banner" and made a much more blunt statement about the whole situation: "While I agree the mishap at the Super Bowl was a huge mistake, the NFL's shallow effort to portray my music as sexually indecent brings to mind another era when innocent artists were smeared with a broad brush by insecure but powerful people. That's not the America I love. . . . I'll sing the national anthem anytime, anywhere, but not for this NFL."[71]

NBC also announced on February 6 that it was cutting a scene from its hit show *ER* in which an elderly woman's bare breast was briefly exposed during emergency treatment, despite the fact that there was nothing remotely salacious about the scene and it was scheduled to be shown after 10:30 PM at night.

"Though we continue to believe the shot is appropriate and in context . . . ," NBC said in a statement, "we have unfortunately concluded that the atmosphere created by this week's events has made it too difficult for many of our affiliates to air this shot."[72]

ABC also joined the not-quite-live trend, announcing that its broadcast of the Academy Awards on February 29 would be delayed five seconds to give the station time to bleep out any inappropriate language by presenters or show host Chris Rock. Given the typical level of profanity in Rock's popular comedy routines, many openly wondered whether a five-second delay would be sufficient.

With its All-Star Game fast approaching (February 14), the National Basketball Association took a look at the lineup for its halftime show—R&B singer Beyoncé Knowles, pop singer Christina Aguilera, and rap duo OutKast—and decided that the lyrics of Knowles's planned song, "Naughty Girl," were too explicit. Knowles agreed to perform her song "Crazy in Love" instead. Like ESPN, TNT is a cable television channel and thus outside the reach of the FCC; nonetheless, TNT announced that it would implement a seven-second tape delay for its broadcast of the show.[73] Despite its precautions, TNT and Knowles nearly made their own wardrobe malfunction headlines. Dancing provocatively in front of a wind machine during her performance, Knowles almost spilled out of her thin halter top. Ironically, one of the people watching from courtside was Janet Jackson, dressed conservatively "in a furry, brown hat, sunglasses and a brown suede jacket with a white T-shirt underneath."[74]

As interesting as media watchers and First Amendment analysts found those developments, the week's real drama focused on what role, if any, Janet Jackson and Justin Timberlake would play in the upcoming 46th Annual Grammy Awards, scheduled for February 8. The fact that the Grammy Awards followed so closely on the heels of the Super Bowl put CBS in a particularly difficult bind. For weeks leading up to and including the Super Bowl, the network had been running provocative ads touting Janet Jackson's appearance at the Grammy Awards to introduce a special award to the legendary R&B singer Luther Vandross (1951–2005). Rumors had also circulated that Jackson and Timberlake would reprise their Super Bowl appearance by performing a duet to open the telecast.[75]

Further complicating matters for CBS was the fact that the Grammy Awards are someone else's party. The ceremony is organized and hosted each year by the National Academy of Recording Arts and Sciences. In the immediate aftermath of the Super Bowl incident, the academy seemed more bemused than anything else. As a spokesperson for the academy told the cable news show *E!* on February 3, "If we took everyone who is controversial off the show, no one would perform."[76]

But for CBS, the issue was much more serious, given the very real possibility of substantial FCC fines and a hostile political reaction by an increasingly conservative Capitol Hill. On Tuesday, February 3, the network announced that for the first time, it would impose a five-minute delay during the Grammy broadcast to give the network time to edit out or bleep any inappropriate material (a step that Jay Leno gleefully described as a "booby trap").

At the same time, CBS quietly entered into negotiations with both Timberlake and Jackson regarding their scheduled appearances at the Grammys. Even as early as February 3, rumors were circulating that CBS intended to pressure the academy to uninvite Jackson; however, a source close to CBS reportedly said that "the network has no objections to Timberlake."[77]

At the beginning of the week, Jackson appeared to be making some effort to remain a part of the Grammy Awards. On Monday evening, she issued a statement in which she took full responsibility for the breast-baring incident. "The decision to have a costume reveal at the end of my halftime show performance was made after final rehearsals. MTV was completely unaware of it. It was not my intention that it go as far as it did. I apologize to anyone offended—including the audience, MTV, CBS and the NFL."

MTV was apparently pleased with Jackson's version of the event. That same evening, MTV elaborated on its postgame apology, posting a page on its Web site that said:

MTV was as surprised and shocked as anyone last night. Janet Jackson acknowledged that we had no prior knowledge of her plans. We will continue to investigate the circumstances.

Our goal with the Super Bowl Halftime show was to produce an entertaining stage experience with a positive message about empowerment and voting. We are disappointed that this message has been overshadowed by the unfortunate incident.

MTV apologizes again to anyone who was offended.[78]

On Tuesday, February 3, Tom Freston, chairman and CEO of MTV Networks, went even further, telling a panel of entertainment executives that the music network was "punk'd by Janet Jackson," a reference to MTV's own comedic show *Punk'd* that films and airs practical jokes played on celebrities by actor Ashton Kutcher.[79]

As the week progressed, however, it became clear that a not-so-subtle public relations battle was being waged by the two performers, and that Timberlake was clearly winning. In an interview with KCBS-TV in Los Angeles on Tuesday, February 3, Timberlake made it clear that his assessment of the "wardrobe malfunction" had changed dramatically from his post–halftime show conversation with *Access Hollywood*'s Pat O'Brien. He told the KCBS reporter that he was "completely embarrassed" by what happened and added that he understood that a lot of people were offended, including his own family.[80]

After explaining that he got a call from Jackson and her choreographer with the idea for doing a "costume reveal," which Timberlake thought would leave a red lace bra over Jackson's breast, he described his reaction onstage: "[I] got to the field. Went on stage. Was in the moment and when what happened happened, I was completely shocked and appalled and all I could say is 'Oh my God! Oh my God!'"[81]

Later that same night, Jackson's publicist distributed to media outlets a videotaped version of her apology. On camera, a conservatively dressed and very somber, even downcast Jackson essentially repeated her earlier printed statement. "I am really sorry if I offended anyone," she said. "That was truly not my intention." She did not make any further public comments that week.

Timberlake, CBS, and the academy were all highly motivated to reach some satisfactory resolution that would allow Timberlake to appear at the Grammy Awards. Not only was Timberlake scheduled to perform, but he had also been nominated in five different categories. Even a single Grammy Award could mean millions in additional album sales for Timberlake, and it would be particularly embarrassing to miss out on the actual presentation of a trophy. Moreover, both CBS and the academy were loathe to lose one of the evening's main attractions, a rising star particularly popular with younger viewers.

Jackson was in a very different position. Although a multiple past winner at the Grammys, she was not nominated in any category in 2004 (although, as numerous columnists suspiciously pointed out, she was scheduled to release a new album, *Damita Jo*, on March 30). Her one announced role at the Grammys required little more than a couple of minutes in front of the teleprompter. When the academy announced on Wednesday that Vandross had not recovered sufficiently from his earlier stroke and would not be attending the Grammy Awards at all,[82] any leverage Jackson might have had effectively vanished.

As early as February 3, an academy press release offered the first tangible suggestion that Jackson might not appear at the Grammys: her name (but not Timberlake's) was conspicuously absent from the list of performers, presenters, and celebrity hosts scheduled to appear at the awards.[83] Ron Roecker, the spokesperson for the academy, tried to downplay the significance of the omission, but inadvertently underscored the difference in how the two performers were being treated: "There's always lots of controversy. They're musicians, for goodness' sake. And there's such a big difference, no disrespect to the Super Bowl, to putting a stage on Astroturf than an appearance at the Grammys. It's a live show, so, yes, it's unpredictable, but we have things in place. This is all about the music, not the controversies. It's about celebrating Justin's music."[84]

Neither the Academy of Recording Arts and Sciences nor CBS, it seemed, was in any hurry to celebrate Janet's music just then.

Within twenty-four hours, both *Access Hollywood* and *Entertainment Tonight* broke the news that Timberlake had agreed to CBS's conditions. They also reported that Jackson had refused to apologize again and that her invitation had been revoked.[85] According to sources cited by London's *Mirror*, CBS was being pressured by unnamed "Government censors" to drop the singer from the broadcast, and that the network was increasing its pressure on the academy.[86]

When the news broke that the academy was dropping Jackson from the Grammy program, her boyfriend, music producer Jermaine Dupri, announced that he was resigning from his position as president of the academy's Atlanta chapter.

"[T]here appears to be a double standard," Dupri said. "I cannot stand by and watch a fellow member of the music community be used as a scapegoat. It comes down to the issue of fairness. Despite it all, what is happening is not fair."

Others agreed with Dupri's assessment. "What did Justin Timberlake know and when did he know it?" columnist Kaye Grogan asked. "Was he a co-conspirator or was it a last minute extemporaneous move on his part? What-ever . . . he has not received the same scornful contempt Jackson has had to endure."[87] Congressman Bobby L. Rush (D-IL) objected to the way in which some people were referring to the incident. "My friend from Nebraska, Mr.

Terry, and others have made comments calling the incident at the Super Bowl the Janet Jackson incident. Well, where is Justin Timberlake? I am utterly astonished that Mr. Timberlake has been given, in my estimation, a proverbial slap on the wrist while Janet Jackson has been substantially punished. This seems to me continues a pattern of the double standards that I fought against most of my life."[88]

On the morning of Sunday, February 8, CBS issued a statement with its version of the week's negotiations:

> Throughout the week, CBS and The Recording Academy have been evaluating and deliberating the appropriateness of Janet Jackson and Justin Timberlake appearing at "The 46th Annual Grammy Awards." CBS had serious reservations about their scheduled appearances; however, we respected the Recording Academy's wishes to produce the program they originally intended. Ms. Jackson and Mr. Timberlake were invited to participate in the show as long as they agreed to apologize on the air for what happened during our Network's broadcast of the "Super Bowl Halftime Show." Ms. Jackson declined the invitation. Mr. Timberlake accepted.[89]

Despite the network's concerns, the show went off without a hitch. Timberlake received two Grammy Awards, first for Best Pop Vocal Album for his 2002 debut solo album *Justified* (which has sold over seven million copies worldwide), and then for Best Male Pop Vocal Performance for his single "Cry Me a River." After opening the envelope and seeing the name of the winner for the second award, presenter Jakob Dylan (Bob Dylan's son) offered Timberlake one simple word of advice: "Behave."

Timberlake clearly had no intention of doing anything but. As he accepted the award, Timberlake made his promised apology: "I know it's been a rough week on everybody," he said. "And what occurred was unintentional, completely regrettable and I apologize if you guys were offended."[90] And with those words, the curtain fell on one of the more remarkable weeks in American entertainment and political history.

The music and recording industry, gathered safe and warm at the Grammys in the Los Angeles Staples Center, gamely tried to ignore the growing legislative and bureaucratic rumblings from Washington. Other incidents had blown over in the past, and many in the industry undoubtedly thought that the same thing would happen this time. Ultimately, that may still prove true, but in the short term, Congress and the FCC reacted with an unparalleled level of ferocity.

If there is anything positive that can be said to have come out of the Jackson/Timberlake incident, it is the fact that the nation has been given an opportunity to examine in some detail its attitude toward government regulation of speech in general and broadcast media in particular. However unwittingly, Timberlake and Jackson laid bare the central question of a representative democracy. In a nation where freedom of speech is one of the first principles secured by the Bill of Rights, how is it that any agency of the federal government has the authority to punish broadcasters for what they put on the air? The answer to that question lies in the complicated fabric of the nation's political, religious, and social history.

Chapter Two

From Henry VIII to the FCC

Tracing the Origins of American Efforts to Legislate Decency

It is by a mutual consent, through a special overvaluing providence and a more than an ordinary approbation of the
Churches of Christ, to seek out a place of cohabitation and
Consortship under a due form of Government both civil and
ecclesiastical. In such cases as this, the care of the public
must oversway all private respects, by which, not only conscience, but meer civil policy, doth bind us.

—Hon. John Winthrop, Esq.[1]

The consequences of divorce are always unpredictable. But few marital
breakups have rippled through history with the intensity and duration of the
efforts of Henry VIII (1491–1547) to end his first marriage to the Spanish
princess Catherine of Aragon (1485–1536). To a remarkable degree, the battles
today over decency in American culture are a direct descendant of the efforts
of a frustrated (and lustful) monarch to provide his country with a prince and
heir. Understanding the cultural and religious changes that stemmed from
Henry's frustration offers valuable insights into our present morass.

The marriage of Henry VIII and Catherine on June 11, 1509, was his first
but her second. She had previously been married, at sixteen, to Henry's older
brother Arthur (1486–1502). Normally, it would not have been possible for
Henry, king or no, to marry his former sister-in-law, as royal marriages at the
time required the approval of the pope, and the Catholic Church did not

Anthony Comstock, special inspector for the United States Postal Service and secretary to the New York Society for the Suppression of Vice.

approve of matches between two such closely related people. Catherine, however, averred that her first marriage had not been consummated (Arthur, fifteen when he married, had died roughly six months after the wedding from fever), and the pope reluctantly gave his approval to her match with Henry.

Over the course of their twenty-four-year marriage, Catherine was pregnant at least seven times, but only one child, Mary (1516–1558), survived past infancy. This deeply concerned both Henry and his court. The House of Tudor's hold on the throne was not particularly secure, and Henry was determined to provide a male heir to rule England. In 1526, concluding that the aging Catherine was unlikely to have another child—much less a boy—Henry began an amorous pursuit of Anne Boleyn (ca. 1501/1507–1536), one of the queen's handmaidens. Over the next seven years, Henry engaged in complicated and ultimately futile negotiations with Rome to have his marriage to Catherine annulled.

In January 1533, a frustrated Henry quietly married the pregnant Anne and had his hand-selected archbishop of Canterbury, Thomas Cranmer (1489–1556), declare his marriage to Catherine null and void.[2] In September, Anne bore Henry their only child, Elizabeth (1533–1603). After learning what Henry had done, an outraged Pope Clement VII (1478–1534) excommunicated him in July 1533, but the English parliament, at the urging of Henry's chancellor of the exchequer, Thomas Cromwell (ca. 1485–1540), responded by passing the Act of Supremacy in 1534. The legislation effectively separated England's church from Rome and established the English monarch as the head of the Church of England.

While the political and social significance of Henry's repudiation of Rome cannot be easily underestimated, it is worth noting that the Anglican Church initially did not stray far from its Catholic roots. Henry himself was no fan of the Protestant Reformation launched by Martin Luther (1483–1546); in fact, Pope Leo X (1475–1521) had awarded Henry the title *fidei defensor* (defender of the faith) for his learned attacks on Protestantism. Under Henry, the birthdays of some saints were stricken from the church calendar and pilgrimages were abolished, but otherwise the average priest or nun would have been perfectly comfortable at an Anglican service.

During the brief rule of Henry's son Edward VI (1537–1553) (born to Henry's third wife, Jane Seymour [ca. 1508/1509–1537]), however, the Anglican Church swung much more heavily toward Protestantism. That move was swiftly and bloodily reversed when Edward's Catholic half sister, Mary (daughter of Catherine of Aragon),[3] took the throne following his death in 1553. During Mary's brief rule, Catholics struggled to reunite England with the pope, and Mary ordered the execution of more than three hundred religious opponents. But Mary's time on the throne was also short; she died in 1558 and was succeeded by her Protestant half sister, Elizabeth I, whose reign oversaw what many consider to be the "golden age" of the British empire—the Elizabethan era.

Among her other accomplishments, Elizabeth brought a final end to papal control over the English, or Anglican, Church. She reinstituted the use of the Book of Common Prayer first introduced under Edward, demanded oaths by public officials acknowledging her sovereign control over the Church, and replaced many Roman Catholics at court with Protestants.

In the eyes of some English Protestants, however, neither Elizabeth nor her successor, James I of England (1566–1625), did enough to purge the Anglican Church of the excesses that had motivated Martin Luther's Protestant Reformation in the first place. Inspired in particular by the writings of French theologian John Calvin (1509–1564), these Protestants sought to "purify" the Anglican church and bring it more closely in line with the strict doctrines and practices set forth in the New Testament.

Even among the so-called Puritans, however, there was some skepticism about their ability to reform the Church of England. Some felt that however lofty and noble the goal, it would be impossible to strip the Church of its pomp and papistry. The only solution, they argued, was to separate from the Church altogether and to establish a new church, a church "free from state power and royal control."[4] It was a profoundly radical idea, and one that would have long-term consequences for the course of church and state development in the New World.

The Separatists (as these defiant Puritans were called) were painfully aware that their disapproval of the Queen's church was viewed as tantamount to disapproval of Queen Elizabeth herself, something not cheerfully tolerated by the Crown. In the early part of the seventeenth century, under constant fear of arrest by the local sheriff, one small congregation of Separatists met in secret near Nottingham, at the home of William Brewster (ca. 1566–1644), to debate how best to proceed. In 1607 the tiny congregation elected to migrate to Holland, settling first in Amsterdam and then, when the larger city proved too full of earthly temptation, relocating to nearby Leyden. Their hope was to return home once the Church of England demonstrated either greater purity or the Crown practiced greater religious tolerance.

As the years passed, however, the Church showed no signs of greater purity nor the Crown of more tolerance. Out of a sense of desperation, driven in part by the steady cultural assimilation of their children into the Dutch population, a portion of the Leyden congregation resolved on a pilgrimage to the English colony of Virginia in America.[5] Emigrating to the New World would give them the opportunity to structure their church as they saw fit, far from the watchful eye of the Crown or the local sheriffs. After sixty-four days at sea, the diminutive *Mayflower* dropped anchor off the coast of America, albeit some six hundred miles north of the original destination.

When the weary and storm-tossed passengers of the *Mayflower* finally stepped ashore at Plymouth on December 26, 1620, they faced a difficult and painful future: four of their company had died aboard the ship, and half of the remainder died in the first few winter months. Clustered on a rocky shore thousands of miles from home, with winter pressing in and woefully inadequate food, these Pilgrims, as they came to be known, were saved in equal measure by the indigenous peoples who befriended them and the deep, passionate faith that had driven them to the New World.

"A DUE FORM OF GOVERNMENT BOTH CIVIL AND ECCLESIASTICAL"

The modern American endorsement of freedom of religion notwithstanding, neither the Pilgrims nor the other Puritans who eventually followed were inspired by what one would describe as a liberal faith. In 1630 an English attorney named John Winthrop (1587/8–1649) led seven hundred Puritans to the New World to set up the Massachusetts Bay Colony and establish a "Godly church," far from what he considered to be the corrupted and altogether too papish Anglican Church. During the voyage, Winthrop drafted and delivered a sermon summarizing Puritan values and underscoring the historic opportunity they faced: "For we must consider that we shall be as a city upon a hill. The eyes of all people are upon us. So that if we shall deal falsely with our God in this work we have undertaken, and so cause him to withdraw his present help from us, we shall be made a story and a by-word through the world. We shall open the mouths of enemies to speak evil of the ways of God, and all professors for God's sake. We shall shame the faces of many of God's worthy servants, and cause their prayers to be turned into curses upon us till we be consumed out of the good land whither we are a-going."[6]

From the start, the Massachusetts Bay Colony was as close to a true theonomy as this country has ever seen (with the possible exception, at various times, of portions of Utah under the Mormon Church). Political suffrage was limited initially to members of the church, which in turn was limited to people "who could claim the full experience of individual spiritual regeneration." As of 1640, that meant that only 8 percent of the colony's population was considered to be full citizens and permitted to vote.[7] Civil authorities were expected to suppress "corrupt opinions" that conflicted with Puritan doctrine, and taxes were levied to support the church. The only thing that kept the colony from becoming a full-fledged theocracy was the Puritan belief, earned from hard experience, in the separation of church and state—church officials were barred from serving as civil magistrates.[8]

In a remarkably short time, however, a quiet rebellion arose against the religious restrictions on political franchise. The leading complainants were the colony's increasingly wealthy merchants, who chafed at the requirement of a personal spiritual experience as a prerequisite for voting. Their concerns were acknowledged in the Halfway Covenant, which authorized participation in the church and community for those "goodly people" who were merely baptized Christians. The next logical step occurred in 1693, when the English Act of Toleration was imposed on the colony; under the terms of the act, ownership of property replaced the religious criterion of baptism as the qualification for citizenship. In an early test of New World values—the preeminence of strict theology or financial resources—economics won.

The defenders of a stricter view of Puritanism viewed both the Halfway Covenant and the Act of Toleration with unconcealed contempt. Old North Church ministers Increase Mather (1639–1723) and his son Cotton (1663–1728), for instance, waged a lengthy but ultimately futile campaign to resist the forces of religious and political liberalism that were reshaping the colony. Among other things, they urged residents to report neighbors who swore or blasphemed, a policy that gave tacit encouragement to the Salem witch trials in 1692 (during which nineteen people were hanged and one pressed to death by stones).[9] In 1701, however, Increase Mather lost his position as president of Harvard University and, with his son in tow, stormed off to New Haven, Connecticut, to assist in the founding of Yale University, which they envisioned as a more theologically rigorous institution.[10]

One of the most concrete examples of the changing political and religious climate in the colony occurred in 1711, when the political leaders of the Massachusetts Bay Colony adopted what is generally considered to be the New World's first antiobscenity ordinance:

> Whereas evil communications, wicked, profane, impure, filthy and obscene songs, composures, writings or prints do corrupt the mind, and are incentives to all manner of impieties and debaucheries, more especially digested, composed or uttered in imitation or in mimicking of preaching, or any other part of divine worship, every person or persons offending in any of the particulars aforementioned shall be punished by fine to Her Majesty not exceeding twenty pounds or by standing on the pillory once or oftener, with an inscription of his crime in capital letters affixed over his head, according to the discretion of the justice in quarter sessions.[11]

The adoption of the ordinance makes it clear that eighty years after the founding of Winthrop's "City on a Hill," the colony's political leaders still took seriously their obligation to enforce the moral precepts of the Puritan Church. But the more significant implication of the ordinance is the fact that for the first time, church and political leaders felt it was necessary to reinforce the authority of the church through civil legislation. For the next two centuries, with relatively few exceptions, religious leaders and social activists would continue to seek the assistance of civil government when their own efforts to impose a particular moral code were failing.

To Save a Nation's Soul: The Birth of Social Evangelism

The real significance of the Halfway Covenant lay not merely in the fact that it made the Mathers apoplectic but in its role in the origins of evangelicalism in America. The person most typically credited with coming up with the idea of the Halfway Covenant is the Reverend Solomon Stoddard (1643–1728/9), pastor of the Northampton Church in western Massachusetts's Pioneer Valley. Observing a decline in the number of attendees at church and concerned about the generally diminishing religiosity of the colony's second and third generations, Stoddard introduced two innovations: first, he began offering communion to everyone who had been baptized and had grown up in the church; and second, he proposed to increase the number of conversions in his congregation by employing "a style of preaching that appealed not to dry intellect but to living experience, to fear of damnation and hope of heaven."[12]

After fifty-five years as pastor of the Northampton Church, Stoddard was replaced by his grandson, the Reverend Jonathan Edwards (1703–1758), in 1729. Four years later, a religious revival began in Northampton under the spell of Edwards's powerful preaching. A typical example of Edwards's revivalist sermons can be drawn from his most famous work, "Sinners in the Hands of an Angry God":

> O sinner! Consider the fearful danger you are in: it is a great furnace of wrath, a wide and bottomless pit, full of the fire of wrath, that you are held over in the hand of that God, whose wrath is provoked and incensed as much against you, as against many of the damned in hell. You hang by a slender thread, with the flames of divine wrath flashing about it, and ready every moment to singe it, and burn it asunder.

By 1739 the fire Edwards had lit in Northampton had expanded into a region-wide phenomenon known as the Great Awakening. Over the next twenty years or so, pockets of revivalism and evangelism flared up throughout the colonies, but by the late eighteenth century, as mercantilism and revolution increasingly occupied the attention of the populace, the movement largely died out. Nonetheless, the impact of the religious revival lingered—no less an observer of the American Revolution than John Adams (1735–1826) argued that the seeds of the political rebellion were planted by the first Great Awakening.[13]

If Adams was correct in his assessment, then the law of unintended consequences imposed a harsh penalty on the Congregationalist churches from which both the Great Awakening and the American Revolution to some degree flowed. Beginning first in the Virginia legislature in 1786 and then in the federal Bill of Rights five years later, measures were adopted to guarantee freedom of religion. The battle against the establishment of a state or federal religion was led primarily by Thomas Jefferson (1743–1826) and James Madison (1751–1836), both of whom strongly opposed the role that the official Church of England had played in the southern colonies.

These concerns were far less common in Massachusetts, Connecticut, and New Hampshire, where the state-supported Congregationalist churches were not an extension of a foreign government but were instead the backbone of colonial communities and, in their own right, ardent supporters of the Revolution. Nonetheless, over a period of years, state financial support was slowly withdrawn from the New England churches.[14] The removal of churches from the public dole did not, as some had feared, cause them to wither and die. To the contrary, the great Presbyterian minister Lyman Beecher (1775–1865) conceded that the decision in 1818 to cut the bonds between the state of Connecticut and the Congregationalist Church imbued local churches with renewed vigor and enthusiasm. "It cut the churches loose from dependence on state support," Beecher wrote. "It threw them wholly on their own resources and on God."[15]

In the early to mid-nineteenth century, this enthusiasm was expressed in a renewal of religious fervor designated as America's Second Great Awakening. But unlike the first revival, which focused almost entirely on the personal experience of conversion and salvation, this upsurge in religious fervor was marked by the profound belief that the nation's soul could be saved as well. At first, the staggering number of civic organizations and associations that arose during the Second Great Awakening were focused on spreading the gospel and converting the irreligious and the misguided. Over time, however, these same groups began advocating for the adoption of laws and public policies to end various social ills, ranging from the abuse of alcohol to slavery.

One of the more interesting aspects of the Second Great Awakening is that it was as much a technological revolution as a social one. In 1816, for instance, the American Bible Society was founded to distribute inexpensive copies of the scriptures around the country. Similarly, in 1825, the American Tract Society was established to publish "short, plain, striking, entertaining, and instructive Tracts." Thanks to advances in printing technology, a ten-page tract could be produced for a single penny, making it affordable for the society to print the tracts themselves and give them away for free.[16] "Evangelicals were among the first to take advantage of this development. Ignited by the power of the Word to save souls, their associations pioneered in the newest machines and techniques of printing and forms of organization and distribution. In the process they helped to revolutionize publishing and advance literacy in America."[17]

Four hundred years earlier, when Johannes Gutenberg (ca. 1398–ca. 1468) had designed and built his revolutionary printing press, the first book printed was the Bible. But within a decade, the list of printed works included Giovanni Boccaccio's (1313–1375) *Decameron*, a notoriously salacious and highly anti-clerical work that was rigorously suppressed. Similarly, the nineteenth-century improvements in modern printing technology driven by the evangelical tract societies led to an upsurge in the availability of salacious books and pamphlets that were far closer to the *Decameron* (if less well written) than to the Bible.

As a result, in urban areas around the country, movements arose to combat the forces of immorality threatening to ensnare young men and women. To an unprecedented degree, either before or since, these efforts were funded and led by evangelical businessmen, who were motivated in equal measure by their belief in the uplifting power of the gospel and their pragmatic need for a reliable workforce.

THE YOUNG MEN'S CHRISTIAN ASSOCIATION AND THE NEW YORK SOCIAL REFORMERS

Of all the organizations founded to improve the moral environment in post–Industrial Revolution cities, it is the Young Men's Christian Association that has lasted the longest and has had the greatest cultural impact. Originally founded in England and now 162 years old, the YMCA has a presence in all fifty of the United States and in 120 countries around the world.

The organization was founded in July 1844 by a British draper, George Williams (1821–1905), who as a young man traveled to London for work. In his early days in the city, he described himself as a "careless, thoughtless, godless, swearing young fellow," but not long after arriving in the city, he found God and became a devout Christian. Concerned about the working and living conditions for young men in the city, Williams organized a prayer group of his fellow employees to provide an alternative to immoral amusements like the pub and the pool hall.[18]

By 1851 the charismatic thirty-year-old Williams was the head of an organization of fifty-one YMCAs in Britain, with a combined membership of twenty-seven hundred. That same year, Prince Albert (1819–1861), Queen Victoria's consort, helped lead a campaign to conduct a grand exhibition in London of the nation's art and manufacturing. On May 1, 1851, Queen Victoria (1819–1901) opened the Great Exhibition at the Crystal Palace, a mammoth cast-iron and glass enclosure covering 772,784 square feet. The gutters alone stretched thirty miles. Underneath the capacious roof, seventeen thousand exhibitors presented a bewildering array of goods and services to the public. By the end of the exhibition, more than six million people had come through the Crystal Palace doors.[19]

Among the exhibitors was the London YMCA, equipped with pamphlets and tracts about its Christian mission. With the help of exhibition visitors from around the world, the YMCA quickly began to spread beyond the borders of England. By the end of the year, two YMCAs were founded in North America: the first was established in Montreal on November 25, 1851, and the second in Boston on December 29.[20]

One of the millions who attended the Great Exhibition was a New York importer named George H. Petrie (1828–1902). He picked up one of the London YMCA's tracts and, upon his return to New York, called together some friends to discuss the possibility of creating a New York chapter. Over the course of the following year, Petrie and his friends developed a plan to promote "the improvement of the spiritual, mental and social condition of young men." Although supposedly ecumenical in intent, the espoused purpose of the New York YMCA was "to promote evangelical religion," and, more specifically, evangelical Christianity.

The New York chapter of the YMCA opened its doors in September 1852 in the Stuyvesant Institute on Broadway. In addition to its campaign "to seek out young men" and help them find lodging, employment, and Christian associates, the YMCA's board of managers also "set up committees in charge of the association's rooms, library, publications, and lecture series."[21]

In relatively short order, two young men emerged as the leaders of the New York YMCA: William E. Dodge Jr. (1832–1903) and Morris K. Jesup (1830–1908). Dodge was the son and namesake of a wealthy merchant philanthropist who had helped found the New York branch of the American Tract Society in 1827, as well as some of the city's most important evangelical organizations.

Jesup, too, came from evangelical roots, but from far different social circumstances than Dodge. Born in 1830, he was raised in the stern strand of Connecticut Congregationalism that prevailed in the late 1700s and early

1800s, a region steeped in the passions of the Second Great Awakening. At the age of seven, Jesup moved to New York with his mother, and at the tender age of twelve began work as a clerk for Rogers, Ketchum & Grosvenor, a manufacturer of locomotives and cotton-mill gins.[22] By the time he joined with Dodge, George Petrie, and others in founding the YMCA, the twenty-two-year-old Jesup was already a partner in a prosperous railroad supply firm called Clark & Jesup. He was well on his way to becoming one of the wealthiest merchants of late nineteenth-century New York, and a leading example of the era's seamless mix of business and Christian evangelicalism.

From its earliest days, the New York YMCA was concerned about the issue of immorality and its effects on young men in the city. The organization's concern was heightened by the onset of the Civil War, with its accompanying breakdown of social order and mores in the ranks. At the start of the war, Jesup helped lead the formation of the United States Christian Commission, an organization devoted to ministering to Union troops through meetings, the distribution of Bibles and hymnbooks, the operation of soup kitchens, and some nursing. During the conflict, a total of five thousand volunteers helped distribute roughly $5.5 million in donations and supplies.[23]

One of the primary concerns of the US Christian Commission during the Civil War was the type of reading material available to soldiers. The publishers of salacious books and titillating photos found a particularly ready market for their products in encampments and on the front lines. In *The Story the Soldiers Wouldn't Tell: Sex in the Civil War*, Thomas Lowry lists the contents of one soldier's carefully saved catalog: "The personal effects of Pvt. Edmon Shriver of Company F, 42d Ohio, contained the 1863 catalog of G. S. Hoskins and Co., also of New York City. The book selection contains twenty-three titles, including *Fanny Hill*, *The Lustful Turk*, and *The Libertine Enchantress*[.] For $1, one could purchase *Matron's Manual of Midwifery*, *Prostitution in Paris*, *Male Generative Organs*, or *Aristotle Illustrated*. For only 50¢, one could choose among nine titles, including *Venus in Cloister*, *The Marriage Bed*, *Secret Passions*, and *Physiology of Love*."

Hoskins offered other merchandise as well: "spicy" song books, French tobacco boxes (in the shape of "human manure"), marked playing cards, transparent playing cards water-marked with naked women, French ticklers, love powders, false mustaches, three types of condoms, and stereoscopic pictures at $9 a dozen.

For only $3 a dozen, a soldier could receive, postpaid, *cartes de visite* of "London and Paris voluptuaries," portraying "the mysteries and delights of naked female beauty, male and female together and separate." The pièces de résistance were microscopic photos, set in stickpins, showing, when held close to the eye, "two or more figures photographed from life, engaged in sexual enjoyment."[24]

Other catalogs offered a similarly broad array of indecent literature and racy photographs of both foreign and domestic origin. Given the fact that the French had released the details of Louis Jacque Mandé Daguerre's revolutionary photographic technique only twenty-four years earlier, the range of poses and variety of devices for displaying photographs was really quite astonishing.

Not surprisingly, members of the military command were not thrilled with this booming trade. In a diary entry dated June 8, 1963, Marsena Patrick, the provost marshal for the Union's Army of the Potomac, wrote: "Amongst other things, I have seized upon and now hold, large amounts of Bogus jewelry, watches, et cetera, all from the same houses that furnish the vilest of obscene books, of which I have made a great haul lately." His entry for June 10 described the disposition of the books: "There has been a bonfire in the rear of my tent, burning up a large quantity of obscene books, taken from the mails."[25]

Prior to the Civil War, nobody seems to have given much thought to the fact that the nation's postal system was being used to distribute pornography. But in 1864, Postmaster General Montgomery Blair (1813–1883) appeared before Congress to ask for its assistance in stopping the "great numbers of obscene books and pictures" being mailed to soldiers in the army,[26] a proposal that was actively supported by the New York YMCA. Congress responded promptly by attaching to a broader piece of postal legislation its first prohibition against the mailing of obscene literature. Violation of the statute was a misdemeanor punishable by a fine of up to $500 and/or imprisonment for up to a year.[27]

Despite the passage of the revised postal law, it was clear to the leaders of the New York YMCA that the city was still awash in licentious publications. A report prepared in 1866 for the YMCA's executive committee concluded that "[t]he debasing influence of these publications cannot be over estimated: they are feeders for brothels." To further its fight against indecency and obscenity, the New York YMCA lobbied heavily for an obscenity bill in the New York legislature, which finally passed a law in 1868. Even with the new state law, however, enforcement was lax, and, in 1872, the YMCA board of directors created a Committee on Obscene Literature to examine what might be done.[28] Largely through happenstance, the committee found its solution in the person of a twenty-eight-year-old dry goods clerk named Anthony Comstock.

Zealotry Unleashed: Anthony Comstock Goes Postal

The twin strands of Puritanism and progressive reform found fertile soil in the mind and soul of Anthony Comstock, and combined in him to create an individual of strongly noble aspirations and deeply destructive execution. In large part because of his vocational excesses, no other individual has since been similarly vested with such unlimited authority over the hunt for and the prosecution of the indecent and obscene. And yet, his immense, bewhiskered shadow has lingered for more than a century, offering an object lesson for would-be reformers and content producers alike.

Anthony Comstock was born on March 7, 1844, in the small Connecticut town of New Canaan. The town, originally established as Canaan Parish by the Connecticut colonial legislature in 1731, is in the far southwest corner of the state, in what is now one of the country's wealthiest counties, Fairfield County (also known informally as the Gold Coast). At the time of Comstock's birth, however, the area was primarily agricultural with a steadily growing shoe-making industry. His parents, Polly Lockwood and Thomas Anthony Comstock, were moderately affluent farmers of Puritan descent and active members in the community's Congregationalist Church.

Like Morris Jesup, although some fourteen years younger, Comstock was imbued with the stern Congregationalist ethos of his native Connecticut from an early age. The younger man was also influenced by the fact that he grew up in the midst of the first wave of the American temperance movement. In 1825 one of the first tracts distributed by the American Tract Society argued for the benefits of abstinence. Temperance societies formed in most of the states, leading to the adoption of the first Prohibition law in 1846 in Maine. Pastor Lyman Beecher, an ardent temperance supporter, loudly praised the state for its action: "This thing of God, that glorious Maine law was a square and grand blow between the horns of the devil!"[29] Over the next ten years, thirteen states (including Connecticut) followed Maine's example. For Prohibitionists, however, these early legislative victories proved illusory; by the Civil War, the laws had either been vetoed or repealed in most jurisdictions.[30]

Despite the uneven success of the temperance movement, Comstock was such an ardent supporter that at the relatively young age of eighteen he raided a local seller of spirits and broke up his stock. During his stint in the Civil War, Comstock infuriated his fellow soldiers by accepting each day's ration of whiskey and pouring it onto the ground untasted. By all accounts, he remained abstemious throughout his life.[31]

During his last few months in the Union army, Comstock's efforts to organize prayer meetings and bring preachers to the troops led to his appointment as a voluntary agent for the Christian Commission. His diary from that time demonstrates that his efforts were not always well received. His compatriots teased him about being a "Christian," fought with him when drunk, and literally tried to smoke him out of his bunk, an event that Comstock—a notoriously bad speller throughout his life—described as the "boys were iniatiating me."[32] It is not difficult to imagine this being a lonely and oppressive time for Comstock, but the faith and drive that sustained him throughout his service in the Union army would serve him in good stead.

Roughly a year after he was mustered out of the army, Anthony Comstock arrived in New York armed with only a $5 loan from a Norwalk, Connecticut, banker. For the next five years, Comstock's life consisted of a series of dry-goods jobs, frugal living, and then a $500 down payment on a house in Brooklyn and marriage to Margaret Hamilton. Comstock would launch his moral campaign here, with the support of the Congregational minister William Ives Budington and of the Brooklyn branch of the YMCA.[33]

Comstock first went after the saloons in his neighborhood that opened on Sunday in violation of the Brooklyn blue laws. After a drawn-out but successful battle, he next turned his attention to the extensive and open sale of licentious materials. His first recorded challenge to booksellers occurred on March 2, 1872, when he asked a New York police captain and a reporter from the *New York Tribune* to accompany him to two stationery stores well known for their sale of "obscene" books and pictures. After Comstock purchased samples of the offending materials, the police captain arrested six employees from the two stores under the authority of the 1868 New York obscenity law, which the YMCA had championed.[34] Two weeks later, Comstock made his first appearance in the pages of the *New York Times* when it was reported that his complaint had led to the arrest and prosecution of three people charged with selling "articles of an obscene character."[35]

During the raid on March 2, Comstock learned the name of William Haynes, the prolific publisher of prurient books, and resolved to have him arrested. At some point during that month, a store owner and middleman named E. M. Grandin sent Haynes a note, saying, "Get out of the way. Comstock is after you. Damn fool wont look at money." Haynes died the same evening that he received Grandin's note.[36] Despite Haynes's death, Comstock resolved to purchase and destroy the steel plates used to print the illicit books, and promised to pay Haynes's widow (and business partner), Mary Haynes, $650 for them.

The problem, however, was that Comstock did not have enough money to make the purchase. According to Comstock's semiofficial biographer, Charles Trumbull, Comstock submitted an appeal for funds to purchase the Haynes plates to R. R. McBurney, secretary of the Young Men's Christian Association of New York. While passing McBurney's desk soon thereafter, Jesup happened to see the letter, and was intrigued by Comstock's account of his battle against indecent literature. Jesup visited Comstock at work, introduced himself, and invited Comstock to present his request for funds at a meeting of other philanthropists at Jesup's house. After listening to Comstock's description of the immoral book trade and his efforts against it, Jesup and the YMCA agreed to provide Comstock with $650 to purchase the plates used by William Haynes and $150 to compensate Comstock for his time.[37]

Trumbull reports that a short time after the meeting at Jesup's house, "Mr. Comstock had an experience that deepened his faith in God's guidance and in prayer." He had not yet finalized the purchase of the book plates, but while heading to work one morning, Comstock had a sudden impulse to go instead to Balchen Place, Brooklyn (the street on which the Hayneses lived). As he stood speaking with Mrs. Haynes at her front door, Comstock saw outside a wagon loaded with engraved printing plates. He reportedly seized control of the wagon and drove it to the YMCA, where the plates were stored until their destruction with acid at the Brooklyn Polytechnic Institute on April 6, 1872.[38]

Comstock's successful capture and destruction of the Haynes plates made it clear to Jesup and the other directors of the YMCA that they had found a powerful instrument for their goal of moral reform. Jesup helped raise funds to provide Comstock with a salary of $1,950 for the balance of 1872 and $3,000 for 1873, along with an expense account "for detecting and punishing offenders and for destroying stock seized."[39] In addition, the directors recruited Comstock, along with McBurney and New York lawyer Charles E. Whitehead, to lobby for a federal version of the 1868 New York obscenity law, since neither they nor Comstock felt that the existing federal law was strong enough to prevent the volume of indecency traveling through the mails.[40]

Upon his arrival in Washington in late January 1813, Comstock spent a day on the floor of the House of Representatives, displaying a collection of the types of materials seized during his raids. To assist him in the drafting of his proposed antiobscenity legislation, he obtained the help of the widely regarded New York lawyer Benjamin Vaughan Abbott (1830–1890) and, remarkably, US Supreme Court justice William Strong (1808–1895), who made sure that Comstock's bill was in the proper form for Congress.[41]

On February 6, 1873, A. H. Byington, the editor of the *Norwalk Gazette*, helped Comstock obtain the use of the vice president's room of the floor of the US Senate. Comstock used the space to lay out his trophies, and his diary describes the reaction of the senators: "About 11:30 went up to the Senate with my exhibits. A. H. Byington of Norwalk very kindly aided me by securing the Vice-President's room and inviting Senators out to see me. I spent an hour or two talking and explaining the extent of the nefarious business and answering questions. . . . All were very much excited, and declared themselves ready to give me any law I might ask for, if it was only within the bounds of the Constitution. I also saw the Vice-President [Schuyler Colfax].[42] All said they were ready to pass my bill promptly this session."[43]

Senator William Windom (R-MN) (to whom Comstock had been introduced by Justice Strong) presented Comstock's bill in the Senate on February 11, 1873. A similar version of the bill had previously been introduced in the House of Representatives by Clinton L. Merriam (R-NY). [44] After some legislative wrangling, the bill, which quickly became known as the Comstock Law, was signed into law by President Ulysses S. Grant on March 3, 1873. It was, coincidentally, the one-year anniversary of Comstock's first amateur obscenity raids.

Immediately after the passage of the Comstock Law, Senator Windom and Representative Merriam joined forces to petition Postmaster General Marshall Jewell to appoint Comstock a special agent of the US Post Office to enforce the law, which he did. Comstock accepted the position, but only on the condition that he not draw a salary lest there be charges of favoritism or patronage. It was understood by all concerned that Comstock would be compensated instead by the YMCA (and, later, by the separately incorporated New York Society for the Suppression of Vice). It was an arrangement that was eminently satisfactory to all sides: Comstock received financial backing for his moral crusade, the YMCA received the force of federal law for its work, and both Congress and the YMCA received the services of an indefatigable moralist.

Chaos in the Airwaves

Despite Comstock's objective successes (tons of allegedly indecent materials destroyed, dozens of people successfully prosecuted, and a legislative legacy that persists today), the battle that he waged was fundamentally unwinnable. Even at a time when the distribution of allegedly indecent materials was limited to books, pamphlets, prints, and photographs, it was simply impossible for him to eliminate all of the potential "traps for the young." [45] And during Comstock's own lifetime, two nearly simultaneous inventions presaged even greater challenges in limiting the spread of indecency: radio and motion pictures (the latter is discussed in the following chapter).

In 1894 Guglielmo Marconi (1874–1937), a young Italian electrical engineer, developed a system that enabled him to send a radio signal from one point to another. Like the concepts behind many great inventions, the transmission of a radio signal is deceptively simple. In fact, the marvelous Web site HowStuffWorks.com offers instructions for constructing "the simplest radio":

- Take a fresh 9-volt battery and a coin.
- Find an AM radio and tune it to an area of the dial that produces only static.

- Now hold the battery near the antenna and quickly tap the two terminals of the battery with the coin (so that the terminals are connected for an instant).
- A crackling noise will come out of the radio's speaker, caused by the connection and disconnection of the battery terminals by the coin.[46]

These instructions describe the process for creating a "spark transmitter" and replicate (in very basic form) the essence of Marconi's 1894 invention. By itself, the process of using sparks to generate static is not very useful, but Marconi realized that the production of a spark could be regulated to transmit the patterns of Morse code, which is how he transmitted a message first across the Italian hills near his home and later across the Atlantic. (In general, as Marconi discovered, size matters—the bigger the spark, the greater the distance covered by the signal.) Rebuffed by his native Italy when he tried to sell his invention to the national government, Marconi sought his economic fortune first in Britain (where he helped construct the first radio factory in 1898) and then in America, where he founded the American Marconi Company in 1899. He was all of twenty-five at the time.

Marconi's invention of wireless telegraphy led to an amateur and commercial radio boom that mirrored the craze surrounding photography fifty years earlier and anticipated the frenzy over the World Wide Web a century later. The simplicity of setting up a radio transmitter and receiver to exchange messages quickly led to the development of a three-pronged wireless industry in the United States consisting of government stations (primarily belonging to the navy), nascent commercial operations, and large numbers of amateurs of widely varying abilities. By January 1910, for instance, the so-called Wireless Association of America laid claim to more than three thousand members,[47] while two years later Hugo Gernsback (considered by many to be the Father of Amateur Wireless) offered "his heartiest congratulations to the 400,000 American amateurs" on the passage of a bill officially recognizing their status.[48]

The popular enthusiasm for Marconi's wireless telegraphy, or radio, quickly raised resource management issues on a national and ultimately international scale. As opposed to other media (such as newspapers, books, photographs, or even movies), the number of people who can effectively use broadcast frequencies is limited by the fact that there are a finite number of electromagnetic frequencies available. The range of frequencies that we commonly describe today as "radio" consists of those frequencies that can be generated by applying an alternating current of electricity to an antenna (approximately 9 kilohertz to just above 300 gigahertz).[49]

Complicating matters is the fact that not all frequencies behave in a similar fashion. Marconi was ultimately awarded a Nobel Prize for discovering (among other things) that lower radio frequencies (with correspondingly longer wavelengths) travel not only through the air but also through the ground along the curve of the earth, vastly increasing the distance over which such signals can be detected. In general, the lower the frequency, the farther a signal of a given power can travel by means of "ground waves."

Operators of early radio transmitters, both amateur and professional, naturally gravitated toward the lower frequencies so that they could maximize the reach of their stations through the advantageous use of ground waves; not surprisingly, this quickly led to considerable interference among radio stations.[50] As early as 1906, trade publications had begun to complain about the rising levels of signal noise. "We believe strongly in the potency of individual effort, and look with distrust upon too intimate Governmental control of private enterprise," the editors of *Electrical World* said. "Nevertheless, the time has now come when in wireless telegraphy it is either regulation or chaos, and of the two the former is certainly to be preferred."[51]

The proper form that wireless regulation should take, however, was not at all clear to Congress. It is important to note that when the issue of radio regulation was first being debated, Congress did not have the assistance of extensive committee staffs, think tanks, or large numbers of lobbyists to help educate them about technical issues. At the same time, Washington was receiving considerable pressure from the international community as well. There was grumbling that despite sending delegates to two international wireless conferences, one in 1903 and the other in 1906, the US government had not yet done anything significant to either promote or regulate wireless communication.

THE FEDERAL RADIO COMMISSION AND THE FEDERAL COMMUNICATIONS COMMISSION

Congress took the first small steps toward regulating the new medium by adopting the Wireless Act of 1910. The bill was inspired in large part by a well-publicized collision between two ocean liners, the White Star Line's RMS *Republic* and the *Florida*, an Italian immigrant ship. The collision made headlines around the world in large part due to the heroics of the *Republic*'s Marconi wireless operator, Jack Binns, who sent out a distress signal ("CQD") from his sinking ship. He stayed at his post for nineteen hours, guiding rescue ships through dense fog to the *Republic*; his heroism earned him congressional accolades, a ticker-tape parade, and the lifelong nickname "CQD Binns."

Despite the evident value of wireless, the Wireless Act of 1910 was far from comprehensive: its main provision was to require ships to carry wireless sets.[52] In fact, the Department of Commerce and Labor's Bureau of Navigation did not even established a radio service to enforce the requirements of the Wireless Act until 1911.[53]

Recognizing that more needed to be done in the area of wireless telegraphy or "radio," as it was coming to be known, Congress began work on An Act to Regulate Radio Communication. By the spring of 1912, much of the work on the bill had been completed; however, a second marine tragedy helped speed the bill's passage.

On the night of April 14, 1912, at about 11:40 PM, the RMS *Titanic* (the brand-new flagship of the White Star Line) scraped alongside an iceberg in the North Atlantic Ocean, tearing a series of holes in its forward bulkheads. The ship was on its maiden voyage from Southampton, England, to New York City, and was just over twelve hundred miles from its destination. Although the ship had been widely described as "practically unsinkable" (the qualifier was frequently omitted) and despite the fact that the holes together measured just twelve square feet (smaller than most beds), the damage was sufficient to overcome the *Titanic*'s highly touted design. Just two hours and forty minutes after first striking ice, the *Titanic* sank to its final resting place more than two miles below the waves, taking over fifteen hundred people with it.

The sinking of the *Titanic* threw into stark relief just how chaotic the wireless situation had become. The White Star Line complained to President Taft that the number of people sending information and breaking into transmissions made it "practically impossible to get any reliable information by wireless."[54] The president himself was frustrated by his inability to get accurate information about the fate of his military aide, Major Archibald Butt, who was returning from Europe on the White Star liner.[55] The chief engineer for the navy, Hutch I. Cone, was quoted as saying, "This wireless chaos that places human lives at the mercy of irresponsible operators who are beyond control of the government or any regulation is particularly outrageous at such a time as this. It is precisely what is bound to happen when there is no regulation by law, and it will happen again unless some means of regulation is prescribed."[56]

The Radio Act of 1912 would almost certainly have passed on its own merits, but the confusion and interference that accompanied the *Titanic* disaster helped speed its adoption by Congress. Less than three months later, on August 13, 1912, Congress approved the so-called Radio Act, and the law was signed by President Taft the same day (although it did not officially take effect until four months later).

The "merits" of the Radio Act, however, proved to be less than impressive. The language of the act was frequently vague and confusing, reflecting Congress's uncertain grasp of the new technology. Moreover, the act was premised on the increasingly outdated concept of stations communicating directly with each other (for the purpose of relaying of messages)—using frequencies of their own choosing—rather than broadcasting radio signals for general reception. Congress tried to minimize interference among stations by dividing the usable radio spectrum into four segments: a particular valuable and useful segment for exclusive government use, two segments on either side of the government range for commercial use, and a single wavelength (1500 khz), generally considered to be useless, for transmissions by amateurs. (Despite the fact that amateurs had played a critical role in the development of wireless technology, the Radio Act of 1912 was a clear statement by Congress that their presence was no longer welcome on the airwaves.)[57]

The problem, unfortunately, was that the new technology continued to befuddle Congress. Not unlike the challenges posed today by Internet and computer technology, the pace of change in radio technology only exacerbated the legislature's dilemma. Senator Key Pittman (D-NV) undoubtedly spoke for many of his colleagues when he complained: "I do not think, sir, that in the 14 years I have been here there has ever been a question before the Senate that in the very nature of the thing Senators can know so little about as this subject."[58]

Following the end of World War I (during which the federal government suspended all private and commercial radio broadcasts), Secretary of Commerce Herbert Hoover convened a series of conferences in an ultimately futile effort to resolve the contentious issues of interference and frequency piracy (when more powerful stations simply overrode weaker ones). Hoover's authority to deal with the problem of radio was badly undercut in 1926, when both a federal court and acting US attorney general William J. Donovan concluded that the Radio Act of 1912 did not give him the authority to assign specific frequencies to particular radio stations.

The discussion of Hoover's authority accelerated an ongoing debate in Congress over how to resolve the issue. From the start, the debate over radio reform was colored by concerns regarding Secretary Hoover's personal political ambitions and the ambitions of the politicians drafting the legislation. The idea of a radio commission gained support in large part because of the concern that if appointed "radio czar," Hoover would be in a position to use radio to benefit either his own campaign or those of his fellow Republicans. Similar concerns undoubtedly dampened enthusiasm for putting radio under the control of the Interstate Commerce Commission, given the fact that the chair of the Senate Interstate Commerce Committee, James E. Watson (R-IN), had his own presidential aspirations.[59] But at the other end of Pennsylvania Avenue, President Calvin Coolidge, a strong pro-business Republican, made it clear that he did not favor the establishment of another independent commission, citing what he perceived to be problems in the operation of both the Interstate Commerce Commission and the Federal Trade Commission.[60]

Another significant issue underlying the debate was what role, if any, government should play in regulating radio. In resolving that issue, two forces often antagonistic to each other combined to shepherd a compromise bill through Congress. On the one hand were the business owners who had invested hundreds of millions of dollars in the infrastructure of radio and were deeply concerned that the ongoing chaos in the airwaves (particularly from smaller stations and low-power amateurs) would ruin the industry through continued interference with commercial signals. And on the other hand were political progressives, who believed in the possibilities and benefits offered by radio, but only if it were administered in the "public interest, convenience and necessity."[61] Implicit in that standard was that broadcasters would refrain from or be punished for airing material that was not in the public interest. Ironically, then, the "progressive" goal of putting the radio industry under the supervision of the federal government, rather than permitting unfettered capitalism, carried with it the cost of a limitation on what could be said on the air.

Despite his reluctance to do so, President Calvin Coolidge signed the Radio Control Law on February 23, 1927, creating a five-member Federal Radio Commission to supervise a reorganization of the radio airwaves. Under the terms of a legislative compromise, the Radio Commission was supposed to operate for just a single year and then turn over its authority to the Secretary of Commerce.[62] As often happens in Washington, however, the commission was granted a series of extensions, and was finally replaced in 1934 by the more comprehensive Federal Communications Commission.

In the Radio Control Law, Congress included language requiring equal opportunity for politicians (but only "legally qualified candidates," which further limited the range of political speech), and forbidding the utterance of any "obscene, indecent or profane" language. From the start, the latter clause in particular raised concerns. Not long after the signing of the bill, the *New York Times* featured an editorial declaring that "[t]he listener has, of course, instant protection from all these invasions of his privacy. A turn of the hand upon the dial and these demons of the air are dismissed."

"The peril," the *Times* warned presciently, "comes from the insidious propagandist, the alluring demagogue, the covert advertiser, the fatuous entertainer and the debaser of the arts."[63] Sadly enough, a nearly identical editorial could be published today, nearly eighty years later.

Print shows satire of American women from Edenton, North Carolina, pledging to boycott English tea in response to a Continental Congress resolution in 1774 to boycott English goods. (Library of Congress)

Chapter Three

Religious Boycotts and Corporate Self-Censorship

Private
Efforts to Cleanse
American Culture

I wish to join the Legion of Decency, which condemns vile and unwholesome motion moving pictures. I unite with all who protest against them as a grave menace to youth, to home life, to country and religion.

I condemn absolutely those salacious motion pictures which, with other degrading agencies, are corrupting public morals and promoting a sex mania in our land.

I shall do all that I can to arouse public opinion against the portrayal of vice as a normal condition of affairs and against depicting criminals of any class as heroes and heroines, presenting their filthy philosophy of life as something acceptable to decent men and women.

I unite with all who condemn the display of suggestive advertisements on billboards, at theatre entrances and the favourable notices given to immoral motion pictures.

Considering these evils, I hereby promise to remain away from all motion pictures except those which do not offend decency and Christian morality. I promise further to secure as many members as possible for the Legion of Decency.

I make this protest in a spirit of self-respect, and with the conviction that the American public does not demand filthy pictures, but clean entertainment and educational features.
—Pledge of the Catholic Legion of Decency, 1934[1]

During the summer of 1880, Captain Charles Cunningham Boycott (1832–1897) was serving as a land agent for Lord Erne. The lord was the holder of large tracts of land in the Lough Mask area of County Mayo in western Ireland. The region, like much of Ireland at the time, was riven by political and social turmoil. A campaign was being waged by the Irish Land League to provide better economic conditions for the country's tenant farmers. Among other things, the campaign called for the "3F's": "fair rent, fixity of tenure, and free sale."[2] At the instigation of reform activist Michael Davitt (1846–1906), the tenant farmers working Lord Erne's land refused to bring in that year's harvest. Captain Boycott tried to disrupt the reform movement and in response Davitt organized a campaign of community ostracization. The land agent was ignored by his neighbors, refused service by shop owners, and isolated at church. At Lord Erne's request, the British government ultimately stepped in to resolve the situation, sending fifty Protestants from Ulster to harvest his crops and a mixture of British soldiers and policemen to protect the harvesters. The captain soon departed Ireland for Britain, leaving behind only his contribution to the English language: the phrase "to boycott."

More than a century before Lord Erne's oats and potatoes lay moldering in the fields, commercial ostracization had already proven to be a powerful tool of social protest and change. In 1768 Boston merchant John Hancock helped organize a boycott of the tea sold in the colonies by the British East India Company. One of his major reasons for doing so was his outrage over the admittedly accurate charges by the British that he was a smuggler. Over the next five years, the company's sale of tea in the American colonies dropped from 320,000 pounds to 520 pounds, leaving the company with warehouses filled with unsteeped inventory and enormous debts (and, in the process, turning the colonies—and eventually the United States—into a nation of coffee drinkers). When the British government tried to force tea shipments down the throats of the colonialists in Boston, a group of Bostonians disguised as Native Americans stormed three ships on the night of December 16, 1773, and tossed the tea overboard. The "Boston Tea Party" infuriated the British government, which promptly shut down the port of Boston. Up and down the Atlantic coast, the colonial boycott on tea expanded to a general refusal to purchase British goods of any description, a development that helped precipitate the American Revolution two years later.[3]

The two most powerful applications of the boycott occurred in regions of the world far removed from each other but linked by a common goal: the promotion of civil and human rights. In 1921 Mohandas Gandhi advocated a boycott of all foreign-produced goods (but especially British products) as part of his campaign for self-rule in India. And in 1955, the arrest and conviction of

Rosa Parks (1913–2005) for disorderly conduct (for refusing to comply with a Montgomery, Alabama, ordinance requiring African Americans to sit at the back of a bus) triggered a 382-day boycott of the bus system by the African American community. The boycott was led in large measure by a relatively unknown twenty-six-year-old Baptist minister, Martin Luther King (1929–1968), who was inspired by the principles of nonviolence espoused by Gandhi. The success of the Montgomery bus boycott helped propel King to national prominence as a leader of the US civil rights movement.

The success of these social protests have made the boycott a popular tool for a variety of relatively modern causes: the Arab League's nearly half-century boycott of Israeli businesses (and, in some cases, businesses that buy or sell from Israeli businesses); the United Farm Workers' boycott of grapes and lettuce organized in the mid-1960s by Cesar Chavez (1927–1993); and the boycott of South Africa by entire nations in the early 1980s to protest its policy of apartheid. One of the central challenges in organizing and running an effective boycott is asking people to act against their economic self-interest, which by definition is an irrational act in a capitalist economic system. But as the response to those boycotts demonstrates, people can be persuaded to assign an economic value to their ideals of social justice.

Not surprisingly, various groups committed to winning the decency wars have tried to use the boycott as a tool in their efforts to cleanse American culture. While those efforts have had some limited success, the boycott has ultimately failed to make a significant difference in the moral environment of the nation. In response, social and religious conservatives increasingly have replaced the use of the boycott with attempts to pass and enforce increasingly strict federal legislation and regulations.

BOYCOTTING BOOKS: SIX HUNDRED YEARS OF FUTILITY

The medium that has struggled the longest with both religious censorship and boycott is the printed word. For roughly a thousand years, the Roman Catholic Church had the ability to completely control both the content and distribution of books in western Europe. Throughout the long period colloquially referred to as the Dark Ages, the Church was both the preserver and the filter of information. What few books were actually produced during the period were those laboriously hand-copied in the Church's *scriptoria* by someone in a monk's cowl.[4] In its own fashion, the Church performed an invaluable service for intellectual thought by preserving knowledge, but the freedom with which that knowledge was shared was sharply limited.

Two separate developments combined to strip the Church of its near-total control over books. The first was the rise of universities, beginning in Bologna, Italy, in 1139. At first, universities were closely tied to the Church, but over time they became steadily more secular. In the process, the demand for books exceeded the ability of monks to produce them, and budding capitalism took over. University students could either purchase books hand-copied in a local shop or buy paper to make their own copies of a borrowed text. Combined with an increased flow of books from outside Europe (particularly from the mathematically advanced Arab world), the Church's ability to control what people read was greatly weakened.

The second development occurred in the mid-1450s, when Johannes Gutenberg, a native of Mainz, Germany, combined a number of different technologies to construct a device that greatly sped up the production of books: a printing press with movable type. It was hardly accidental that the first European printing press was built in the city of Mainz. Located on the bank of the Rhine River in southwestern Germany, Mainz is widely regarded as the capital of Germany's wine-growing industry, where the region's ubiquitous screw-type wine presses became an integral part of Gutenberg's design.[5]

The significance of Gutenberg's invention lay not merely in the increased speed with which books could be produced—cultural theorist Marshall McLuhan (1911–1980) once estimated that by the year 1500 (less than fifty years after Gutenberg built his first press) there were "fifteen to twenty million copies of 30,000 to 35,000 separate publications"[6]—but also in the sheer simplicity of his design. Given the limited economic and technological capabilities of fifteenth-century Europe, use of the printing press spread with remarkable speed: According to one account, by 1480 there were sixty-eight printing presses in locations ranging from England to southern Italy. Just twenty years later, the number had more than doubled to 140.[7]

The full extent of the printing press's impact on the Church's ability to control written materials became evident in 1520, when Pope Leo X issued the bull Exsurge Domine, which prohibited the printing of all current and future writings by the German theologian Martin Luther. But the theological barn door was already wide open: Leo's bull was released three years after Luther's 95 Theses (which, thanks to the printing press, had crossed Germany in just two weeks and all of western Europe in two months). As the Luther-inspired Protestant Reformation flamed across the continent, the fundamental lesson was that in the short span of seventy-five years, printing technology had spread too far for the Church to effectively control literary content. Although individual authors would continue to feel the lash of the Church's disapproval, or worse (particularly during the Inquisition), literature steadily and irrevocably became a secular phenomenon.

Recognizing its diminishing institutional control over the production and distribution of books, the Church shifted strategies and essentially tried to organize a boycott of unacceptable books. Beginning in 1559, the Catholic Church created and maintained a list, ultimately known as the *Index Librorum Prohibitorum*, of all the books deemed a sin for Catholics to read. Over time, the list became a virtual Who's Who of prominent authors and, as early as the eighteenth century, it was considered something of a professional compliment to be listed.[8] Although the *Index* never achieved its ultimate goal of eliminating objectionable works, it did have some localized success: it could be difficult to find copies of prohibited books in cities with a high percentage of Catholics and strong church leadership.

Thanks in no small part to their common origins, Catholicism and Protestantism shared a similarly dim view of libidinous literature. At first, the New England Congregationalists and the southern Anglicans tried the same approach as the European Catholics, using the disapproval of church leaders to regulate what was read. But when the power of the threat of eternal damnation began to fade, the Protestants took the next logical step of codifying their disapproval in statutes, thus replacing intangible damnation with the far more immediate threat of stocks, bonds, and imprisonment. By 1800 every one of the new American states had a prohibition against obscenity, and as new states joined the union, they invariably followed suit. Moreover, between 1842 and 1956, the US Congress passed twenty different prohibitions of obscenity.[9]

Statutory bans never completely succeeded in preventing the publication or distribution of allegedly "indecent" or "obscene" books. However, for much of the nation's history, such statutes had a chilling effect on the books that could be purchased and read, particularly when the prohibition was enforced with the enthusiasm (and invested authority) of someone like Anthony Comstock. But the strength of the ban on obscene literature began to slip in 1933, when US District Court judge John M. Woolsey (1877–1945) ruled that James Joyce's (1882–1942) novel *Ulysses* was not obscene. Despite Woolsey's ruling, however, literature would remain under threat of obscenity prosecution for years to come. D. H. Lawrence's (1885–1930) *Lady Chatterly's Lover* (1928), for instance, was not published freely in the United States until 1959, and Henry Miller's (1891–1980) *Tropic of Cancer* (1934) until 1960.

Long before the obscenity threat to books was finally lifted, there were occasional attempts to organize boycotts of specific authors. Most of these attempts were local in nature and never had a significant impact on sales. One of the earliest efforts occurred during the trial of Oscar Wilde (1854–1900) in London in 1895 for "gross indecency," when a boycott of his books was organized in Newark, New Jersey, and the city's library trustees ordered the removal of Wilde's name and the name of his books from the library catalog.[10]

His "poems, stories, and plays" were also withdrawn from the public library in St. Louis, Missouri.[11] Similarly, the Derby Neck Free Library in Connecticut expunged Jack London's (1876–1916) books in 1906 after he publicly endorsed socialism.[12] (The resulting publicity, one letter writer pointed out, promptly made London's essay collection on socialism one of the three most-requested books at the New York Public Library.)[13] The same year, noted author Upton Sinclair (1878–1968) was targeted following the publication of *The Jungle*, his exposé of the Chicago meat-packing industry. Library trustees in two major cities, Chicago and St. Louis, concluded that *The Jungle* "was a book unfit for circulation." Sinclair was sanguine about both the boycott of his book and the reasoning behind it. "Now, I share hard fate in good company, and I am aware of the incidental advantages which it brings to my book; and am not sufficiently hypocritical to pretend that I am at all grieved over this abuse of authority. I cannot, however, help noticing the peculiar circumstance—that the only two places in the country which have found 'The Jungle' unfit for circulation are large and important centres of the packing industry!"[14]

Notwithstanding Sinclair's cynical assessment of the power of the meat-packing industry, the most enduring efforts to boycott books in the United States were driven not by corporate policy but by religious doctrine. In 1934 Catholic bishop John Francis Noll (1875–1956) helped found the National Organization for Decent Literature (NODL). Over the next two decades, the NODL established branches in nearly every diocese in the United States. Adopting the model of the Legion of Decency, it printed pledge cards for every parishioner over the age of twelve to sign. Parents were encouraged to administer the pledge to children between the ages of five and twelve.[15]

Over the years, the Catholic Church slowly backed away from the idea of an organized boycott, preferring instead to describe the NODL as a "clearing house for information, suggestions and current news." The American Civil Liberties Union (ACLU) pointed out, however, that booksellers that chose to sell books on the NODL's prohibited list were warned by church officials that parishioners would not buy anything from them.[16] In Detroit, book publishers went to court to prevent a local prosecutor from banning the sale of books on the NODL list; the federal court ruled that the prosecutor could only act in cases where he believed the obscenity law was actually violated.[17]

The broadside by the ACLU and the unequivocal nature of the federal court's ruling in Detroit seemed to take some of the starch out of the NODL's efforts to collar indecent and obscene books. In November 1957, the nation's Catholic bishops reiterated their intent to wage a "war on obscenity," but the influence of recommendations by either the Legion of Decency or the NODL was steadily decreasing.

There was one last concerted effort to limit reading material on a national basis. In February 1959, a group called Citizens for Decent Literature (CDL) was formed in Cincinnati, Ohio.[18] The main force behind the group was a Cincinnati lawyer named Charles H. Keating Jr., who served as CDL's first national chairman. One of the group's first objectives was to link "the wave of juvenile delinquency" to the "cancerously filthy literature" available on the nation's newsstands.[19]

The group hit its pinnacle in 1965. It held a two-day national conference at the Waldorf-Astoria Hotel in New York City, which attracted roughly one thousand attendees. During the conference, Keating announced that the CDL would file an *amicus brief* in eight obscenity cases then pending before the US Supreme Court.[20] Just two years later, however, the use of obscenity law to prevent the distribution or sale of books effectively ended when the US Supreme Court handed down its decision regarding *Memoirs of a Woman of Pleasure*— more popularly known as *Fanny Hill*.

Fanny Hill was written circa 1749 by John Cleland (ca. 1709–1789), an Englishman who at the time was languishing in debtor's prison after a failed career with the British East India Company. The novel had a long history of censorship and suppression, thanks largely to its now quaint (but still quite explicit) descriptions of sexual activity.[21] In fact, one of the first obscenity prosecutions in the United States involved *Fanny Hill*, when two traveling booksellers were charged in 1820 with selling copies of the novel to Massachusetts farmers.[22]

In 1963 G. P. Putnam's Sons published *Fanny Hill* in Boston, and the Massachusetts attorney general filed a lawsuit alleging that the book was obscene. At the time, the prevailing test of obscenity had three parts: (1) the dominant theme of the material taken as a whole appeals to a prurient interest in sex; (2) the material is patently offensive because it affronts contemporary community standards relating to the description or representation of sexual matters; and (3) the material is utterly without redeeming social value.[23]

During the *Fanny Hill* trial, evidence was offered regarding the novel's literary merit and historical significance, but the Massachusetts Supreme Judicial Court rejected the value of the evidence. "We do not interpret the 'social importance' test," the court said, "as requiring that a book which appeals to the prurient interest and is patently offensive must be unqualifiedly worthless before it can be deemed obscene."[24]

Justice William Brennan (1906–1997), writing for the Supreme Court, said flatly that the Massachusetts court had erred. "A book cannot be proscribed," Justice Brennan said, "unless it is utterly without redeeming social value."[25] Since the Massachusetts trial court conceded that *Fanny Hill* had at least a "modicum of literary and historical value," the declaration that it was obscene was erroneous.

The "utterly without redeeming social value" standard enunciated by Justice Brennan sounded the death knell for the prosecution of literature on obscenity grounds. A little over a year later, the Court relied on the *Memoirs* case to throw out the conviction of Robert Redrup, a New York newsstand clerk who was convicted of selling two pulp novels—*Lust Pool* and *Shame Agent*—to an undercover policeman.[26] Most prosecutors reasonably concluded that if a book like *Lust Pool* was not "utterly without redeeming social value," then there was little chance that the Supreme Court would find any book obscene.

The Supreme Court was not alone in recognizing that the time had come to stop banning literature on the grounds of obscenity. In the wake of the Second Vatican Council, the Catholic Church essentially reached the same decision in 1966. The head of the Church's Congregation of the Faith, Alfredo Cardinal Ottaviana (1890–1979), announced that no further additions would be made to the *Index Librorum Prohibitorum* and that it no longer had "the force of law" within the Catholic Church.[27] Despite the removal of the threat of excommunication, however, individual Catholics had and still have an obligation to avoid reading anything that might endanger their faith or morals.

Although both the NODL and the CDL lingered on for a few years following the Supreme Court's *Fanny Hill* decision, there was clearly a growing national consensus that literature should not be banned. Consequently, the likelihood that any group could effectively organize a national book boycott, slim to begin with, largely vanished. There are simply too many potential sales outlets for even the most objectionable book, and, far more important, the idea of a book boycott struck too closely to the fundamental ideal of the First Amendment.

THE LEGION OF DECENCY GOES TO THE MOVIES (AND IS NOT AMUSED)

Although the Catholic Church had effectively lost its battle against heretical and indecent literature some centuries before the founding of the United States, it still retained enormous cultural power, particularly in the decades immediately following the great immigrations of European Catholics in the mid- to late-nineteenth century. Beginning in the 1930s, the newly activist American Catholic Church began an effort to shape the content of popular culture. Using a well-timed and highly successful boycott as its launchpad, the Church succeeded for the better part of thirty years in restraining the content of Hollywood's movies. Its control over the medium was never as complete as it would have liked, however, and in the end, a combination of much more powerful economic and cultural forces destroyed the Church's ability to mold the medium.

Motion pictures were perceived as a threat to decency by the watchdogs of cultural morality from the very moment of their invention in the late nineteenth century. There was a nearly instantaneous awareness that a technology consisting of the projection of larger-than-life images to an audience in a darkened hall had the power to shape societal values and undercut traditional norms of behavior.

The first hint of where that power might lead occurred in the early summer of 1896, when inventor Thomas Alva Edison (1847–1931) asked May Irwin (1862–1938) and John C. Rice (ca. 1858–1915), the stars of Broadway's hit play *The Widow Jones*, to reenact the play's final scene, a lingering kiss, on film for his Kinetoscope theaters. The twenty-second-long film was an absolute sensation: movie patrons professed to be shocked, newspapers editorialized against it, and preachers denounced it from the pulpit, arguing that it would encourage moral decay. In a pattern that continues unabated to the present day, however, the moral outrage of social and religious leaders had little effect, apart from helping to promote the movie. *The Kiss* was Edison's top-grossing film in 1896.

Whether or not any impressionable youth were taught how to kiss by Edison's movie, filmmakers had no trouble absorbing the film's other valuable lesson: racy films were box office gold. *The Kiss* was quickly followed by other provocative movies, including *Fatima Dances* (1897), a thirty-second demonstration of a "couchee-couchee" dance by Fatima, one of the sensations of the Columbia World's Exposition in Chicago in 1893,[28] and *Orange Blossoms* (1897), "a pantomime of a bride's wedding night preparations," which was banned by the New York police and destroyed by court order.[29]

The increasingly stern warnings of religious leaders and social activists about the immoral content of the movies and the threat they posed to decent society were almost entirely ignored. The number of movie theaters—quickly known to all as nickelodeons in honor of their typical admission charge—exploded across the country: by 1906 there were already some five thousand nickelodeons across the United States; in 1908 that number had doubled, with more than two hundred thousand people attending a motion picture each day.[30]

Not surprisingly, the obvious popularity and staggering revenues of the new medium only heightened the concerns about its corrupting influence. As social reformers frequently pointed out, the very success of motion pictures stemmed from the fact that they were designed for mass consumption, often with little or no pretension to artistic merit. The silent film ("talkies" were not developed until the late 1920s) was a particularly accessible medium, even for the waves of immigrants arriving in America with little or no knowledge of English. And even the poorest dockworker or cleaning maid could usually scrape together the nickel required to pay for a Saturday evening's entertainment. As James Skinner noted in *The Cross and the Cinema*, underlying these concerns was a healthy dose of class prejudice: "In short, it was the great unwashed who patronized the picture shows, uncritically and with deplorably enthusiastic regularity. It was the moral duty of their betters, protests from libertarians to the contrary, to save them from their baser instincts."[31]

Given that so many people were reluctant to be saved from their baser instincts, the task of protecting the public from the charlatans of film was daunting (reformers face a similar problem with the Internet today). Nonetheless, both religious leaders and social progressives undertook the challenge with vigor. In a particularly churlish move, New York mayor George B. McClellan Jr. (1865–1940) shut down all of the city's motion picture theaters on Christmas Eve, 1908. He cited inadequate fire exits and the extreme flammability of the film itself as the primary reasons, but it was clear that concerns over decency also played an important role: "Because of the serious opposition presented by the rectors and pastors of practically all the Christian denominations in the city," McClellan said, ". . . I will revoke any of these moving-picture show licenses on evidence that pictures have been exhibited by the licensees which tend to degrade or injure the morals of the community."[32] The film industry rushed into court and persuaded a judge to issue an injunction ordering the theaters reopened on December 26.[33]

Generally, however, the preferred approach for movie opponents was the creation of state and local censorship boards that were given the authority to approve or disapprove of films. Chicago led the way in November 1907, giving the city's police chief the authority to shut down any movie he felt was "immoral" or "obscene." In a relatively short time, more than one hundred communities around the country had established local censorship boards, along with a number of states: Pennsylvania was the first, in 1911, and was quickly followed by Ohio (1913), Kansas (1913), and Maryland (1916).

The film industry filed a legal challenge to Ohio's state censorship law, but in 1916 the US Supreme Court upheld the statute. In the process, the Court ruled that movies were not entitled to First Amendment protection since they are not "part of the press of the country [or] organs of public opinion."

"They are mere representations," the Court said, "of events, of ideas and sentiments published and known, vivid, useful and entertaining no doubt, but, as we have said, capable of evil, having power for it, the greater because of their attractiveness and manner of exhibition."[34]

The revenues of the growing industry made it absolutely clear just how attractive motion pictures were to the public. In the battle over Mayor McClellan's Christmas Eve shutdown, one of the major arguments raised against the mayor was economic. An attorney for a coalition of "moving picture men" told the *New York Times* that "[t]his sort of treatment can go in Russia, but it can't go in this country. There are 12,000 men employed in the 550 places."[35]

Clearly intrigued by the attorney's comment, the *Times* began investigating the economics of the decade-old movie industry, and a few days later published an overview of its findings. Among other things, the paper estimated that more than $40 million had been invested in facilities and equipment, that over one hundred thousand people were employed nationwide (earning a total of $2 million per week in wages), and that each week 45 million people attended a picture show, resulting in weekly movie revenues of $3 million.

Relatively little of those revenues, at first, flowed to the actors. As one studio stage manager put it, "[m]ost of the principals are trained actors. There are always enough of them idle in the city who are willing to earn from $5 to $10 by rehearsing a few days, then going through the pantomime seen in the pictures."[36] But the concept of celebrity that Oscar Wilde had launched in London in the 1890s quickly reached Hollywood, to the enormous benefit of some. Charlie Chaplin (1889–1977), for instance, debuted in 1914 his soon-to-be-trademark character the Little Tramp. Just three years later, he became the first actor to sign a movie contract for $1 million (just over $15.2 million in 2005 dollars).[37]

The fact that Chaplin could command such a salary was a testament not only to his popularity but also to the popularity of motion pictures in general, which were generating enough revenues to cover that kind of paycheck. The industry's income was also sufficient to fund a trade association to lobby on its behalf. The leading motion picture companies, along with the National Board of Censorship, formed the Motion Picture Board of Trade of America on September 9, 1915. The expressed purpose of the group was to challenge censorship legislation and support court challenges when necessary.[38] Its first work, however, would be "a campaign to further the political interests of candidates who are known to be opposed to legislation that would hurt the motion picture business."[39] In the argot of Hollywood, "A PAC Was Born."

The movie industry spent its money well. In 1916 the first serious federal censorship bill was proposed by Dudley M. Hughes (D-GA) (1848–1927). As chairman of the House Committee on Education, he held six nights of hearings on indecency in the movies in January, during which a large producer of films was quoted as saying that "50 per cent. of the exhibitors wanted pictures to be risque, so as to better please their patrons."[40] In May, Chairman Hughes introduced a bill calling for the creation of a federal film commission that would license films for shipment in interstate commerce unless "such film or a part thereof is indecent, immoral, inhuman . . . or is of such character that its exhibition would tend to corrupt morals or incite to crime." Pictures depicting prizefights or bullfights were also barred.[41] Hughes did not succeed in getting his bill through the full House, however, and no similar initiative was undertaken in the Senate. Hughes himself served just one more term before losing a reelection bid in 1918.

The most serious challenge to the movies stemmed in large part from the industry's own outrageous behavior. During the so-called Roaring Twenties, following World War I, fan magazines built a large and enthusiastic readership by chronicling the lifestyle excesses of the film industry's increasingly wealthy stars. An avid following also developed for stories about Hollywood's disappointed hopefuls, the hundreds and thousands of young people (mostly women) who flocked to southern California in the typically vain hope of becoming the next Mary Pickford (1892–1979) but who all too often wound up as "working girls," in every sense of the phrase.[42] But even these stories, as compelling and often tragic as they were, paled in comparison to the scandals that rocked the movie industry in the early twenties.

In 1921 the immensely popular silent film star Roscoe "Fatty" Arbuckle (1887–1933) was tried three times for the manslaughter death of actress Virginia Rappe (1895–1921), who had died from suspicious internal injuries at the end of a raucous Labor Day weekend party at the St. Francis Hotel in San Francisco. The trials, which were filled with a salacious mix of Hollywood high life, debauchery, and sexual innuendo, were covered in breathless detail by the William Randolph Hearst national media chain (the Fox Network of its day). Although Arbuckle was ultimately acquitted at his third trial (the jury returned its verdict in just six minutes and apologized to Arbuckle for his ordeal),[43] the news coverage had long since convicted the rotund actor in the court of public opinion.

Hard on the heels of Rappe's death came the news of the murder of well-known director William Desmond Taylor (1872–1922) on February 1, 1922 (still unsolved), and the morphine-related death on January 18, 1923, of Wallace Reid (1891–1923), a handsome and enormously popular action-film star. The Taylor trial in particular was a media sensation, replete with shocking disclosures of his abandonment of his first wife, numerous affairs, and riotous living.

As tragedies and scandals swirled around them, film producers recognized that some action was required. In 1921 legislators in thirty-nine states introduced nearly one hundred bills providing for censorship of the movies, and some were calling once again for federal action.[44] The producers reorganized their increasingly ineffectual trade association into the Motion Picture Producers and Distributors of America (MPPDA) and hired an experienced politician to run it. In March 1922, Will Hays (1879–1954), an elder in the Presbyterian Church and former postmaster general under President Warren G. Harding (1865–1923), was named president of the MPPDA.[45]

Hays's leadership, political experience, and evident religious faith provided immediate benefits to the movie industry, as he successfully led a referendum campaign in Massachusetts to overturn a proposed state censorship board (one of the first times a censorship proposal was defeated). In fact, Hays helped the industry completely stem the tide of governmental involvement: no more state censorship boards were created after Hays was hired by the MPPDA.[46]

Admittedly, not all of Hays's ideas worked out. One of the more bizarre public relations proposals he considered—even before he started work—was the idea of constructing a movie production lot and village on Long Island "with Puritanic standards of life" to help overcome the public perception of Hollywood's immorality. At the top of the list of proposed buildings was an ecumenical Community Church, where all could attend services. Other planned construction included houses for the technical staff, mansions for the stars, schools, and, of course, a motion picture theater. Part of the studios' motivation, not surprisingly, was also economic: concerned about the costs of operating in California, they increasingly believed that they could make movies for less in New York, particularly given the abundance of hungry actors in the "legitimate theaters" in Times Square.[47] Hays's village, however, never left the drawing board.

There was one more serious attempt to create a federal film commission not long after Hays was hired. A bill to establish such a commission was drafted and promoted in 1926 by Rep. William D. Upshaw (1866–1952) (D-GA), an evangelist and strong supporter of Prohibition (he was described at the time as "the driest of the dry"). After multiple hearings, however, the Upshaw bill was shelved by the House Education Committee, in part because of opposition to film censorship by President Calvin Coolidge (1872–1933), a Republican well known for his belief that "the business of America is business." As the committee voted to table the legislation, the irrepressible Fiorello LaGuardia (1882–1947) (D-NY) defended the decency of motion pictures by suggesting that they could serve an educational purpose: "There is nothing unnatural about kissing. If some husbands would learn from the stage and the pictures just how to kiss and then go home and practice on their wives, there would be happier homes and fewer divorces."[48]

Religious groups vehemently disagreed. As early as 1922, the General Assembly of the Presbyterian Church had called on its members to boycott "suggestive and unclean movies." Arguing in favor of the resolution, the Reverend Dr. Gustav A. Briegleb (1882–1943) anticipated the crux of the coming battle between Hollywood and religious organizations. "It is office receipts that count. If the Church of Jesus Christ spoke out as it should against indecent movies we would have decent movies in ten days. The only thing the movie people are afraid of is local censorship. The movies are here to stay, but we want clean movies."[49]

At the time the Presbyterian General Assembly issued its call for boycott, Hollywood was averaging forty million paid admissions per week.[50] As the Reverend Briegleb no doubt was aware, the audiences were not pouring in to see uplifting tales of moral redemption, they were coming to see films with, among other attractions, nude bathing scenes (*The Branding Iron* [1920], *The Isle of Love* [1922]); a naked Lilith from the Garden of Eden (*The Tree of Knowledge* [1922]); and the passionate lover Rudolph Valentino (1895–1926) (*The Sheik* [1921], *Blood and Sand* [1922]).

Despite the content of the films pouring off the movie lots in California, Hays was doing his best to fend off the threat of a boycott and hostile legislation. In 1924 he proposed that the studios submit to his office "a synopsis of every play, novel, or story under consideration for a future film." The Hays Office would review the proposals and eliminate any ideas or treatments that were unacceptable. Under what became known as "The Formula," the Hays Office rejected 125 proposed films; nevertheless, the project was viewed as a failure by religious leaders and social moralists.[51] Recognizing that critics were unimpressed with the movie industry's efforts, Hays replaced The Formula in 1927 with the "Don'ts and Be Carefuls." The "Don'ts" was a list of eleven themes that were simply forbidden: "pointed profanity; any licentiousness or suggestive nudity—in fact or in silhouette; the illegal traffic in drugs; any inference of sex perversion; white slavery; miscegenation; sex hygiene and venereal diseases; scenes of actual childbirth—in fact or in silhouette; children's sex organs; ridicule of the clergy; [and] willful offense to any nation, race, or creed." Themes on the "Be Carefuls" list could appear in films, but moviemakers were cautioned on how they presented such material. These cultural landmines included use of the flag, sedition, arson, theft, man and woman in bed, the sale of women, deliberate seduction of girls, and excessive kissing.[52] The efficacy of these guidelines, however, was fatally undercut by the fact that compliance was voluntary and the Hays Office had no enforcement mechanism.

In 1929 Martin Quigley (1890–1964), a Catholic publisher of movie trade newspapers, and the aptly named Reverend Daniel A. Lord (1888–1955), a Catholic theologian and professor of English at St. Louis University, collaborated on a revision of the Don'ts and Be Carefuls. In April 1930 the two presented the Hays Office with a document titled the "Motion Picture Production Code."[53]

The new code not only laid out the general philosophical principles underlying movie censorship but also provided specific guidelines on how various controversial topics were to be treated. The code covered most of the same themes as The Formula and the Don'ts/Be Carefuls, but in greater detail.

Although the code raised hopes for a cleaner Hollywood, it initially appeared to be no more effective than its predecessors: by the end of the decade, Americans were buying ninety million(!) movie tickets per week so that they could watch even more daring films:

- *Hell's Angels* (1930), featuring the buxom Jean Harlow (1911–1937) and her immortal question, "Would you be shocked if I put on something more comfortable?"
- *The Blue Angel* (1930) and *Morocco* (1930), both featuring the compelling Marlene Dietrich (1901–1992), who shocked audiences of the latter film by dressing in a tuxedo and kissing another woman in a cabaret scene
- *Pandora's Box* (1928), a German silent film starring Louise Brooks (1906–1985) "as an amoral and insatiable cabaret star/prostitute named Lulu
- *Madam Satan* (1930), a Cecil B. DeMille (1881–1959) production most notable for its licentious party scene aboard a zeppelin[54]

Hays was coming under increasingly strong attack from both politicians and religious leaders, and it looked like his tenure would be brief. But economic forces soon intervened. By the end of 1932, weekly attendance at the movies was down 40 percent from its high of nearly one hundred million just two years earlier. The Great Depression was gathering strength, and studios were now saddled with the cost of adding sound to their films and audio equipment to their chains of theaters.[55] In 1933 nearly one-third of the nation's movie theaters shut their doors.[56] For years, high profits had helped the studios resist moral pressure, but the economic downturn left them unusually vulnerable.

The studios' vulnerability, ironically, was heightened by the introduction of sound in films in 1927. When films were silent, a local censorship board might demand cuts (where objectionable pieces of the film were literally snipped away and two ends rejoined), but the film could most likely still be shown in something close to its original form.[57] Once sound was introduced, however, a single cut could ruin a film and require expensive reshooting of entire scenes. With the production costs of films skyrocketing, movie studios were much more motivated to make films that met with censor approval before they were released to the public.

The American Catholic Church was under pressure of its own. In October

1933, the pope's personal representative in the United States, Amleto Giovanni Cardinal Cicognani (1883–1973), announced at the Conference of Catholic Charities that "Catholics are called by God, the Pope, the bishops, and the priests to a united and vigorous campaign for the purification of the cinema, which has become a deadly menace to morals."[58] A month later, the Church responded to this papal challenge by forming plans to create a Legion of Decency. The legion was formally organized in April 1934, and Archbishop John T. McNicholas (1877–1950) of Cincinnati drafted the pledge quoted at the beginning of this chapter. Over the next two years, an estimated ten million Catholics took the pledge orally or in writing, along with a smaller number of Protestants and Jews.[59]

As a general expression of Catholic disapproval, the Legion of Decency was a powerful force, but it was still not powerful enough by itself to make the studios change their films. The major blow came on May 23, 1934, when Dennis Joseph Cardinal Dougherty (1865–1951), archbishop of Philadelphia, ordered the city's 823,000 Catholics to boycott all movies. This was not merely a polite request: Cardinal Dougherty declared in his message that the boycott was "a positive command, binding all in conscience under the pain of sin."[60]

The impact was dramatic and swift. The Hays Office estimated that ticket sales in Philadelphia dropped between 15 and 20 percent in the early days of the boycott and that, by July, sales at the city's Warner Brothers Stanley Theater had dropped from $41,000 to $7,000 per week. All together, the weekly revenue loss for Warner Brothers was estimated at $175,000. The efforts of studio cofounder Harry Warner (1881–1958) to arrange a conciliatory meeting with Cardinal Dougherty were unsuccessful.[61]

The Philadelphia boycott nominally remained in effect until Cardinal Dougherty's death in 1951, but even by the fall of 1934 the sales figures for movie tickets made it clear that Catholics were slowly trickling back into the theaters. Ultimately, the boycott was probably unsustainable due to a lack of a reasonable entertainment substitute; there was radio, of course, but it paled in comparison to the visual wonders of the big screen.

Nonetheless, the Philadelphia movie boycott accomplished its primary goal. It played a significant, even critical, role in persuading Hollywood to accept a much more rigorously enforced moral code. In June 1934, the Studio Relations Committee was reformulated as the Production Code Administration (PCA) under the supervision of a devout Catholic journalist named Joseph I. Breen (1890–1965). The code was amended to require preapproval of the PCA before shooting could begin, and PCA approval of the final product. Any MPPDA theater that showed a film without a PCA seal could be fined up to $25,000.

Since before the American Revolution, no single religion had ever exercised so much control over a particular communication medium.[62] By the end of 1934, a Catholic censor was enforcing the provisions of a Catholic-drafted moral code under the watchful gaze of the Catholic-led Legion of Decency.[63] Not surprisingly, the decisions of Breen and the PCA almost immediately came under attack by filmmakers wanting to go further than the code allowed, and eventually, the economic conditions that had made the studios so vulnerable abated. Nonetheless, for the better part of twenty-five years, the code set the initial parameters for what was made and seen in America's movie theaters.

CORPORATE SELF-CENSORSHIP OF RADIO AND TELEVISION

For quite a long time, neither radio nor television raised anything approaching the level of decency concerns that so quickly attached to other media. One reason was the specter of the government. Both the 1927 Radio Act and the 1934 Communications Act made it clear that the federal government did not have the power to censor broadcasts in advance. At the same time, however, both the Federal Radio Commission and then the Federal Communications Commission could punish "obscene, indecent or profane" broadcasts after the fact, with sanctions ranging from a fine to license revocation.

A far more compelling reason for on-air decency, at least in the early years of radio and TV, was financial. As radio station networks (or "chains," as they were called then) developed, the investment of companies like the Radio Corporation of America or the National Broadcasting Company ran into the millions of dollars. The owners and managers of the growing networks were reluctant to run any risk that their investment would be damaged by an unguarded word.

The other critical part of the financial picture is that unlike the film industry, radio and television are sponsored media. Radio and television shows are paid for (to one degree or another) by companies that buy advertising time associated with those shows. The advertisers, therefore, had a vested interest in the content of the shows and the public reaction to what was broadcast. This was particularly true when a single advertiser would sponsor an entire show, a practice that was common throughout the late 1950s. The combination of financial investment and deference to the concerns of advertisers meant that broadcasters were extremely sensitive about the material that went out over the air. As a result, it was far more likely that shows would be censored by the stations themselves rather than in response to a listener boycott.

One of the earliest incidents of radio self-censorship involved the broadcast by Station WELK of a talk given by US general Smedley D. Butler

(1881–1940) in 1931 to the Philadelphia Elks Club. Describing an assault on Fort Riviere in Haiti by the US Marines in 1915 (for which he had received the Congressional Medal of Honor), General Butler said that he hesitated as he and a detachment of marines approached a drain leading into the fort. "Then," the general told his audience, "I saw Sergeant Russell L. Iams looking at me as if to say to himself, 'Hell, if you're not going through, get out of the way and let me go on.'"

Unbeknownst to General Butler, the WELK radio announcer then interrupted his speech and issued an apology: "Ladies and gentlemen of the radio audience, I regret it has been necessary for us to cut Major General, or General Major, Butler, or whoever he is, off the air for the use of indecent and obscene language. We have warned him that if he again resorts to the use of such language we will cut him off permanently." Upon learning that his speech had been censored, an outraged General Butler demanded and received a broadcast apology for the censorship.[64]

Congressman Emmanuel Celler (1888–1981) (D-NY), who represented Brooklyn in Congress for fifty years, was a particularly strong critic of corporate censorship. Mere weeks after the formation of the Federal Radio Commission in 1927, he sent it a letter asking that an investigation be undertaken of censorship of talks aired by Station WEAF in New York.[65] In a lengthy interview with the *New York Times* a few months later, Representative Celler listed a number of specific instances in which various radio speakers (including himself) had been censored by radio stations for political reasons or out of fear that "it was not an appropriate time for such remarks." Celler told the *Times* that radio "offers an unexcelled medium for educational work," but that such work "cannot be performed if the ideas of some are refused while the propaganda of others is being broadcast."[66]

Thanks to the radio industry's sensitivity to possible offense, consumer-led boycotts of radio shows or stations were rare. It didn't take listeners long, however, to realize that their purchasing power gave them a potential powerful weapon. In 1929 the NBC radio network announced plans to shift the broadcast of the enormously popular *Amos 'n' Andy* show from 11 PM (EST) to 7 PM, which meant that in the west, the show would air during work hours. An estimated one hundred thousand people protested the planned change, and many threatened to boycott the toothpaste company that sponsored the show. An arrangement was quickly worked out to broadcast the show in the evening on the West Coast.[67]

As the cultural battle over the movies heated up in the early 1930s, the radio industry watched with concern. Although the Legion of Decency never targeted radio specifically, five orchestra leaders and radio broadcasters organized "The Committee of Five for the Betterment of Radio" to prevent attacks on the industry for indecency. The group, consisting of Richard Himber (1900–1966), Rudy Vallee (1901–1986), Paul Whiteman (1890–1967), Guy Lombardo (1902–1977), and Abe Lyman (1899–1957), agreed to meet each week to review newly published songs. Publishers would be asked to change any song titles or lyrics found objectionable, and if the publisher refused, the song would be placed on a "banned" list. Orchestra leaders around the country promised not to perform banned songs on the radio.[68]

John Royal (1886–1978), vice president of the National Broadcasting Company, praised the work of the Committee of Five: "We have always maintained a censorship of song. We have condemned many and have caused many to be rewritten. Every new song we look over and if any suggestive lines are found they are killed or changed. We have often warned that dance band leaders have used too many double-meaning titles and songs. We are pleased that they are beginning to see the light."[69]

Another short-lived consumer boycott of radio arose in New York in 1940, when the New Rochelle Woman's Club announced their "I'm Not Listening" campaign to protest the broadcast of what they described as "cheap love dramas" during the morning and afternoon. The boycott received an unusually frank response from Donald S. Shaw, executive vice president of the local station, WMCA: "We are in the broadcasting business to make money," Shaw said, "and dripping dramas pay for the worthwhile programs that don't pay their way." He added that the sponsor of the love dramas, a leading soap company, had conducted a survey and found that "they sell soap—and plenty of soap."[70]

With the introduction of commercial television in 1940, federal regulators and station censors now had to worry not only about what audiences might hear but what they might see (a transition not dissimilar to what Hays wrestled with when sound was introduced in the movies). The dubious honor of being the first person to be actively censored by a television network is arguably held by Eddie Cantor (1892–1964), a popular vaudeville star who went on to enormous success in radio, film, and television.[71] On May 25, 1944, Cantor was scheduled to perform his Broadway hit song "We're Having a Baby (My Baby and Me)" on his NBC show, *Time to Smile*. Less than an hour before the live show aired, NBC told Cantor to drop the song from the show. Cantor refused, saying that he and his duet partner, Nora Martin, did not have time to rehearse a new number. NBC allegedly relented, but as Cantor and Martin were singing, network engineers pressed a button that cut the audio feed to prevent the home audience from hearing these allegedly indecent lines:

Martin: "Thanks to you, my life is bright. You've brought me joy beyond measure."

Cantor: "Don't thank me. Quite all right. Honestly, it was a pleasure."

Martin: "Just think, it's my first one."

Cantor: "The next one's on me."

Cantor's hips were as much a problem for NBC as his lips; during a dance sequence later in the show the network kept its cameras carefully above his waist. (Some years later, a young singer from Memphis, Tennessee—Elvis Presley—would spark the same reaction by CBS and the *Ed Sullivan Show*.)

"I'm blazing mad," Cantor told the *Times*, "at fellows who tell you it's all right and then sneak around and cut you off. Of course, NBC has the right to say we don't use the lyrics, but when little Hitlers tell you you can't do it just as you're going on, that's tough."[72]

Perhaps not entirely coincidentally, Cantor played a leading role in eliminating one of the financial incentives for checks on program content. In 1954 he left his regular slot on NBC's *Colgate Comedy Hour* and announced that he would produce a program that would be sold to individual sponsors in various cities across the country, rather than to a single sponsor who would support the program across an entire network. Individual stations that purchased Cantor's program would make a greater profit, and Cantor could avoid what the *Times* described as the "vagaries and whims of an individual sponsor."[73] It was a marketplace solution that also recognized varying attitudes toward the question of program content (and of decency) around the country: what sells soap in Los Angeles, California, obviously, will not necessarily move product in Peoria, Illinois.

Consumer boycotts were not always inspired by lurid lyrics or suggestive dance moves. The Beatles learned that an unguarded comment, even in the 1960s, could become a public relations nightmare. In a 1966 interview with the *London Evening Standard*, band member John Lennon (1940–1980) spontaneously offered his assessment of Christianity: "Christianity will go. It will vanish and shrink. I needn't argue about that: I'm right and I will be proved right. We're more popular than Jesus now; I don't know which will go first— rock'n'roll or Christianity. Jesus was all right, but his disciples were thick and ordinary. It's them twisting it that ruins it for me."[74]

Across the American South, already being referred to by some as the Bible Belt, the reaction was swift. Dozens of radio stations announced that they would no long play the group's music. Some stations felt that wasn't a strong enough response and announced that they were planning public bonfires for the group's albums and photos.[75] The protests, however, did little to dent the Beatles's status as the most popular band of the late twentieth century.

By the early 1970s, the power of the boycott as a tool of wide-scale cultural change (never enormously strong to begin with) largely vanished, chiefly because of the inability of individual groups to inflict sufficient economic harm on a producer, distributor, or sponsor of allegedly indecent content. On both television and radio, individual syndication of programs gave way to multiple sponsorship (through sixty- and thirty-second ads) of each episode, making it that much harder to exert influence over stations and networks. In future decades, various groups (and in particular, religious conservatives) only rarely used boycotts or the threat of boycotts in an effort to promote their cultural agenda. Frustrated by their vain attempts to persuade their own followers to simply "turn the dial" or not purchase the products helping to pay for objectionable content, religious conservatives increasingly looked instead to the federal and state governments to impose their cultural values on the entire country.

Barry Goldwater greets an Indianapolis crowd during a campaign tour in October 1964. (AP photo/file)

Chapter Four

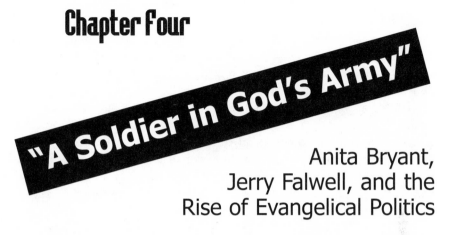

"A Soldier in God's Army"

Anita Bryant,
Jerry Falwell, and the
Rise of Evangelical Politics

Mine eyes have seen the glory of the coming of the Lord;
He is trampling out the vintage where the grapes of wrath are
    stored;
He has loosed the fateful lightning of his terrible swift sword;
His truth is marching on!
        —Julia W. Howe, "Battle Hymn of the Republic," 1861

"I n your heart, you know he's right." The slogan for Republican presidential candidate Barry Goldwater (1909–1998) was at best cold comfort on the morning of November 4, 1964. The conservative icon and Republican presidential nominee had waged a vigorous campaign for the presidency. But, a year after succeeding the slain John F. Kennedy (1917–1963), President Lyndon Johnson (1908–1973) swept back into office with one of the largest popular and electoral victories in American history. Johnson received 61 percent of the popular vote (the highest total in 140 years), and outpolled his opponent in forty-five out of fifty states. The margin in the Electoral College was even more daunting, with Johnson receiving 486 votes to Goldwater's 52.

Johnson's platform was a total refutation of everything on which Goldwater had campaigned: voluntary participation in Social Security, school vouchers, a flat tax, resistance to federal enforcement of civil rights, and his advocacy of tactical nuclear weapons in Vietnam and willingness for NATO commanders to act similarly in Europe. Johnson's campaign was particularly successful at raising concerns about Goldwater's nuclear temperament, first by running the infamous "Daisy Girl" commercial, which first showed a young girl counting the petals she pulled off a flower and then a jarring countdown to a nuclear explosion,[1] and then by parodying Goldwater's own slogan with the derisive "In your guts, you know he's nuts."[2]

For social conservatives, it was heady stuff to finally have a national candidate to promote their issues, but the morning after the 1964 presidential election, the country veered sharply to the political Left. President Johnson's embrace of the Civil Rights Act and his vision of a "Great Society" represented the greatest endorsement of governmental activism since President Franklin Delano Roosevelt's New Deal. The goal of the Great Society, Johnson said, was "to put an end to poverty and racial injustice."

Aided by a strongly Democratic Congress, President Johnson created a cabinet-level Department of Housing and Urban Development in 1965, and implemented a wide array of new programs: Volunteers in Service to America (VISTA) (1964), the Job Corps (1964), Upward Bound, the Neighborhood Youth Corps, Head Start, and Medicare/Medicaid (1965). As a follow-up to the Civil Rights Act, Johnson also promoted the Voting Rights Act, which outlawed literacy tests as a prerequisite for voter registration and imposed federal supervision and voter registration in areas where less than 50 percent of eligible voters were registered. The spiraling cost of the Vietnam War kept Johnson from funding the Great Society as fully as he would have liked; nonetheless, after his reelection in 1964, the federal government veered so far to the Left that some commentators concluded that conservatism as a political force was dead.

That conclusion was buttressed by the cultural changes taking place across the country. The 1967 "Summer of Love" alone was a high-decibel, highly sexed, just plain high refutation of everything for which the gray-flanneled 1950s had stood. The once-mighty influence of the Legion of Decency had largely vanished. Under the new leadership of former Johnson aide Jack Valenti, Hollywood and the Motion Picture Association of America were on the verge of abandoning precensorship in favor of a postproduction age rating system that freed up filmmakers but put more of a burden on parents to monitor what their children were watching. In the music world, musicians were making the often-jarring transition from the sock hop to Woodstock. Even television, typically the slowest-moving medium, was playing with cultural limits, from the pointed and often-censored political commentary of the *Smothers Brothers Show* to the leering double entendres of *Rowan & Martin's Laugh-In*.

While it may have been fashionable to blame Goldwater for the Great Society and the cultural upheavals of the 1960s, neither of course was actually his fault. Moreover, the setback to Republicans proved merely temporary; clearly, it was from the radioactive crater of Goldwater's presidential ambitions that the conservative movement eventually rose, Phoenixlike, to its electoral success. Four years before his defeat, Goldwater's 1960 bestseller, *The Conscience of a Conservative*, was ghostwritten by speechwriter L. Brent Bozell, now the highly influential head of the Parents Television Council. The book became required reading for all so-called movement conservatives in the 1960s. Pat Buchanan, who read *The Conscience of a Conservative* during his undergraduate years at Georgetown University, described the book as the movement's "New Testament."[3]

Another avid reader in 1960 was Phyllis Schlafly, then a housewife in Alton, a small town in south-central Missouri. Four years later, Schlafly wrote a small book titled *A Choice, Not an Echo*. She identified a split in the Republican Party between the so-called Rockefeller Republicans, who represented the liberal, mostly northeast wing of the party, and true conservatives like US senator Barry Goldwater (R-AZ). The 75-cent pamphlet, which Schlafly self-published, sold three million copies and made her a national figure. It also sparked one of the few genuine drafts of a presidential candidate, as a collection of young conservative politicians—inspired both by Schlafly's book and its impressive reception—pushed Goldwater to represent them on the national stage.[4] When Goldwater captured the nomination on the first ballot at the Republican National Convention in San Francisco, he paid homage to the impact of Schlafly's book by describing his candidacy as "a choice, not an echo."[5]

In California, a moderately successful B-movie actor (and former Democrat) named Ronald Reagan (1911–2004) became cochairman of California Republicans for Goldwater. In 1964 he developed a stump speech that began with this proud declaration: "I am going to talk of controversial things. I make no apology for this. . . . This is the issue of this election: Whether we believe in our capacity for self-government or whether we abandon the American Revolution and confess that a little intellectual elite in a far-distant capital can plan our lives for us better than we can plan them ourselves."[6]

Reagan's cinematically polished delivery and enthusiastic support of Goldwater attracted the attention of both the national campaign and conservative donors, who identified him as one of the party's rising stars. Reagan was invited to make one of the nominating speeches for Goldwater in September at the Republican National Convention, and used his growing notoriety to launch a campaign for governor in California. Just two years later, he was elected by a margin of more than a million votes.

Funding a Revolution: Tapping Corporate Conservatives

Reagan's victory in California was a remarkable achievement for conservatives and it encouraged their belief that the movement could achieve similar success at the national level. Conservative activists recognized, however, that even if they succeeded in electing conservative leaders, most of the intellectual support for actually governing at the federal level came from many of the same institutions and foundations that had supported the creation of the Great Society. In order fundamentally to change the federal government, they needed to build a network of think tanks, foundations, and academic programs to parallel the ones supporting liberal ideas.

The intellectual firepower needed to stock such a network was steadily growing. In 1951, for instance, William F. Buckley Jr. wrote *God and Man at Yale: The Superstitions of "Academic Freedom,"* in which he criticized Yale University in general and various professors in particular for their rejection of student religious beliefs and their focus instead on teaching liberal values. (Buckley thus served as a model for the future founding of Accuracy in Academia, the conservative faculty watchdog group.) The book clearly threw Yale on the defensive: an alumni committee was convened that concluded that the university, ironically founded 250 years earlier expressly to promote conservative theological views, "has no Communist on its faculty, has no faculty member seeking to undermine democracy, has not engaged in 'intimidation' that might affect academic freedom, and currently has a religious life that is 'deeper and richer' than it has been in years."[7]

Buckley's next book, which he cowrote with his brother-in-law L. Brent Bozell, was called *McCarthy and His Enemies: The Record and Its Meaning.* The book was an attempt to defend not only Senator Joe McCarthy (1908–1957) but, more important, the occasionally excessive methods he used to improve America's security and defeat communism.

"McCarthyism, then, is a weapon in the American arsenal," Buckley and Bozell wrote. "[A]s long as McCarthyism fixes its goal with its present precision, it is a movement around which men of good will and stern morality can close ranks."[8]

The following year, Buckley launched the *National Review*, furnishing the growing ranks of conservative anticommunists with their own weekly journal. A half century later, the *Review* is still widely considered to be one of the nation's most influential periodicals. A memorandum issued at the time by Buckley stated that the intent of the journal was "to change the nation's political and intellectual climate—which at present, is preponderantly leftist."[9]

The *National Review* laid some of the groundwork for the conservative intellectual revolution, but it had help. The upheavals and apparent break-down of social order during the late 1960s also persuaded some liberal, or at least moderate, intellectuals—most notably Irving Kristol, Norm Podhoretz, and Nathan Glazer—to conclude that under both Roosevelt (the New Deal) and Johnson (the Great Society), government's reach had far exceeded its grasp. Combined with their ardent anticommunism, their advocacy for a more restricted view of government earned them the sobriquet of neoconservatives or, simply, neocons.[10] Both individually and collaboratively, these fathers of the neocon movement set out to promote their expansive vision of unexpansive government.

Joining them in the battle was a former journalist named Paul Weyrich, who in 1967 came to Washington, DC, to serve as press secretary for Senator Gordon Allott (1909–1989) (R-CO). Despite the enthusiasm generated three years earlier by the Goldwater campaign, the capital city was still, in the words of the *National Review*'s Buckley, "an utterly inhospitable place" for a young conservative.[11] Congress was solidly Democratic and increasingly liberal, and the Republicans were, in the eyes of the hard-core conservatives, still offering far more "echoes" of Democrats than actual conservative choices.

Senator Allott's support of the civil rights movement earned him an invi-tation to a 1969 ad hoc meeting of liberal policy groups—the Brookings Insti-tution, the American Civil Liberties Union, and the National Committee for an Effective Congress—to discuss strategies for defeating an unpopular housing initiative proposed by President Nixon. For Weyrich, it was a political epiphany. "There before my eyes was unveiled how the other side operated," he later said. "It was the single most important meeting I have attended in my political lifetime." It became Weyrich's mission to replicate for conservatives the network of think tanks, policy groups, op-ed writers, and congressional aides that had helped drive two decades of liberal legislation.[12] In the process of accomplishing his goal, Weyrich and his allies also built the recruiting cen-ters for a generation trained to do battle in the ideological war over decency.

His first steps were modest. Weyrich's work on the Hill had brought him in contact with a legislative assistant to Rep. Bill Colmer (1890–1980) (D-MS) named Trent Lott, whom Weyrich described as "sharp, articulate, and absolutely solid on the issues." (Lott, then a Republican, would replace Colmer in the House in 1972 on the strength of Nixon's coattails.) Together with an Allott speechwriter named George Will, the three founded the Conservative Lunch Club of Capitol Hill. From the start, it was an unqualified hit. "[W]e were thrilled with the turnout for that luncheon," Weyrich said. "Sixty Hill staffers attended." Over the next three years, the Conservative Lunch Club produced a major policy program each month for its attendees.[13]

With the subsequent establishment of two conservative legislative support groups, the House Republican Study Committee and then the Senate Republican Steering Committee,[14] Weyrich was well on his way to establishing the type of conservative policy infrastructure that he had envisioned in 1969. The next step was a conservative think tank to provide intellectual competition for the venerable Brookings Institution, which for much of the 1960s had been associated with the conservative wing of the Democratic Party. Weyrich was not the only one who identified this need. In a memo to President Richard Nixon (1913–1994) in March 1970, speechwriter Pat Buchanan told the president that "[t]here is a clear national need for a Republican conservative counterpart to Brookings which can generate ideas Republicans can use [and] which can serve as a repository of conservative and Republican intellectuals."[15]

The creation of a serious think tank, however, requires serious money. Fortunately for Weyrich and his cohorts, their campaign to create a neoconservative infrastructure neatly overlapped similar concerns in the conservative segment of the business community. In August 1971, a Richmond, Virginia, corporate lawyer named Lewis Powell (1907–1998) wrote a confidential five-thousand-word treatise for the US Chamber of Commerce titled "Attack on the American Free Enterprise System." In it, Powell called on the chamber to commit itself to a program of assisting corporations in recapturing the ground that had been lost to consumer and environmental groups, all with the aid of a mendacious media. To accomplish that goal, Powell recommended a pro-business campaign, consisting of the promotion of conservatism on college campuses, a push for more favorable coverage by the media and scholarly journals, the organized support of sympathetic candidates, and the pursuit of "neglected opportunities in the courts."

With a forthrightness missing from most of the contemporary discussion of conservative courts, Powell recognized that "[u]nder our constitutional system, especially with an activist-minded Supreme Court, the judiciary may be the most important instrument for social, economic and political change." It didn't hurt the chamber's subsequent efforts that Powell himself was nominated to the Supreme Court two months later by Richard Nixon, and began serving on January 7, 1972.

Powell's memorandum (which was published about a year after his appointment) was inspiring enough to open the hearts and wallets of a number of conservative and very wealthy business owners and philanthropists, including: Richard Mellon Scaife (Pittsburgh, Pennsylvania), Lynde and Harry Bradley (Milwaukee, Wisconsin), the Smith Richardson family (North Carolina), John Olin (New York), David and Charles Koch (Wichita, Kansas), and Joseph Coors (1917–2003) (Colorado).[16] It is worth pointing out that in the century since George Petrie had founded the New York YMCA, concern for the social, moral, and financial welfare of employees had fallen well down the list of ownership concerns.

Weyrich and Coors had already collaborated on one policy project in 1971 when they founded Analysis and Research, Inc., a short-lived conservative research group. But in late 1972, Weyrich read a letter sent by Coors aide Jack Wilson to Senator Allot's office, asking for advice on how Coors's money could be used to promote conservative causes.[17] For Weyrich, the timing was perfect: his services as a press secretary were no longer needed since, despite the Nixon landslide that year, Senator Allott had just lost a close election to a relatively unknown Democrat, Floyd Haskell (1916–1998). Weyrich invited Wilson to Washington and explained how conservatives needed an outside policy organization to counter the ones on the Left. A short time later, Joseph Coors came east as well, and after meeting with Weyrich and assorted conservative legislators, decided to donate $250,000 to launch a new conservative think tank called the Heritage Foundation.[18]

Over the next few years, Coors's initial investment was supplemented by $900,000 from Richard Mellon Scaife, the multimillion-dollar heir of Judge Thomas Mellon (1813–1908), who founded the family bank in Pittsburgh. Both Scaife and his mother, Sarah Mellon Scaife (1903–1965), were enthusiastic supporters of Goldwater, contributing both funds and their airplane to his campaign. Former Republican hatchet-wielder David Brock (and, more recently, the Benedict Arnold of the neocons and a founder of the Left-leaning Media Matters in America) argued that Scaife's ensuing thirty-year "war over American values" was born out of his anger over Goldwater's loss. "[It] left Scaife bitterly determined," Brock said, "to fight liberalism and discredit its idea of achieving social advances through government."[19]

Thanks to his large personal fortune (estimated in September 2005 to be approximately $1.2 billion, tying him for 283rd place on the *Forbes* list of the 400 richest Americans)[20] and his family's control of several charitable foundations, Scaife over the years has become one of the most reliable and generous sources of funding for the political Right. Since its founding, Scaife has donated over $23 million to the Heritage Foundation alone; out of the three hundred right-wing advocacy groups listed in the 1999 Directory of Public Policy Organizations, 111 had received contributions directly from Scaife or Scaife family foundations.[21] One reporter estimated that over the course of thirty years, Scaife and three Scaife family charities—the Carthage, the Allegheny, and the Sarah Scaife foundations—have donated some $200 million to conservative groups.[22]

As a proponent of conservative ideology, the Heritage Foundation took its place beside the American Enterprise Institute, a right-wing, extremely pro-business think tank founded in 1943 by Lewis H. Brown (1894–1951). The organization had languished for some years until the Howard Pew Freedom Trust, using funds derived from the Sun Oil fortune, helped revive it in the mid-1970s with donations totaling $6 million. Also coming onboard at the same time was the Cato Institute, a libertarian/conservative public policy research foundation cofounded in 1977 by Edward H. Crane and billionaire David H. Koch.

Shortly after the establishment of the Heritage Foundation, a rift developed between Weyrich and some of the foundation's financial supporters over whether the foundation should expand its mission to promote conservative positions on various social issues. Weyrich left the Heritage Foundation and with the continued support of Joseph Coors founded two new groups: A political action committee called the Committee for the Survival of a Free Congress and a think tank called the Free Congress Research and Education Foundation. Out of those two groups evolved the Free Congress Foundation, for which Weyrich served as president for twenty-five years, from 1977 to 2002.

In less than a decade, thanks in large part to the impressive resources of conservative business owners, the vision of Weyrich, Buchanan, and others for a network of conservative organizations to counter the long-standing primacy of liberal think tanks had been realized. The success of the conservative organizations was confirmed in a handbook published by Americans for Democratic Action (ADA), titled the *Citizen's Guide to the Right Wing*. In it, the ADA listed the major conservative organizations and complained that "in Congress, their associates, a small group of extreme conservatives, have frightened and harassed what was expected to be the most progressive Congress in our recent history into a state of political shock."[23] Clearly, the donors' money was well spent.

MUSTERING THE TROOPS: THE LAUNCH OF THE CHRISTIAN CRUSADE

While the neocons were building the intellectual framework needed for a political resurgence, religious conservatives were also beginning to flex their ideological muscle. For the better part of a generation, following the public relations debacle of the Scopes "monkey trial," American fundamentalists and religious conservatives had avoided the political arena. In the late 1950s, however, the rise of the Cold War motivated some religious conservatives to reconsider the idea of political involvement. With the United States locked in a fierce global struggle with "godless communism," who better than evangelical Christians to join the ranks for God and country?

Few enlisted in the ideological war with more enthusiasm than the Reverend Billy James Hargis (1925–2004), the evangelical leader of the strenuously anticommunist Christian Crusade. In 1950 Hargis was a pastor in the Disciples of Christ Church in Sapulpa, Oklahoma, when the idea occurred to him "to become an anti-Communist evangelist." With the inadvertent help of the US government, his profile rose quickly.

"My biggest break," Hargis said, "so far as promotion is concerned, came in 1953. I got the idea of ballooning Bibles into the Iron Curtain countries from West Germany." The incident made Hargis a celebrity.[24]

But the risks that religious conservatives faced in returning to the political arena were not limited to scornful editorials and mocking commentaries. Under federal law, tax-exempt organizations are forbidden from most forms of lobbying and virtually all types of political activity. The line between Hargis's ministry and his political activities had always been thin, even to the most casual observer. The Internal Revenue Service, of course, is not a casual observer, and in 1964 the agency concluded that Hargis and the crusade's parent organization, Christian Echoes National Ministry, Inc., had engaged in "excessive levels" of political activities. Reverend Hargis strenuously disagreed, arguing that the IRS action was in fact an attempt by the Johnson administration to stifle dissent.

"If the administration can close down an opposing voice," Hargis asked, "doesn't this set a precedent? Couldn't a conservative administration close down an opposing voice?"[25]

Hargis appealed the IRS ruling and announced that if the decision was upheld, he would file suit to revoke the tax-exempt status of groups like the National Council of Churches and the Southern Christian Leadership Council, both of which Hargis accused of engaging in liberal political activity.[26] After the IRS rejected Hargis's appeal on October 22, 1966, Hargis challenged the ruling in federal court.

It should be noted that the loss of tax-exempt status had little effect on the finances of the Christian Crusade. In 1969 a mailing list of over two hundred thousand people was helping the crusade pull in more than $2 million per year in operating funds, enough to found the group's American College, employ a staff of more than one hundred people, and fund four groups who traveled around the country warning "patriots" about the looming dangers of "liberals" and the pending "Communist take-over." The crusade's business activities were so lively, Reverend Hargis bragged to the *Times*, that the organization had leased a computer (long before computers were in widespread use) to help with the workload.[27]

Seven years after the IRS's final decision, the Supreme Court refused to hear Hargis's appeal of a Tenth Circuit Court of Appeals decision that upheld the IRS decision; the only justice to vote for taking the case was William O. Douglas

(1898–1980).[28] As the case wound through the courts, there were ironies aplenty: Hargis's appeal was supported by virtually every major religious group in the country, including the National Council of Churches, which he had earlier threatened to sue. The year before the Supreme Court vote, when Hargis moved his American College to Tulsa, Oklahoma, one of the college's first extracurricular activities was the "Committee to Impeach Justice Douglas."[29]

Some religious conservatives followed Hargis into the political battle over communism, and others were politicized by social issues: the rise of feminism in the mid- to late-1960s, the final rejection of state bans on the teaching of evolution in 1968, the elimination of state support for religious schools in 1971, and the upholding of a right to abortion in 1973. Still others found inspiration during 1976 in the campaign and nomination for president of Jimmy Carter, a born-again Southern Baptist. The early evangelical enthusiasm for the former Georgia governor, however, quickly waned due to his refusal to unequivocally condemn abortion and his confession—in *Playboy*, no less!— that he had "looked on a lot of women with lust" and "committed adultery in [his] heart many times."[30] But for most religious conservatives, the two issues that finally destroyed the barrier between private faith and political activism were the proposed IRS crackdown on private religious schools and the growing gay rights movement.

In the wake of the US Supreme Court decision in *Brown v. Board of Education of Topeka,*[31] the nation's schools were ordered to desegregate "with all deliberate speed." Ten years after *Brown,* however, just 1 percent of African American students in the South attended racially mixed schools. With the passage of the 1964 Civil Rights Act, the Justice Department was given the authority to file lawsuits to enforce desegregation, and the government was instructed to withhold federal funds from segregated schools. The law resulted in some modest progress; by 1968, 10 percent of African American children were attending desegregated schools.[32] At the same time, however, many communities around the nation (though primarily in the South) were establishing private, whites-only schools to avoid the requirements of court-ordered desegregation. In 1967, at the urging of Senator Russell Long (1918–2003) (D-LA), the IRS granted tax-exempt status to virtually all such schools.[33]

By 1970 an estimated three hundred to four hundred "white" or "seg" academies had been founded, and Robert H. Finch (1925–1995), President Nixon's Secretary of Health, Education, and Welfare, announced that the administration was considering a move to end the tax exemption for the schools.[34] The announcement set off an argument in the administration, since the IRS questioned whether it had the power to revoke the tax-exempt status of the schools. Just one week after Finch's comments, however, a federal court ruled that the tax-exemption policy constituted indirect support by the government for unlawful behavior.[35] Initially, the Justice Department considered an appeal of the ruling; in midsummer, however, the IRS announced that it was reversing its position and revoking the tax-exempt status of private schools that practiced racial discrimination. Four years later, the IRS adopted additional regulations prohibiting church-affiliated primary and secondary schools from discriminating as well. The agency said that religions would not be able to claim that such discrimination was required by their religious beliefs.[36]

A federal lawsuit in 1977 successfully argued that private schools were still discriminating. With the active encouragement of the federal courts, the IRS issued strict (and complex) new regulations in 1978 to require all private schools, including those affiliated with religious organizations, to demonstrate that they were taking aggressive steps to promote racial integration. Among other things, schools were required to implement outreach programs and establish scholarships specifically for black students. The IRS threatened to strip away the tax-exempt status of any schools that did not comply.

The proposed regulations outraged white religious leaders of virtually every denomination, but the reaction was particularly strong among evangelical churches, whose ministers organized a protest campaign to Congress that generated over one hundred and fifty thousand letters. Despite the fact that the IRS revised its regulations to make them less strict, less than a year later, both the House and the Senate adopted legislation barring the Internal Revenue Service from taking any action on the tax exemptions of any private schools.[37] In succeeding years, conservative legislators attached riders to annual appropriations bills that effectively mandated tax exemptions for all private schools that simply declared themselves nondiscriminatory.[38]

The battle over private school tax exemptions gave religious conservatives a crash course in realpolitik. When evangelical leaders saw what they had wrought with postcards and letters, they quickly realized that the same tactics could be applied to other social issues that had a political dimension—and that the energy and fervor of their congregations could play an important role in influencing those public debates.

At the forefront of this new political entanglement was a young Baptist minister in Lynchburg, Tennessee, named Rev. Jerry Falwell. At the height of the controversy over the segregation academies, his television ministry, *The Old Time Gospel Hour*, ran a series of special features on the tax-exempt issue, and was widely credited with inspiring thousands of evangelicals to contact their congressional representatives to protest the IRS's regulations.

This was Falwell's second successful political battle in less than a year; during a warm Miami summer in 1977, he had stood shoulder-to-shoulder with

Anita Bryant as she fought the recognition of gay rights in Miami-Dade County, Florida.

"Breakfast without Orange Juice Is Like a Day without Sunshine"

In the months leading up to the Super Bowl in 1976, the National Football League faced two problems: First, the game was the first major cultural event in the country's bicentennial year, and the league felt that its halftime show should offer a somewhat fancier salute to the nation's birthday than yet another marching band. The second problem was one of the NFL's own making, albeit inadvertently. In 1971 Don Weiss (1926–2003), public relations director for the NFL and one of Commissioner Pete Rozelle's (1926–1996) ablest assistants, suggested using Roman numerals to designate each Super Bowl—the 1971 game became "Super Bowl V" and the first four games were retroactively designated "I" through "IV."[39] Unfortunately, however, this change meant that the bicentennial championship would be known as "Super Bowl X," and the concern at the notoriously conservative NFL headquarters was that the game would be associated, however jokingly, with the term "X-rated."

Rozelle and Weiss found a potent antidote for any possible off-color jokes: Up with People, a touring singing group known around the world for their relentlessly perky lyrics and squeaky-clean image. The wholesome troupe had its origins in the mid-1960s, when it was founded by Dr. J. Blanton Belk as a counter-counterculture response to the growing student unrest on the nation's college campuses. In addition to the group's success—the organization had five different troupes touring the world at the same time and was pulling in over $30 million a year in revenues—Up with People had proven that it was a good match for the polyester-clad "I'd Like to Teach the World to Sing" cheerfulness of the early 1970s.

Joining Up with People for the halftime festivities was the well-known Florida orange juice pitcher and born-again Christian, Anita Bryant, thirty-six, performing her signature song, the "Battle Hymn of the Republic." A former Miss Oklahoma and second runner-up in the 1959 Miss America competition, Bryant had parlayed her singing performance at the national pageant into a recording contract, and she quickly developed a very successful professional singing career. She had several gold albums and at the height of her popularity in the late 1960s was outselling other well-known artists like Ray Charles (1930–2004), Perry Como (1912–2001), and even Elvis Presley (1935–1977).[40] Bryant frequently joined comedian Bob Hope (1903–2003) on his

USO tours to perform for servicemen around the world, and when President Lyndon Johnson died in January 1973, she performed the "Battle Hymn of the Republic" during his funeral in Stonewall, Texas.[41]

By the time Bryant performed at Super Bowl X, however, she was probably better known for her advertising career than for her singing. Over the years, she had appeared in ads for a variety of companies, including Coca-Cola, Kraft Foods, Holiday Inn, and Tupperware. But above all else, Bryant was the face and voice of the Florida Citrus Commission, the state agency responsible for promoting Florida's most famous crop. For eight years—a near-eternity in television time—she strolled through the Florida orange groves, singing "Come to the Florida sunshine tree" or stood by a well-laden breakfast table, reminding viewers that "breakfast without orange juice is like a day without sunshine." According to a 1970 survey, 75 percent of US television viewers could identify both Bryant and her product, which in turn led Florida governor Reubin Askew to quip: "People connect orange juice, Florida and Anita Bryant so much that it becomes difficult to decide which to visit, which to listen to, and which to squeeze."[42]

As the final notes of her stirring halftime performance gave way to thunderous applause, no one in Miami's Orange Bowl Stadium, including Bryant, could have imagined that it would be the last time that "America's Sweetheart" would sing on a national stage. Over the course of the next three years, Bryant's voice would be uplifted not in song but in vigorous and often harsh protest, as she spearheaded a campaign to overturn a Miami-Dade County ordinance prohibiting discrimination against gays "in housing, public accommodation and employment."[43] In the process, she helped launch or galvanize not just one but two national movements: the evangelical Christian movement and, ironically, the gay rights movement itself. As Robert Kunst, one of the leaders of the Miami gay rights coalition opposing Bryant, told the *New York Times* in 1977: "The truth is that Anita Bryant is the best thing that ever happened to us."[44]

The ordinance against which Bryant campaigned so strongly was adopted by the Miami-Dade County Commission on January 18, 1977, by a 5–3 vote after what was described as "an emotional two-hour hearing." It was immediately clear that the issue would not end there.

"We're not going to take this sitting down," Bryant said. "The ordinance condones immorality and discriminates against my children's rights to grow up in a healthy, decent community."[45]

Bryant then proceeded to pour every ounce of her celebrity capital into a fight to overturn the gay rights ordinance. Following the commission's decision, she helped found a group called Save Our Children and served as the group's leader. Bryant made no secret of the group's intention to oppose homosexual rights not just in Miami but throughout the country: "If homosexuality were the normal way, God would have made Adam and Bruce. This has become a national fight. I've spoken all around the country. We've gotten more than 20,000 letters and taken in about $40,000 from more than 40 states. It won't stop here in Florida. We're setting up to go national."[46]

The Save Our Children campaign started with a petition drive to force a referendum on the ordinance. In order to put the issue before the voters, Save Our Children needed the signatures of ten thousand registered voters. Bryant and her followers managed to collect sixty thousand signatures, mainly at area churches. As a result of their efforts, a vote on the ordinance was scheduled for June 7, 1977. The group also secured the support of Governor Askew, who told reporters that if he lived in Miami, he would vote for the ordinance because "I do not want a known homosexual teaching my child."[47]

With the preliminaries out of the way, the attention of the region and the entire nation turned to the battle over the referendum. On the eve of the vote, one observer estimated that, largely thanks to Bryant, Save Our Children had raised a campaign fund of nearly $200,000, with at least a third of the money coming from out of state. The pro-ordinance forces did even better, collecting as much as half of their $300,000 bankroll from outside Florida.[48]

Despite their fund-raising success, however, the ordinance supporters lost badly when the vote was taken on June 7, 1977. The ordinance was repealed by a 2–1 margin, a victory that had Bryant dancing a jig in her twenty-seven-room Miami Beach mansion. Both she and ordinance supporters made it clear that the Miami vote was merely the beginning of a national debate over gay rights.

"The campaign has motivated gay people politically," said John W. Campbell, one of the ordinance's prominent supporters, "not merely in Florida but all across our nation and even in Europe. We're going national now. We've got more than $50,000 left, more than any gay group has ever had before."[49]

As promised, Anita Bryant took her campaign against homosexuality from one end of the country to the other. But as activists pointed out, by providing a face and a focal point for newly politicized gays, she did more to galvanize the gay rights movement than any other single person. Within weeks of the Miami vote, pro-gay activism was evident across the country: three thousand gays protested her in Houston; forty thousand gays marched for rights in San Francisco; and for the first time, gays were openly trying to use the boycott to effect social change, first by not drinking the orange juice promoted by Anita Bryant and, second, by not buying products advertised on ABC's sitcom *Soap*, since many in the gay community objected to the stereotypical portrayal of the show's gay character.

For Bryant, the defeat of the Dade County ordinance proved to be a victory both personally and painfully Pyrrhic. Just before the vote, she told reporters her bookings were already down 70 percent. A month afterward, her agent (who was married, ironically, to one of the county commissioners who supported the ordinance) announced that his agency would no longer represent her. When the boycott of Florida orange juice by gay groups slowly gathered steam in August, Governor Askew gave Bryant an at best lukewarm endorsement, saying that Bryant's role as spokesperson should continue only as long as sales remained steady. And in October, her meringue-covered profile was flashed around the world by United Press International when gay activist Tom Higgins hit her in the face with a pie before a concert in Des Moines, Iowa.[50]

By February 1978, Bryant had lost every nonreligious singing concert, had been dropped as a television commentator for the Orange Bowl on New Year's Day, and was performing primarily at small religious revivals around the country, where she was paid out of contributions by the audience.[51] Her contract with the Florida Citrus Commission was allowed to expire at the beginning of 1980, and she and her husband/manager Bob Green divorced that same year. Bryant's divorce did not sit well with her Christian audience, and her once-flourishing musical career largely dried up.

FALWELL AND THE FOUNDING OF THE MORAL MAJORITY

When Jerry Falwell returned to his ministry in Lynchville, Virginia, after the successful battle in Miami, he carried with him the conviction that it was time for evangelicals to abandon their long-standing disdain for politics and engage the political process. This was not an uncontroversial decision; already, Falwell's forays into the political realm had earned him criticism from "true fundamentalists" like Bob Jones Jr. and his son, Bob Jones III, who believed that evangelicals in general and ministers in particular should stay out of politics.[52]

Falwell, however, had been laying the groundwork for a political organization for some time. In 1976 he traveled around the United States on a road show called "America, You're Too Young to Die!" At each stop, he presented his argument that "[a]ny diligent student of American history finds that our great nation was founded by godly men upon godly principles to be a Christian nation. Our Founding Fathers . . . developed a nation predicated upon Holy Writ."[53] Along the way, Falwell also made a point of meeting "with local ministers and lay leaders who were committed to political action."[54]

Heady with the successful fights over tax exemptions and gay rights, Falwell sensed a crucial opportunity and, unlike Anita Bryant, he had the network and resources to put his plans into effect. Whereas Bryant was largely dependent on performance fees or donations from either secular or religious music audiences that numbered in the low thousands, Falwell could count on the estimated $1 million per *week* brought in by his televised appeals for donations: his appeals were carried on over 320 stations per day and reached upwards of 15 million faithful viewers per week.[55]

In May 1979, Falwell invited leading conservatives to a meeting in Lynchburg. Chief among them were: Howard Phillips, the national director of the Conservative Caucus; Ed McAteer, president of the Memphis-based Religious Roundtable; Paul Weyrich, president of the Free Congress Foundation; Richard Viguerie, the conservative direct-mail guru; and Robert Billings, head of the National Christian Action Council. During the meeting, Paul Weyrich said that there was a large number of average Americans who agreed with the positions of both religious and economic conservatives—a "moral majority" of voters just waiting to be tapped. Falwell latched onto Weyrich's phrase and at a rally on the steps of the US Capitol soon afterward announced that he had founded the Moral Majority to combat the rise of "humanism" in American society.

The founding of the Moral Majority was a lesson in superb political timing. For much of the decade, the United States had been wrestling with a creeping national malaise that began when President Richard Nixon resigned in disgrace in 1974, continued through the ignominious end of the Vietnam War in 1975, and culminated in the humiliating capture and hostage-taking at the US Embassy in Tehran on November 4, 1979. Adding to the national feeling of dissatisfaction were concerns over energy issues and the economy: the Arab oil embargo of 1973 and 1974 triggered a period of stagflation (flat economic growth combined with skyrocketing double-digit inflation) that President Carter was unable to remedy during his administration.

Thanks to Falwell's existing mailing list of contributors to *The Old Time Gospel Hour*, the Moral Majority quickly became a political powerhouse. By mid-January 1980, the group claimed seventy thousand supporters and a budget of $1 million, which it allocated to four areas of concentration: education, lobbying, the endorsement of candidates, and legal aid for religious issues in court.[56] In early June, the group orchestrated a startling takeover of the Republican state convention in Alaska, ensuring that all of the convention's national delegates were pledged to Falwell's presidential pick, Ronald Reagan.[57]

Just three months before the 1980 election, Falwell said that the membership of the Moral Majority had climbed to four hundred thousand and that the group had taken in $1.5 million in donations. He also reported that the Moral Majority was organizing political action committees in every state to promote favorable candidates and had registered three million new voters. One of the states in which the Moral Majority had an immediate impact was Iowa, in which as many as eighty thousand new voters may have registered in time for the Republican primary. Although the more moderate George H. W. Bush defeated Reagan in the Republican presidential primary, the votes of Reagan's supporters were credited with helping Rep. Charles Grassley, himself a lay preacher, outpoll the more moderate Tom Stoner by a 2–1 margin in the Senate primary.[58] (Grassley went on to defeat the incumbent, Senator John Culver, in the general election and, twenty-five years later, is still serving in the Senate.)

In his one debate with President Carter on October 28, 1980, Ronald Reagan aptly captured the disgruntled mood of the country by asking voters one simple question: "Are you better off now than you were four years ago?" In November, voters emphatically answered Reagan by giving him a solid popular-vote victory over Carter, 51 percent to 41 percent. The Electoral College results were even more impressive: Reagan received 489 electoral votes to Carter's 49. Reagan's victory was attributed to a number of different factors, including his relentlessly optimistic outlook, his promise to restore America's greatness and rebuild its military, his promise to end "big government," and his belief that the nation's economic health could be restored through application of the principles of "supply side economics."

The Moral Majority, however, had a much simpler explanation for Reagan's victory: they selected him and propelled him to victory. As the Reverend Jerry Falwell later put it in a fund-raising letter:

> Our first priorities were voter registration and the selection of a "champion" to support for the presidency in November 1980. We organized quickly in all 50 states, eventually enlisting about 100,000 pastors, priests, a few rabbis and millions of grassroots Americans around our agenda. We chose Ronald Reagan in 1980 as our flag bearer and we were "off to the races."
>
> The rest is history. Ronald Reagan was elected. Twelve liberal senators were unseated. The national media declared that the "religious right" was born. Faith and family social issues became front burner political issues, with Roe vs. Wade in our crosshairs from Day One.[59]

In a remarkably short time, however, it would become clear to religious conservatives, as it had to so many before them, that there was a vast gulf between political influence and the adoption of public policy. It would also become clear that although conservatives were starting to win significant political victories, the battle over decency was headed in a decidedly different, market-driven direction.

"The Man with the Golden Gut" Invents "Jiggle TV"

At the same time that neocons were working strenuously (and successfully) to make Washington less inhospitable for themselves and that religious conservatives were organizing for battle, a series of changes was taking place in the media and in society in general that would ultimately make conservatives across the country far less comfortable. In particular, the nascent gay rights movement, born over a series of riotous nights outside the Stonewall Inn in New York in 1969, was slowly gathering steam; ironically, evangelical Christians would soon push it into the spotlight. Movie themes were more sexual than ever—in 1969 *Midnight Cowboy* became the only X-rated film to win a Best Picture Oscar, and the XXX-rated *Deep Throat* made millions from mainstream audiences in 1973. Music was undergoing its own revolution: the Beatles, Simon & Garfunkel, and the Monkees all broke up in 1970, the same year that several popular singers (Janis Joplin, Jim Morrison, and Grace Slick) were all fined for using obscenity during public performances.

But in terms of overall cultural impact, no medium changed quite so dramatically and so completely during the decade than television. In the aftermath of the 1960s, *Ozzie and Harriet* moved out of the neighborhood, and *Mary Tyler Moore* moved in. The *Ed Sullivan Show* had just one year left, and *Gomer Pyle, U.S.M.C.* was mustered out. NBC introduced a series of gritty crime dramas, including *McCloud* and *Columbo*, and CBS premiered the frank and often painfully relevant *All in the Family*, which spent the next six years as the top Nielsen-rated television show. Spinning off from the *All in the Family* was *Maude*, which intensified the debate over social realism on the small screen (the lead character, played by Beatrice Arthur, was an outspoken proponent of women's liberation, a staunch Democrat, and was depicted in 1972 as choosing to have an abortion after getting pregnant at age forty-seven).

Congressmen (particularly those with teenage kids) were certainly not unaware of the changes taking place in popular culture, but there was relatively little they could do. In 1969 Senator John Pastore (1907–2000) (D-RI) floated a plan to have the National Association of Broadcasters prescreen television programs before they aired.[60] As columnist Jack Gould pointed out, the virtue of "self-regulation" would be undercut by the fact that the screening would be done by an organization that also lobbies on behalf of the broadcast industry on Capitol Hill, which would make it unduly sensitive to the tastes and preferences of legislators. "That the two functions can be realistically separated," Gould wrote, "is pure naiveté and Senator Pastore, one hopes, would be the first to sense the practical perils of such a move."[61]

Whether or not Senator Pastore was in fact the first to see the problems in his proposal, the plan died a quiet and unlamented death. In fact, there was really only one thing that concerned legislators could do—call the Federal Communications Commission on the carpet and demand a plan to do something about the perceived increase in sex and violence on television. In 1974 Senator Pastore and Rep. Torbert H. MacDonald (1917–1976) (D-MA) (the respective chairmen of the Senate and House Communications Subcommittees) both instructed FCC chairman Richard E. Wiley to report back to Congress by December 31 on specific actions the FCC could take to protect children from "violent, obscene or indecent materials."[62]

A couple of months past the deadline, Chairman Wiley told Congress that the networks and the National Association of Broadcasters had agreed to institute a "family viewing hour" at the start of prime time, during which they would limit the broadcast of material unsuitable for children. However, Chairman Wiley noted that any attempt by the FCC or Congress to specify what is or is not appropriate for children "might involve the Government too deeply in programming content and raise sensitive First Amendment issues."

"[P]arents in our view," Wiley wrote, "have—and should retain—the primary responsibility for their children's well-being."[63]

The "family viewing hour" notwithstanding, the rush toward more sexual sitcoms accelerated as the decade progressed. In theory, there were three broadcast networks in 1974, but one of them—ABC—was so consistently and distantly third that it often barely registered in the ratings. The industry joke was that "if they put the Vietnam War on ABC, it would get canceled in thirteen weeks." To remedy matters, the "alphabet" network persuaded CBS programming chief Fred Silverman (who had been responsible for overseeing the hit shows *All in the Family* and *Mary Tyler Moore*) to switch shops.[64] As he began work at his new job, Silverman quickly recognized that in order to change ABC's fortunes, a radically new approach was needed. He decided that the network would be the first to design shows specifically targeted at the so-called power buyers—the eighteen- to thirty-year-old demographic that is most attractive to national advertisers.[65]

In the early 1970s, the concept of audience demographics was still a relatively new idea and effective counting of the total audience itself was only a decade old. In the early 1960s, the ACNielsen Company of Chicago, Illinois, developed the first effective system for recording which channels specially selected televisions were watching at any given time. The audience totals compiled by Nielsen enabled the broadcast networks to have some idea of what to charge advertisers for different shows; thus, advertising rates could be based on whether the show was first, second, or third in its time slot and on the number of people actually watching.[66]

Over the course of the decade, Nielsen made its data more useful by breaking down the total audience for each show into different age groups. Advertisers quickly realized that not all age groups were created equal: there was far greater potential profit, for instance, in advertising on shows that appealed to people with more disposable income. In turn, the networks recognized that they could attract more advertisers (and charge higher advertising rates) by creating programs that appealed to the most affluent and liquid demographic, eighteen- to thirty-year-old males. So compelling was this idea that CBS, for instance, canceled a number of popular shows in the 1970s— *Petticoat Junction* (1970), *Green Acres* (1971), and *Gunsmoke* (1975)—when it concluded that despite good overall ratings, the percentage of younger viewers was simply too low.[67] The first two shows may have been no real loss in artistic terms, but it is not clear that the youth-oriented replacements were any better.

Silverman didn't need to take a poll to figure out what types of shows would appeal strongly to eighteen- to thirty-year-old men. For a year, Aaron Spelling had been shopping a show called *Alley Cats*, which featured the crime-fighting exploits of three attractive female detectives. Silverman's predecessor at ABC, Michael Eisner, allegedly told Spelling that it was "one of the worst ideas" he had ever heard, but Silverman gave the go-ahead to shoot a pilot episode.[68] The show, renamed *Charlie's Angels* at the suggestion of cast member Kate Jackson, debuted on March 21, 1976, and was an instant ratings hit, with over half the TVs in America tuning in.[69] Television critics generally agreed with Eisner's assessment, but Silverman had convincingly demonstrated that when it came to marketing to eighteen- to thirty-year-olds, less (i.e., fewer bras) was more.

The success of *Charlie's Angels* was part of a remarkable run for ABC. The network had already made substantial gains in the ratings by producing enormously popular comedies like *Happy Days* (1974) and *Laverne & Shirley* (1976), but the introduction of "jiggle TV" took ABC to a new ratings peak. In 1977 the network added to its jiggle quotient by launching *Three's Company*, a madcap situation comedy about a man pretending to be gay so that he could share an apartment with two attractive female roommates. Even the network's dramas turned somewhat racier. That same year, Robert Urich starred in *Vega$*, playing a detective fighting crime in the neon city with the help of his attractive former showgirl sidekick.

One positive side effect of ABC's growing audience strength was that it had the creative freedom to try some serious and provocative programming. Despite the growing gay rights controversy, the network felt that it could ignore a threatened boycott and stick with a show (*Soap*) that featured an openly gay character. It could also take dramatic chances: Silverman gave the green light to a number of potentially controversial but highly acclaimed miniseries, including *Rich Man, Poor Man* (1976) and Alex Haley's *Roots* (1977). The latter series, which ran for eight consecutive nights, was remarkable not only for its gripping, even cathartic examination of slavery in America (the finale is still the third-highest rated show ever), but also for the fact that it was the first time that naked female breasts were intentionally shown on a network broadcast. (If the FCC received any complaints, they didn't do anything about it.)

From a financial perspective, Silverman's decision to focus on eighteen- to thirty-year-olds was a tremendous success. At the end of the 1976–77 television season, ABC was number one in the Nielsen ratings for the first time, displacing CBS from its twenty-year perch, an accomplishment that earned Silverman the cover of *Time* magazine and the nickname "the man with the golden gut."[70] More important, the network's revenues exploded. When Silverman started at ABC, the network was earning about $29 million in profits. Just two years later, ABC reported profits of $165 million. In 1978 ABC could claim a remarkable fourteen out of the top twenty prime-time shows.[71]

There are few industries that produce more replication than network television. After enviously watching ABC's success with younger viewers, both NBC and CBS tried the same strategy to attract younger viewers, with only middling results. In 1978 CBS introduced *WKRP in Cincinnati*, which relied in no small part on the physical attributes of buxom actress Loni Anderson. The show developed a solid following, but was never a tremendous hit. NBC took an edgier route, hiring comedian Richard Pryor (1940–2005) to star in the *Richard Pryor Show* during the 1977–78 season. However, the network quickly realized that it couldn't broadcast the vast bulk of Pryor's graphic and unexpurgated comedy routines, and only four of the planned ten episodes were even produced.[72] Writer Joseph Lelyveld described one of Prior's final tapings: "It's original, funny, sometimes moving, superior to the Pryor that NBC has shown, and scatological in the extreme—a powerful assertion of individuality even when it turns nasty, as it finally does. And, of course, it's absolutely unusable by any imaginable network canon. . . . Out of the first 65 minutes Pryor performs, his producer salvages exactly 22 words."[73]

Even though the NBC and CBS experiments largely failed in the short term, the rumble in Silverman's golden gut was music to television executives' ears; all three networks were now sold on sex as a theme in their programming decisions. In the coming years, as other types of media increasingly pecked away at the broadcast television audience, the networks would increasingly turn to sexual themes and situations (replete with well-toned bodies) to bolster their sagging market share.

The basic structure of television economics would intensify this trend. Although advertising rates for national advertisers are based on Nielsen samplings taken throughout the year, the rates for local advertisers are set during just four weeks a year, in February, May, July, and November. Since rates are based on the number of viewers, networks have gotten into the habit of scheduling "edgy," often outrageous episodes or specials during each "sweeps week." This has had a consistently downward ratcheting effect on the artistic value of televised content. When a show, particularly a popular one, crosses each season's equivalent of the "son-of-a-bitch" barrier (a phrase *Maude* was the first to use in the early 1970s), it's tough to go back. For the networks, lowbrow was the new high.

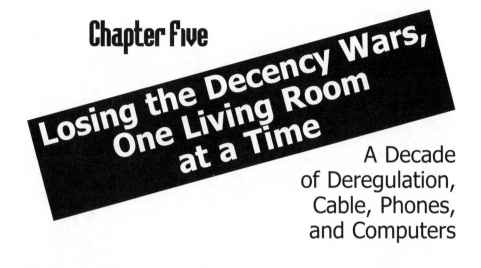

Chapter Five

Losing the Decency Wars, One Living Room at a Time

A Decade of Deregulation, Cable, Phones, and Computers

onald Wilson Reagan was sworn into office as the fortieth president of the United States on January 20, 1981. For religious conservatives in general and the Moral Majority in particular, it was a glorious day, one that truly offered the promise of "A New Beginning"—the slogan plastered on banners throughout Washington, DC. This president, this "Great Communicator," was going to right the American ship of state, restore the nation's glory, and reverse its decline into secularism and moral decay. When the hostages being held by Iranian militants were released within minutes of Reagan's inauguration, it was perceived by many as an unusually direct sign of divine approval.

In the heady days following Reagan's election, religious conservatives made no secret of their political wish list and the expectation that it would be delivered unto them. The list included defeat of the Equal Rights Amendment, a constitutional amendment permitting prayer in schools, a constitutional amendment banning abortion (or, failing that, Supreme Court reversal of *Roe v. Wade*), the banning and aggressive prosecution of nonchild pornography, and an unequivocal rejection of gays and gay rights. While there may have been some realists in the movement who understood the gulf between election and enactment, much of the rhetoric made no concession to compromise.

Gary Jarmin, political director for the political and educational group Christian Voice, told the *New York Times* that Reagan's election "points to the beginning of a new era." The Moral Majority's Reverend Falwell announced

Tipper Gore, testifying before the Senate Committee on Commerce, Science, and Transportation on September 19, 1985, about the dangers of "porn rock." (*Broadcasting & Cable*)

that it was "the greatest day for the cause of conservatism and American morality in my life."[1] A few days later, Falwell stood on the steps of the New Jersey State House in Trenton and preached "against abortion, pornography, and homosexuality." He explicitly warned liberal legislators to "examine their records and get in step with conservative values or prepare to be unemployed."[2]

Even before the transition was well under way, however, more seasoned political observers questioned how much of the religious conservative agenda would actually be implemented. Activists might have dismissed the comments of the *Washington Post*'s liberal columnist David Broder, who wrote that "Reagan and the Republicans face a fateful choice in which agenda they accept. . . . To put it as directly as possible, if they choose the economic agenda, they have a chance of success that can broaden their constituency and give them a leg up on the Democrats in the struggle for the future of American politics. If they choose the social agenda, they will squander their energies in what is probably a losing cause, divide their own ranks and alienate the very voters who could make them the majority party of the next three decades."[3]

The preelection comments of *Wall Street Journal* reporter Albert R. Hunt, however, should have been a wake-up call. Hunt pointed out that between Reagan's two marriages, he had something of a reputation as "one of Holly-wood's well-known ladykillers," which made it "disingenuous for the Gipper to pretend he's a moral cousin of the Rev. Jerry Falwell. . . . I have watched and thought about Ronald Reagan a lot during the past year. Still, I'm uncertain whether he would be a good or bad President. But I do feel confident that at least two groups would have their expectations dashed by a Reagan presidency. They are his harshest critics and his most zealous supporters."[4]

It did not take long for Reagan's "zealous supporters" to feel the disap-pointment of unmet expectations. As the transition team began staffing the new administration, religious and social conservatives complained that rela-tively few from their ranks had been tapped. By contrast, Reagan drew fairly heavily from the so-called Ford wing of the Republican party, leading *Conser-vative Digest* editor John Lofton to grouse, "Sometimes I wonder how much of a Reaganite Reagan really is, and unfortunately those times are becoming more frequent."[5] Conservative direct mail expert Richard Viguerie was even more direct. "This administration is clearly not a conservative administration. The people who elected Ronald Reagan, who have stuck with him for over 16 years, got kicked in the teeth."[6]

President Reagan and his staff cannot be accused of entirely ignoring the policy goals of religious conservatives. During its eight years in power, for instance, the Reagan White House worked hard to appoint more conservative judges to the federal bench (although its success at the Supreme Court level was decidedly mixed). Most notably, in the spring of 1984, Reagan personally pushed for the adoption of a constitutional amendment to allow school prayer (albeit after his reelection campaign was under way). Ironically, Reagan's efforts to placate his religious conservative supporters in that instance actually may have backfired; he rejected efforts by members of his own party in the Senate, including Orrin Hatch (R-UT), to draft a constitutional amendment that used the phrase "moment of silence" instead of prayer. Despite the White House's lobbying and the day-long presence of pro-prayer demonstrators out-side the Capitol, the amendment failed to get the two-thirds majority required to send it to the states.[7]

The disappointment of religious conservatives intensified over the course of Reagan's presidency. A typically disgruntled analysis was written by John McLaughlin in a 1985 article for the *National Review*, in which he pointed out that while Reagan had run on the Republican antiabortion plank and had authored a book while in office titled *Abortion and the Conscience of the Nation*, little else had been done. "That's how Reagan treated social issues at the level of talk," McLaughlin wrote. "Action was a different story; namely, precious little. In fact abortion typifies the President's all-talk, little-action approach to social issues."[8] As conservative activist Dan Arico bluntly observed at the Conservative Political Action Conference in Washington, DC, in the spring of 1987, "Ronald Reagan has turned out to be so disappointing."[9] And that was a full year before the news broke that throughout her husband's presidency, First Lady Nancy Reagan had consulted an astrologer about her husband's daily schedule —a practice condemned in the Old Testament as worshiping a false god.[10]

A good argument can be made that religious conservatives had something of a "false god" problem of their own. Syndicated columnist Cal Thomas, who was serving as a vice president in the Moral Majority at the time of Reagan's inauguration, aptly summarized how Reagan had played the serpent to the religious conservatives' Eve: "As I'd travel around the country, I'd go into churches and I'd see featured prominently in the office of a hallway a picture of the pastor with Reagan. Nothing wrong with that, but that happened so many times that I think Christian people were sucked into the political process so that it became primary in their lives, and a moral and spiritual power that should've been theirs, to [enable them to] speak truth to power, seemed to be put on the back burner, because Ronald Reagan became the surrogate Messiah."[11]

In political terms, the problem for religious conservatives was that they mistook both the country's mood and the core nature of Reagan's conservatism. Unquestionably, President Reagan saw the electoral importance of the conservative social agenda and learned the lines well, but he was at heart a Goldwater neoconservative, right down to the offhand jokes about using nuclear weapons.[12] His election in 1980 had far more to do with the country's desire to restore American preeminence in the world, defeat communism, and improve the nation's faltering economic prospects than with so-called moral values. And once in office, Reagan and his advisers (most of whom were themselves far more neoconservative and economically conservative than religious) demonstrated their awareness of that fact by making it clear that any push to promote a conservative social agenda would have to take a backseat to Reagan's economic program. Clinton adviser James Carville may have coined the phrase "It's the economy, stupid," but behind every successful president is a staff that understands that credo instinctively.

The emphasis of the Reagan administration on neoconservative and economic conservative issues undercut the religious conservative social agenda in two different ways. First, it limited the amount of time that the administration could devote to social conservative issues (even if it had wanted to do so). And second, although it wasn't always immediately apparent, some of the goals of economic conservatives were directly at odds with the objectives of social conservatives.

Many of the profound cultural changes that took place during the 1980s (most of which were anathema to religious and social conservatives) were well beyond the control of the Reagan administration—or, in fairness, any presidential administration. But it is also undeniably true that the Reagan administration's enthusiastic support for governmental deregulation—long a goal of economic conservatives—encouraged and helped finance a series of technological developments that gave the pornography industry direct access to every living room and bedroom in the country. At the same time, consolidation of broadcast media shifted programming choices away from local communities into control booths often thousands of miles away.

By the time Ronald Reagan rode off into the sunset to his California ranch, it was clear that while religious conservatives might have won the battle to elect a sympathetic president, they were steadily losing the broader decency wars.

"I Want My MTV!"

In 1950 a tower was constructed in Lansford, Pennsylvania, to pick up broadcast television signals and distribute them to local residents by coaxial cable. The system, known then as community antenna television (CATV), was designed to provide remote viewers with a cleaner and more reliable signal than they could get over the airwaves. From that modest beginning, CATV (or, as we know it today, cable television) has grown into an entertainment behemoth: as of the summer of 2005, the cable television industry had an estimated seventy-two million subscribers, and seven out of ten homes in the United States were wired for cable.[13]

In the late 1970s and early 1980s, however, cable television was suffering from the same economic slowdown that was plaguing other sectors of the economy. In 1977, for instance, there were 12,168,450 cable subscribers, reaching 16.6 percent of the households with TV. By the end of 1980, the number of subscribers had risen to just 17,671,490, with a television market penetration of 22.6 percent.[14] Certainly, some signs of progress, but definitely not a robust and dynamic growth curve.

While the often conflicting demands of the FCC and different local communities undoubtedly made things more complicated for the cable industry, the more significant issue was that for the first thirty years of cable's existence, the only thing it really offered was better reception for network television. For much of the country, rabbit-ear antennae were more than adequate for receiving broadcasts by the small number of available channels.

That slowly began to change in the late 1970s, when Time, Inc., launched the Home Box Office (HBO) cable channel. It grew in just six years from a small, struggling pay-TV service in New York to a nationwide cable channel capable of financing its own original films. The company's first three independent projects were financed in 1978: *The Bell Jar*, *The Wild Geese*, and *Watership Down*. It was a wildly eclectic group of films—the first about a suicidal New England young woman, the second about a group of aging British mercenaries hired to overthrow an African dictator, and the third about a down of animated rabbits. But the advent of these films showed a glimmer of the growing economic strength of cable in general and HBO in particular. Eager to tap into the growing demand for movies on cable, the media giant Viacom decided to expand its own experimental movie channel, Showtime, to a national audience later that same year.

With the movie channels blazing the way, other specialized channels began to come onboard. In 1980 Atlanta entrepreneur Ted Turner gambled that consumers would pay for a twenty-four-hour, all-news network. Within just four years, Turner was proven right when CNN first began to earn a profit. In August 1980, HBO offered further evidence of its remarkable growth by launching Cinemax, the first movie channel offered to cable subscribers as a separate purchase.[15]

Over time, each of these new cable channels—and the dozens that followed—would play a role in the nation's growing decency wars. But in the short term, there was no cable channel that offered a more direct assault on the nation's sense of decency than Music Television (MTV).

The cable music revolution began in 1977, when a joint venture known as Warner Amex Cable (started with investments from Warner Communications and American Express) launched QUBE, the country's first interactive cable television system. Based in Columbus, Ohio, the system offered a variety of different channels, including one called Sight on Sound, which gave viewers a chance to vote for their favorite musicians and songs. Although the QUBE system itself was an expensive failure and was shut down in 1984,[16] its music channel was so popular that Warner Amex invested $30 million to launch it as a stand-alone cable channel on August 1, 1981. When it rolled out, the channel was initially available to 1.5 million cable subscribers.[17]

There's some debate among cable industry analysts about the role that MTV actually played in the growth of cable in the United States. Some suggest that in terms of actual audience size, "MTV never achieved the ratings or the national coverage that was supposed to make it a significant advertising buy."[18] Others, like Robert Thompson, director of the Center for the Study of Popular Television, argue that MTV was in fact the catalyst for the entire industry. As he told the *Miami Herald* in 2004: "MTV was really the fuse that finally lit the cable revolution. Cable had been around for a while, with a lot of people deciding not to take it. In 1981, MTV finally comes up with something you really can't get anywhere else. Everybody under 18 is screaming for it. I think an awful lot of people finally got their houses wired for cable thanks to MTV."[19] It was, if nothing else, a classic example of how the elusive "buzz" can influence an entire industry.

There is no disagreement, however, that MTV did have at least one measurable economic impact, even beyond the sheer number of kids who were begging their parents to sign up for cable so that they could watch the latest Michael Jackson video. As MTV steadily spread across the country's cable systems, the music industry quickly noticed that when a band's video played on MTV, its albums flew off the shelves of the nation's music stores.[20] This was a huge issue for artists and recording studios. Record sales had peaked in 1978 at $4.1 billion per year, and by 1982 had slumped to $3.6 billion. In 1984, just three years after MTV debuted, the sales of records and cassette tapes soared to $4.2 billion, at that time a new high.[21]

The surge in record sales helped underscore the fact that MTV had its finger firmly on the pulse of a very specific demographic—the twelve- to thirty-four-year-olds interested in contemporary music. Although advertisers were still hesitant about the value of advertising on cable, MTV was a compelling purchase for companies for a number of reasons: the ability to direct ads at a narrowly targeted audience, that audience's willingness to spend money, and the low cost of purchasing time on the music network. The last factor may have been the most compelling: a thirty-second advertisement on MTV cost just $1,000 in 1982, compared to the $175,000 fee for a comparable spot during the popular prime-time drama *Dallas*. Six months after its launch, MTV could list over one hundred major national brands that had purchased advertising time. Neither MTV nor cable as a whole represented a major threat to broadcast television ad dollars at that point: altogether, cable took in $129 million in 1981, compared to the $12.7 *billion* that advertisers paid that same year for time on broadcast networks. Nonetheless, the first whispers of competition were being heard in network headquarters.[22]

As MTV's phenomenal growth continued—nine million subscribers after eighteen months, twelve million before its second year ended—it began to alter not merely the television universe but the musical one as well. Even well-established bands began experimenting with video to promote their new albums, and the number of rock tours began to decline thanks to the more favorable economics of MTV's twenty-four-hour concert (a tour might be seen by as many as one hundred thousand people, a fraction of MTV's regular audience). Some critics even began to wonder if the new video format was damaging the art of song writing.[23] As MTV's popularity grew, its groundbreaking visual style also began to creep into the broader culture. The successful movie *Flashdance* (1983) was modeled on MTV's video style, and, in September 1984, NBC introduced *Miami Vice*, aiming quick-cut edits of Miami's drug trade and Don Johnson's natty linen blazer squarely at MTV's now twenty-four million subscribers.[24]

The one thing about MTV that caught everyone's attention was sex. No one should have been surprised that videos made by rock musicians for rock music fans would be laced with near-nudity and sexual imagery—such themes had been the staples of songs, to one degree or another, for centuries. But the addition of a visual component made the issue that much more visceral, particularly for the millions of parents who had given in to MTV-driven pleas for cable television in the first place.

When Ted Turner announced on November 1, 1984, that he was launching MTV's first twenty-four-hour competitor, the Cable Music Channel, he explicitly stated that the videos aired each day "would not contain the same levels of sex and violence contained in MTV's." Turner quickly proved that at least when it comes to entertainment, cleanliness is next to bankruptcy. Just thirty days later, Turner announced that the assets of the Cable Music Channel had been sold to MTV for $1 million and that MTV had agreed to purchase $500,000 in advertising on Turner's other networks.[25]

"It's Only Rock and Roll," So "We're Not Going to Take It!"

One of the most obvious effects of MTV's introduction of video to rock was a steady trend toward increasingly outrageous music and styles. With music videos repeating several times a day (and when MTV started, several times per hour), there was a premium on outrageousness—violence, sex, and so on—to keep viewers glued to their couches and to generate buzz.

At the same time, the music video network's debut coincided with (and accelerated) rock's transition from new wave to heavy metal bands like Def Leppard, Iron Maiden, Guns N' Roses, Kiss, Metallica, Nazareth, Quiet Riot, Van Halen, and Mötley Crüe. With their long hair, monsterish costumes, loud volume, and violently antisocial lyrics, laced with themes of violence, drug use, casual (and often kinky) sex, and suicide, the growing popularity of heavy metal bands began raising the blood pressure, ironically enough, of the once-hippy baby boomers who were now trying to rear their own teenage children.

In May 1985, a group of twenty or so influential mothers gathered at St. Columbia's Church in Washington, DC. Under the leadership of Tipper Gore (wife of Senator Al Gore), Susan Baker (wife of Treasury Secretary James Baker), and Nancy Thurmond (wife of Senator Strom Thurmond [1902–2003]), the group founded the Parents Music Resource Center (PMRC). The meeting was organized by Gore, who was reportedly horrified by the lyrics that she heard on her daughter's copy of *Purple Rain* (1984). Exhibit A in Gore's "chamber of horribles" was the song "Little Nikki," in which Prince sings about meeting a girl named Nikki in a hotel lobby, where he sees her masturbating with a magazine.

Thanks in large part to the group's political connections, the PMRC was able to quickly mount a massive and aggressive public relations campaign against the record industry. Members were interviewed by a variety of major news outlets, including *Newsweek*, the *Washington Post*, and *National Public Radio*.[26] Declaring that sexually explicit lyrics were "porn rock," the PMRC stated with remarkable precision that "8 percent of all rock lyrics were objectionable."[27] Alarmed by the rapid rise of the group and their obvious political clout, Edward Fritts, president of the National Association of Broadcasters, sent a warning letter to 806 radio and television owners and 45 record company executives. Fritts's warning was largely ignored by the record companies, but a number of broadcasters (leery, no doubt, of possible action by the FCC) started editing objectionable songs or striking songs from their playlists.[28]

With the obvious threat of political action lurking in the background, the PMRC demanded that the recording industry take a number of different steps, including printing lyrics on record albums, pressuring broadcasters not to play "controversial" videos or songs, placing labels on albums containing explicit lyrics, putting albums with explicit covers out of sight, and implementing rating systems for both albums and concerts.[29] As a demonstration of its political clout, the PMRC persuaded the Senate Committee on Commerce, Science, and Transportation to schedule a hearing on September 19, 1985, to take testimony on music lyrics and proposed systems for either rating music or applying parental warning labels.

It was an indication of how the nation's economic landscape had changed that the PMRC, unlike the Catholic-led Legion of Decency, never advocated that parents simply boycott unacceptable music. Much of the reason may well have been the group's awareness that a call for a boycott of "porn rock" would have failed miserably. Even in a pre-Internet world, there were simply too many outlets for music sales; there were no substitutes for a particular band's music; it would have been too difficult to inflict noticeable economic harm on massive recording companies; too few parents had the time or inclination to prescreen their children's music; and, given the growing economic resources of teens, many would simply have purchased the tapes or CDs themselves. And, in fairness, there's hardly a unanimity of opinion on the harmfulness of rock music, unlike, for example, in the early 1930s, when the view that movies were indecent was much more widely held. The popular columnist Ann Landers (1918–2002) asked for reader response to the charge that rock music was responsible for teen suicides and drug abuse, and out of her first twenty thousand responses, the letters ran 90–1 in support of rock.[30] A summary of Landers's correspondence hardly qualifies as a scientific study, but given her typically older and more conservative readership, it is clear that public support for the PMRC's campaign was underwhelming.

So, rather than using the economic decisions of thousands of individual households to bring about cultural change, the PMRC used the threat of federal legislation in order to extract concessions from the recording industry. As with so many of the decency battles in Washington, when everything was said and done, the benefits of the PMRC's campaign were largely political rather than cultural.

Musicians of every description were outraged by the PMRC's attack, and, not surprisingly, a number of fairly unflattering songs were written about the PMRC in general and Tipper Gore in particular (the ultimate revenge of artists). In addition, Danny Goldberg, the owner of Gold Mountain Records, helped organize managers, radio executives, publishers, and artists into an opposition group that he called the Musical Majority.[31] But while recording industry executives may generally have agreed with their musicians, they had two major concerns: first, the collective political firepower of the PMRC leadership made it at least possible that Congress could be persuaded to pass censorship legislation (which would be expensive to fight in court, even if the outcome would likely be favorable), and second, the recording industry was currently lobbying Congress for a surtax on tape recorders and blank cassettes to compensate the industry for lost revenues from the taping of albums. As a result, the recording industry was far more conciliatory to the PMRC than it might otherwise have been.[32]

Even before the Senate hearing convened, the president of the Recording Industry Association of America (RIAA), Stanley M. Gortikov, sent a ten-page letter to the PMRC, rejecting most of its proposals but promising that record companies would put a label on album and cassette covers to warn parents of explicit lyrics. The RIAA agreed to work with the PMRC on appropriate wording.[33]

Despite the RIAA's concession on labeling, the Senate Committee went ahead with its hearing. The witness list was a remarkable study in contrast: representatives from the PMRC and the national Parent Teacher Association on one side, and three musicians—Frank Zappa (1940–1993), Dee Snider (from the group Twisted Sister), and John Denver (1943–1997)—on the other.

Susan Baker testified that the nation faced a "proliferation of songs glorifying rape, sado-masochism, incest, the occult and suicide by a growing number of bands."[34] Frank Zappa responded by asking where the line should be drawn: "Where do you stop and start? Does 'Puppy Love' mean bestiality? Does 'On the Good Ship Lollipop' mean a psychedelic trip?"[35] Both Dee Snider and John Denver argued that if parents were concerned about lyrics, they should listen to albums first themselves, rather than asking the government to censor music.

The concept of parental responsibility was apparently lost on some legislators. Senator Paula Hawkins (R-FL) stirred partisan supporters when she "played two rock video tapes and held high some posters for rock albums she consider[ed] obscene."[36] Democrats were just as censorious: "It is outrageous filth, and we must do something about it," Senator Ernest F. Hollings (D-SC) thundered. "If I could find some way constitutionally to get rid of it, I would."[37] But despite an implied threat from Senator Jim Exon (1921–2005) (D-NE) that in the absence of improvements by the music industry, "there might well be legislation,"[38] the hearings adjourned without any specific recommendations. Part of the reason may well have been an awareness on the part of the senators that any legislation they crafted would have been instantly challenged and almost certainly declared unconstitutional. Ira Glasser, executive director of the American Civil Liberties Union, neatly summarized the real purpose of the hearing: "What they are doing is using the threat of legislation to force voluntary compliance. And the threat of legislation doesn't exist, since no such legislation would survive a constitutional challenge. The only purpose is to try and create self-censorship in the music industry."[39] Senator John C. Danforth (R-IN) implicitly conceded Glasser's point when he said that "[t]he be-all and end-all of everything is not Congressional legislation. The purpose of the hearing is to provide a forum."[40]

Despite the high-profile hearing and implicit threat of legislation, the PMRC was not very effective in getting the record industry to adopt most of its agenda. While the two sides were able to agree on language for the voluntary labeling program ("PARENTAL ADVISORY—EXPLICIT LYRICS"), the so-called Tipper stickers (which are still in use today) do not contain any ratings or additional information about the nature of the explicitness. There is also no consistent practice regarding the publication of lyrics, the other major concession the group sought.

Some PMRC activists were upset that the record industry successfully resisted the creation of a movie-style rating system for albums, but Tipper Gore pronounced herself satisfied: "[The labels] speak to our solution perfectly. We are firmly opposed to censorship. We don't want legislation. All we ever wanted was for companies to voluntarily provide consumer information so that we could make an informed choice in the stores."[41]

That generally reasonable position presupposes, of course, that when consumers walk into a store, the choice to purchase a stickered CD is available. One of the direct (and completely foreseeable) consequences of the adoption of the Tipper stickers was that a number of stores announced that they simply would not carry any music bearing a parental advisory label. Today, the two leading abstainers, the notoriously conservative Wal-Mart and KMart, also happen to be among the largest retail outlets for music. Together, they sell as much music as traditional music stores. A decision by Wal-Mart or KMart to carry or not carry a particular CD exerts a strong gravitational effect on artists, by forcing them to change or "bleep" their lyrics just enough to remain unstickered and on superstore shelves.

Retailers are naturally entitled to set whatever standards they feel are appropriate for the products they sell, and artists are equally free to conform to those standards or not. In some cases, artists have dealt with content restrictions by creating two versions of their work, one for conservative retail outlets and one for everywhere else. What is troubling about the "porn rock" controversy is that while Gore and the PMRC may not have wanted government censorship, the fact that their campaign was backed by an implied threat of federal legislation led directly to a reduction in consumer choice. Given the PMRC's initial complaints and the group's effect on the marketplace, Gore's protestations against censorship seem somewhat disingenuous.

WHAT'S THAT COMMISSION REPORT DOING UNDER YOUR MATTRESS?

The PMRC's high-profile attack on the music industry coincided with and undoubtedly bolstered the efforts of religious conservatives to get the Reagan administration to join the growing antipornography movement. Under President Reagan's first attorney general, William French Smith (1917–1990), the Justice Department had not made the prosecution of obscenity cases a high priority, so religious conservatives were getting increasingly impatient. According to Father Morton A. Hill (1917–1985), founder of the antipornography group Morality in Media, "The token enforcement mentality of the U.S. Department of Justice has become so entrenched that only intervention by the President himself can change it."[42]

In March 1983, Father Hill obtained that intervention by arranging a meeting with President Reagan and various agency heads at the White House. Together with other national leaders of the antipornography movement, they asked the president to appoint a coordinator to organize the activities of various federal agencies and promote aggressive obscenity enforcement. Following the meeting with Father Hill, President Reagan created a White House Working Group on Pornography in June and, in December, told a gathering of US attorneys that there should be more aggressive enforcement of obscenity laws.[43]

The Reagan administration's most significant action against the pornography industry was probably the least heralded. In the fall of 1984, just one month before his reelection, President Reagan signed the Comprehensive Crime Control Act, a massive piece of legislation designed to reorganize and tighten the federal criminal code. At the last minute, Senator Jesse Helms (R-NC) added an amendment to include "obscenity" among the list of crimes covered by the federal Racketeering Influenced and Corrupt Organizations (RICO) statute. The amendment dramatically increased the potential penalties for federal obscenity convictions from five to twenty years. More significantly, it gave the Justice Department the ability to seek the forfeiture of any financial or physical assets related to an obscenity conviction.

In addition to adding obscenity to RICO, Congress that same year passed the Child Protection Act, which authorized prosecutions for the production, distribution, or receipt of child pornography even when it would not be judged obscene under the standard enunciated in 1973 by the Court in *Miller v. California*.[44] Congress also removed the requirement that child pornography be produced for commercial purposes before being prosecutable and increased the age limit for involvement in the production of sexually explicit material from sixteen to eighteen. By limiting child pornography prosecutions to "visual depictions," Congress essentially codified the long-standing trend of exempting literary works of any description from obscenity prosecutions.

While almost no one seriously questioned the value of cracking down on child pornography, religious conservatives continued to push the Reagan administration for a more broad-based campaign against hard-core adult pornography. In mid-May 1984, the Justice Department organized a seminar for state and federal prosecutors on how to prosecute obscenity cases more effectively. Later that year, during the signing ceremony for the Child Protection Act, President Reagan declared that "[i]t's time to stop pretending that extreme pornography is a victimless crime." He announced that he was ordering his attorney general, William French Smith (1917–1990), to establish a commission to study the effects of pornography on society. The final formation of the attorney general's Commission on Obscenity and Pornography was handled by Smith's replacement, Edwin Meese III, and became known as the Meese Commission. At the head of the eleven-person commission was Henry E. Hudson, chief county prosecutor from Arlington County in northern Virginia. During his tenure, he developed a reputation as an ardent pornography foe, and said that his appointment was in part justified by the fact that Arlington County no longer had a single adult bookstore or massage parlor. The other ten members of the commission were also heavily slanted toward the antipornography camp, including, most notably, the extremely conservative James C. Dobson, founder of Focus on the Family. Hudson estimated that the commission would spend $400,000 to $500,000 and produce its report in a year.[45]

The commission immediately launched into what became one of the most wide-ranging investigations of the pornography industry in America. One of the first groups it met with was the Parents Music Resource Center, which sat down with commissioners in June 1985 to outline concerns about the sexual explicitness of rock music.[46] After two public hearings in Washington, the commission took its show on the road, reviewing law enforcement procedures in Chicago, inquiring in Houston about the effects of pornography on human behavior, investigating commercial production and distribution of pornography in Los Angeles, examining the issue of child pornography in Miami, and looking into the role of organized crime in pornography in New York.[47] It was a busy time for antipornography activists: at the same time that the Meese Commission was traveling around the country, the PMRC was appearing before the Senate Committee on Commerce to present its testimony on "porn rock."

Even before the commission issued its report, it sparked controversy and a lawsuit. In February 1986, Alan Sears—the commission's executive director and a tough antipornography prosecutor from Kentucky—sent a letter on commission stationery to a number of major booksellers and convenience store chains. The letter stated in part that the commission had "received testimony alleging that your company is involved in the sale or distribution of pornography." The letter continued: "This commission has determined that it would be appropriate to allow your company an opportunity to respond to the allegations prior to drafting its final report section on identified distributors. Failure to respond will necessarily be accepted as an indication of no objection."

Included in the letter were excerpts from the testimony of the Reverend Donald Wildmon, a member of the commission himself and a longtime antipornography crusader and founder of the National Federation for Decency. In his remarks, Wildmon characterized a number of companies as "distributors of pornography" and explicitly labeled Southland Corporation (the operator of the large chain of 7-Eleven stores) as one of "the leading retailers of porn magazines in America."[48]

Within a few weeks of the letter, a number of major retailers—including Southland Corporation, Revco Drug Stores, Rite Aid Drug Stores, People's Drug Stores, and Stop-N-Go—announced that they would no longer carry adult magazines.[49] Outraged over the Sears letter (and the fact that adult magazines had been dropped from thousands of stores), the American Booksellers Association and *Playboy* announced in May 1986 that they were suing the commission on the grounds that it "was illegally attempting to suppress sexually explicit books and magazines."[50] Even some members of the commission later said that they were upset that the threatening letter had been sent out, particularly since it omitted the fact that the damning testimony had been received from a member of the commission itself (Wildmon).[51]

The controversy over the Meese Commission and its occasionally heavy-handed investigative tactics may have played a role in the outcome of a June 1986 referendum vote in Maine on a proposal to make the selling or promotion of obscene material a felony. The referendum was defeated by a 2–1 margin, with an unusually high number of people—38 percent—casting ballots in the primary election.[52]

Just before the commission issued its final report, US District Court judge John Garrett Penn agreed with *Playboy*. He ordered the commission to delete its "blacklist" of "identified distributors" and to publicly retract the Sears letter. He also stated that *Playboy* was likely to prevail on the merits of its claim that it is unconstitutional for the federal government to restrain or suppress "nonobscene, constitutionally protected" publications.[53]

That left the commission's report a little lighter when it was issued on July 10, 1986. Nonetheless, it was still an impressively large document. Logging in at 1,960 pages, the majority report concluded that some types of pornography can lead to acts of sexual violence. The commission also called for much more rigorous enforcement of obscenity laws and, in particular, laws relating to child pornography. To buttress its findings, "[t]he report lists the titles of 2,325 magazines, 725 books and 2,370 films found in ['adults only'] stores, and it contains detailed, explicit descriptions of the activities depicted in these publications and films."[54] The commission's descriptions were so explicit, in fact, that many religious bookstores refused to stock copies of the final report for fear of offending their customers.[55]

To combat the problems of pornography that it identified, the commission listed ninety-two separate recommendations, ranging from grassroots opposition (including picketing and boycotts) to the adoption or revision of state and federal laws to toughen penalties and extend obscenity law to new technologies such as cable and satellite, and, in general, calling for far greater attention to the issue of pornography at all levels of government.[56]

Not every recommendation discussed by the commission made it into the final report. Both Chairman Hudson and Executive Director Sears, for example, pushed hard throughout the year for a commission vote in support of a national ban on the sale of vibrators and anything else used to stimulate the genitalia. (One commissioner allegedly wisecracked, "Does that include my hand?")[57] The idea was strenuously opposed by three of the commissioners and despite repeated discussion, was never brought to a vote.[58]

Of greater significance was the fact that despite all the publicity, relatively few of the ninety-two recommendations made by the commission were actually implemented. The most concrete outcome of the commission's work was the establishment in October 1986 of a team of federal prosecutors to specialize in pornography cases. Known as the National Obscenity Enforcement Unit, the ten-member group was charged with assisting federal pornography prosecutions around the country, including a high-profile case arising from the discovery that popular porn star Traci Lords was under age eighteen when she made nearly eighty X-rated movies.[59]

COURTING CONSERVATIVES: BATTLING FOR THE SOUL OF THE SUPREME COURT

Unquestionably, the single biggest disappointment for religious conservatives during Reagan's administration was the nomination of Sandra Day O'Connor to the US Supreme Court in 1981. Although President Reagan reportedly conferred with Reverend Falwell by telephone for an hour prior to announcing his choice (which itself raised separation-of-church-and-state hackles),[60] Falwell publicly characterized her nomination as a "disaster," which in turn prompted Senator Goldwater to acerbically declare that the minister deserved a "kick in the ass" (O'Connor was from Goldwater's home state of Arizona). The primary concern for religious conservatives was O'Connor's history of involvement in feminist causes, including support for the Equal Rights Amendment, and her support for abortion rights. The National Right to Life Committee promised to vigorously oppose her nomination, saying that "[t]his appointment is a grave disappointment to the pro-life public nationwide."[61] Nonetheless, O'Connor benefited on Capitol Hill from the enthusiastic support of Senator Goldwater and was confirmed on a 99–0 vote by the Senate.

When another vacancy opened up on the Supreme Court, President Reagan saw an opportunity to mend some fences with his religious conservative base and atone for what many considered to have been an overly hasty selection process driven more by O'Connor's gender than her convictions. On July 2, 1987, Reagan announced that he was nominating US Court of Appeals judge Robert H. Bork to replace the retiring Lewis Powell.

For religious conservatives (and to some extent economic conservatives as well), it would have been difficult to find a more exciting nominee—Bork was widely regarded as a deeply committed conservative with a powerful and wide-ranging intellect. More important, his writings and speeches made it clear that he would decide constitutional issues based on his interpretation of the original intent of the framers.[62] For liberals, the most significant consequence of his originalist views was that there is no "right to privacy," since that phrase does not actually appear in the Constitution. This raised particular concern about the Court's continued support for *Roe v. Wade*, which relies heavily on the Court's determination that for a portion of each pregnancy, the decision about whether to have an abortion lies within a woman's right to privacy. The worries of pro-choice advocates were well-founded. In testimony before Congress in 1981, Bork gave the opinion extremely short shrift. "I am convinced, as I think almost all constitutional scholars are, that *Roe v. Wade* is an unconstitutional decision, a serious and wholly unjustifiable judicial usurpation of state legislative authority."[63]

Not surprisingly, liberals were appalled by Reagan's decision to nominate Bork. The call to battle was most fiercely sounded by Senator Edward "Ted" Kennedy (D-MA), who declared his opposition to the nominee on the floor of the Senate within minutes of the announcement at the White House. "Robert Bork's America is a land in which women would be forced into back-alley abortions, blacks would sit at segregated lunch counters, rogue police could break down citizens' doors in midnight raids, schoolchildren could not be taught about evolution, writers and artists could be censored at the whim of government and the doors of the federal courts would be shut on the fingers of millions of citizens."[64]

Led by TV producer Norman Lear's People for the American Way, a coalition of socially liberal groups launched an unprecedented campaign to persuade the Senate to block Bork's nomination.

The battle over Bork's nomination was, up to that time, the most contentious and bitter debate over an appointment to the Supreme Court in US history. There was, of course, ample ammunition. Over the years, Bork had testified frequently before Congress, had written extensively, and was the author of numerous appellate court decisions (prompting a trend in recent years toward less literary nominees). Throughout the nomination proceedings, excerpts of his writings were interpreted and misinterpreted by groups from one end of the political spectrum to the other.[65] With legislative work and other nominations piling up on Capitol Hill, the high-pitched struggle over Judge Bork finally came to an end on October 23, 1987, when the Senate rejected his nomination by a vote of 58–42.

Things continued to go badly for the White House and its religious conservative allies: on October 29, President Reagan nominated US Court of

Appeals judge Douglas H. Ginsburg in Bork's place (whom Reagan promised opponents would "object to as much as they did [Bork]").[66] Just a week later, however, the news broke that Ginsburg had smoked marijuana as recently as 1979, when he was working as a law professor at Harvard. The following day, he withdrew his nomination.

Even before the news broke of his drug use (a particular embarrassment to the strongly antidrug Reagans), the nomination had not been well received. Apart from concerns about the relative inexperience of the forty-one-year-old appellate judge, religious conservatives were upset by reports that Ginsburg's wife, a doctor, had performed abortions. One of Reagan's key liaisons to the religious conservative community was Gary L. Bauer, who at the time was serving in the administration as assistant to the president for policy development. He said that conservative support for Ginsburg had been "mixed" from the start, and that conservatives felt that the marijuana disclosure was "a disaster for the [Reagans'] anti-drug efforts."[67]

The withdrawal of Ginsburg left Reagan in a difficult position. With his second term drawing to a close and an election year looming, senators on both sides of the aisle warned that if the White House did not send up a name that could command wide support, it might not be possible to fill the Powell vacancy before the end of Reagan's term.

Reagan heeded their advice and picked Anthony M. Kennedy, a judge on the US Court of Appeals for the Ninth Circuit who had been near the top of the list from the start. The appeals court is based in San Francisco, California, and the president had known Kennedy for more than twenty years. Before making any announcement, however, Kennedy was invited to Washington for a particularly thorough review of his background.[68]

The rumors that Reagan was planning to select Kennedy did not sit well with some religious conservatives. Senator Jesse Helms, who along with Ed Meese had been a strong supporter of Daniel Ginsburg, announced that he had called the White House and told the president "No way, Jose, can I support [Kennedy]."[69] Helms's remarks led to the postponement of a preconfirmation meeting between Kennedy and the conservative senator out of concern that it would appear that Helms had veto power over the White House's Supreme Court nominations.

During his confirmation hearing before the Senate Judiciary Committee, Kennedy assured the panel that his understanding of the term "liberty" as it is used in the Constitution includes the "protection of a value we call privacy." Kennedy also disputed a report by columnist Cal Thomas that Kennedy had told Senator Helms that his Catholic beliefs would lead him to vote against *Roe v. Wade*. (Years later, James Dobson would offer religious conservatives similar assurances about nominee Harriet Miers before her withdrawal.) Judge Kennedy's statement was an unequivocally clear refutation of the efforts of religious conservatives to impose an anti-*Roe* litmus test on judicial nominees:

> It would be highly improper for a judge to allow his or her own personal or religious views to enter into a decision with respect to a constitutional matter. If I had an undisclosed intention or a fixed view on a particular case, an absolutely concluded position, perhaps I might be obligated to disclose that to you.
>
> I do not have any such views with reference to privacy or abortion, therefore I would not attempt to try and signal by inference or indirection, my views.

Kennedy went on to add that he had not made any promises to Reagan, Helms, or anyone else about how he might vote on specific issues, and that he "would consider it highly improper to do so."[70]

Despite Kennedy's insistence on keeping an open mind about issues that might arise before the Court, not a single conservative vote was cast in opposition to his appointment to replace Lewis Powell on the US Supreme Court. The unanimous vote (97–0) in the spring of 1988 marked the end of Reagan's appointments to the High Court. Once again, the reach of the religious conservative wing of the Republican Party had exceeded its grasp of reality: the willingness or even the ability of a struggling administration to fight for the movement's most important issue.

THE PRIVATIZATION OF PORNOGRAPHY: VCRS, PHONE SEX, AND BBSS

In the meantime, a variety of technological innovations was driving a social and cultural revolution far broader and more pervasive than the issues being debated in Washington. MTV—and cable in general—was merely the loudest and most visible of the technologies shaping culture during the Reagan administration. Three other technologies—one maturing, one developing, and one just being born—each contributed to the fundamental shift in personal entertainment taking place in the 1980s.

The most significant change by far was the enthusiastic consumer adoption of the videocassette recorder. The home recording of television dates as far back as 1965, when Sony introduced the Videorecorder, a device capable of storing up to one hour of television on a magnetic tape reel. *Time* reported that in eight months, Sony sold one thousand Videorecorders at $1,345 each, and that "[a] new rental market is opening up for TV-taped plays, operas and movies."[71]

The first videocassette recorder was introduced by Philips in 1972, but it was quickly overtaken by Sony, which introduced its Betamax videocassette system in 1975. The devices retailed for about $1,300 and Sony sold one hundred thousand of them in just two years. In 1976, however, the Victor Company of Japan (JVC) introduced its Video Home System (VHS) and quickly overtook Sony for one simple reason: the VHS machines could record for twice as long as Betamax. By 1984 Sony's share of the VCR market was just 7 percent and falling fast.[72]

The reaction of the two film industries—Hollywood's and the adult's "Silicone Valley"—to the growing popularity of the VCR could not have been more different. Fearing rampant piracy of its films, Hollywood threw open the shark tank and spent millions of dollars in legal fees in an unsuccessful attempt to persuade federal courts to either ban the VCR or compel royalty payments on the sale of VCRs, blank videocassettes, or both.[73]

Adult filmmakers, however, quickly realized that VCRs offered an opportunity to repackage the myriad films collecting dust in their warehouses. Given that the VHS format offered more room for content and was slightly cheaper, the adult industry gravitated toward the JVC technology. The adult industry's format choice clearly played a meaningful role in the marketplace triumph of VHS over Betamax, since 90 percent of the videocassettes purchased in 1976 and 1977 were adult titles.

The shift from public to private consumption of pornographic films was one of the most significant cultural changes of the late 1970s and early 1980s. It was undoubtedly cold comfort, but religious conservatives had at least one reason to cheer the rise of the VCR: it essentially wiped out the nation's adult theaters. As former *Screw* publisher Al Goldstein observed in a 1981 interview with the *New York Times*: "I'd hate at this moment to be the owner of a porno theater. Their obsolescence is inevitable. Some people say I'm a doomsayer, but I think the technology speaks. X-rated films should never have been seen in theaters anyway. It's O.K. to see a horror film in a theater, but the point of a porno film is to turn you on, and a theater isn't the best place for that. The ideal context is the home."[74]

It quickly became clear that millions of people agreed with Goldstein. People who would never have ventured into the red light district of a nearby city were much more willing to nip in and out of the local video store's adult section and watch a film at home. To service consumers who lived in more restrictive states, rentals of adult videos by mail were available as early as 1979.[75] In New York City, the first video rental store, Video Shack, specialized entirely in adult tapes. By 1981 industry analysts were estimating that between 25 and 50 percent of all videotapes sold in the United States were X-rated, usually at prices between $70 and $100 per tape. Three years later, the pornography industry's share of the video market had dropped to 15 percent—Hollywood was finally catching on[76]—but the raw number of adult films being produced was more than enough to keep the Meese Commission busy.

Many people have observed that a desire to play X-rated videotapes at home was a significant factor in the rapid consumer acceptance of the VCR. But for technology companies, the counterexample may have been even more compelling. There was a brief flurry of consumer interest in the videodisk technology marketed by RCA and Pioneer in the early 1980s, but when those companies refused to license their technology to producers and distributors of X-rated films, consumers chose videocassette recorders over videodisk players in overwhelming numbers, and the videodisk became a quaint technological footnote.[77] It was a mistake that the later developers of CD-ROMs and DVDs would not make.

By 1986, when the work of the Meese Commission was completed, VCRs were in 40 percent of American homes; just two years later, that number rose to 62 percent.[78] But even with those impressive numbers, the VCR was not the leading source of sexual content for Americans. That honor, for a short time at least, went to a technology that was in virtually every home in the country: the telephone. Thanks to the deregulation efforts of the federal government, it was this technology that first enabled the pornography industry to distribute sexually explicit content directly into homes across the United States.

The remarkably swift rise of phone sex can be traced, in large part, to an antitrust lawsuit launched by the Justice Department against AT&T in November 1974, just three months after the resignation of President Nixon. The litigation persisted until January 1982, when AT&T agreed to divest itself of the regional Bell Companies in exchange for the opportunity to enter the computer business. The breakup of AT&T became official on January 1, 1984, just three weeks prior to the start of President Reagan's second term.

Even before Ma Bell sent her Baby Bells out into the world, the subsidiaries were looking for new revenue streams. On the West Coast, Pacific Bell leased a high-volume telephone line to Sable Communications, a subsidiary of the ironically named New York–based Carlin Communications (of no apparent connection to comedian George Carlin, whose "Filthy Words" monologue a few years earlier had led to a crackdown on radio indecency). Sable used the lines to provide sexually explicit, prerecorded phone messages; callers were charged a special fee, which was billed by Pacific Bell and divided between the phone company and Sable.[79] By 1986–87, Pacific Bell was earning $13.5 million in profits per year from its involvement in the dial-a-porn business.[80]

On the East Coast, there was so much interest in the so-called audiotext business that New York Telephone decided to hold a lottery for potential lessees of the high-volume lines. At the time, porn actress Gloria Leonard was serving as publisher of the adult magazine *High Society*, and she entered the company into the New York Telephone lottery and won. The magazine company began using the line to give readers previews of its upcoming issues. Leonard, however, had the idea of having each month's centerfold record a one-minute message, and the results, she said, were phenomenal: "[When] it became the centerfold's voice, the number of calls that were coming in were just mind-boggling. We were blowing out business circuits for like a five-block radius. Then technology was introduced that made it possible to charge for the calls, and it turned out that the Pentagon had run up about 20 or 30 thousand dollars in one month making calls to our number; ABC Television had to put a block on its 976- capabilities because all of its employees were spending a great deal of the day listening to these messages, so it was creating a great furor."[81] By one estimate, *High Society* was soon earning $8,000 per day with its phone sex line.[82] That estimate was in keeping with other reports: investigators told the Meese Commission that Carlin Communications was getting six to seven million calls and grossing $130,000 per month.

Unlike with other technologies, Congress reacted fairly quickly to the rapid growth of the phone sex industry. When the FCC determined in May 1983 that existing federal law did not cover phone sex, Congress amended the Communications Act of 1934 to make it a crime to make "obscene or indecent" phone calls for commercial purposes to persons under the age of eighteen.[83]

Over the next six years, Congress, the FCC, and the courts wrestled with how best to carry out Congress's intent. In 1988, impatient with the back-and-forth between the FCC and the Second Circuit Court of Appeals, Senator Jesse Helms (R-NC) offered an amendment to a school funding bill that banned "indecent" or "obscene" phone calls to anyone of any age. The Helms Amendment passed the Senate by a 98–0 vote, and was subsequently adopted by the House of Representatives.

By the time Congress finally acted, however, the phone sex industry was already a $2.4 billion business,[84] and the new law did little to slow it down. The heavy-breathing crowd did take a hit in the summer of 1989, when the United States Supreme Court ruled in *Sable Communications v. FCC*[85] that Congress did have the authority to make "obscene" phone calls illegal. However, the Court also held that Congress had overstepped its bounds by trying to make merely "indecent" phone calls illegal. Writing for a largely unanimous Court, Justice Byron White made it clear that "[s]exual expression which is indecent but not obscene is protected by the First Amendment."[86] The Court did not specifically define the word "indecent" in the *Sable* case, but presumably was using the common understanding: "not decent; especially: grossly unseemly or offensive to manners or morals."[87]

Over time, revenues for phone sex (indecent or otherwise) steadily declined, but not in response to congressional action. Instead, the shrinkage in the industry's profits stemmed from the competition it received from the next significant blending of technology and sex: the personal computer.

Hollywood's efforts to portray new technologies are often amusing or absurd (or both), but there are occasions when Tinseltown gets it exactly right. In the 1983 film *War Games*, Matthew Broderick's high school–age character has an early model personal computer and modem installed in his bedroom. He uses the modem to dial into his school's computer to correct "mistakes" in his report card and to randomly search different area codes for other modem-equipped computers (a practice that became known as *war dialing* in honor of the movie). During one search, his computer accidentally dials into a North American Aerospace Defense Command (NORAD) computer called the War Operation Plan Response (W.O.P.R.),[88] which is linked to the nation's nuclear missiles. Broderick begins playing what he thinks is a World War III simulation with the W.O.P.R., but the computer treats it as a real crisis. As the W.O.P.R. steadily counts down to Armageddon, Broderick and classmate Ally Sheedy must find the W.O.P.R.'s mysteriously missing designer to help shut down the program.

Apart from the fact that most computer geeks at the time would have cheerfully traded a ten-meg hard drive and their *good* keyboard to spend a week running around the Northwest with Ally Sheedy, *War Games* mostly got it right. The marriage of personal computers and modems began during a weekend snowstorm in January 1978 in Chicago, Illinois, when Ward Christensen and Randy Seuss, fellow members of the Chicago Area Computer Hobbyists Exchange (CACHE), joined forces to create the world's first computerized bulletin board system (CBBS). Seuss configured a computer so it could answer phone calls from other computer users with modems, and Christensen wrote the software that allowed callers to (e)nter, (r)etrieve, or (k)ill messages. Even more significantly, as it turned out, a short time earlier Christensen had written a program called "xmodem," which allowed files to be transferred from one computer to another across phone lines.[89] And in one other bit of foreshadowing, Christensen's CBBS software even had a decency filter: if a visitor used what Christensen thought was inappropriate language in a message, the call was automatically terminated.[90] In fairly short order, bulletin board systems began springing up around the country and users started exchanging messages, text files, programs, and even love notes with other computer users, most of whom they had never met.

The big-screen coolness factor of *War Games*, combined with steadily dropping equipment costs (when the movie came out, a computer user could get a three-hundred-baud modem for as little as $100),[91] helped make computer bulletin boards the Next Big Thing. By 1983 a software program called Fido enabled individual bulletin board systems to communicate with each other. The resulting national network, FidoNet, was in many ways the popular precursor to the World Wide Web, which Timothy Berners-Lee was just then in the process of developing in Switzerland.

The rapid growth of computerized bulletin board services presaged the Web's enormous popularity as well. In just ten years, the CBBS created by Seuss and Christensen was joined by roughly six thousand other systems across the nation; by the end of the Reagan administration, a veteran of *Boardwatch* magazine estimated that there were fifteen thousand BBS systems in operation.[92]

Remarkably, given the slow transmission speeds and comparatively crude graphical capabilities of computer displays in the mid-1980s, law enforcement was already expressing concern about the use of BBSs to distribute child pornography and other sexually explicit materials. A typical warning came from Robert Showers, the head of the US Justice Department's National Obscenity Enforcement Unit. "You can actually reproduce a picture on the computer," Showers told the *Los Angeles Times* in 1987. "You can produce the child pornography and send it from one computer terminal to the other. I think law enforcement is just beginning to get the intelligence information on the use of computers in child pornography."[93]

By the end of the decade, there were an estimated twenty-four thousand computer bulletin board systems in operation around the country, and a number of the largest and most successful purportedly made a significant portion of their million-plus revenues from the exchange of sexually explicit images.[94] Whether they specifically intended to be or not, computer bulletin board systems were on the leading edge of the second major expansion of pornography production and consumption.

It was, in sum, a discouraging end to a surprisingly bad decade for religious conservatives. Millions had been donated to the Moral Majority and the Reagan campaign, hours and hours had been spent leafleting and manning phone banks, heartfelt votes had been cast, but in the end, while neoconservatives could revel in the pending collapse of the Soviet Union and economic conservatives could toast a supply-sided economy from a yacht off the shore of Fisher Island, religious conservatives were left with three new Supreme Court justices, only one of whom (Antonin Scalia) was a reliable conservative voice; the other two (O'Connor and Kennedy) accepted the concept of a right to privacy and its implied consequence—in other words, no outright reversal of *Roe*. The nation's kids were still listening to "porn rock," the pornography industry was flourishing, television was a disaster, heavy-breathing porn stars were just an 800-number away, and with a quick trip to the local video store, every living room could be converted to a *Pussycat Theater*.

Many religious conservatives no doubt wondered, with justification, that if things went this badly under their supposed champion, how much worse would it get when Reagan left?

Donald Wildmon, speaking at a press conference for the Coalition for Better Television in 1981. (*Broadcasting & Cable*)

Chapter Six

The Post-Reagan Hangover

A Four-Year Rearguard Action against Cultural Indecency

Initially, you sought freedom. In the process, you gained power. And with power, a small minority now want control. There are those who would seek to impose their will and dictate their interpretation of morality on the rest of society. There are those who would forget the need for tolerance.
—Vice President George H. W. Bush, 1987[1]

Ronald Reagan's decisive victory over Walter Mondale in the 1984 election left religious conservatives even more deeply convinced of their electoral power than they had been four years earlier, despite the lack of concrete progress on most of their social agenda. Just under 80 percent of white evangelical voters cast their ballots for Reagan/Bush.[2] As a result, religious conservative voters clearly provided the margin of victory in several congressional races (including, most significantly, the reelection of Jesse Helms [R-NC]). Religious issues and debates over the role of religion in politics dominated the 1984 campaign, and even Democratic candidates Walter Mondale and Geraldine Ferraro made a point of repeatedly professing their respective faiths (Methodist and Catholic) on the campaign trail. Ferraro in particular had a difficult path to tread. As a pro-choice Catholic, she was pointedly criticized by New York's archbishop John Cardinal O'Connor (1920–2000) for her stand on abortion. Cardinal O'Connor did not threaten her with excommunication (a possibility he raised for pro-choice politicians in 1990).[3] However, he did question "how a Catholic in good conscience can vote for a candidate who explicitly supports abortion."[4]

The high-profile role of religion in the 1984 election enabled religious conservatives to put their disappointment in the Reagan administration behind them. They quickly began searching for a 1988 presidential candidate who would reliably and aggressively promote their agenda. Almost immediately, however, it became apparent that there was no one individual upon whom religious conservatives could collectively agree. Normally, of course, a sitting vice president would be the presumptive nominee, particularly in the generally deferential Republican Party. But Christian (and party) principles notwithstanding, all too many religious conservatives continued to be suspicious of the depth of Bush's conservative beliefs and still bore a grudge for his insufficiently deferential attitude toward the movement after Reagan's initial victory.

The generally frosty relationship between Bush and the Republican Party's conservative activists was an unavoidable consequence of both style and substance. Religious conservatives and the so-called Reagan Democrats never quite managed to embrace George H. W. Bush, a Northeastern establishment candidate with more than a whiff of Rockefeller about him. Many agreed with William Loeb (1905–1982), the deeply conservative and often acerbic publisher of New Hampshire's *Manchester Union-Leader*, that Bush was "the candidate of liberals, elitists, eastern newspapers [except his, of course], and 'clean fingernails' Republicans."[5] The fact that Bush was a jogger, a member of the relatively staid Episcopal Church, and fond of overly cute phrases like "the big Mo" (to describe his campaign's growing momentum) didn't help.

On paper, Bush's positions on most policy issues were far closer to Reagan's than not, but Bush parted company with Reagan on at least two issues of great importance to religious conservatives: his opposition to the adoption of a constitutional amendment outlawing abortion and his support for the passage of the Equal Rights Amendment. Even when speaking about issues on which he and conservatives agreed, one reporter noted that "[Bush] chooses moderate language to explain conservative positions, and that does not assure the right. . . . Also, in speaking of foreign policy decisions he disapproves of, he does not portray them in apocalyptic, Communists-vs.-free-world terms."[6] As much as anything else, it was Bush's lack of evangelical fervor that concerned religious conservatives; such mild-mannered discourse was simply not compelling to a wing of the party energized by weekly fire-and-brimstone sermons.

Reagan, of course, was nothing if not fervent, an accomplished speaker who galvanized conservative audiences. And in direct contrast to Bush, Reagan not only campaigned in favor of an antiabortion amendment but went even further by offering verbal support for the idea of a constitutional convention to consider the idea if Congress refused to pass such an amendment. He repeatedly promised antiabortion activists that he would "use the power and the prestige of the presidency to push for an amendment if he is elected."[7] The fact that Reagan didn't in fact follow through on his rhetoric only served to make religious conservatives more insistent on ideological purity in prospective nominees for the 1988 election.

Bush's personal history as a Republican presidential candidate added to suspicions that he lacked the requisite purity. During the 1980 primary, for instance, the more conservative routes to the White House were staked out by Reagan and Rep. Philip M. Crane (R-IL), an eleven-year veteran of the House who had worked as director of research for the Goldwater campaign before winning a special election to replace Rep. Donald Rumsfeld. The liberal wing of the Republican Party was represented by Senator Howard Baker (R-TN) and, to some extent, by Rep. John B. Anderson (R-IL), who started his campaign for president in the Republican primary but then ran as an independent in the general election. That left Bush with little choice but to present himself as the moderate alternative.

At the start of the long campaign, where exactly Bush fell on the Republican political spectrum was unimportant, given the fact that early polls placed his support somewhere between 3 percent and below 1 percent. Many early assessments of the race, in fact, did not even mention him, despite the fact that he had held numerous high-level Washington positions and had been actively considered as a vice presidential choice by Richard Nixon (twice) and Gerald Ford. By the end of November 1979, however, the well-organized and increasingly well-funded Bush campaign was starting to show results, and there was already talk about how Bush could finish a strong second or even win the Iowa caucuses in January 1980.[8]

Thanks to good groundwork and indefatigable campaigning, Bush did in fact win in Iowa, a victory that catapulted him into the top echelon of the Republican presidential race. But it turned out to be the high point of his campaign. His new prominence brought him under strafing attacks from the Left and the Right (one of the chief drawbacks to moderation), and a series of missteps left voters with the impression of a campaign in sudden disarray and a candidate without firm, well-thought-out positions. Reagan, who rarely lacked for decisive policy proclamations, trounced Bush in the New Hampshire primary and, by late spring, had built an insurmountable lead in convention delegates. Apart from a late-night convention speech traditionally accorded to losing primary candidates, no one expected to hear much more from Bush following his withdrawal from the primary campaign.

In the argot of the Beltway, one of the leading synonyms for political power is *access*, the ability to get a meeting with someone in a position of authority (and, in particular, the president). In the summer of 1980, the growing electoral influence of religious conservative groups gave leaders like Jerry Falwell and Paul Weyrich an impressive level of access to the highest Republican political circles. When Reagan, the presumptive Republican nominee, was weighing his vice presidential options, he invited a number of the movement's leaders—including Falwell, Weyrich, Richard Viguerie, and Howard Phillips— to his suite in Washington's Renaissance Plaza Hotel. There was some division on who Reagan should select, but uncharacteristic unanimity on who should *not* be picked: Senator Howard Baker and George H. W. Bush were both widely viewed by religious conservatives as too liberal on most social issues.[9]

Religious conservatives, however, quickly got a lesson in *realpolitik*: access may be a synonym for power, but it is not the same thing. After initially taking the unusual step of discussing with former president Gerald Ford the possibility that he might join Reagan's ticket as vice president, the Republican nominee picked up the phone and asked Bush to be his running mate.

"Out of a clear blue sky," the startled Bush said, "Governor Reagan called me up and asked if I would be willing to run with him on the ticket. I was surprised, of course, and I was very, very pleased. I feel honored."[10]

Religious and social conservatives were, to put it mildly, appalled. Howard Phillips, executive director of the American Conservative Union, groused that Reagan "sounded like Winston Churchill but behaved like Neville Chamberlain." There were rumblings of a possible "Helms for Vice President" floor fight, which faded when Bush promised to support the Republican platform (some of which flatly contradicted his campaign positions) and when Senator Helms was given a last-minute speaking slot at the convention.[11]

In the hurly-burly of the presidential election, religious conservative concerns about Bush were put aside in the interests of a Reagan victory over Jimmy Carter. But the old suspicions and antagonisms came rushing back when Bush was assigned the utterly thankless task of making it clear that the administration would not be under the control of any specific interest group. It is, unfortunately, one of the fundamental rules of presidential politics: the vice president is in charge of bearing unpleasant truths to the president's supporters, including the news that their priorities might not match the checklist on the president's desk blotter.

Still, religious conservatives can be forgiven for thinking that Bush seemed to take a little too much delight in the task. Just one week after the 1980 election, for instance, Vice President–elect Bush used a Houston press conference to declare firmly that the Reagan White House in general and he in particular would not be a captive of religious conservative groups. He brushed aside possible retribution by religious conservatives for deviation from their agenda: "I take violent exception to certain individuals in some of these groups, some of their positions, and have stated it publicly and am not intimidated by those who suggest I better hew the line. Hell with them."[12]

SLOUCHING TOWARD G. H. W. BUSH: RELIGIOUS CONSERVATIVES EMBRACE PRAGMATISM

Comments like that go a long way toward explaining why Bush appeared so far down the list of potentially interesting candidates for religious conservatives in the 1988 Republican presidential primary. Bush was not entirely without support among the Christian right: shortly after Reagan's reelection, none other than Moral Majority leader Jerry Falwell announced that he was backing Vice President George H. W. Bush for president in 1988. At the time, however, that was a fairly lonely position in the evangelical wing of the Republican Party.

In the early stages of the primary campaign, the leading contender among both religious and economic conservatives was Rep. Jack Kemp (R-NY). The influential group Christian Voice, for instance, declared that it was enthusiastically throwing its support behind the former Buffalo Bills quarterback. According to Gary Jarmin, the chief lobbyist for Christian Voice, Christians were going to carry Kemp to the end zone: "You heard it here. We are going to swamp the caucuses in Iowa. Jack Kemp is going to get it."[13]

Still other religious conservatives believed that the best strategy to promote their social agenda would be to support a candidate drawn from their own ranks. In the spring of 1985, mere weeks after Reagan's second inauguration, friends and associates suggested to Dr. Marion G. "Pat" Robertson that he consider running for president in 1988. It was an idea that the articulate and successful televangelist found more than a little tempting.

Robertson's prominence among religious conservatives was largely a result of his groundbreaking success in using television to promote his ministry. A graduate of Yale Law School and a minister in the Neopentecostal[14] movement, Robertson was the founder and charismatic leader of what some called the "fourth network," the Christian Broadcast Network. Robertson began his electronic ministry in 1959, when he scraped together the money to purchase a defunct television station in Portsmouth, Virginia. The following year, the nation's first Christian television station, WYAH, began broadcasting. Struggling to keep the station on the air during its first few months, Robertson came up with the idea of asking seven hundred subscribers to send in just $10 per month. The idea was a tremendous success; the donations poured in, leading

Robertson to rename his main television show *The 700 Club*. In the process, Robertson also demonstrated the power of televised fund-raising to the growing number of electronic ministers.

Twenty-five years later, the fifty-six-year-old Robertson was head of a religious/commercial empire grossing between $200 and $230 million per year in revenues. His donor base was reportedly as large as that of the Republican National Committee, and his show claimed an audience of 7.2 million viewers per week (although audience levels for cable shows are notoriously difficult to measure). When asked about a possible run, Robertson told the *Washington Post* that he was praying about it and that "he believes that God will ultimately decide whether he should do it and will convey His decision during one of their conversations."[15]

Also clearly believing, however, that God helps those who help themselves, Robertson had already begun laying the secular groundwork for a presidential run just weeks after Reagan took the oath for his second term in January 1985: "In addition to praying," the *Post* said, "he has purchased a twenty-four-seat jet aircraft; set up a precinct-based organization called the Freedom Council; provided preliminary funding for a think tank, the National Perspectives Institute; and developed strong ties to such Washington-based New Right leaders as direct-mail specialist Richard Viguerie, Paul Weyrich of the Free Congress Foundation, and Howard Phillips of the Conservative Caucus."[16]

Robertson seemed poised to get off to a flying start in mid-1986, when his supporters set the stage for an upset victory in the selection process for Michigan delegates to the national GOP convention. When the dust settled later that fall, however, Robertson was ranked third behind Bush and Kemp with single-digit support.[17] In polls taken through the end of the year, neither Robertson nor Kemp succeeded in breaking into double-digit territory.

With the ostensible conservative champions floundering in the early days of the 1988 campaign, religious conservatives indulged in flirtation with one other serious candidate. In a windowless basement office in the West Wing, former Nixon wordsmith Pat Buchanan was serving as White House communications director. Like an ideological Sergeant York, Buchanan had spent November and December leaping out of his foxhole to vigorously defend President Reagan from critics of the Iran-Contra scandal. Although opinion was hardly unanimous, most conservatives loved the uncomplicated clarity of Buchanan's language and his "us vs. them" passion for his principles. Admittedly, Buchanan was not a member of one of the evangelical Protestant sects that made up so much of the American religious conservative movement, but he was (and is) a deeply conservative Catholic.

Although he mostly covered Reagan's left flank, Buchanan was more than happy to frag a few fellow conservatives, particularly in Congress. In an op-ed piece for the *Washington Post*, Buchanan wrote: "With a few exceptions—J. Strom Thurmond and Ted Stevens come to mind—the whole damn pack has headed for the tall grass." In his inimitably pugilistic[18] fashion, Buchanan went on to add: "In recent years, Republican candidates have taken to prattling about at election time about their devotion to 'family values.' But among the first of those values is family loyalty. And when a mob shows up in the yard, howling that the head of the household be produced, the sons do not force the Old Man to sit down at a table and write up a list of his 'mistakes.' You start firing from the upper floors."[19]

The romance with Buchanan, however, went unrequited. He announced at the end of January 1987 that he would not run, fearing that his candidacy would doom the insurgent run of Representative Kemp against Vice President Bush. It was a noble gesture, but Kemp had bigger issues than a possible Buchanan challenge from the Right. Kemp's campaign struggled against Bush's enormous incumbent resources and more centrist message, and, ultimately, Kemp withdrew after a thin showing in the Super Tuesday round of primaries in March 1988. Robertson also did relatively poorly on Super Tuesday but waited until April to acknowledge the obvious and end his campaign.

With Robertson's departure from the race, Vice President Bush was left with an unimpeded path to the Republican nomination. But Bush found himself with less ideological freedom than he'd had as Reagan's vice presidential choice. With a potentially close race shaping up for November, Bush was in no position to boldly resend his 1981 "hell with them" message to religious conservatives. Under the direction of Republican strategist Lee Atwater (1951–1991), Bush began a carefully constructed campaign to assure religious conservatives and other members of the party's far right wing of his loyalty and commitment to their social agenda. His most significant gesture occurred in mid-August, when he announced that he had chosen Senator Dan Quayle to serve as his running mate. Unlike his predecessor, who had felt confident enough to defy his religious conservative base and select a vice president who he felt would moderate his own conservative image, Bush was more worried that his conservative supporters might simply stay home, which he knew he could not afford. Conservative leaders were delighted. Phyllis Schlafly noted approvingly that Quayle "brings youth, attractiveness, conservative image . . . all the elements of a great and winning ticket." Former Bush opponent Pat Robertson was also pleased: "In areas like abortion, school prayer, that sort of thing, he's right down the line with evangelicals."[20]

Long before Quayle's selection as vice president, the wing of the Republican Party that William Safire described as the "True Believers" demonstrated the strength of their "win wish"[21] by supporting Bush over more staunchly conservative but arguably less electable candidates like Kemp and Robertson. In November, Quayle's support for the religious conservative agenda mollified the True Believers and helped them overcome their reservations about the top of the ticket. Quayle's support, combined with the apparently unbearable prospect of an administration led by Massachusetts governor Michael Dukakis, led so many of the True Believers to turn out on Election Day that Bush actually wound up with a greater percentage of evangelical votes than Reagan received in 1984. In the end, however, it would prove to be a shotgun wedding.

PACKING UP THE REVIVAL TENT: THE CHRISTIAN COALITION REPLACES THE MORAL MAJORITY

The election of George H. W. Bush as president in 1988 should have solidified Jerry Falwell's position as the leading political force in the Christian Right. Almost alone among his evangelical peers, he had been an early and enthusiastic supporter of Bush's presidential bid. His endorsement played a critical role in the early days of the GOP primary by helping to mute criticism from other factions in the religious conservative movement and by limiting the drift of evangelistic voters from Bush to fellow televangelist Pat Robertson.

But the two years prior to the 1988 election had been extremely difficult and draining for Falwell. In November 1985, for instance, the support of the Moral Majority was cited as a factor in the defeat of Virginia gubernatorial candidate Wyatt B. Durrette. A poll taken by the *Richmond Times-Dispatch* during the campaign found that 51 percent of voters were less likely to support a candidate carrying a Falwell endorsement.[22] Even more troubling, no doubt, was a finding by Republican pollster Robert Teeter that on a scale from 0 to 100, the general public approval rating of Falwell was 33.1, well below Senator Ted Kennedy's 54 and Ronald Reagan's 68.3.[23]

Implicitly acknowledging the public relations problem, Falwell announced in January 1986 that the Moral Majority would be folded into a new organization called the Liberty Foundation. "We are not disbanding or retreating," Falwell told reporters. He stressed that the new organization would expand on the Moral Majority's work by including activism on behalf of President Reagan's Strategic Defense Initiative (SDI, better known as the "Star Wars" program) and Falwell's own controversial support of the Nicaraguan contras and the (repressive) governments in South Africa and the Philippines. Some observers, however, pointed out that the change of emphasis was driven as much by revenue concerns as principle; right-wing fund-raisers told the *Post* that neoconservative political issues like SDI were producing higher donations than the traditional religious conservative concerns of pornography or abortion.[24]

The name change, however, did little to improve Falwell's fund-raising for political activities. Despite a high-profile (and widely criticized) speech by Vice President Bush at the Liberty Foundation's launch in January 1986, the organization struggled to gain a foothold among the growing number of conservative political action groups. The Liberty Foundation's fiscal problems were mirrored by downturns in the financial fortunes of all the major televangelists: In the summer of 1986, for instance, Falwell laid off 225 employees from his show *The Old Time Gospel Hour* and from his Liberty University. All told, Falwell said, he was trying to cut $10 million in costs from his organization's $100 million budget. Over at the Christian Broadcasting Network, Pat Robertson announced that he was planning a similar level of cuts, shaving $24 million from an annual budget of $200 million.[25]

Wrestling with the devilish details of a single multimillion-dollar, largely donation-based operation would have been ample reason for Falwell to pull back from the public stage. But in March 1987, he received a phone call from televangelist Jim Bakker, asking Falwell to step in and take control of the massive PTL (Praise the Lord) operation run by Bakker and his wife, Tammy Faye. The request stemmed from the fact that Bakker was resigning his ministry in the wake of the disclosure that he had paid $265,000 to a church secretary, Jessica Hahn, to cover up a sexual encounter with her in 1980.

Bakker's indiscretion with Hahn proved to be merely the tip of a large and increasingly ugly iceberg. Over the next six months, Falwell and the PTL's reconstituted board of directors discovered massive misappropriation of church funds, including salary payments to the Bakkers of $1.6 million in 1986 alone (despite televised claims by the Bakkers that they merely took a "living salary" from the weekly donations). From the start, rumors flew that rival televangelist Jimmy Swaggart[26] was attempting a hostile takeover of the PTL so he could benefit from Bakker's theme park, Heritage USA, and his large cable network. As the scandal unfolded over the summer, the ministry was rocked by additional charges that Bakker frequented female *and* male prostitutes, that high-ranking church officials had engaged in wife-swapping, and that the aggressively mascaraed Tammy Faye was battling a seventeen-year addiction to prescription drugs.[27]

By the end of the year, Falwell (whom Bakker also ultimately accused of trying to steal the PTL for himself) had had enough. The effort to run two enormous religious organizations was both physically and emotionally draining. In October, he resigned as the head of the PTL, and in November stepped down from both the Moral Majority and the Liberty Foundation. In a rueful acknowledgment of the impact of the PTL scandal, Falwell told a radio audience that "[w]e're no longer breaking new ground. It's no longer as glamorous to be in the religious right."[28]

Things got steadily worse for religious conservatives over the next year. On February 21, 1988, Assemblies of God minister Jimmy Swaggart confessed on air to an "unspecified sin" (which in fact involved a series of liaisons with prostitutes in Louisiana) and temporarily left his ministry. Just three days later, the United States Supreme Court (unanimously!) overturned a $200,000 emotional distress verdict that Falwell had won against the Christian Right's *bête noire*, publisher Larry Flynt, for a fake advertisement in *Hustler* that suggested Falwell lost his virginity to his own mother in an outhouse. In April, Robertson's campaign was steamrolled by Vice President Bush. And in early 1989, Jim Bakker was convicted of conspiracy and mail fraud and sentenced to forty-five years in prison.[29]

But in the ashes of these various punch-line debacles were the seeds of renewal, the most important of which was the political education that the Robertson campaign provided to an up-and-coming corps of religious conservatives across the country. Falwell may have blazed the trail of evangelical involvement in politics, but it was Pat Robertson who took the next step by turning the machinery of his campaign into a tool not merely for registering voters but for recruiting candidates. In 1989 Robertson handed his presidential mailing list to the Dorian Gray–like Ralph Reed with instructions to turn it into a conservative grassroots organization called the Christian Coalition.

At the relatively tender age of twenty-eight, Reed was a seasoned veteran of the College Republican National Committee (CRNC), an organization devoted to promoting conservative activism on campus. In 1981 he and conservative activist Grover Norquist helped Jack Abramoff win the chairmanship of the CRNC; two years later, Abramoff appointed Reed to succeed Norquist as the CRNC's executive director. At about the same time, Reed experienced a religious conversion that resulted in his becoming a born-again Christian and a member of the Evangel Assembly of God in Camp Springs, Maryland. For a while, one acquaintance said, the conversion experience made the normally hard-driving Reed a somewhat less effective political operative: "[He] was completely insufferable for about a year [after his conversion]. Because he was all full of the milk of human kindness, he wanted to forgive everybody. . . . Anyway, he got over that."[30]

A more typical (and arguably less Christian) comment was Reed's own characterization of his political methodology, first made in 1991 and often repeated: "I want to be invisible. I do guerilla warfare. I paint my face and travel by night. You don't know it's over until you're in a body bag. You don't know until election night."[31]

The combination of Robertson's 1988 political groundwork and Reed's organizational skills (ninja or otherwise) proved to be devastatingly effective: within five years, the Christian Coalition was one of the most powerful political organizations in the country and reported to the *New York Times* that it had "1.4 million supporters, a mailing list of 30 million, and 1,100 chapters in 50 states."[32] By focusing on the nuts and bolts of political campaigning, the coalition helped the religious conservative movement overcome the sex, drug, and false-eyelash excesses of some of its high-profile leaders. In the process, however, it took religious conservatives farther from the basic evangelical mission of individual salvation and more deeply into the compromising morass of cultural cleansing.

TRYING TO TAME THE TUBE

Much of the strength of the Christian Coalition comes not merely from its individual members but also from the other religious conservative groups with which it is affiliated. Effective political alliances are often strongest when there is shared anger over a burning issue. For religious conservatives, one of the longest-burning issues has been the level of indecency on broadcast television. Not surprisingly, much of the most heated activism in this area dates from the creation of "jiggle TV" by programming guru Fred Silverman at ABC.

The longest-active and best-known campaigner for TV decency is the Reverend Donald E. Wildmon, the conservative United Methodist minister from Tupelo, Mississippi. In 1976, just when the nation was tuning into *Three's Company* and *Charlie's Angels*, Wildmon founded the National Federation for Decency (NFD). Relatively speaking, "jiggle TV" has been nearly as good to Wildmon as it was to ABC. After Wildmon quit his ministry to work on the NFD full-time in 1977, his household was scraping by on his wife's $10,000 salary as a home economics teacher and roughly the same amount from his royalties on seventeen religious books Wildmon had authored. By the end of 1978, however, Wildmon told the *Wall Street Journal* that he had raised over $35,000 in dues from the NFD's three thousand members. Over the next twenty-five years, according to the Southern Poverty Law Center, Wildmon's anti-indecency campaign grew from its shoestring origins to a mini-empire with 100 employees, regular appearances on 200 radio networks, and a monthly mailing of 180,000 newsletters.[33]

The NFD and Wildmon claimed success for their campaign in early 1978, when the national retailer Sears announced that it was pulling its advertising from *Three's Company* and *Charlie's Angels*. Sears denied that its withdrawal had anything to do with the NFD, but Wildmon pointed out that Sears made the announcement the same day the NFD was scheduled to start picketing Sears headquarters in Chicago. "Now do you think it's a coincidence?" he asked rhetorically. "We definitely had an impact."[34]

Shortly after Reagan's inauguration in 1981, Wildmon joined forces with Jerry Falwell and Phyllis Schlafly and roughly 150 other conservative groups to form the Coalition for Better Television (CBTV). Although Wildmon was selected to serve as chairman of the new group, the mediagenic and politically savvy Falwell quickly became the public face of the organization. He said that the purpose of the CBTV was to pressure advertisers and networks to eliminate "offensive" programs, and announced that the organization was preparing to launch a boycott of a major sponsor that summer.[35]

There was some suggestion at the time that the formation of the CBTV was as much about money and politics as it was about media decency. As *Washington Post* television analyst Tom Shales pointed out: "What appears to have happened is that war against television has become an industry unto itself. . . . The Coalition may be guilty of trying to capitalize on the hate side of America's love-hate relationship with television merely as a means to construct a vast political base, a righteous class whose members will be continually called upon to perform at the ballot box or the mailbox as if signaled by a Pavlovian bell."[36]

Richard Viguerie perhaps unintentionally gave credibility to that analysis when he neatly summarized the benefits of the interwoven relationships between the Moral Majority and groups like the National Federation of Decency: "The networks may beat us—they may, after three or four years still have their sex and violence on television—but in the meantime, Jerry Falwell and others may increase their list of supporters by three-, four- or five-fold. And we can do something the networks cannot do, which is get involved in political campaigns."[37]

Viguerie's analysis was a little naive; even though networks could not openly endorse specific candidates, no one seriously questions the ability of networks to get their views heard in Washington. But his basic point is just as true today as it was back then—the names and addresses of the people who support one cause (liberal or conservative) are all too often passed around to sympathetic organizations looking to swell their own ranks.

The CBTV's threatened boycott in the summer of 1981 never materialized. At a June 29 press conference, Wildmon said that the CBTV's monitoring of television that spring had produced a list of companies that sponsored the most offensive material. However, Falwell and Wildmon refused to release the list, saying that to do so would be the equivalent of calling for a boycott. There was widespread speculation, particularly by the networks, that the CBTV called off its planned boycott out of fear that it would fail miserably. However, both

Wildmon and Falwell disputed that and said that their campaign had already produced results. They cited Procter & Gamble's decision to pull advertising from fifty network shows and said that thirty to forty unnamed companies had done the same. All three networks said the latter claim was simply false.[38]

The Moral Majority and the CBTV came to a parting of the ways in January 1982, when Falwell announced that his organization would not support a planned national boycott of advertisers scheduled to begin in March. Although Wildmon said that the organizations parted on congenial terms, he took a backhanded swipe at Falwell by saying that "the organization may not be with us, [but] basically the people who make up the Moral Majority are."[39] Disregarding the loss of the Moral Majority's promised $2 million in support, Wildmon launched a boycott of NBC and its then-parent company, RCA. Among other things, Wildmon demanded "a downplay in future programs of sex, violence, and profanity as 'a part of the plot'; . . . the withdrawal of ads for all feminine personal hygiene products; and a cessation of 'discrimination against Christian characters . . . values and . . . culture.'"[40] Eight months later, even Wildmon conceded that the boycott had made little difference in the content of NBC's shows, but he said that the boycott would continue indefinitely. Wildmon also claimed that his group was responsible for a slump in RCA's sales of consumer electronics, which the company and other industry analysts blamed instead on a sharp rise in foreign competition.[41]

Without question, the stridency and officiousness of Wildmon's diatribes against popular culture made it relatively easy for the networks and mainstream media to dismiss them. His high-profile service on the Meese Commission, including his somewhat unsavory role in the Justice Department's threat to magazine retailers, further damaged his effectiveness as a moral crusader. But in mid-January 1989, another activist joined the battle against television smut, one who was less easily dismissed by the networks and their advertisers: Terry Rakolta, a telegenic forty-one-year-old, upper-middle-class housewife and mother of four from the wealthy Detroit suburb of Bloomfield Hills.

One evening, Rakolta sat down with her three youngest children to watch television and saw an episode of Fox Television's *Married . . . With Children* in which the show's obnoxious husband, Al Bundy, tries to buy his wife—the sweet but coarse mom, Peg Bundy (played with over-the-crop-top exuberance by Katey Sagal)—a discontinued bra model at the fictitious "Francine's of Hollywood." The double entendres began with the store's motto, "If you've got the boulders, we've got the holders," and went downhill from there. Among other things, the show featured a male stripper in a G-string, a man at Francine's wearing a garter belt and nylons, and a young woman who removed her bra with her back to the camera.[42]

Outraged by the show's raunchy humor, Rakolta launched a highly public letter-writing campaign to persuade the show's advertisers to withdraw their support. She had some initial success, as Procter & Gamble, McDonald's, Tambrands, and Kimberly-Clark all announced that they were pulling their advertisements from *Married*. Ira C. Herbert, president of Coca-Cola, USA, personally wrote a letter to Rakolta, in which he said that he was "corporately, professionally and personally embarrassed" that an ad for Coca-Cola had appeared on the show.[43]

The fact that several corporations reacted so quickly and so publicly to the complaints of a disgruntled mother was front-page news. The same day the story broke, Rakolta was asked to appear on ABC's *Nightline*.[44] Rakolta wasted no time declaring victory: "It restores my faith in the big American product companies," she beamed.[45]

The timing of Rakolta's television decency campaign was unusually propitious; there was little serious debate that broadcast television was more salacious than ever before. Thanks to a series of breathless articles in mainstream media and additional media appearances on talk shows like *Donahue*, Rakolta was quickly dubbed the head of a new movement against crass content, and she managed to attract an impressive number of supporters for her television decency campaign.

Network executives themselves conceded that there were a number of factors contributing to public concern about television content: cost-saving cuts in their standards and practices divisions that resulted in more salacious material on air; parents who were increasingly concerned about the effects of violent and sexual programming on their children; and the increasing public hostility to "tabloid TV" shows. Some analysts blamed the perceived rise in television indecency on Reagan-era deregulation, while others pointed to increasing competition from cable television and the VCR.[46]

Regardless of the precise reason, Rakolta had clearly succeeded in tapping into a reservoir of viewer discontent. At the beginning of May, Rakolta announced that she was forming a group called Americans for Responsible Television (ART) and a week later was given at least partial credit for ABC's remarkable inability to find a single sponsor for *Crimes of Passion II*, a planned sequel to the previous season's popular show featuring reenactments of various violent crimes. The show was pulled from the network's schedule at the last minute.[47]

But in the end, Rakolta's campaign suffered the same fate of previous television improvement efforts, and her faith in corporate America proved to be somewhat misplaced. Despite press releases and promises to the contrary, only two companies actually pulled their ads in response to Rakolta's campaign, accounting for all of forty-five seconds of commercial support in *Married's* entire season. In addition, most of the other companies, including the apologetic Coca-Cola, didn't actually promise to pull their advertisements; instead, they simply promised to decide on an episode-by-episode basis whether to run their ads, and most of the time opted to do so.[48]

Thanks in large part to the publicity generated by Rakolta's boycott efforts, *Married* jumped from the eighty-eighth show nationally to twenty-seventh, and stayed on the air for ten more seasons (a longer run than many classic and less salacious sitcoms, including *I Love Lucy* and *The Mary Tyler Moore Show*).[49] Along the way, it became the first Fox television show to hit the top 20.[50]

Despite the commercial success of *Married*, Rakolta soldiered on. By 1993 ART claimed nearly one hundred thousand members, and Rakolta was lobbying in Washington for a renewal of the family viewing hour and for legislation designed to limit violence on television. Although ART still appears on some television decency resource lists, it appears to have largely ceased operation.

As with so many other decency battles, the winner in this struggle was determined by economics. The chief reason that *Married*—which its own crew nicknamed "The Anti-Cosby Show" during its first season—survived so long was that it did particularly well with younger viewers. As television analyst Larry Gerbrandt aptly observed, "The MTV generation appreciates a little sicker sense of humor."[51] Recognizing the appeal of *Married* to that most coveted of advertising demographics, the networks and advertisers rolled out a succession of sitcoms aimed at the darker side of family life: *Roseanne* (ABC, 1988), *The Simpsons* (Fox, 1989), *Beavis and Butthead* (MTV, 1993), and *Family Guy* (Fox, 1999).

Favorable newspaper articles and choice talk show slots notwithstanding, Rakolta and ART were simply never able to inflict enough economic pain on either advertisers or networks, particularly when their own activities helped to make their targets more popular.

"MY TAX DOLLARS PAID FOR THAT??": THE BATTLE OVER THE NATIONAL ENDOWMENT FOR THE ARTS

At about the same time that Rakolta was launching her one-person letter-writing campaign to television advertisers, the Reverend Donald Wildmon was calling on his members to write Congress to protest some of the government's funding choices in the arts. In January 1989 a traveling exhibit of photographs opened at the Virginia Museum of Fine Art in Richmond. The exhibit was the product of a collection of $15,000 grants given to various photographers in 1987 by the Southeast Center for Contemporary Art, using funds provided by the National Endowment for the Arts (NEA). Among the photographs was an image that on its surface was fairly unremarkable: a slightly streaky, reddish orange–tinged shot of a plastic crucifix.

The photo, however, had a provocative title—"Piss Christ"—and an even more provocative methodology: the image's distinctive color resulted from the fact that the crucifix was photographed in a jar of artist Andres Serrano's urine. The photograph sparked little comment during its national tour, but at some point in early 1989 (months after the exhibit had closed), both the image and its funding source came to the attention of Reverend Wildmon. Not long after the publicity debacle involving his role on the Meese Commission, Wildmon had changed the name of his organization from the National Federation for Decency to the American Family Association (AFA).

In April, Wildmon wrote about "Piss Christ" in his AFA newsletter and urged members to send protest letters to members of Congress. On May 18, 1989, Senators Helms and Alphonse D'Amato (R-NY) rose in the Senate to denounce the artist for taking the photo. D'Amato went so far as to tear up a copy of the exhibit catalog on the Senate floor[52] and derided the National Endowment for the Arts for funding what he called "a deplorable, despicable display of vulgarity."[53] After the public protest by Helms and D'Amato, roughly 50 senators and 150 representatives contacted the NEA to protest the grant and ask pointed questions about the agency's funding procedures.[54]

The controversy over the Serrano photo was particularly ill-timed for the NEA. The agency's longtime chairman, Frank Hodsall, had recently resigned, and President Bush was still considering possible replacements. Although President Reagan had startled nearly everyone by proposing a slight increase in the 1990 NEA budget just before he left office, Congress had not yet acted on the recommendation. And on top of everything else, the NEA itself was up for reauthorization, a process that Congress was required by statute to undertake every five years. Supporters of federally supported art were painfully aware that there was a cadre of legislators eager to save $170 million by eliminating the NEA altogether.[55]

The situation quickly worsened. On June 12, 1989, the director of Washington's Corcoran Gallery of Art, Christina Orr-Cahall, announced that she was canceling a planned exhibition of Robert Mapplethorpe's (1946–1989) photography titled The Perfect Moment. The show, scheduled to open on July 1, had been organized by the Philadelphia Institute of Contemporary Art on the strength of a $30,000 grant from the NEA. Mapplethorpe, who had died in March 1989 from complications stemming from AIDS, was a widely admired artist whose photography featured, among other things, themes of homoeroticism, sadomasochism, and child nudity.

Without question, The Perfect Moment contained some challenging examples of Mapplethorpe's artistic vision—one man urinating into the mouth of another, for instance, or the iconic self-portrait of the artist himself bent over with a bullwhip sticking out of his rectum. The Corcoran's skittishness, however, took people by surprise. The gallery was not the first stop for The Perfect Moment; the photographs had previously been exhibited in Philadelphia and Chicago without controversy.[56] Moreover, the Corcoran itself did not receive any money from the NEA to host the Mapplethorpe exhibit. In a classic bit of Orwellian logic, however, Orr-Cahall said that the museum was canceling the show in order to save it.

"It certainly wasn't going to be a climate in which he [Mapplethorpe] could be presented as an artist in his own right," Orr-Cahall told the Times. "We're about education, we're not about hyperbole. That's why I think we're acting responsibly not playing into that."[57]

Few people bought the idea, however, that the Corcoran's action wasn't an attempt to appease the conservatives who were fulminating a few blocks down Pennsylvania Avenue. The gallery's decision was particularly suspicious given the fact that it receives much of its operating budget directly from Congress through the National Capital Arts and Cultural Affairs program. In the arts community, the protest over Orr-Cahall's decision was both swift and vociferous. A typical reaction was voiced by Robert Miller, a New York art dealer who represented Mapplethorpe: "When one thinks of the terrors that Washington generates and sends out into the world, the thought that depiction of the human body might be disturbing to Washington seems ludicrous."[58]

Officials at other museums questioned the decision to cancel a scheduled show for political reasons, while artists and members of the gay and lesbian community offered more pungently phrased reactions.[59]

As a spokesman for Senator Helms accurately predicted, the Corcoran's cancellation was "not the end of the matter." On June 30, the night before the show was supposed to open, a crowd of roughly nine hundred people gathered outside of the Corcoran and used theatrical equipment to project fifty-foot-high images of Mapplethorpe's work onto the facade of the gallery. Members of the crowd were pleased by the news that the Washington Project for the Arts (WPA) planned to host the exhibit later in the summer but dismayed that the Corcoran Gallery had so quickly crumbled in the face of senatorial disapproval.[60] When the show opened on July 21 at the WPA, Washingtonians voted with their feet: the gallery, which normally has between 40 and 80 visitors per day, had 5,500 visitors in the first three days of the show alone.[61]

Despite the overwhelming public response to the Mapplethorpe exhibit, however, the NEA was still facing heavy sledding on Capitol Hill. Conserva-

tive legislators demanded that the NEA either change its standards and procedures for awarding grants or see its budget slashed. In mid-July, the House
rejected efforts to cut the NEA budget by as much as 10 percent but did
approve a $45,000 reduction—an amount equal to the combined grants for the
Serano and Mapplethorpe exhibits. As Congressman Charles Stenholm (D-
TX) noted, "[r]eally, it's a shot across the bow. It's sending the appropriate
message without shooting everything in sight."[62]

The NEA faced a more serious threat on the other side of the Capitol. At
the end of July, a Senate appropriations subcommittee recommended imposing
a five-year ban on any grants to the institutions that had funded the two photographers.[63] At the same time, Helms introduced an amendment to the
NEA's funding bill that would have prohibited the NEA from providing
funding for "obscene or indecent materials."[64] To help promote his legislation,
Helms took a page from Anthony Comstock's playbook: he created a portable
"chamber of horrors" (a pamphlet of four Mapplethorpe photos from the
exhibit) that he kept in his Senate chamber desk to show wavering members.

Initially, Helms made some progress in his campaign against the NEA; both
the House and the Senate approved restrictions on NEA grants, with the Senate
adopting the particularly stringent language proposed by Helms. But by the end
of what *New York Times* columnist Anthony Lewis aptly described as the "Summer
of the Booboisie,"[65] cooler heads were prevailing. When the House of Representatives debated whether to replace its grant limitation language with the Helms
Amendment, the battle against the senator's proposal was led by Sidney R. Yates
(1909–2000) (D-IL), who said that it "goes way beyond pornography and estab-
lishes a pattern of censorship." The leading proponent of the Helms Amendment,
Dana Rohrabacher (R-CA), warned legislators that their votes against the
amendment would be perceived by conservative groups as a vote "to prevent
restrictions on the NEA's sponsorship of obscene and indecent art."[66] Despite the
threat, however, the House refused to support the Helms Amendment.

Helms did not give up his battle to impose content restrictions on the
NEA. When conferees from the two Houses met to sort out their differences
on NEA financing, Helms mailed a copy of his Mapplethorpe pamphlet to each
member of the committee.[67] After extensive debate, however, the conference
committee recommended dropping virtually all of Helms's language, leaving in
place only a prohibition against the federal funding of "obscene" art, as that
term is defined by the US Supreme Court. The revised language was subsequently adopted by both the House and the Senate.

During the ongoing congressional debate over the Helms Amendment,
the Corcoran Gallery quietly issued a formal apology for canceling the show,
and just before Christmas 1989, to no one's great surprise, Orr-Cahall resigned

as the gallery's director. With the passage of the NEA funding authorization, things appeared to be settling down on the arts front. It was, however, merely the eye of the storm.

In April 1990 the national tour of the Mapplethorpe exhibit reached the city of Cincinnati, Ohio. After touching off the political firestorm in Washington, The Perfect Moment had traveled to Hartford, Connecticut, and Berkeley, California, where it had been received with minimal objection. In Cincinnati, however, Police Chief Lawrence Whalen announced his intention to seize any obscene photographs from the exhibit, which was scheduled to open at the Cincinnati Contemporary Arts Center (CCAC) on April 6. "The people of this community," Whalen declared, "do not cater to what others depict as art."[68] That claim, at least, was open to debate: a preview of the show at the CCAC drew 5,000 people, and another 2,700 showed up for the exhibit's first day.[69]

On the morning the Mapplethorpe exhibit opened, a Hamilton County grand jury indicted the gallery and its director, Dennis Barrie, on two misdemeanor counts each of pandering obscenity and using minors in pornography. Later that same day, members of the Hamilton County Sheriff's Department braved a crowd of one thousand shouting protestors and shut down the Arts Center for an hour and a half in order to gather evidence for trial. The images of armed officers closing an American art gallery were far more shocking and disturbing to most Americans than anything actually hanging on the gallery walls. Cincinnati graphic artist Richard Ringo offered a typical comment: "Just as totalitarianism is crumbling in Eastern Europe, we have it right here in Cincinnati."[70]

Despite the county's indictments, a federal district court judge enjoined Cincinnati from shutting down the Mapplethorpe exhibit, and blocked Hamilton County prosecuting attorney Arthur M. Ney Jr. from seeking additional indictments.[71] While the two sides began preparing for trial, the exhibit continued to draw large crowds; over twenty-three thousand viewed Mapplethorpe's photographs in the show's first two weeks alone. It also did not escape notice that later that summer, while Cincinnati was prosecuting its Contemporary Arts Center for alleged pandering, the Mapplethorpe exhibit was welcomed in, of all places, Boston, with its lengthy history of cultural censorship. In fact, the local Public Broadcasting Station, WGBH, went one step further: the station broadcast the most controversial images from the exhibit as part of its 10 PM newscast on July 31, 1990, the night before the exhibit opened. Calls to the station ran 5–1 in favor of the broadcast, and a representative for the Federal Communications Commission said the agency had not received any complaints. Not surprisingly, WGBH's announcement of its plans to broadcast the controversial Mapplethorpe photos doubled the news program's normal ratings.[72]

Back in Cincinnati, the trial of Barrie and the Contemporary Arts Center got under way on Monday, September 24. The prosecution's case was based on 7 images taken from the 175 that made up The Perfect Moment exhibit. Two photographs depicted partially nude children, and five showed scenes the *New York Times* described in an elliptical manner: "one shows a man urinating into the mouth of a man kneeling before him; the others show anal and penile penetration with unusual objects." The fact that the trial was focused on specific photos was seen as an important pretrial victory for the prosecution; the defense had argued that the challenged photos should be seen in the context of the entire exhibit and not as individual objects.[73] But Judge David J. Albanese ruled that "[e]ach photograph has a separate identity. Each photograph has a visual and unique image permanently recorded." He also pointed to the fact that each of the challenged photographs was framed individually and had been collected separately.[74]

The bulk of the trial consisted of a parade of defense witnesses, mostly other museum directors, who attempted to explain the significance of Mapplethorpe as an artist and the artistic value of the individual photographs. Prosecutor Frank Prouty made a practice of asking each defense witness a series of standard questions about art, including "[w]hat are the formal values of the picture where the finger is inserted in the penis?" The original organizer of the exhibit, Janet Kardon, offered a typical answer, saying that "[i]t's a central image, very symmetrical, a very ordered, classical composition."[75] In rebuttal, the prosecution team offered the testimony of Dr. Judith Reisman, a researcher for Reverend Wildmon's American Family Association, who testified that by hanging the images, the museum and Barrie were encouraging the activities depicted, including the abuse of children.[76]

After impassioned closing arguments by the two sides, the judge instructed the eight-person jury (four men and four women) to disregard any personal feelings they might have about Mapplethorpe's photos and limit their analysis to whether any of the photographs violated the standard for obscenity established in 1973 by the US Supreme Court in *Miller v. California*. After two hours of deliberation, the jury returned and unanimously declared the museum and Barrie "not guilty" on all counts. Interestingly, once the jury verdict was handed down, even the *New York Times* felt a little freer to describe the Mapplethorpe photos in more detail than it had previously.[77]

FROM BULLWHIP TO PITCHFORK: HOW ROBERT MAPPLETHORPE HELPED DEFEAT A PRESIDENT

Much to the irritation of religious conservatives, Helms's proposal to bar NEA grants to "obscene or indecent" works of art was opposed not merely by the usual liberal suspects but also by President George H. W. Bush's nominee to lead the NEA. At his confirmation hearing in September 1989, John Frohnmayer told members of the Senate Labor and Human Resources Committee that the Helms Amendment would be "extremely difficult to administer." In response to a question posed *advocatus diaboli* by Senator Ted Kennedy, who asked why the NEA should fund potentially objectionable art, Frohnmayer replied: "I do not believe in funding obscene art, but I do believe that there ought to be artistic freedom and tolerance so that we can operate on a continuum that starts, on the one hand, with public trust and public money, and goes to the other extreme of complete and unfettered artistic freedom."[78]

The following spring, when testifying on a proposed reauthorization of the NEA, Frohnmayer told a House committee that the Bush administration was proposing legislation for the arts endowment that did not contain any restrictions on content. [79] He also made a point of taking a few sideswipes at religious conservatives, telling Congress that information provided by Wildmon's American Family Association and Robertson's *700 Club* about NEA grants was simply incorrect.[80]

Frohnmayer's testimony was front-page news and set off a firestorm of criticism from religious conservatives groups. The White House switchboard received a large number of calls protesting Frohnmayer's statements, and Robertson made a point of taking both the NEA and Frohnmayer to task on *The 700 Club*. The controversy highlighted Bush's effort to find a middle ground on some issues in preparation for his 1992 reelection campaign; at the same time however, it also underscored the long-standing cultural differences and class issues between Bush and religious conservatives.[81]

Frohnmayer's job over the next two years did not get any easier. Helms and other conservative members of Congress continued to push for tighter content restrictions, while artists and liberal members of the arts community complained about Frohnmayer's efforts to enforce the existing law. Particularly disliked was a requirement established by Frohnmayer in 1990 that all grant recipients sign a pledge not to produce obscene art. Just a few months later, the pledge requirement was thrown out by a federal district court, which ruled that the Helms-sponsored ban on obscene art was an unconstitutional violation of artists' free speech rights.[82] Once again, the religious conservative agenda, even when it yielded legislative results, struggled to survive in the harsh light of constitutional analysis.

Frohnmayer was in an impossible political situation, and given his near-total inability to please both conservatives and the arts community, it is unlikely that his tenure would have lasted much longer than it did. But there were two specific events that greased the skids for his departure.

First, in an almost poetic example of bureaucratic self-immolation, Frohnmayer approved a $25,000 postproduction grant for a film aptly titled *Poison*, an interweaving of three stories loosely based on the writings of France's Jean Genet (1910–1986). The film was a grand prize winner at the 1991 Sundance Film Festival. A couple of its scenes, displaying sexual relationships in prison, set off charges by religious conservatives that Frohnmayer was now an executive producer of government-financed homosexual pornography.

Ralph Reed, executive director of the Christian Coalition, offered a typically blunt assessment: "This guy has got to go. Can you be more politically reckless and arrogant than to defend a tax-funded porno flick on Good Friday?"[83]

The second critical event for Frohnmayer was the outcome of the 1992 New Hampshire Republican primary. As a sitting president, Bush commanded slightly more deference than he did in 1988, but he was still vulnerable to attacks from the Right (Patrick Buchanan) and the way Far Right (former Ku Klux Klan and neo-Nazi David Duke). Of the two, Buchanan was obviously the more serious threat, as he proved in New Hampshire: the conservative talk show commentator and quintessential protest candidate received 40 percent of the votes cast. The morning-after spin was all about the "jarring political message" that Bush had received, and Bush himself admitted that "I understand the message of dissatisfaction."

The bulk of the dissatisfaction, undoubtedly, was over the anemic performance of the economy through much of 1991 and 1992 (thus inspiring James Carville's mantra "It's the economy, stupid"), as well as Bush's economically sound but politically destructive decision to reverse his no-new-taxes pledge.[84] But there was also widespread concern in the Bush camp that Buchanan was going to use the NEA in general and Frohnmayer in particular as a campaign issue in the more conservative South.

Buchanan, however, did not wait to get below the Mason-Dixon line to make the NEA an issue. Just two days after the New Hampshire primary, Buchanan lambasted Bush for his support for the endowment and described it as "the upholstered playpen of the arts and crafts auxiliary of the Eastern liberal establishment." The following morning, Frohnmayer was called into the White House and told to take one for the team. Following this meeting, a press release was sent out in which Frohnmayer said that a decision had been made that "May 1, 1992, should be my departure date."[85]

Not surprisingly, advisers to President Bush were concerned that the decision to jettison Frohnmayer would be seen as a purely political response to Buchanan's insurgency. They insisted that, in fact, the personnel change had been planned well before the New Hampshire primary. Almost no one believed them. As Rep. Sidney Yates put it, John Frohnmayer was "a victim on the altar of Pat Buchanan and the conservative wing of the Republican party."[86] The *New York Times* described Frohnmayer's firing as a "public execution," and praised the embattled director's farewell speech, in which he criticized "the lunacy that sees artists as enemies and ideas as demons." It was a speech, the *Times* said, that "put President Bush to shame for the graceless, naked capitulation to his right-wing challenger, Patrick Buchanan."[87]

Arguably, the moment of political panic that led to Frohnmayer's abrupt dismissal did more damage to Bush's reelection campaign than anything the NEA had funded over the past three years. There should have been no illusions in the White House that regardless of who was running the NEA in early 1992, the federal funding of art was going to be a campaign issue for Buchanan. This was, after all, a candidate who routinely promised his audiences that "[w]hen I get to be President, we're going to shut that place down, then padlock it and fumigate it." In the week leading up to the Georgia primary, the Buchanan campaign began airing a political advertisement accusing President Bush of using the endowment to invest taxpayer dollars in pornography and blasphemy.

More important, the manner in which Frohnmayer's firing was handled violated one of the central tenets of Republican philosophy: no negotiations with terrorists, political or otherwise. This was, ironically, a principal that Buchanan himself had inimitably espoused during the Iran-Contra controversy, when he called on congressional Republicans to resist the mob "yowling that the head of the household be produced." But now, of course, Buchanan was at the head of his own mob, and while Bush did start firing from the upper floors, he was using staff people for ammunition.

The eventual crumbling of Buchanan's campaign in 1992 had far less to do with enthusiasm for Bush than it did with voter concern over Buchanan's isolationist impulses and cultural censoriousness. Although Buchanan did not win a single primary, his acidic fusillades clearly damaged Bush, both by contributing to a public perception of electoral weakness and by forcing the president farther to the Right in order to limit the encroachment of Buchanan's campaign on the ranks of the True Believers.

Buchanan's final blow to Bush came at the Republican National Convention in Houston in August. Accorded a prime-time speaking slot in deference to his showing in the primaries and his popularity among a critical wing of the party, Buchanan presented a speech that can best be described as "Sinners in the Hands of an Angry Talking Head." He reiterated his long-standing belief that "[t]here is a religious war going on in our country for the soul of America. It is a cultural war, as critical to the kind of nation we will one day be as was the Cold War itself." As only he can, Buchanan made it absolutely clear where the cultural battle lines should be drawn:

> Like many of you last month, I watched that giant masquerade ball at Madison Square Garden—where 20,000 radicals and liberals came dressed up as moderates and centrists—in the greatest single exhibition of cross-dressing in American political history. . . .
>
> The agenda Clinton & Clinton would impose on America—abortion on demand, a litmus test for the Supreme Court, homosexual rights, discrimination against religious schools, women in combat—that's change, all right. But it is not the kind of change America wants. It is not the kind of change America needs. And it is not the kind of change we can tolerate in a nation that we still call God's country.[88]

As he had throughout the primaries, Buchanan electrified the religious and social conservatives who had supported him. But the barely contained anger and the sheer pugnaciousness of his speech did irreparable damage to Bush's reelection prospects, already struggling under the weight of a poor economy. The mob had finally made it through the front door.

Chapter Seven

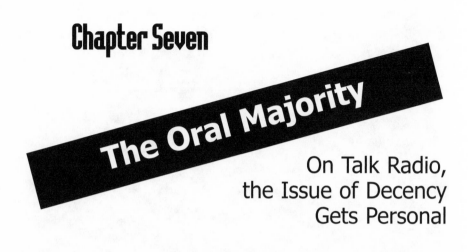

The Oral Majority

On Talk Radio, the Issue of Decency Gets Personal

I'm not gonna be open-minded or tolerant or all that bilge!
—Conservative radio talk show host Rush Limbaugh[1]

Many of the battle lines—regional, cultural, religious—in American politics today can be traced to one simple physical fact: watt for watt, AM radio waves travel much farther than FM radio waves. Depending on geography, weather conditions, time of day, and so on, an AM signal can travel more than ten times farther than an FM signal. A strong FM station in Boston, for instance, can barely be heard in Springfield, just 60 miles to the west, whereas an AM station transmitting from the same location might be heard in Detroit, nearly 750 miles away.

The radio revolution at the turn of the twentieth century was sparked (literally) by Guglielmo Marconi's discovery of amplitude modulation (AM) radio. The remarkable range of AM transmissions was a fortunate bonus that helped spur public acceptance of radio by making it possible for signals to be heard in rural and remote areas of the country. When the Federal Communications Commission was created by Congress in 1934, one of the first major technical issues it had to address was whether to allocate space on the electromagnetic spectrum for a new type of radio signal, based on frequency modulation (FM). The inventor of FM radio, Major Edwin H. Armstrong (1890–1954), told the FCC that if commercial FM stations were given permission to operate, many urban radio stations would switch from AM to the "perfect medium" of FM.[2]

Radio talk show host Rush Limbaugh talks on a phone as House Speaker Newt Gingrich gestures during a break in taping of NBC's *Meet the Press*, Sunday, November 12, 1995, in Washington, DC. (AP photo/Doug Mills)

Armstrong's claim of perfection was based on the fact that FM transmissions are less subject to interference than AM transmissions and, more significantly, are capable of reproducing stereophonic sound. (At the time of its introduction, FM was frequently referred to as "high fidelity" or "full fidelity" radio.) But while there was a brief flurry of interest in FM following World War II, consumer attention was focused instead on the nearly simultaneous introduction of television. In 1958, twenty-five years after their invention, FM receivers made up just over 3 percent of radios sold and, as late as 1973, still accounted for just 30 percent of the listener market.[3]

The slow growth of FM wasn't entirely a result of market forces and consumer choice. When the FCC began issuing FM licenses in the 1940s, the majority of them were purchased by the owners of AM stations, who were concerned that they would lose listeners (and advertisers) to the new medium's superior reception and sound quality. To save money, station owners typically broadcasted the same programs over both their AM and FM frequencies.

The relatively small number of independent FM stations concentrated on broadcasting classical music and other content that benefited from FM's superior sound quality. The limited appeal of the programming helped to keep the audience small, which in turn kept the cost of FM receivers high and therefore less attractive than AM receivers. Given the content, equipment cost, and generally urban setting of FM, it didn't take long for the medium to develop an elitist reputation.[4]

Hoping to broaden the appeal of FM and spur the growth of the medium, the FCC ruled in 1966 that any FM station that merely duplicated an AM station's programming would be required to produce at least 50 percent original content by the end of the year or risk losing its broadcast license. Some stations responded by simply broadcasting AM programs a day later on their FM stations, but the FCC ruling unquestionably increased the variety of programming available on FM. As *Business Week* described the shift, "[t]he cloistered little world of FM radio has been invaded—by rock-'n'-roll, hockey game play-by-plays, and sexy girl announcers making slightly off-color remarks."[5] Little did they know.

The FCC's efforts to boost FM's popularity through more diverse program requirements were stunningly successful. Aided by a variety of other cultural trends—population shifts from rural areas to cities and suburbs, the skyrocketing popularity of musical groups like the Beatles and the Rolling Stones (whose sound quality mattered to their audiences), and generally falling equipment prices—FM's share of the radio audience steadily grew to more than 70 percent in just twenty years. FM's rapid increase in market share was mirrored by AM's precipitous descent into the broadcasting cellar. The split in advertising dollars—the economic engine of radio—was similar: FM earned an estimated $4.8 to 5 billion in 1987 compared to AM's $1.7 to 1.9 billion. The burning question among broadcasters was no longer how to prop up FM but instead how to salvage AM, a medium whose increasingly gray-haired audience seemed on the verge of dying out.[6]

The industry itself had some ideas. Efforts were under way to reduce AM interference through the use of more advanced transmitters, and several systems were competing to add stereo sound to the AM band. The inability of the AM industry to settle on a single stereo standard from the five competing systems, however, delayed the successful implementation of AM stereo. Many AM station owners expressed frustration over the fact that the FCC, consistent with the Reagan administration's deregulatory philosophy, chose to wait for the marketplace to determine the best standard, rather than resolving the dispute itself. Wayne Vriesman, vice president of the Tribune Broadcasting Company's radio group, described the FCC's refusal to mediate the AM stereo dispute as a disaster. "We lost years through that process."[7]

But what deregulation tooketh away, it also gaveth back, in spades. Recognizing the unintended consequences of its boost to FM in the 1960s, the FCC began considering proposals to ease regulatory restrictions on AM stations. In 1985, for instance, the commission widened the AM spectrum to make room for more radio stations.[8] The following year, the FCC released a 116-page report containing a variety of recommendations intended to relax AM regulations, including easing restrictions on multistation ownership, allowing some daytime-only stations to expand to nighttime, permitting stations to buy more outside content, and allowing stations on the same frequency but in different cities to carry the same content at the same time. The latter move favored radio networks distributing programming from a central location. Many analysts argue that centralization of radio programming has played a significant role in changing broadcast decency standards, as radio networks became less responsive to local standards.

The overall goal of AM deregulation, FCC chairman Mark Fowler said, was to make it easier for AM station owners to compete financially with their advertising-rich competitors on the FM dial. "Without financial viability," Fowler said, "you don't have diversity of voices."[9] In January 1987, the FCC also announced that it was beginning a comprehensive review of its ownership regulations, on the theory that the regulations were making it more difficult for television and radio broadcasters (particularly AM) to be financially competitive with other types of media, including cable and video.

While these various initiatives undoubtedly helped AM station owners by reducing the operating costs for individual stations (and offering the prospect of efficiencies of scale), the real salvation of AM radio lay in another piece of significant Reagan-era FCC deregulation: the abandonment of the commission's sixty-year-long commitment to fairness on the airwaves.

THE DEATH OF FAIRNESS

When Congress established the Federal Radio Commission (FRC) in 1927, it charged the commission's board to consider "public convenience, interest, or necessity" when allocating radio frequencies. As the commission struggled to follow Congress's instructions, it concluded that one of its duties was to enforce simple fairness: "public interest requires ample play for the free and fair competition of competing views, and the commission believes the principle applies . . . to all discussions of importance to the public."[10] As a result, the Federal Communications Commission (the FRC's successor) decreed that radio stations could not "advocate" but instead were required to present "all sides fairly, objectively, and without bias."[11]

From the start, broadcasters hated the so-called Fairness Doctrine. They resented the implication that they were in need of greater supervision than other media (most notably newspapers, to which the Fairness Doctrine did not apply); they resented the monitoring and regulation of their content; and, perhaps most of all, they resented the cost, either in putting together the content necessary to satisfy the Fairness Doctrine or in providing free airtime to competing views. And, of course, the legal costs of dealing with the incessant demands for "equal time" were exorbitant. Quite frankly, the Fairness Doctrine was a burden for the FCC as well, since resolving disputes over charges of imbalance and enforcing the provision of "equal time" was an onerous and almost entirely thankless task.

The only significant court challenge to the Fairness Doctrine arose, not surprisingly, out of the bitter 1964 presidential election between Barry Goldwater and Lyndon Johnson. On November 25, 1964, the Reverend Billy James Hargis delivered an installment of his "Christian Crusade" radio broadcast. One subject of his commentary that day was author Fred J. Cook, who had recently written a book titled *Goldwater: Extremist on the Right*. In his brief remarks, Hargis leveled a variety of inflammatory charges against Cook, including claims that Cook had been fired from a reporting job for making false charges, that he had worked for a "Communist-affiliated publication," that he was a defender of alleged Soviet spy Alger Hiss (1904–1996), and that he had written a book intending to "smear and destroy Barry Goldwater."[12]

When Cook learned of Hargis's attack, he wrote to a number of stations that had carried the Hargis broadcast, requesting free airtime under the Fairness Doctrine in order to respond to the charges. Station WGCB in Red Lion, Pennsylvania, was one of those stations, but owner Rev. John Norris refused to provide Cook with free time (although he did reportedly offer to charge Cook the same amount he charged Hargis—$7.50 for fifteen minutes).[13] Cook filed a complaint with the FCC, which ruled that under the Fairness Doctrine WGCB was required to provide him with free airtime. Norris promptly appealed the decision to federal court. The case worked its way up to the Supreme Court, which in 1969 upheld the FCC's decision and ruled that the Fairness Doctrine was "both authorized by statute and constitutional." Writing for a unanimous court, Justice Byron White (1917–2002) concluded:

> Nor can we say that it is inconsistent with the First Amendment goal of producing an informed public capable of conducting its own affairs to require a broadcaster to permit answers to personal attacks occurring in the course of discussing controversial issues, or to require that the political opponents of those endorsed by the station be given a chance to communicate with the public. *Otherwise, station owners and a few networks would have unfettered power*

to make time available only to the highest bidders, to communicate only their own
views on public issues, people and candidates, and to permit on the air only those
with whom they agreed. There is no sanctuary in the First Amendment for
unlimited private censorship operating in a medium not open to all. "Freedom
of the press from governmental interference under the First Amendment does
not sanction repression of that freedom by private interests."[14]

Despite the Court's stately language, the effect of the ruling was simply to
uphold the constitutionality of a rule adopted by the commission; the Court did
not conclude that fairness itself is a constitutional requirement. A few years
later, the intellectual and political underpinnings of the Fairness Doctrine were
badly damaged by an investigation conducted by former CBS journalist Fred
Friendly (1915–1998).[15] In the course of investigating the *Red Lion* case in the
mid-1970s, Friendly discovered that Cook's request for equal time was part of a
much larger coordinated campaign by Democrats to use the Fairness Doctrine
to harass radio stations carrying conservative commentary. His conclusion was
that rather than promoting balanced discussion of controversial topics, the Fairness Doctrine "has on occasion been perverted—used for political purposes."

In early 1963, for instance, the Kennedy White House coordinated an
effort to use the Fairness Doctrine to counter conservative opposition to a
nuclear test ban treaty with the Soviet Union. "The campaign resulted in a
dramatic number of broadcasts favoring the treaty in areas of the country,"
Friendly wrote, "where such views might otherwise not have been heard."[16] It
is a little unclear why Friendly characterized that outcome as a "perversion" of
the Fairness Doctrine—after all, the entire point of the doctrine was to ensure
that listeners were exposed to competing ideas regarding issues of national significance, a category into which airborne nuclear testing surely fits. But clearly,
Friendly found the use of the Fairness Doctrine for covert partisan political
purposes to be unacceptable.

The Kennedy White House also concluded that its use of the Fairness
Doctrine helped pass the test ban treaty, although the size of the vote (90–9)
suggests that there were other equally if not more plausible reasons for ratification. Concerns over the possible health effects of nuclear tests, for instance,
were not limited to the nascent environmental movement, and fear from the
preceding fall's Cuban missile crisis was still fresh in everyone's memory.

Nonetheless, given the success of the ratification campaign, the Democrats continued to monitor conservative broadcasts through the 1964 election
and to use the Fairness Doctrine to demand equal time. Wayne Phillips, a publicist hired to coordinate the campaign by the Kennedy White House, reported
after Johnson's reelection that Fairness Doctrine requests had resulted in more
than seventeen hundred free radio broadcasts of anticonservative material.

"[E]ven more important than the free radio time," Phillips wrote, "was the effectiveness of this operation in inhibiting the political activity of these right-wing broadcasts."[17] (In many cases, stations simply dropped conservative commentators to avoid having to air liberal responses.)

The dispute between Cook and Hargis was a direct result of the Democratic "fairness" campaign. The Democratic National Committee (DNC) worked closely with Cook, hiring him to write articles critical of the Right and preordering fifty thousand copies of his book on Goldwater, a move that guaranteed that it would be published.[18] Radio monitors hired by the DNC were the first to hear Hargis's attack on Cook, and the DNC helped Cook file his Fairness Doctrine request. Cato Institute analysts Thomas W. Hazlett and David W. Sosa argued that as a result of Cook's request, "the majority of stations stopped carrying Hargis's commentary, thus providing the very chilling effect the Supreme Court had failed to find evident in [Red Lion]."[19]

By the time Ronald Reagan was elected president, the clamor from broadcasters to jettison the Fairness Doctrine was growing increasingly loud. The new president's deregulatory philosophy was an inspiration to many people, but it would be difficult to find a more enthusiastic adherent than Mark Fowler, the man President Reagan selected in 1981 to lead the FCC. A former disc jockey from the 1960s, "Madman Mark" Fowler came to the commission with a deep-seated distrust of government regulation of broadcast media. Famous for his declaration that a television is a mere "appliance . . . a toaster with pictures," Fowler considered his own government regulators to be the equivalent of censors who "have no place in a democratic, free society."[20]

Near the top of Fowler's list of unnecessary and harmful FCC regulations was the Fairness Doctrine. In Congress, Senator Bob Packwood led an investigation by the Senate Commerce Committee that was designed to show that the Fairness Doctrine in fact wasn't "fair" and that it actually suppressed speech. The gist of the report was that the doctrine discouraged media outlets from airing specific opinions about important public issues due to a reluctance to offer equal time. Relying on the Commerce Committee's research, the FCC issued its own lengthy "Fairness Report," in which it concluded that the long-standing doctrine did inhibit the ability of the public to hear dissenting viewpoints.

The FCC also ruled that the scarcity argument relied on by the Supreme Court in the Red Lion case was no longer supported by the evidence: among other things, the FCC pointed to a 48 percent rise in radio stations, a 44 percent increase in television stations, and a 195 percent increase in the number of cable channels. In late 1986, the deregulatory forces got some help from the US Court of Appeals for the DC Circuit, when Judges Antonin Scalia and Robert Bork upheld a ruling by the FCC in which the commission refused to extend the Fairness Doctrine to a new broadcast technology.[21] It was a precursor of the commission's intent to abandon the doctrine altogether.

Concerned by the evident direction in which the FCC was moving, Congress belatedly stepped in to try to protect the Fairness Doctrine. In April 1987, the Senate voted 59–31 to require the FCC to enforce the doctrine, and, in early June, the House followed suit on a vote of 302–102. However, President Reagan vetoed the legislation on June 20, 1987, declaring that the law was unconstitutional. "In any other medium besides broadcasting," the president said, "such Federal policing of the editorial judgment of journalists would be unthinkable."[22] There was some discussion of trying to override the president's veto, but it was clear that the pro-fairness forces simply did not have the votes. The doctrine was formally buried on August 4, 1987, when the FCC unanimously repealed the regulations requiring broadcast fairness.[23]

AM TALK RADIO FINDS ITS VOICE

Although few fully realized it at the time, the elimination of the Fairness Doctrine was an enormous going-away present from President Reagan to his most ardent (if somewhat disappointed) followers and, ultimately, to AM station owners as well. More than any other regulatory change enacted by the FCC, the abandonment of broadcast fairness helped lay the groundwork for a conservative "coup de talk." Among other things, it has helped make American politics more antagonistic, confrontational, and bitterly partisan.

Well before Fowler took on the Fairness Doctrine, talk radio was a staple of AM radio. The chief reason is, of course, that talk is in fact cheap. It is far less expensive to pay someone to talk for three hours and take some phone calls from listeners than it is to pay royalties on three hours of music. In addition, talk is better suited to the monophonic sound of AM; a conversation doesn't sound significantly better in stereo than it does in mono. AM also particularly thrives at night, when its signal can bounce off the ionosphere and carry hundreds of miles, and nighttime, of course, is better suited to the mellow musings of a Paul Harvey or Larry King than the high-decibel offerings of Billboard's latest chart-topper.

It was no accident that AM radio talk show hosts, even before the abandonment of the Fairness Doctrine, tended to be fairly conservative. In general, station owners were more likely to hire commentators and hosts who shared a pro-business, antigovernment, low-tax view of the world. Such views were also more appealing to AM's generally more rural listeners, many of whom had their own suspicions of central government and dislike for taxes. And although the new generation of talk show hosts began emerging on the airwaves at the very end of the Reagan administration, they still viewed themselves as political revolutionaries, agitating against the forty-year domination of Congress by Democrats.

That self-perception and the potential political power of talk radio were driven home in February 1989, when Congress debated giving itself a 51 percent pay raise, from $89,000 to $135,000 per year. A semiorganized coalition of talk show hosts across the country helped stir up so much public protest that the plan was voted down by both the House and the Senate. In Detroit, Station WXYT's Roy Fox encouraged listeners to send tea bags to Congress to protest the plan, and encouraged other talk show hosts to spread the idea. By one estimate, over one hundred and sixty thousand tea bags were mailed to Congress, many with Fox's suggested inscription: "Read My Tea Bag! No 50% Raise."[24] Following the vote, Jerry Williams, a longtime "radio activist" on Boston's WRKO, invited fifty other politically active talk show hosts to Boston for an informal conference on Patriot's Day, 1989, to discuss other issues on which the hosts might work together.[25]

Out of the growing cacophony of talk radio, however, one booming voice quickly became the dominant spokesperson for modern conservatism: Rush Hudson Limbaugh III, the self-described "most dangerous man in America." While doing a talk show in Sacramento, California, in 1988, Limbaugh was approached by Ed McLaughlin, a former president of ABC network radio. The two came up with a novel marketing scheme: to offer radio stations across the country a three-hour daytime talk show hosted by Limbaugh. It was a bold venture because, at the time, talk radio was almost exclusively a local phenomenon, with each host covering a specific geographic region. But Limbaugh's undeniable radio talent and brash ability to tap into conservative dissatisfaction—with George H. W. Bush, the National Endowment for the Arts, the Democratic Congress, gays, feminists, and liberals in general—struck a powerful chord. Within just two years of leaving Sacramento, Limbaugh could claim an audience of 1.3 million listeners daily, earning him a yearly salary of roughly $500,000.[26] Two years later, on the eve of the 1992 election between President Bush and Arkansas governor Bill Clinton, Limbaugh's show was carried by more than five hundred radio stations to twelve million listeners per week.[27] "With talent on loan from God,"[28] Limbaugh laughingly declared, he had succeeded in making himself a national cultural and political force. Many a dyspeptic liberal looked forward to the day when God would call in his marker.

Some of the liberal antipathy toward Limbaugh can be ascribed to little more than simple jealousy, an understandable emotion given the fact that Limbaugh's diatribes were earning him a six-figure salary; that his book *The Way Things Ought to Be* opened at number six on the *New York Times* bestseller list in 1992; that his public speeches commanded fees of $25,000; and that a speaking tour, "Rush to Excellence," not only sold out its tickets but also did a boffo business in T-shirts and bumper stickers.[29] Other critics raised concerns about Limbaugh's belief—at most half-joking—that he was the only news source his listeners needed. "You don't have to read the newspapers," he said in his heyday in the early 1990s. "I read them for you and tell you what to believe."

But what was particularly galling to many people was—and still is—the unapologetic harshness with which Limbaugh discussed issues, people, and groups with whom he disagreed. Feminists were famously dubbed "femi-Nazis" by the twice-divorced host; environmentalists were "extremist wacko-nut-cases"; liberals were "compassion fascists," with many hailing from San Francisco, "the West Coast branch of the Kremlin"; and even ice cream moguls Ben & Jerry got the Limbaugh treatment: "long-haired, maggot-infested, dope-smoking hippies." Limbaugh delivered his epithets with enough good humor to credibly act wounded when accused of being mean-spirited, but there is a stiletto-sharp quality to his gibes.

Admittedly, Limbaugh can hardly be blamed for inventing attack radio: as far back as the 1930s, Father Charles Edward Coughlin (1891–1979) used his enormously popular radio show (at its peak, an estimated one-third of the nation listened) to argue, among other things, that the persecution of the Jews in Nazi Germany was essentially justifiable retribution for their persecution of Christians. In the late 1960s, television and radio host Joe Pyne (1925–1970) thrilled his Los Angeles audiences by inviting what the *Washington Post* described as "the beat-niks, kooks, and exhibitionists" into his studios and raking them with aggressive questions and sarcastic put-downs. The problem, the *Post* reported, was that Pyne imitators were springing up across the country, and some Washington-area radio stations even instructed their hosts to "be controversial." "Safeguards are few. Name-calling is prevalent. Some broadcasters have eagerly taken to the substitution of collective ignorance for what was once individual wisdom."[30]

Precisely the same phenomenon occurred following Limbaugh's meteoric success, and it is not unfair to lay at least some of the blame for the decline in broadcast civility and the general sense of decency at Limbaugh's door. Around the country, spurred by dreams of high ratings, station owners rushed to fill their hours of talk radio with the most aggressive, antigovernment, liberal-baiting hosts they could find. Those were heady times for conservative talk show hosts; not only were ratings and revenues soaring but one of their own, Pat Buchanan, was storming through the 1992 presidential primaries and lobbing verbal hand grenades at everything from the excesses of the National Endowment for the Arts to illegal immigrants. Clearly, pandering to voter anger and disaffection with government was becoming a growth market.

And what a growth it was. In 1986, just before the abandonment of the

Fairness Doctrine, there were roughly two hundred radio talk shows; eight years later, there were over one thousand, of which about 70 percent were conservative.[31] The success of Limbaugh's national syndication model also changed the shape of talk radio since it encouraged the development of a number of other national programs, hosted by people ranging from Don Imus to Pat Buchanan to G. Gordon Liddy. Syndicated programs proved particularly popular with local station owners because they were even cheaper than live talk show programs. In addition, advances in satellite and computer technology made it increasingly easy to run syndicated programs automatically, which further reduced the need for station personnel.[32]

The outcome of the 1992 election, in which Bill Clinton edged past President Bush by five and a half percentage points (43 to 37.4), only added fuel to the conservative talk radio phenomenon. As Limbaugh and his fellow hosts gleefully pointed out, not only was Clinton a minority president but the Democrats lost nine seats in the House of Representatives (the first loss by a winning presidential party since 1960) and failed to pick up any Senate seats. And while openly hostile to the possible passage of Clinton policy initiatives like gays in the military or national healthcare, most conservative talk show hosts recognized that Clinton's election was a "Conservative Talk Radio Full Employment Act." What better goad to Limbaugh's audience of self-described "ditto-heads" than a liberal baby boomer president with an alleged history of insufficient fidelity, insufficient military service, and insufficient inhalation? That President Clinton brought with him into the White House a feminist lawyer spouse who viewed the presidency as a partnership ("two for the price of one," in Bill Clinton's own memorable words) was simply too good to be true.

TALK RADIO THROWS ITS WEIGHT AROUND

The two years following Clinton's election were the high-water mark for conservative talk radio in general and Limbaugh in particular. When it was discovered that Clinton's first nominee for attorney general, Zoë Baird, had hired illegal aliens as a chauffeur and a nanny, conservative talk radio helped galvanize popular opposition that sank her bid. During the debate over Clinton's proposal to allow gays to serve openly in the military, discussion of the topic on talk radio generated thousands of calls to Congress.[33] Restaurants around the country opened "Rush Rooms" so that fans could gather to listen to his show,[34] and Republican political consultant Roger Ailes urged Limbaugh to consider a bid for the 1996 GOP presidential nomination (Limbaugh declined, saying he "couldn't afford the pay cut").[35]

Unable to slow conservative gains in the broadcast booth (and worried about the voting booth), liberals themselves sought refuge in legislation. One of the first initiatives that Clinton supported after being elected president, not surprisingly, was the Fairness in Broadcasting Act of 1993. Few people, of course, had more reason to dislike conservative talk radio than President Clinton. The talk radio trade journal *Talkers* conducted a survey in April and May 1993 and concluded that Clinton was, in the words of editor Michael Harrison, "the most bashed individual in talk radio the past three years." Given the recent growth of talk radio, Harrison added, "[h]e is likely the most bashed individual in talk radio history."[36]

The legislation, which essentially tried to erase six years of unfortunate broadcasting history (at least for liberals), was introduced in the Senate on February 4, 1993, by Senator Ernest F. Hollings (D-SC). The text of the bill was short and to the point: "A broadcast licensee shall afford reasonable opportunity for the discussion of conflicting views on issues of public importance." In his inimitable fashion, Limbaugh proudly declared that Hollings's legislation was the "Hush Rush" bill, and L. Brent Bozell, then head of the Media Research Center, said that conservative shows would be canceled because station owners would be unable to find liberals capable of producing the same type of ratings generated by conservative hosts.[37]

The Fairness in Broadcasting Act passed the Senate in September 1993 and appeared headed for easy passage in the House. Throughout the month of October, however, Limbaugh and Michael Harrison, host of *The Talk Radio Countdown Show*, helped lead a conservative talk show campaign against the bill. Listener calls and letters running four to one against the bill flooded Congress. By Halloween, congressional aides conceded that conservative talk show hosts had made the potential cost of supporting the legislation too high for most representatives.[38] The bill was allowed to die quietly in committee.

The talk show campaign against the Fairness in Broadcasting Act was merely a warm-up for the 1994 midterm elections. Six weeks prior to the election, Rep. Newt Gingrich (R-GA) proposed a series of legislative initiatives that he dubbed (on the strength of careful focus group testing) the "Contract with America." Among other things, the contract proposed congressional term limits, tax cuts, balanced budget legislation, and the elimination of nonessential services. In an impressive blending of technology and campaigning, Gingrich set up a Contract Information Center to repeatedly fax press clippings and information about the contract to five hundred radio talk show hosts around the country, many of whom simply read the information directly into their microphones. Limbaugh in particular promoted the contract heavily on his show and frequently conferred with Gingrich on the progress of the campaign.

Among religious conservatives, there was some concern that Gingrich's Contract with America concentrated almost exclusively on economic issues and made no significant mention of the social concerns of religious conservatives. Both Ralph Reed of the Christian Coalition and Paul Weyrich of the Free Congress Foundation warned Republicans that they should not take the religious conservative wing of the party for granted. Reed assured his supporters that he had commitments from the Republican leadership that they would address the school prayer issue within the first hundred days of the election. Gingrich also tried to reassure nervous religious conservatives by stressing his belief in the importance of religion in America. At a speech at the Heritage Foundation prior to the election, Gingrich talked about "a vision of an America in which belief in the Creator is once again at the center of defining being an American."[39]

Gingrich's contract proved to be one of the most successful political ideas in American history. Midterm elections are usually a low point for the party in the White House, but Republicans gained a stunning fifty-four seats in the House and eight seats in the Senate, giving them majority control of both houses of Congress. In January 1995, Newt Gingrich was elected as the first Republican Speaker of the House in forty-two years, and grateful Republican representatives voted Limbaugh "an honorary member of the freshman class" of representatives.

While acknowledging the importance of both the contract and conservative talk radio in the election outcome, religious conservatives made it clear that in their opinion, they themselves were the critical piece of the Republican victory. Ralph Reed specifically praised conservative talk radio for helping to turn out "white evangelical born-again Christians": Talk radio, Reed said, "has become the chief alternative means of communication to the establishment media for grassroots conservatives."[40] Nonetheless, Reed pointed to the fact that 70 percent of born-again Christians voted Republican, and that they were the deciding factor in twenty-five Republican House victories as well as a number of state races (including the victory of John Ashcroft in the Missouri Senate race).[41]

"Other than my wedding night," Reed gloated following the election, "this is as good as it gets."[42]

As it turned out, however, Reed suffered from a case of premature exultation, as the religious conservative movement was left standing at the altar once again. The promised legislation to introduce a school prayer amendment did not materialize in the first hundred days, or in the hundred days that followed. Just weeks after the election, the nation's thirty GOP governors raised concerns with Gingrich that an effort to pass a school prayer amendment would distract

Congress from passing necessary economic reforms. Michigan governor John Engler summed things up concisely by saying, "If we don't deal with the economic issues, we'll need more than prayer to solve our problems."[43] By April 1995, Gingrich was publicly musing on the Sunday talk shows that perhaps an amendment was not necessary to protect children who pray in school. He also repeated his long-standing opposition to organized prayer by school officials.[44]

After growing increasingly impatient for some action from the Republican majority on school prayer and other key social issues, Reed and the Christian Coalition attempted to put some additional pressure on Congress in May 1995 by announcing a "Contract with the American Family," in which they listed their top ten legislative priorities, including a constitutional amendment for "religious equality" (but not, interestingly, a school prayer amendment), limitations on the right to abortion, implementation of school vouchers, restrictions on pornography on cable television and the Internet, and abolishment of both the federal Department of Education and the National Endowment for the Arts.[45]

Although the Contract with the American Family attracted a fair amount of media attention, it made even less headway in Congress than the more economically oriented original. Two years later, when the 1996 presidential election rolled around, Gingrich could point to only two items on the Contract with America that had made it into law: a ban on unfunded federal mandates and a requirement that Congress adhere to the requirements of federal employment laws. Neither was likely to get religious conservatives out of bed on election day.

PUBLIC DIS-COARSE: THE TRASHING OF AMERICA'S AIRWAVES

Along with so much else in the media, the standards regarding personal invective have changed over the years. In March 1974, the Federal Communications Commission announced that its Broadcast Bureau had proposed a $1,000 fine against a New York radio station, WMCA. The offense? In a show broadcast a year earlier, acerbic talk radio host Bob Grant described Rep. Benjamin S. Rosenthal (D-NY) as a "coward" for refusing Grant's invitation to appear on his show to debate the merits of an ongoing national meat boycott. The FCC later dropped the fine but ruled that under the Fairness Doctrine, Straus Communications, Inc., the owner of WMCA, should have notified Representative Rosenthal of Grant's comment and offered him an opportunity to respond on air.

That was essentially the last time that the FCC tried to fine a station for the content of a host's personal attack on someone. Two years later, the US Court of Appeals in Washington, DC, overturned the commission's decision.

The initial determination of whether a personal attack requires a response, the Court said, is up to the broadcaster, not the FCC. The commission should judge the "objective reasonableness" of the station's decision and not substitute "its own judgment."[46] The appeals court decision became one more contributing factor to the eventual growth of attack radio.

In the winter of 1994, with the Republicans firmly in control of both houses of Congress, conservative and religious talk show hosts were suddenly deprived of one of their favorite targets, a Democratic Congress. Conservative feet could still be held to the fire, of course, and ritual potshots could still be taken at well-dented targets like Senator Ted Kennedy (D-MA), but conservative talk show hosts trained their fire farther down Pennsylvania Avenue: at Bill and Hillary Clinton and the people who supported them. Now giddy with the perceived power of kingmakers and basking in the benevolent eye of Newt, some conservative talk show hosts began pouring out the venom that had long bubbled just beneath the surface of their shows. In Virginia, newly hired talk show host Oliver North (best known for his role in the illegal sale of arms during the Iran-Contra affair) joked about "a job opening at the White House" following the suicide death of presidential aide Vince Foster (1945–1993).[47] In San Francisco, the self-described "Compassionate Conservative" Mike Savage labeled local gay-rights leaders "gay and lesbian Nazis, I don't know what else to call them, they're trying to steal our freedom."[48] Various hosts referred to Clinton as the "Coward in Chief," and Limbaugh derisively called the Clinton's adolescent daughter, Chelsea, "the White House dog." Bob Grant, still on the air after all these many years, often announced some variation of the theme, "I'd like to get every environmentalist up against a wall and shoot 'em."[49]

Remarkably, despite their long-standing concerns about decency in the media and in society in general, very few of the nation's religious and social conservative leaders stepped forward to call for a reduction in the harshness of talk radio. Much of that reticence undoubtedly had to do with the fact that the religious conservative wing of the party hoped to benefit politically from the efforts of conservative talk show hosts. But the other main reason that religious conservative leaders did not condemn the language and vitriol of conservative talk radio is that many of them were indulging in it as well. Randall Terry, founder of the militant antiabortion group Operation Rescue and also a nationally syndicated radio host, announced in an interview that "Bill Clinton is a tyrant; he's a monster. The Bible commands us to expose the wicked." Pat Robertson described the inauguration of Clinton in 1992 as a "repudiation of our forefathers' covenant with God."[50]

But perhaps the most virulent of the religious broadcasters was none other than the Reverend Jerry Falwell, who in May 1994 spent hours on his television show offering an anti-Clinton videotape, *Bill and Hillary Clinton's Circle of Power*, in exchange for "donations" of $40 plus $3 shipping and handling. (The sale of *Circle of Power* coincided with a $500,000 fundraising campaign by Falwell on behalf of his cash-strapped Liberty University.)[51] The tape, produced by a California-based conservative group called Citizens for Honest Government, accused Clinton of a wide range of crimes, including sexual harassment, drug smuggling, intimidation of political opponents by physical force, and even murder: "Hello. My name's Larry Nichols. Some of you have read about me or seen me on TV. People are dead in Arkansas. There are people in —— that are dead, yeah. When I started this, I knew that I might be one of the unsolved mysteries in Arkansas. There were boys on a railroad track. There were countless and countless people that mysteriously died that, as it turned out, had some connection to Bill Clinton. I believe this is going on today."[52]

Thanks to Falwell's hawking, *Circle of Power* reportedly received enough "donations" to ship one hundred thousand copies, which led to the production of a sequel, *The Clinton Chronicles*, that explored the charges in greater depth.[53] That summer, *Time* magazine reported that Rep. Phil Crane (Reagan's chief conservative competitor in 1980) distributed copies of the *Chronicles* tape to fellow Republicans in Congress, along with a cover letter praising the videotape.[54]

Clinton tried to stay above the fray, but by the summer of 1994 his patience was clearly wearing thin. While flying to St. Louis at the end of June, Clinton called the nonpartisan KMOX talk show *Morning Meeting* from Air Force One and used the opportunity to criticize conservative broadcasters in general and Limbaugh and Falwell in particular. "[I]f you look at how much of talk radio is just a constant, unremitting drumbeat of negativism and cynicism," the president said, "you can't—I don't think the American people are cynical, but you can't blame them for responding that way." In a speech later that evening, the president added that talk radio "may be fun to listen to, but it's tough to live by."[55]

Conservative talk shows hosts were gleeful that they had managed to irritate their nemesis, and collectively told him to stop whining about his treatment on the air. Limbaugh's response that afternoon was typical: "Aw. [sound of people laughing and groaning in mock sympathy] Isn't that just too bad?"[56] And in response to the president's complaint that there is no truth detector for Limbaugh's show, Limbaugh simply laughed and said, "[t]here is no need for a truth detector. I AM the truth detector!"[57]

But by the spring of 1995, in the midst of the gleeful gibe-talking, some of the comments on conservative talk radio began to give people pause. Mike Savage's fellow host on KSFO-AM, J. Paul Emerson, for example, was fired in February 1995 after calling for AIDS patients to be quarantined and for

Television host Faye Emerson, seen photographed in one of her signature V-neck dresses, ca. 1950. *(Courtesy of Wisconsin Center for Film and Theater Research)*

Michael Powell, who was appointed to the Federal Communications Commission in November 1997 and served as its chairman from January 2001 until his resignation in March 2005. *(Courtesy of the Federal Communications Commission)*

Kevin Martin, who was appointed to the Federal Communications Commission in 2001 and appointed chairman in March 2005 by President George W. Bush. *(Courtesy of the Federal Communications Commission)*

Justin Timberlake holds the awards he won for best male pop vocal performance "Cry Me a River" and best pop vocal album *Justified* at the 46th Annual Grammy Awards, Sunday, February 8, 2004, in Los Angeles. *(AP Photo/Mark J. Terrill)*

Singer Beyonce Knowles performs during halftime of the NBA All-Star game, Sunday, February 15, 2004, in Los Angeles, and nearly suffers her own "wardrobe malfunction." *(AP Photo/Mark J. Terrill)*

Undated photo of author Upton Sinclair, whose book *The Jungle* was removed from library shelves in Chicago and St. Louis due to its criticism of the meat-packing industry. *(Library of Congress/ George Grantham Bain Collection)*

United States General Smedley Butler, ca. 1910. General Butler had the dubious honor of being one of the first individuals to have his live, on-air comments censored by a radio network during a broadcast of WELK in Philadelphia in 1931. *(Library of Congress/George Grantham Bain Collection)*

Will Hays, ca. 1921, former postmaster general of the United States, who served as the first president of the Motion Picture Association of America from 1922 to 1945. *(Library of Congress)*

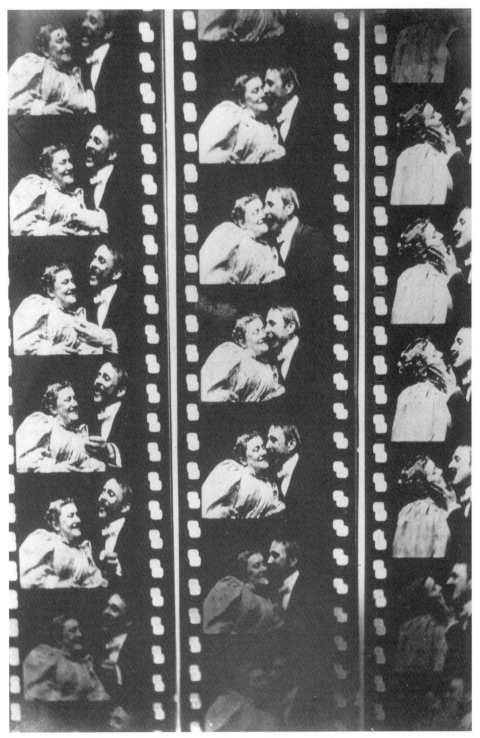

Frames from the Thomas Alva Edison movie *The Kiss* (1894), one of the earliest motion pictures and perhaps the first to stir concerns about the morality of the new medium. *(Courtesy of the US National Park Service)*

Singer Anita Bryant and her then husband Bob Green are shown at a news conference in Miami Beach, Florida, on June 7, 1977. Bryant's group Save Our Children, an organization opposed to gay rights, won the election held in Miami to repeal an antidiscrimination ordinance in Dade County. *(AP Photo)*

The Reverend Jerry Falwell, of the Moral Majority, appears on the set of NBC-TV's *Tomorrow* show, hosted by Tom Snyder, February 5, 1981. *(AP Photo/Suzanne Vlamis)*

US Attorney and Pornography Commission chairman Henry Hudson, *right*, presents a two-thousand-page report to Attorney General Edwin Meese, July 10, 1986, during a news conference in Washington. The conference was held in the Great Hall of the Justice Department; behind the men is the statue known as the *Spirit of Justice*. *(AP Photo/Charles Tasnadi)*

Terry Rakolta, listening to testimony at a US Senate hearing in 1993 on legislation calling for a renewal of the family viewing hour and a reduction of broadcast violence. *(Courtesy of Broadcasting & Cable)*

Raising new concerns in the decency wars: mobile pornography. In the foreground, three late-model cell phones capable of displaying images and video; in the background, the new Apple video iPod, a mobile device specifically designed to store and display movies. *(Used by permission of AVN Online)*

Although the efforts of the Meese Commission reduced the sales of adult magazines, it did not succeed in eliminating them. Twenty years later, they can be found in greater variety and in more mainstream outlets than ever before. The most serious threat adult magazines face is not government censorship but competition from the Internet. *(Copyright © Jordan S. Douglas 2005)*

Outgoing Christian Coalition president Ralph Reed, *left*, talks with television evangelist Pat Robertson during a dinner in Reed's honor in Atlanta, Friday, September 12, 1997. Reed had recently announced that he was resigning from the Christian Coalition after nine years as its president to form a political consulting firm. *(AP Photo/John Bazemore)*

With the *Spirit of Justice* statue behind him, Attorney General John Ashcroft addresses employees on November 8, 2001, in the Great Hall of the Justice Department in Washington. *(AP Photo/Kamenko Pajic)*

Attorney General John Ashcroft, speaking in the Great Hall of the Justice Department in Washington on February 20, 2002. Behind the $8,000 drape are two statues, the female *Spirit of Justice* and the male *Majesty of Law*. *(AP Photo/Joe Marquette)*

A photograph of a fossil of *Olenellus thompsoni*, a trilobite common in the Lower Cambrian period, roughly 550 million years ago. The fossil was found in York, Pennsylvania, approximately eight miles from Dover, the site of the 2005 trial over the mandatory teaching of "intelligent design." *(Copyright © Jordan S. Douglas 2005)*

Participants in a Vermont civil union share a kiss over a piece of cake. *(Karen Pike, © Karen Pike Photography, 2005)*

describing gays as "sick" and "pathetic."[58] Even more people questioned the role of conservative talk radio following April 19, 1995, after Timothy McVeigh detonated a truckful of explosives outside the Alfred P. Murrah building in Oklahoma City, killing 168 people (most of them federal employees). Many in the nation were horrified when syndicated host (and convicted Watergate burglar) G. Gordon Liddy, just five days after the bombing, advised a caller on how best to resist raids by "jack-booted" federal agents: "They've got a big target on there: ATF [Bureau of Alcohol, Tobacco, and Firearms]. Don't shoot at that because they've got a vest on underneath that. Head shot, head shots." The following day, Liddy told another caller that the head was too small a target, "so you shoot twice to the body, center of mass, and if that does not work, then shoot to the groin area." A number of stations pulled Liddy's show, and in a few markets, even Limbaugh's.[59] Despite the fact that Liddy was suggesting a violation of one of the better-known Commandments, there was still no widespread condemnation from religious conservative leaders.

At a speech in Des Moines, Iowa, a few days later, a tired and husky-voiced President Clinton inveighed once again against the harshness of talk radio:

> We hear so many loud and angry voices in America today whose sole goal seems to be to try to keep some people as paranoid as possible and the rest of us all torn up and upset with each other. They spread hate. They leave the impression that, by their very words, that violence is acceptable. . . . I'm sure you are now seeing the reports of some things that are regularly said over the airwaves in America today. Well, people like that who want to share our freedoms must know that their bitter words have consequences, and that freedom has endured for more than two centuries because it was coupled with an enormous sense of responsibility.[60]

The Scaife–Goat Chronicles

Unfortunately, President Clinton's moral credibility to criticize the excesses of conservative talk radio, never terrific to begin with, was about to utterly vanish. The damage was in no small part self-inflicted, thanks to his own overly generous contribution to American cynicism about politics in general and politicians in particular. Wholly apart from his actual conduct, both before and during his presidency, his later finger-wagging statement to the White House press corps on January 26, 1998, that "I did not have sexual relations with that woman, Miss Lewinsky," was definitely a low point in presidential press conferences.[61] At the same time, however, it is clear that various social and religious organizations, think tanks, talk show hosts, televangelists, and law firms did in fact coalesce into what Hillary Clinton so memorably described the following morning as a "vast right-wing conspiracy that has been conspiring against my husband since the day he announced for president."[62]

The opening salvo had actually occurred four years earlier in January 1994, when David Brock wrote an article for the conservative magazine *American Spectator* alleging that Clinton had used Arkansas state troopers to arrange sexual liaisons with various women, including "a woman named Paula."[63] The so-called Troopergate article was one of the first elements of a campaign by the *Spectator* known as the "Arkansas Project." According to various estimates, philanthropist Richard Scaife donated over $2 million to the magazine to support a lengthy and ultimately futile investigation of the Clintons in the hopes of turning up evidence of various misdeeds.[64] Nonetheless, thanks to Brock's passing reference to Paula Jones, Scaife got much of what he wanted: a long-simmering scandal that nearly stripped Clinton of the presidency.

From the start, both religious and social conservatives played a central role in the promotion of Jones's lawsuit against the president. Her press conference announcing that she was the "Paula" referred to in Brock's article, for instance, was held several weeks later at the 1994 Conservative Political Action Conference in Washington, DC.[65] In May, after filing her lawsuit against the president in Little Rock, Arkansas, Jones was featured in the *Circle of Power* tape promoted by Jerry Falwell, and had guest appearances on Falwell's *Old Time Glory Hour* and Pat Robertson's *700 Club*.[66] Her first two attorneys, Gil Davis and Joe Cammarata, were recruited by Jerome Marcus, a Philadelphia attorney with extensive ties to the conservative legal community in Washington, including Federalist Society heavyweights like Ken Starr, Ted Olson, and Robert Bork.[67]

Clinton had his own stable of high-powered lawyers, led by the blustery Bob Bennett, who spent much of his time in the first three years of the lawsuit trying to get it delayed until Clinton left office. He succeeded in dragging matters past the 1996 election, when Clinton defeated Senator Bob Dole (R-KS), but in June 1997, the US Supreme Court ruled that a sitting president is not immune from civil lawsuits. With the prospect of a trial looming, settlement talks got serious, and by September the two sides had essentially reached an agreement in which Clinton would pay Jones $700,000 and offer a statement somewhat short of an apology but expressing regret for the damage done to Jones's reputation. According to a report by *U.S. News & World Report*, Davis and Cammarata were in the hole for $800,000 in legal fees, and they recommended to Jones that she accept the settlement.[68]

Enter one of the chief beneficiaries of the Jones case: Ann Coulter, an attorney for conservative nonprofit public interest law firm Center for Individual Rights and a commentator for MSNBC.[69] At the suggestion of a friend,

George Conway, Coulter became one of the so-called elves who provided behind-the-scenes legal assistance to Davis and Cammarata as the case was winding its way up to the Supreme Court. Conway was an active member of the Federalist Society (as was Coulter), and when the time came for the Supreme Court argument, he arranged a coaching session for the two attorneys with Ted Olson and Robert Bork.[70]

Along with Susan Carpenter-McMillan, a conservative Los Angeles columnist and rabid Clinton foe, Coulter persuaded Jones to disregard the advice of her attorneys and reject the proposed settlement. In fact, *Newsweek* reporter Michael Isikoff, who wrote a widely read book about the case, *Uncovering Clinton*, identified Coulter as the person who leaked the news that Jones could identify a "distinguishing characteristic" on the president's body as a result of his sexual advance, in an effort to sabotage the negotiations.[71] "We were terrified that Jones would settle," Coulter admitted to Isikoff. "It was contrary to our purpose of bringing down the President."[72] Frustrated by Jones's rejection of their recommendation to settle and the growing influence of both Coulter and Carpenter-McMillan, Davis and Cammarata requested permission to withdraw from the case, and were allowed to do so.[73]

With the departure of Davis and Cammarata, the role of religion and conservative partisanship in Jones's suit grew even stronger. In mid-September, Donovan Campbell Jr. traveled to Los Angeles to meet with Paula Jones at the suggestion of his friend John Whitehead, founder of the Rutherford Institute, an evangelical Christian answer to the ACLU. The Rutherford Institute frequently referred cases to Campbell, who worked for a devout Christian law firm in Texas called Rader, Campbell, Fisher & Pyke. Whitehead reportedly promised that the Rutherford Institute would cover Campbell's fees in representing Jones.[74] The involvement of the institute raised the specter of the *Clinton Chronicles* once again, which the institute had reviewed extensively in its June 1995 magazine. The institute's articles quoted Falwell in detail and described the charges raised by the videotape as "disturbing."

Whitehead later said in an interview that he expected that the Rutherford Institute would lose money on the Jones litigation, which he estimated would cost another $200,000 to take to trial. To help defray costs, Whitehead mailed out a million letters signed by Paula Jones, describing in elliptical terms what had happened to her and asking for donations. "Although you shouldn't have to suffer the lurid details," she wrote, "you should know that Governor Clinton made unwanted sexual advances toward me."[75] Whitehead later conceded, according to the *Washington Times*, that even if Jones's appeal didn't immediately raise enough money for Rutherford (the final tab was over $300,000), it would brighten the fund-raising prospects of the institute down the road.[76]

In fact, during its four-year run, the Jones case became something of a cottage industry for many of the people involved. In 1994 Jones hired Cindy Hays to set up a legal defense fund; in July 1997 Carpenter-McMillan took over as chairman of the fund, while Hays remained as director.[77] Between 1994 and 1997 the proceeds of the fund helped defray some of Davis and Cammarata's costs. After the lawyers were excused from the case, the Rutherford Institute began raising funds for Jones's legal bills, while Jones signed a contract to have Bruce W. Eberle & Associates, Inc., a McLean, Virginia, fund-raising outfit with numerous conservative clients, handle fund-raising for her Legal Defense Fund. Under the terms of the contract, Jones was paid $100,000 from the proceeds of the fund-raising, with another $200,000 guaranteed. Eberle earned 8 cents for each solicitation processed, as well as various fees from various services provided by companies affiliated with Eberle & Associates. Although Jones assured contributors that donations were being used to pay her legal expenses, the Rutherford Institute's Whitehead said that they had not received any money, and he threatened to file a fraud complaint with the Internal Revenue Service.[78]

Things rapidly got worse for Jones. On April 1, 1998, US District Court judge Susan Webber Wright dismissed Jones's lawsuit, saying that she had failed to make even the most basic show of sexual harassment. To avoid an appeal, President Clinton paid a settlement of $850,000, the bulk of which was divided among Davis and Cammarata; Rader, Campbell, Fisher & Pyke; and the Rutherford Institute. Jones reportedly received just $200,000 from the settlement.[79]

THE END OF PUBLIC DECENCY BUT THE RETURN OF PRIVACY?

The impact of the Jones litigation on the general sense of decency in America was bad enough. Ann Coulter's leak of the president's supposed "distinguishing characteristic" forced Bob Bennett to defend the president's physical normality on *Face the Nation*: "This is awful to even have to discuss this—but the plaintiff has forced this on us—in terms of size, shape, direction, whatever the devious mind wants to concoct, the President is a normal man."

"Maybe I simply feel sorry for us," *New York Times* columnist Maureen Dowd wrote, "not only for the lost dignity of the Presidency but for the lost dignity of the citizenry. The President of the United States should not be publicly strip-searched."[80]

Far worse, however, was about to come. When Rader, Campbell, Fisher & Pyke took over Jones's case, they began an aggressive campaign to find other women who would make similar claims against the president in an effort to show that Jones's alleged harassment was part of a pattern or practice of behavior. They received help from across the conservative spectrum: The Free Congress Foundation (FCF), for one, released a radio advertisement in the fall of 1997 that asked conservative talk show audiences, "Have you been sexually harassed by the President of the United States?" The FCF—which was founded by Paul Weyrich and is one of the many conservative groups funded in part by Richard Scaife—set up a hotline to take complaints, which the FCF said it would investigate. No "authenticated" claims turned up in the hotline's first week, according to FCF media director Bradley Keena.[81]

But the exhaustive exhumation of the president's past did turn up results. Before leaving Jones's case, Cammarata issued a subpoena to a woman named Kathleen Willey, whom Cammarata believed would testify that she had been groped by the president during a visit to the White House. Willey denied the allegation. However, during his own investigation of the Clinton case, *Newsweek* reporter Michael Isikoff interviewed a woman named Linda Tripp, who at the time of Willey's visit with Clinton was serving as an executive assistant in the White House Counsel's office. Tripp told Isikoff that she saw Willey leave the Oval Office disheveled but "flustered, happy, and joyful." Tripp's ostensible purpose was to reject any suggestion that Willey was harassed, but, of course, her account lent credibility to claims that the president lacked the ability to control his libido.[82]

There is little question that Bob Bennett is a superb lawyer, but in the days following the revelation of Willey's identity, he made one devastating mistake: "I smell a rat," he flatly declared. "Linda Tripp is not to be believed."[83] Unbeknownst to Bennett or anyone else, Tripp had recently befriended a young White House intern named Monica Lewinsky while the two were sharing bureaucratic exile at the Pentagon. During the course of their many chats, Lewinsky had revealed to Tripp that she had been involved in an intimate relationship with the president. Angered by Bennett's impugning of her credibility, and with the encouragement of conservative literary agent Lucianne Goldberg, Tripp began secretly taping her phone conversations with Lewinsky.[84]

In October 1997 the Rutherford Institute received an anonymous call advising Jones's lawyers to investigate a woman named "Monica." It didn't take them long to do so, and in December 1997 subpoenas were issued for both Lewinsky and Tripp. On January 16, 1998, the night before a scheduled deposition of President Clinton in the Jones case, Tripp met with Jones's lawyers, who used the information they obtained from her to rigorously grill a surprised Clinton the following morning on specific details of his relationship with Lewinsky.[85]

Clinton's answers in his deposition, when weighed against the information contained on Tripp's tapes, left an impression of something other than complete honesty. Ken Starr, who for the last three years had been trying to determine if the Clintons had acted improperly in connection with a land development in Arkansas known as Whitewater, received permission to expand his inquiry into whether Clinton had lied in the Jones litigation and tried to obstruct justice.

As the sordid details of the relationship between Clinton and Lewinsky made their way into the media—the oral sex, the use of cigars as sex toys, the infamous semen-stained Gap dress—the general state of decency in American society took another serious hit. The political implications of the Lewinsky scandal, of course, were not lost on conservative operatives. Ralph Reed, who had left the Christian Coalition to become a political consultant, unctuously observed that "[y]ou never want to benefit from something like this," but added that the Clinton-Lewinsky scandal would "mobilize our base and turn swing voters off."[86]

To the utter bewilderment of many religious conservatives, however, it didn't quite work out that way. The reports of what took place between Clinton and Lewinsky were dismaying, of course; they revealed deep-seated strains of recklessness and self-indulgence in the president. But the ferocity with which the president's political enemies pursued him, and their willingness to wallow in the most unexpurgated details, deeply offended much of the country's basic sense of fairness and, yes, decency. (And, of course, it didn't hurt that by most measures—a shrinking deficit, low energy prices, inflation under control, a healthy stock market—Clinton's administration was doing fairly well.)

Much of the damage was done by the Right's favorite attack dog, AM talk radio. G. Gordon Liddy started referring to the White House's "Oral Office" and mused about getting his hands on the president's little black book.[87] Washington DJ Billy Bush (a first cousin of President George W. Bush) launched a series of Lewinsky-oriented stunts on his radio show *Billy Bush and the Bush League Morning Show*, one of which involved throwing a life-sized cutout of Lewinsky in front of a vehicle carrying her mother.[88] Station KIIS in Los Angeles held a Lewinsky look-alike contest in which some of the contestants wore kneepads. In New York, WAXQ host Darien O'Toole used language to discuss the incident that the *Washington Post* couldn't (or wouldn't) reproduce: "That skank who was [expletiving] the president. . . . Hillary is gay or frigid. . . . Is the Secret Service going to tell because the president is getting [expletived] by an intern?"[89] Admittedly, the intersection of salaciousness and politics made the regulation of on-air content more difficult, but, still, it is remarkable that the FCC was so notably quiet that summer.

The dissonance between conservative calls for greater decency and their actions culminated on September 9, 1998, when Ken Starr submitted a report to the House of Representatives in which he alleged that on various occasions President Clinton had lied under oath about the nature of his relationship with Monica Lewinsky. In the tradition established by the Meese Commission Report, the document produced by Starr and his staff was remarkable for its salaciousness and graphic nature.

Unquestionably, Americans were disgusted by what took place in the Oval Office, but many were even more disgusted by the lengths to which Starr and other conservatives were willing to go to bring Clinton down. An informal coalition of religious and social conservatives set out to convince Americans that private conduct is a basis for public censure, but, in the end, ironically, they were far more successful in demonstrating to Americans just how tenuous the concept of personal privacy really is.

Senator Patrick Leahy (D-VT) gestures during an address against the recently enacted Communications Decency Act, Thursday, February 15, 1996, at the National Press Club in Washington, DC. (AP photo/ Ron Edmonds)

Chapter Eight

Now Is the Year of Our Dissed Content

Why the
FCC Reenlisted in
the War on Indecency

> The law tells us that we shall have no right of censorship over radio programs, but the physical facts of radio transmission compel what is, in effect, a censorship of the most extraordinary kind.
> —Federal Radio commissioner Henry Bellows, in an address to the League of Women Voters on April 29, 1927

To one degree or another, every communication medium has triggered concerns about changing standards of decency. But it is safe to say that no medium has raised the hackles of religious conservatives and social censors quite so effectively and thoroughly as the Internet. In a remarkably short time, the Internet has not only become a major distribution channel of sexually explicit images, but by its very prominence and pervasiveness it has altered the American cultural landscape. Thanks to the Internet, the challenge of not only enforcing "decency" but even defining it is far more difficult than it was a mere decade ago.

The precise origin of the relationship between the Internet and sexually explicit materials is probably untraceable, but the groundwork was laid in 1979, not long after Chicago programmers Ward Christiansen and Randy Seuss set up the first computer bulletin board system. At Duke University, two graduate students—Tom Truscott and Jim Ellis—developed a software program for exchanging announcements with the nearby University of North Carolina. The system, called "Usenet," was quickly adopted by a variety of other educational institutions and became a popular tool for posting messages on a wide range of subjects, all organized into hierarchical categories by topic, or "newsgroups." It's not surprising that sex proved to be a popular topic; what is mildly surprising is that sex did not get its own newsgroup until April 3, 1988, when an alt.sex topic was created by Digital Equipment Corporation employee Brian Reid.[1] By 1995 Reid estimated that his alt.sex newsgroup was the second most popular Usenet topic (with six hundred thousand readers), and that three other sexually oriented newsgroups (alt.sex.stories, alt.binaries.pictures .erotica, and rec.arts.erotica) made the top ten list as well.[2]

The willingness of perfect strangers to exchange sexy messages and erotic stories was remarkable enough, but the real seeds of cultural change lay in the popularity of the alt.binaries newsgroups. In the jargon of newsgroups, a "binary" refers to a nontext file, typically either a software program or an image file. The Usenet was not originally designed to handle the distribution of non-text files, but programmers figured out how to convert binary files into plain text, which could then be sent out as normal Usenet messages. Once people realized that they could use newsgroups to exchange scanned images (albeit awkwardly), the era of rapid global distribution of pornography truly began.

The popularity of the binary newsgroups is all the more amazing given just how much work it took to successfully download and view even a single Usenet image. Before an image could be posted to a newsgroup, it typically had to be broken into several segments to meet Usenet limitations on message size. Each segment had to be successfully downloaded and the collection unencoded before the image could be viewed.

Despite the technical hurdles, however, newsgroups like alt.binaries .pictures.erotica were rapidly filled with what one anonymous wag described as "gigabytes of copyright violations" (since most of the images initially posted to the newsgroup were scanned out of adult magazines). From the start, concerns were raised about both the explicitness of the images available online and the easy anonymity of image posting. The *New Republic* reported that one contributor of pornographic images to a Usenet newsgroup was "George W. Bush." "No one suspects the governor [of Texas] of being a pornographer," the magazine said, "but no one can determine the true identity of the person using his name by reading this guy's messages, either."[3]

If the Usenet had remained the main method of distributing pornography across the Internet, the battle over online decency would have been far more muted. But in late 1993, the National Center for Supercomputing Applications released Mosaic, a groundbreaking new program for accessing information on the Internet. Mosaic was the first widely used program to put a graphical interface on the World Wide Web, a part of the Internet that shares information through hyperlinks. Mosaic's combination of multimedia presentation and ease of use helped transform the Internet (and, more specifically, the World Wide Web) from the dusty playground of academics and scientists to a full-fledged cultural phenomenon. In the first year alone following the release of Mosaic, the number of Web sites increased from 623 to 10,022; a year after that, there were 100,000; less than a decade later, in August 2005, researchers estimated that there were more than 70 million Web sites.[4]

Among Mosaic's many other accomplishments, it eliminated most of the technical challenges to accessing sexually explicit images by computer. Computer users no longer had to do anything more complicated than click on a Web page link to view or download sexually explicit images. Moreover, the combination of Web software and the Internet Domain Name System allowed pornographers to create permanent electronic "storefronts," to which consumers could easily and reliably return. Even more significantly, consumers could now explore a wide range of sexually explicit materials without the risk of embarrassment at the local video rental store, or without even so much as a brown paper envelope arriving in the mail.

The combination of easier access and greater privacy was obviously compelling to a large number of people from the very start. By August 1996, online pornography was rated as the third-highest moneymaker on the Web (behind computer products and travel), with an estimated $51.5 million in revenues.[5] Just four months later, the *Boston Globe* estimated that the online adult industry's revenues were closer to $100 million.[6]

From the creation of alt.sex in 1988 to the release of Mosaic in the fall of 1993, the spread of pornography largely went unnoticed by the media and general public. But in the months that followed, the issue of "cyberporn" exploded onto the national consciousness with nearly the same rapidity as awareness of the Web itself.

THE COMMUNICATIONS DECENCY ACT: THE BATTLE OVER DOT-COM DECENCY

The first great decency battle over the Internet stemmed from research done by Martin Rimm, a Carnegie Mellon University (CMU) graduate student. While conducting a study of pornography on the Internet in 1994, Rimm compiled statistics on how often specific sexually explicit images were downloaded. He believed that this would provide a measure of the popularity of different sexual practices. During the course of his research, he told the CMU administration that many of the images being distributed across the school's network were arguably obscene under state law (examples included child pornography and bestiality). After looking into Rimm's claim, the administration agreed, and the school's academic council voted to shut down all of the alt.sex newsgroups. After outraged protests from students, faculty, the American Civil Liberties Union, and the newly formed Electronic Frontier Foundation, CMU backed down and restored access to all of the newsgroups.[7]

The coverage of the CMU controversy apparently caught the attention of Senator Jim Exon (D-NE), who introduced a bill on January 30, 1995, to make it a felony to knowingly use a telecommunications device to make, create, solicit, or initiate "any comment, request, suggestion, proposal, image, or other communication which is obscene, lewd, lascivious, filthy, or indecent" to someone under the age of eighteen. With this bill, known as the Communications Decency Act (CDA), Exon proposed to do for online pornography what the US Supreme Court had already said Jesse Helms could not do for phone sex: make the electronic transmission of mere indecency a crime.

"I'm not trying to be a super-censor," Exon said. "The first thing I was concerned with was kids being able to pull up pornography on their machines."[8]

In the summer of 1995, the US Senate was working on a massive telecommunications reform package that *Broadcasting & Cable* magazine later said "relaxes ownership rules for the broadcasting industry, provides rate deregulation for cable, and lays the groundwork for an end to the local telephone monopoly." Following successful negotiations between the House and Senate over various provisions, Rep. Thomas Bliley (R-VA), chairman of the House Commerce Committee, described the Telecommunications Act as "the first major over-haul of the telecommunications law since Marconi was alive and the crystal set was state of the art."[9]

On June 14, 1995, Senator Patrick Leahy (D-VT) proposed an amendment to the Telecommunications Act that would have instructed the Justice Department to study the application of existing laws, including prohibitions on obscenity, to the Internet. The Senate rejected Leahy's proposal, however, and instead overwhelmingly voted to adopt the measure proposed by Exon and cosponsor Dan Coats (R-IN). During the course of the debate, Senator Exon (like Helms before him) invoked the spirit of Anthony Comstock. On the floor of the Senate, he waved a big blue binder with the word "Caution" stamped on it and urged his colleagues to "[t]ake a look at this disgusting material, pictures which were copied for free off the Internet only this week."[10] He invited his colleagues to stop by his desk to take a look at the "disgusting, repulsive pornography [which] is only a few clicks away from any child with a computer."[11] Supporters of the Exon Amendment also considered adding a provi-

sion to the bill that would have imposed prison terms for cable system operators who transmitted indecent material, but the idea was dropped before the
final vote was taken.[12]

Despite widespread opposition from civil libertarians, free speech activists,
and the Internet community, relatively few senators were willing to oppose the
Exon bill. The leading voice in opposition was Senator Leahy, who pointed out
that among all the senators debating the issue, only six had actually used the
Internet (Exon himself needed the help of a computer-savvy friend to put
together his "Blue Book" of cybersmut).[13] Leahy also introduced a stack of
petitions containing thirty thousand signatures opposing the Exon bill, most of
them signed online by the Internet community. One of the few conservatives
to join Leahy was Senator Orrin Hatch (R-UT), who said that "[i]t's kind of a
game, to see who can be the most against pornography and obscenity. It's a
political exercise, and I'm against it."[14]

When the measure reached the House of Representatives, it was tabled by
Speaker Newt Gingrich, who declared that it was "a violation of free speech
and . . . a violation of the right of adults to communicate with each other."[15]
(*New York Times* columnist Frank Rich even went so far as to call Gingrich "my
new hero" for standing up to a bill that "isn't just cybersilly but plain old-fash-
ioned idiotic.")[16] There appeared to be relatively little enthusiasm in the
House for wading into the murky waters of obscenity law, particularly as it
might apply to a new and still little-understood technology. On June 30, 1995,
Reps. Christopher Cox (R-CA) and Ron Wyden (D-OR), for instance, introduced the Internet Freedom and Family Empowerment Act, which called for
self-regulation on the part of the online adult industry and for the development
of easy-to-use screening software for family computers.[17] The House, however,
never acted on the proposal.

Given Gingrich's open opposition to the Communications Decency Act, it
might have quietly faded away amid the somewhat chaotic debate over the
intricacies of the massive telecommunications bill. But in late June 1995,
advance copies of Martin Rimm's graduate study were leaked to the press. On
July 3, 1995, Philip Elmer-DeWitt wrote a cover story for *Time* magazine titled
"On a Screen Near You—Cyberporn." The image on the cover featured a
google-eyed child staring in shock at a computer screen, his face a sickly green
color. Overnight, the entire dynamic of the Internet pornography debate was
irrevocably changed.

Elmer-DeWitt's article summarized the ongoing battle in Congress over
the CDA and offered readers exclusive excerpts from Rimm's as-yet-unpub-
lished study of Internet pornography. Among Rimm's findings were the following shocking items:

- out of 917,410 items stored in Usenet newsgroups, 83.5 percent were pornographic
- thirteen out of the forty most popular newsgroups at one university specialized in sexually explicit materials
- 71 percent of all Usenet images originated from adult BBS [bulletin board system] services, which make money charging users for access to their materials
- the adult BBS industry was fueled by a demand for deviant images[18]

It was a gripping story, filled with compelling statistics about the impact of the Internet on American sexual mores and, most disturbingly, the threat to children. But unfortunately, much of it was completely wrong. Soon after Elmer-DeWitt's story was published, the Rimm study was thoroughly discredited by more experienced researchers. Critics pointed out that Rimm had selected a nonrepresentative collection of newsgroups (ignoring the hundreds, if not thousands, dealing with nonpornographic subjects); had failed to distinguish between material available on the Internet and material accessible only through password-protected BBSs; and had not established any clear definition for determining what was pornography and what was not. In an analysis conducted a few weeks after the *Time* article, Vanderbilt University professors Donna Hoffman and Thomas Novak concluded that "[m]any of Rimm's statistics . . . are either misleading or meaningless."[19] Based on their research, they estimated that pornographic images made up less than half of 1 percent of the images available on the Web.

Elmer-DeWitt, who covered the ongoing controversy over his story, ruefully noted a short time later that "serious questions have been raised regarding the study's methodology, [including] the ethics by which its data were gathered."[20] In one online conversation, he conceded that he had been warned about possible flaws regarding the Rimm study but said that *Time* was under pressure to go with the story because other newsmagazines were planning similar pieces. Elmer-DeWitt concluded by admitting that "[t]here is nothing I wish I had more than another week to work on that story."[21]

Notwithstanding Elmer-DeWitt's understandable regret, the damage was done. Since the Rimm study apparently ratified every anecdotal story Congress had heard about the World Wide Web, senators and representatives leaped on the report and used it to push the Communications Decency Act to final passage. Senator Charles Grassley (R-IA), for instance, introduced Elmer-DeWitt's entire July 3 article into the *Congressional Record* and characterized Rimm's work as "a remarkable study conducted by researchers at Carnegie Mellon University."[22] There is no evidence, however, that Senator Grassley (or anyone else on Capitol Hill) took any pains to introduce Elmer-DeWitt's follow-up article or to amend the record to reflect the rapidly mounting evidence that the study was deeply flawed.

When the Telecommunications Act was in conference committee, the House accepted the Communications Decency Act as proposed by the Senate. The conference committee made a point of defending its prohibition of indecency on the Internet: "The gravamen of the indecency concept is 'patently offensive.' . . . It is the understanding of the conferees that, as applied, the patent offensiveness inquiry involves two distinct elements: the intention to be patently offensive, and a patently offensive result. . . . [U]se of the indecency standard poses no significant risk to the free-wheeling and vibrant nature of discourse or to serious, literary, and artistic works that currently can be found on the Internet, and which is expected to continue and grow."[23] Interestingly, the conference committee said that the specific intent of the Communications Decency Act was to apply to the Internet the indecency analysis developed by the Federal Communications Commission in its decisions against Pacifica Foundation (involving George Carlin's "Filthy Words" monologue) and Sable Communications of California (involving phone sex).[24] In *Pacifica*, the United States Supreme Court upheld the FCC's application of the indecency standard to a radio broadcast on the grounds that it is a "uniquely pervasive" medium.[25] In *Sable Communications*, however, the Court ruled that it was unconstitutional to restrict adult access to "indecent" phone conversations.[26] By ignoring this important distinction, the conference committee was effectively equating the Internet with broadcast technologies like radio and television rather than the more private technology of the telephone.

To the dismay of civil libertarians, President Clinton signed the Telecommunications Act on February 8, but the Communications Decency Act itself never took effect. The following day, a coalition of groups, led by the American Civil Liberties Union, filed suit to block its implementation. Four months later, a three-judge federal panel issued a preliminary injunction against the law, ruling unanimously that the CDA was an unconstitutional infringement on speech. "As the most participatory form of mass speech yet developed," Judge Stewart Dalzell wrote, "the Internet deserves the highest protection from governmental intrusion. True it is that many find speech on the Internet to be offensive, and amid the din of cyberspace many hear discordant voices that they regard as indecent. . . . Just as the strength of the Internet is chaos, so the strength of our liberty depends upon the chaos and cacophany [sic] of unfettered speech the First Amendment protects."[27]

The following summer, the CDA turned out to be just as constitutionally flawed as people had predicted. In June 1997, all nine members of the Supreme

Court agreed that while Congress had the authority to ban the transmission of obscenity across the Internet, the CDA simply went too far in trying to prohibit the distribution of indecency: "In evaluating the free speech rights of adults, we have made it perfectly clear that sexual expression which is indecent but not obscene is protected by the First Amendment. . . . It is true that we have repeatedly recognized the governmental interest in protecting children from harmful materials. But that interest does not justify an unnecessarily broad suppression of speech addressed to adults. As we have explained, Government may not reduce the adult population to only what is fit for children."[28]

HARMFUL TO MINORS: THE STARR REPORT

Although the Supreme Court's decision rejecting the indecency provisions of the CDA was unanimous, two members of the Court—Justices Sandra Day O'Connor and William Rehnquist—suggested that they would support a ban on indecent speech between adults and minors online. The remarks of the two partially dissenting justices gave a small flicker of hope to those in Congress committed to restricting indecency on the Internet. Within weeks of the Court's decision, Senator Dan Coats was at work on a new piece of legislation officially titled the Child Online Protection Act (COPA) but known more widely as "Son of CDA." Instead of trying to ban indecent speech outright, COPA contained language making it a crime for commercial Web site operators to allow children to have access to material deemed "harmful to minors." The law was modeled on a number of different state laws that use the "harmful to minors" standard to block the display of sexually explicit materials in bookstore windows, display racks, and so on. Joining Senator Coats in pushing the new legislation was Rep. Michael Oxley (R-OH), who flatly declared during the House floor debate that "[u]fortunately, the Web is awash in degrading smut."[29]

Given Oxley's comment, it is more than a little ironic that at the height of the debate over COPA, independent counsel Ken Starr submitted to the House of Representatives his report, detailing the relationship between President Clinton and Monica Lewinsky.[30] Thanks to eight months and $10 million worth of prerelease publicity,[31] the Starr Report was a publishing sensation. Within ten days of the report's release, more than a *million* copies were in print.[32] By contrast, when the Meese Commission released its final report, the federal government sold roughly five thousand copies of the two-volume report in four months, at $35 each. Columnist Michael McManus and Rutledge Hill Press, a small religious publishing house, managed to sell more than thirty thousand copies of their one-volume version of the Meese Report at $9.95, despite the fact that many religious bookstores refused to put the book on their shelves for fear of offending their customers.[33]

The much more intense interest in the Starr Report can be explained in part by its possible role in the removal of a president from office. Most people seemed to recognize that President Clinton's transgressions had relatively little to do with his performance (two weeks after the release of the Starr Report, polls showed that between 60 and 68 percent of the country approved of the job Clinton was doing).[34] But the other chief difference in the public reception of the two government reports is that the Starr Report, for better or for worse, was released into a world starkly changed by the Internet. Beyond the million-plus volumes in print, the Starr Report reached a vast audience of online political junkies and voyeurs now able to spend much of their day following endless permutations of the breaking news.

Other events had helped to raise the profile of the Internet as a source of breaking news: the Mars *Pathfinder* mission in July 1997; the death of Diana, Princess of Wales, on August 31, 1997; and the Winter Olympics in Nagano, Japan, in February 1998. But *l'affaire Clinton* was the first major political controversy to occur in the era of the World Wide Web. Taken together, the Starr Report and the Clinton impeachment helped speed the Net's transition from its early days as a silicon-enhanced *Playboy* magazine to a popular source of breaking political news. The controversy also helped to illustrate both the phenomenal distributive capabilities of the Internet and the compelling nature of the Web's multimedia mix of information. The online service Yahoo! published the entire Starr Report on its Web site within five minutes of receiving the text from Congress. Interest in the independent counsel's report quadrupled the Web traffic at MSNBC's site, while the *Washington Post* reported that its online traffic had tripled.[35]

The fact that the Starr Report was released at around 3 PM on a workday underscored another issue: the distractive power of the Internet in the workplace. By one estimate, American businesses lost $450 million in employee productivity in the two weeks following the release of the Starr Report and the online posting of President Clinton's video deposition before a Washington grand jury. NetPartners Internet Solutions, the producers of Internet filtering software for businesses, estimated that twenty-five million copies of the report and two million copies of Clinton's video testimony were downloaded, with half of the downloads taking place at work. NetPartners also suggested that the real figure might be much higher when soft costs were added, including the impact of the downloads on network resources, employee requests for additional IT support to install software, and damage to workplace morale resulting from the explicit content of the downloads.[36]

As numerous legislators and free speech activists pointed out, many of the downloads of the Starr Report would have been illegal under COPA. "If CDA II [another name for COPA] had been the law this month," said Ronald Weich, a legislative consultant for the American Civil Liberties Union, "even news sites that published the Starr Report and that carry advertising or charge for access might have been subject to criminal prosecution."[37]

Chief among those concerned with COPA's fuzzy language were the very attorneys whose job it would be to enforce it. During Congress's consideration of COPA, the Justice Department raised several specific concerns about the bill's constitutionality. In a seven-page letter to Congress, for instance, Assistant Attorney General Anthony Sutin argued that the bill "contains numerous ambiguities concerning the scope of its coverage," and argued that those ambiguities "might complicate and hinder effective prosecution."[38] The Justice Department also was concerned that the pursuit of online smut would divert attention and resources from other more serious problems, including the fight against child pornography. Those warnings, however, were ignored.

To help promote the passage of COPA, congressional conservatives attached it to a massive spending bill negotiated between Democrats and Republicans in mid-October 1998. (This, of course, is a hoary technique for obtaining political cover on difficult issues.) Although many Democrats on the Hill recognized that COPA was probably as flawed as its predecessor—the Communications Decency Act—they were reluctant to push for its removal during conference committee negotiations. Doing so, they feared, would raise the risk of being portrayed as soft on pornography during the upcoming midterm elections. That was a particularly untenable position given the fact that the House of Representatives was actively weighing whether or not to impeach President Clinton.

The Clinton White House strongly opposed the inclusion of COPA in the spending bill, but the ability of the president to push for elimination of an antipornography measure was also severely hampered.[39] When it came to the subject of indecency, the White House didn't have a lot of political maneuvering room in 1998. President Clinton signed COPA into law on October 21, 1998. Much like the CDA, however, the law has been under litigation since its adoption and has never taken effect.

SLOUCHING TOWARD GEORGE W. BUSH

Not surprisingly, Republicans in general and religious conservatives in particular were looking forward to the 1998 midterm elections. The Democrats were saddled with a president who seemed to epitomize the type of moral decay religious conservatives had been warning of for years, and the GOP leadership was eager to cater to its increasingly impatient ideological base. In May 1988, House majority whip Tom DeLay promised religious conservatives that the Republican congressional leadership "unequivocally give[s] our commitment to work on a long-term basis to take these issues in hand now."[40]

At the Christian Coalition's Road to Victory conference in September 1998, Gary Bauer of the Family Research Council declared that the Clinton administration was a "cultural oil spill," while the Christian Coalition's Pat Robertson chided Clinton for turning the White House into "a sexual playpen." The most popular speech was given by US Senator John Ashcroft (R-MO), who declared that "[t]he sun is setting on the last child of the sixties, Bill Clinton. If there is ever a time to vote your values, it is now."[41]

The enthusiastic reception for Ashcroft underscored the fact that even before the midterm elections, he was the leading contender among religious conservatives for the Republican presidential nomination. Much of Ashcroft's popular standing and fund-raising success with the Christian Right had to do with the fact that throughout 1998, he gave speech after speech decrying the nation's moral decay, which he said began first and foremost with the White House. Ashcroft was one of the first senators to suggest that President Clinton should resign when his affair with Monica Lewinsky became public in early January 1998, telling an enthusiastic crowd at the twenty-fifth annual Conservative Political Action Conference that "[i]t is time for us to say, Mr. President, if these allegations are true, you have disgraced yourself, your office and the office of the presidency, and you should leave."[42] Throughout the remainder of the year, as he traveled around the country, Ashcroft repeated time and again that "[p]ersonal conduct and public life are not divisible." It was a popular line with his audiences.

A member of the large Pentecostal denomination known as the Assemblies of God, Ashcroft enjoyed strong popularity among religious conservatives that dated back to his early days in Missouri state politics. Their support helped him win five statewide races in Missouri (attorney general twice, governor twice, and US senator), and they particularly applauded his unabashed expressions of faith. Throughout his life, Ashcroft integrated his religious beliefs into his public service, most notably by holding voluntary prayer sessions each morning with his staff, both as a Missouri official and a US senator, and by anointing himself with oil prior to taking the state and federal oaths of office.[43] He is also well known for his composition and performance of Christian gospel songs,[44] as well as his participation in the Singing Senators quartet with Trent Lott (R-MS), Jim Jeffords (I-VT), and Larry Craig (R-ID). Not surprisingly, during

Ashcroft's first three years in the US Senate, the Christian Coalition gave him a 100 percent on their voting scorecards "on issues like abortion, education, budget and arts financing."[45]

With the active encouragement of religious conservative leaders like Pat Robertson and James C. Dobson, Ashcroft started exploring the possibility of a presidential run even before President Clinton's reelection in 1996. By September 1998, Robertson was describing Ashcroft as "his current favorite" candidate. He donated $10,000 to Ashcroft's Spirit of America political action committee (as did his daughter), and he actively encouraged other members of the Christian Coalition to contribute as well. He confidently declared to attendees at the Road to Victory conference that "I'm as sure as I'm alive that in the year 2000 we're going to see a born-again Christian sitting in the White House." There is no question that the Christian Coalition's founder believed that person would be John Ashcroft.[46]

To the shock and dismay of most religious conservatives, however, the 1998 midterm elections were something of a disaster for Republicans. Despite predictions that the Clinton scandal would produce a Republican tidal wave, Democrats picked up five seats in the House and did not lose any ground in the Senate. More important, two of President Clinton's fiercest critics were turned out of the Senate—New York's Al D'Amato lost to Charles Schumer and North Carolina's Lauch Faircloth lost to future vice presidential candidate John Edwards. An even more galling defeat occurred in Alabama, where the incumbent Republican governor Fob James campaigned heavily for school prayer and other religious issues. Although he had the enthusiastic support of religious conservative heavyweights like Ralph Reed, Pat Robertson, Jerry Falwell, James Dobson, Phyllis Schlafly, and the Reverend Donald Wildmon, James still lost to Democrat Don Siegelman by sixteen percentage points. All told, in the twenty-eight races specifically targeted by religious conservatives, the Democratic candidates won twenty-two.[47]

Despite the millions that groups like Dobson's Focus on the Family and Bauer's Family Research Council spent on the 1998 races, as many as a third of "Christian conservatives" voted Democratic. Former Christian Coalition head Ralph Reed also had a tough day: in his first election cycle as a political consultant, all of his candidates lost.[48] The popular consensus was that although President Clinton had been subpoenaed by a grand jury to testify about his relationship with Monica Lewinsky in August 1998, his impending impeachment by the House of Representatives (which occurred six weeks after the election) sparked a backlash against the Republican Party. The efforts by House Speaker Newt Gingrich to make the election a referendum on President Clinton left voters frustrated that Congress was not working on more substantive issues.

Shaken by the results of the election, Gingrich announced less than three days later that not only was he stepping down as Speaker (as many religious conservatives were already demanding) but that he was resigning from the House as well.[49] Conservative gloom deepened a few weeks later, when the US Senate acquitted Clinton on February 12, 1999, of all the charges filed by the House.

One of the few postelection bright spots for Republicans was Texas, where Governor George W. Bush had won reelection in commanding fashion, garnering 69 percent of the votes and running strongly in potentially important demographics: 67 percent of women, 70 percent of independents, 60 percent of moderates, 49 percent of Hispanics, and almost one-third of liberal Democrats.[50] Even before the midterm election, Bush had been considered a front-runner for the 2000 nomination on the strength of name recognition alone, and his strong victory on an otherwise bad night for Republicans made him look very viable indeed.

Although the midterm election appeared to strip religious conservatives of some of their power within the party, they nonetheless remained the largest and generally most cohesive of the Republican voting blocs. As a result, they continued to believe that they had the ability to select the Republican presidential candidate. While religious conservatives acknowledged his strong reelection victory, George W. Bush was at best their fourth choice when the serious campaigning for the 2000 nomination began. In the give-and-take that is necessary to govern most states (even one as intrinsically conservative as Texas), Bush had often taken positions that upset the Religious Right. For instance, in June 1997, conservatives felt that he had not pushed strongly enough for tough education standards; in early 1998, Bush refused to pardon death row inmate Karla Faye Tucker despite her prison conversion to evangelical Christianity; and throughout his time in the governor's mansion, he was also charged with not pursuing the Right's antigay agenda with sufficient enthusiasm. Nonetheless, Bush's exit poll numbers had everybody, including religious conservatives, taking a long, hard look at the possibility of a G. W. Bush presidential campaign.

Much like his father in 1988, George W. Bush was ultimately aided by the inability of other candidates to expand their popularity with religious conservatives to other sectors of the electorate. Bush's biggest threat from the Right, John Ashcroft, actually shut down his campaign a good year prior to the 2000 Iowa caucuses. Ashcroft's experience underscored the dilemma that has consistently faced the favorite candidates of the hard-core religious conservatives. He recognized that while his rhetorical attacks on Clinton's private behavior were enormously appealing to religious conservatives, they were too strong for the bulk of the Republican Party, let alone the moderates on which the presidential election would hinge. Earlier, in an attempt to broaden his appeal, Ashcroft had given a speech in December 1998 in which he challenged the Republican Party to be "less divisive" and warned that party members should "never confuse politics and piety."[51] Religious conservatives reacted angrily, interpreting Ashcroft's remarks as an indication that he was backing away from his strict antiabortion position. He was quickly hauled out to the ideological woodshed by Paul Weyrich, a founder of the Free Congress Foundation, who told Ashcroft that "you simply can't afford to have your base in an uproar over speeches you give."[52] The controversy took its toll, and on January 6, 1999, Ashcroft announced at a press conference that he would not seek the presidency and instead would concentrate on his reelection campaign for the US Senate.

The departure of Ashcroft left religious conservatives in a dilemma. There was a brief flurry of interest in the announcement that former vice president Dan Quayle was launching an exploratory bid in February 1999, but after failing to attract enough money or popular support, Quayle pulled the plug in September. Conservative syndicated radio host Alan Keyes impressed a lot of people with his powerful speaking style and debating skills, but his low name recognition and limited resources hampered his campaign and kept his support in the single digits. Pat Buchanan toyed briefly with the idea of seeking the Republican nomination for a third time, but in October 1999 he bolted from the Republican Party and received the presidential nomination of the Reform Party, a mostly libertarian organization founded by billionaire businessman Ross Perot in 1995. Buchanan would ultimately finished fourth in the presidential voting behind Bush, Democratic nominee Al Gore, and Green Party nominee Ralph Nader.

The most natural ideological heir to Ashcroft was Gary Bauer, head of the Family Research Council, a political advocacy group affiliated with James C. Dobson's Focus on the Family. Bauer, the top domestic policy adviser in the Reagan administration in the late 1980s, was selected by Dobson to run the Focus on the Family political office in Washington in 1988. Four years later, Bauer's office was separated from Focus for tax reasons and became an independent entity.[53] But Bauer's candidacy was problematic for a number of reasons. The most obvious was name recognition: although well known and well liked among religious conservatives for his strong antiabortion positions and his support of a constitutional amendment to ban same-sex marriage, very few people outside that community knew his name. Another problem was his association with Focus on the Family leader James Dobson, a strident evangelical who periodically threatened to pull the Republican coalition apart if congressional leaders did not promote a religious conservative agenda. And then there were Bauer's positions themselves. In the wake of the Supreme Court decision overturning Texas's ban on sodomy, for instance, Bauer's antigay rhetoric intensified—he described homosexuality as an "abomination" and said that "[i]t is a subject upon which society cannot afford to be neutral."[54]

Although Bauer's campaign lasted into late February 2000, his departure made more of an impression than his entry. When the Republican primary settled into a *mano a mano* battle between Bush and Senator John McCain, the McCain campaign succeeded in portraying Bush as an extreme conservative, and the Bush campaign succeeded in defining McCain as a "moderate" whose active support of campaign finance reform, among other things, would hurt conservative causes. The Bush campaign's characterizations of McCain were effective, and nearly all religious conservative leaders were lining up behind Bush. Bauer was a notable exception; after shutting down his own campaign, Bauer infuriated many of his conservative friends by endorsing McCain over Bush.[55]

Any hope that McCain had of using Bauer as a bridge to religious conservatives largely vanished on February 28, 2000, when McCain gave a speech describing the Reverends Pat Robertson and Jerry Falwell as "forces of evil," and comparing them to Nation of Islam leader Louis Farrakhan.[56] Bauer initially defended McCain, saying that "if this was an attack on Christian conservatives, I wouldn't be here." But shortly after James Dobson released an extensive rebuttal of McCain's speech, Bauer stopped campaigning for McCain.[57] The maverick Republican's campaign came to a close following the Super Tuesday primaries in March.

REWARDING THE FAITHFUL: ATTORNEY GENERAL JOHN ASHCROFT

More than any other political race in 2000, John Ashcroft's bid for reelection to the United States Senate illustrated the extent to which the pornography industry had quietly edged its way into the American mainstream. During the course of the campaign against Missouri's incumbent governor, Mel Carnahan, Ashcroft ran ads that protested "Hollywood's decaying influence." Ashcroft tried to link Carnahan to Hollywood's immorality and the country's general moral decay by pointing out that Carnahan had accepted donations from Playboy Enterprises president Christie Hefner.

Carnahan responded that the deeply religious Ashcroft's claim to decency was no greater, given that his campaign had accepted donations from Charles W. Ergen, CEO of EchoStar.[58] Dish Network, the satellite subsidiary of EchoStar, was at the time the largest purchaser of adult videos and adult cable channels from New Frontier Media, the Boulder, Colorado-based "media distribution company." Dish Network customers could purchase adult pay-per-view for as little as $6 per movie, or subscribe to New Frontier's Extasy or TeN ("The Erotic Network") for $35 per month.[59]

Ashcroft's campaign tried to argue that there was a difference between producing adult videos, like Playboy Enterprises, and simply reselling already packaged materials.[60] In the end, however, the candidates' spat over who was more favored by the porn industry had little effect; the race was completely upended by the death of Mel Carnahan, his son, and a campaign aide in an October 16, 2000, plane crash, just three weeks before the election. Out of respect, Ashcroft suspended campaigning for more than a week following Carnahan's death, a decision that caused his campaign to effectively forfeit the benefits of nearly $1 million in political advertising. The new governor, Roger Wilson, announced that in the event that Carnahan won the election posthumously, his widow, Jean Carnahan, would be appointed to take his seat until a special election two years later. On November 7, the deceased Carnahan defeated Ashcroft by 48,960 votes, out of a total of 2.3 million cast.

Even as members of the new Bush administration were figuring out the DC transit system and scooping up exclusive apartments in Georgetown, leaders in the religious conservative movement were pushing for a high-level appointment for John Ashcroft. James Dobson, president of Focus on the Family, said that Ashcroft was a "national treasure," and flatly declared that "[i]f I were president-elect, John Ashcroft would be one of the people that I would try to find a spot for."[61]

Not surprisingly, religious conservatives had a specific spot in mind, that of attorney general. After eight years of frustration with the law enforcement priorities of the Janet Reno–led Justice Department, Dobson and other religious leaders were eager for an attorney general whose enforcement priorities would more closely resemble their social agenda. One of the major complaints raised by religious conservatives was their inability to arrange a meeting with Attorney General Reno to discuss their concerns, particularly about online obscenity. The White House reported that during the transition, president-elect Bush, vice president–elect Cheney, and political strategist Karl Rove all received numerous calls from religious conservative leaders urging Bush to appoint John Ashcroft as attorney general.[62] Recognizing a golden opportunity to reward religious conservatives for helping him to overcome the McCain challenge, particularly in South Carolina, Bush sent Ashcroft's name to the Senate as his pick to head the Justice Department.

The Ashcroft confirmation proved to be a bruising battle, one that galvanized activists from up and down the political spectrum. Pat Robertson issued a telephone message to a half-million Christian Coalition supporters in favor of Ashcroft, and the Traditional Values coalition also launched a grassroots campaign to support his nomination. Paul Weyrich said that Ashcroft had "stronger support in the conservative movement than any nominee I can remember in a long, long time." On the Left, pro-choice groups like the National Abortion and Reproductive Rights Action League protested Ashcroft's strong antiabortion stance, and others raised concerns about the potential effect of Ashcroft's strong religious views. "There are legitimate inquiries about how Senator Ashcroft will do his job as Attorney General," Senator Charles Schumer (D-NY) said, "and if they are done in a fair-minded way, nobody should take umbrage."[63]

In the end, Ashcroft received more "no" votes than any nominee in eighty years, but on February 2, 2001, he was confirmed by the Senate, 58–42, to serve as attorney general. He was sworn in that same day by Supreme Court justice Clarence Thomas, and issued a statement promising to "confront injustice by leading a professional Justice Department that is free from politics, that is uncompromisingly fair."[64]

Almost immediately following Ashcroft's appointment, the walls blocking access by religious conservatives to the Justice Department came tumbling down. On May 10, 2001, for instance, Ashcroft and his aides held a meeting with a veritable Who's Who of the religious conservative antipornography movement: Janet LaRue, director of legal activities for the Family Research Council; Bruce Taylor of the National Law Center for Children and Families; Tom Minnery of Focus on the Family; Patrick Trueman of the Family Research Council; and Beverly LaHaye of Concerned Women for America; among others.

LaRue was pleased with the fact that Ashcroft attended the meeting personally and took their concerns so seriously. "He was very attentive, took his own notes, listened, [and] asked good questions," she said after the meeting. "Mr. Ashcroft reaffirmed his commitment to enforce all of the federal laws on obscenity."[65] Religious conservatives came away from the meeting confident that the new Justice Department would launch a vigorous new campaign against the pornography industry, and, in early September of that year, rumors were rife that the Justice Department was in fact on the verge of doing so. But after the morning of September 11, 2001, prosecuting pornographers took a distant backseat to fighting global terrorism and protecting America.

THE BUSH ADMINISTRATION COMMITS STATUARY DRAPE

Even in the midst of the postattack chaos, the Justice Department did strike one blow for decency. Major announcements by Justice Department officials, including the attorney general, usually take place on a stage in the building's

Great Hall. Looming behind the stage are two twelve-feet-tall art deco aluminum statues, which were created as part of a Works Progress Administration project by sculptor C. P. Jennewein (1890–1978) in 1936. One, depicting the *Majesty of Justice*, is a male figure with a cloth wrapped around his torso; the other, the *Spirit of Justice* (also known affectionately as "Minnie Lou"), is a female figure wearing a toga that exposes her right breast.[66]

Over the years, it was something of a sport for Washington political photographers to choose camera angles that included the *Spirit of Justice*'s naked breast above the head of whoever was speaking. In late January 2002, however, photographers were startled to find that large blue drapes had been permanently hung behind the stage, obscuring both the *Majesty* and the *Spirit of Justice* from view. The cost of the new drapes was reported to be $8,650, or $1,375 more than Jennewein had originally charged for the statues themselves.[67] The cover-up of the statues quickly became a cause célèbre and provided ample fodder for late-night comics and liberal columnists. The Justice Department quickly grew so frustrated by the coverage of the incident that it denied permission to the Associated Press to photograph Jennewein's other art in the Justice Department building.[68]

Ashcroft's spokesperson, the aptly named Barbara Comstock, denied that the attorney general had ordered the curtains out of irritation over the persistent presence of Minnie Lou's right breast over his head in photographs. "He doesn't look at his press coverage a lot, himself," she said. "He spends his time dealing with threat assessments and more important business." Comstock said that the decision to install the curtains had been made by a publicity person to provide a better background for TV cameras.[69]

One city that got a particular chuckle over the move to cover the art deco statues in the Justice Department's Great Hall was Cincinnati, a city with its own history of artistic controversy. The *Cincinnati Post* sent reporter Barry Horstman out to review the myriad nude statues that adorn Cincinnati, ranging from "Fountain Square's 131-year-old Tyler Davidson Fountain [which has several nude figures]" to the Cincinnati Art Museum. Even Phil Burress, the head of Cincinnati's Citizens for Community Values, seemed amused: "I think Cincinnatians, because of the battles we've had here over First Amendment rights, know the difference between art and obscenity probably as well as anyone. I'd be shocked if anybody here would make a move against art. If that happens, count us out."[70]

In truth, it does seem relatively unlikely that Ashcroft himself would have actually bothered with a detail like drapes in the Great Hall. But for many people, Left and Right, the redecoration of the Great Hall was a perfect metaphor for Ashcroft's Justice Department. For liberals, the act of obscuring

Justice and Liberty was the physical embodiment of the USA PATRIOT Act, the intrusive antiterrorism legislation that Ashcroft championed just two weeks after 9/11. And for religious conservatives, the drapes came to represent a department and an administration that thought it was enough to substitute symbolism for the action they craved.

Needless to say, when religious conservatives pulled out the stops to support Ashcroft's appointment as attorney general, they expected more activity on the decency front than a few yards of blue cloth. Most antipornography activists understood the shift in the department's priorities following 9/11, but by the fall of 2003 they were impatient for some signs that Ashcroft intended to carry through on his 2001 promise to aggressively enforce the nation's obscenity laws. There was some applause over the August 2003 indictment of Extreme Associates, a West Coast video production company specializing in extremely violent and sexually explicit videos, but groups like Concerned Women for America were still concerned that the Justice Department was not doing enough. The group's chief counsel, Janet LaRue, said that there are "100,000 Web sites offering material that is prosecutable," but added that the Justice Department's threshold for selecting sites to prosecute was set "too high to have any meaningful impact."[71]

It is no coincidence, really, that religious conservatives were expressing their disapproval of the Justice Department's performance at about the same time they were reacting angrily to the FCC's October 2003 decision not to fine NBC and its affiliates for U2 singer Bono's unbleeped expletive at the Golden Globes. With a presidential election looming the following year, religious conservatives were taking stock of the Bush administration and wondering what they had gotten in return for their critical support in the primaries. Religious conservatives felt that they had picked up the pieces after Bush lost the New Hampshire primary to McCain, and helped Bush sweep the South, including Al Gore's native Tennessee, during the general election.

These feelings were not lost on Bush's chief political adviser, Karl Rove, who noted that in 2000 four million evangelical voters stayed home instead of casting their ballot for Bush. Rove held a meeting in Atlanta, Georgia, with evangelical leaders in December 2003 to promote Bush as a man of faith. To help improve the evangelical turnout the following November, the campaign also hired political consultant Ralph Reed to serve as the Bush-Cheney campaign chairman in the South.

"We need to have a very significant effort," Reed said, "to energize and register and turn out to the polls our key supporters, of which they [evangelicals] are clearly an important part, although not the only part."[72]

Rove recognized that the key to energizing the evangelical base was to demonstrate action on issues important to them. There were some items on the religious conservative checklist that Bush could do relatively little about; there were no Supreme Court vacancies to fill in 2003, for instance, and a vote on a constitutional amendment banning gay marriage on July 14, 2004, fell well short of the two-thirds majority needed for passage. However, a president running for reelection has a number of advantages, including both the personal delivery of well-cured pork to key states and the ability to direct branches of his administration to focus on specific issues. It would be unduly cynical to suggest that either the FCC or the Justice Department was serving as an arm of the Bush-Cheney reelection campaign, but there is little doubt that religious conservatives were far happier with both agencies of the federal government during the 2004 campaign than they had been in the three previous years.

THE JUSTICE DEPARTMENT TARGETS ADULT OBSCENITY

The indictment of Extreme Associates in the summer of 2003 was merely the opening salvo of the Justice Department's renewed interest in the pornography industry. In January 2004, John Ashcroft hired Bruce A. Taylor, one of the founding members of the National Obscenity Enforcement Unit (NOEU) established at the recommendation of the 1986 Meese Commission report. There was some ambiguity about exactly what Taylor was hired to do—either "oversee the Department's pornography prosecutions" or serve as "senior counsel to the Assistant Attorney General based in Washington, D.C."—but in either case, it is clear that he was brought onboard the Justice Department to help expand its focus from child pornography to other types of sexually explicit materials.

Jeffrey Douglas, an attorney and chairman of the board of the Free Speech Coalition, argued that Taylor's hiring was a sop by Bush to religious conservatives: "[A]n all-out attack on the [pornography] industry will, of course, galvanize the right, and when you have people in the Justice Department who are operating under the assumption that they are God's agent on Earth, it's a very bad situation."[73]

Most observers believe that one of Taylor's primary responsibilities was to put pressure on Andrew Oosterbaan, longtime head of the Child Exploitation and Obscenity Section (CEOS), to prosecute more nonchild pornography cases. Oosterbaan had frequently come under fire from antipornography activists like Focus on the Family and its legislative arm, the Family Research Council. When John Ashcroft first took office, religious conservatives urged him to replace Oosterbaan with Bruce Taylor, Robert Flores (a former federal prosecutor with NOEU and former vice president/senior counsel of the National Law Center for Children and Families), or Patrick Trueman (a former head of CEOS and senior legal counsel for the Family Research Council). Instead, Ashcroft elected to reappoint the experienced Oosterbaan.

In addition to hiring Taylor, the Justice Department added six FBI agents specifically assigned to investigate nonchild pornography cases. Janet LaRue of the Concerned Women of America applauded the hirings but said that, due to indifference during the Clinton years, the department was fighting an uphill battle. She claimed that during Clinton's eight years in office, more than one million pornographic Web sites appeared online.[74]

Even more resources were added to the fight against nonchild pornography just after Bush's reelection in 2004. Included in a massive appropriations bill was enough money for the Justice Department to hire seventeen new attorneys to prosecute both child and nonchild pornography cases, along with ten additional FBI agents. Congress also approved an allocation of $2.6 million to improve the equipment and resources at CEOS.

STERN WORDS FROM THE FEDERAL COMMUNICATIONS COMMISSION

As impressive as the changes were at the Justice Department, the shift in the FCC's attitude toward broadcast indecency was even more dramatic, and the statistics bear repeating:

- in 2002 the FCC handed out seven Notices of Apparent Liability (NALs) and called for forfeitures of $100,000
- in 2003 three NALs were issued and $440,000 in forfeitures were assessed
- in 2004 eleven NALs, and forfeitures of $7.7 *million*

Thanks to the unpopularity of the FCC's Enforcement Bureau decision in the Bono expletive case, some of the impetus for a crackdown on broadcast indecency came directly from Congress. Rep. Fred Upton (R-MI), chairman of the Telecommunications and Internet Subcommittee, told the *Chicago Tribune* that when Congress reconvened in late January 2004, he intended to introduce legislation to increase indecency fines by a factor of ten.[75] Upton also announced that he was scheduling a hearing on January 28 to chastise the FCC and take testimony in support of his proposed legislation.

"As a father of two young children, I especially find the use of the 'f-word' and other obscenities on broadcast television wholly unacceptable," said

Upton. "As Chairman of the Telecommunications and Internet Subcommittee, I will have a public hearing on this matter January 28th to hold the FCC accountable for their enforcement policy and am hopeful that the full Commission will, in fact, reverse the Enforcement Bureau's decision."[76]

The FCC clearly got the message. On the day before Upton's hearing convened, the FCC demonstrated its renewed commitment to fighting indecency by announcing two Notices of Apparent Liability: a relatively minor $27,500 fine against Young Broadcasting of San Francisco, Inc., and a massive $755,000 charge against Clear Channel Communications, Inc.—at the time the largest fine ever levied by the FCC against a broadcaster.

The smaller of the two fines assessed on January 27, 2004, was against a San Francisco television station, KRON-TV. This violation graphically illustrates how the climate for indecency had changed since the Bono exclamation. During its *KRON 4 Morning News* show on October 4, 2002,[77] the station interviewed two performers with the popular stage production *Puppetry of the Penis*. During the course of the interview, the performers offered to demonstrate for the hosts what the stage show cheekily describes as "the ancient Australian art of genital origami." The actors (who showed up for the television interview clad only in superhero-style capes), turned away from the cameras, and proceeded to manipulate their genitals into a number of different shapes, including the "Eiffel Tower, a hamburger, a baby kangaroo, public figures and movie characters." In the process of turning toward the hosts, however, the penis of one of the performers was briefly (but fully) exposed on television.[78] An offended viewer complained to the FCC's Enforcement Bureau about both the interview itself and the exposure of the performer's penis on air.

On March 18, 2004, the FCC issued three more decisions: one that reversed the Enforcement Bureau's decision on the Bono expletive, one that assessed a $55,000 fine against two radio stations for broadcasting the sounds of a couple having sex, and one that assessed Infinity Broadcasting $27,500 for a 2001 show by radio personality Howard Stern in which he discussed various slang terms for body parts and sexual acts.

This was hardly the first time that Stern's show had been fined by the FCC. In fact, since 1990 Stern had racked up $2.5 million in indecency fines. It is doubtful that Infinity was particularly upset by the fines, given how lucrative Stern's show was for the broadcasting company. Even though his ratings showed some signs of slippage in 2004, *The Howard Stern Show* was still pulling in $100 million in revenues for Infinity (which, incidentally, is a subsidiary of Viacom, which also owns MTV and CBS).[79] Given those earnings, and given Infinity's overall revenues of $2.1 billion in 2004,[80] it is clear that even an occasional high-profile fine from the FCC was not a big deal for the radio network.

But Stern himself was increasingly tired of dealing with the FCC and worrying about what it might do in response to his show. After being suspended in February by Clear Channel when a caller used a racial epithet on his show, Stern began musing on air about being fired by Infinity and/or Clear Channel, or simply quitting radio altogether. But a different solution presented itself: in October 6, 2004, Stern announced that he had signed a ten-year contract with Sirius Satellite Radio for $500 *million*. Satellite radio, as Stern gleefully pointed out, is beyond the FCC's jurisdiction (although some members of Congress have suggested trying to change that). Stern's first broadcast on Sirius occurred in January 2006.

The Stern soap opera was entertaining, but the most anticipated decision by the FCC during its 2004 orgy of indecency fines concerned, of course, the Super Bowl halftime show. After an eight-and-a-half-month investigation, the commission issued a Notice of Apparent Liability and Forfeiture against the twenty televisions stations owned by Viacom and CBS Network Stations.

In the FCC's view, a number of factors supported a finding of indecency. First, the FCC flatly declared that "the Jackson/Timberlake segment is both explicit and graphic." CBS tried to defend itself by arguing that the broadcast of Jackson's bare breast lasted for only 19/32 of a second, but the FCC was not impressed. "Although the exposure was brief," the commission ruled, "it was clearly graphic." The commission ruled that "throughout the Jackson/Timberlake segment, the performances, song lyrics and choreography discussed or simulated sexual activities." Finally, the commission noted that the pulling of Jackson's bra cup by Timberlake coincided with the lyrics "gonna have you naked by the end of this song." As a result, the FCC concluded that the purpose of the act's nudity was "to pander to, titillate and shock the viewing audience."[81]

The commission then turned to the issue of the appropriate level of fine to levy against Viacom and CBS. As part of its determination, the commission is allowed to adjust the level of the fine based on various aggravating factors. In this particular case, the commission had no difficulty whatsoever finding factors that aggravated it.

Throughout the investigation, Viacom and CBS strenuously denied that they had any foreknowledge of the nudity at the end of the act, and pointed to the fact that Jackson had accepted full responsibility for the event. Even while conceding that the onstage flash might have been the idea of one or both of the performers, the commission concluded that CBS and MTV "were well aware of the overall sexual nature of the Jackson/Timberlake segment and fully sanctioned it—indeed, touted it as 'shocking' to attract potential viewers."

Not surprisingly, the FCC's skepticism toward CBS and MTV was heightened by MTV's Web site. A preview of the halftime show was headlined "Janet

Jackson's Super Bowl Show Promises 'Shocking Moments.'" Just one hour after the finale of the Jackson/Timberlake act, MTV revised the headline of the page to read "Janet Gets Nasty" and added new text, including: "Jaws across the country hit the carpet at exactly the same time. You know what we're talking about. Janet Jackson, Justin Timberlake, and a kinky finale that rocked the Super Bowl to its core. . . . MTV was Super Bowl central, so armchair quarterbacks, fair weather fanatics and fans of Janet Jackson and her pasties were in the right place."

CBS tried to argue that the references to "shocking moments" and "jaws dropping" referred to the surprise appearance of Justin Timberlake, since MTV had been playing up the surprise-guest angle all week. (There was no reference, interestingly, in the FCC decision to the MTV's praise of Jackson's "pasties.") Regardless, the FCC was not buying the network's defense of the Web site article:

> In sum, even assuming that neither CBS nor MTV had advance knowledge that Ms. Jackson's breast would be exposed during her broadcast performance, the record clearly establishes that officials of CBS and MTV did have prior knowledge of, indeed were intricately involved in the planning process for, and tacitly approved, the sexually provocative nature of the Jackson/Timberlake segment. Moreover, they extensively promoted this aspect of the broadcast in a manner designed to pander, titillate and shock. Viacom made a calculated and deliberate decision to air the Jackson/Timberlake segment containing material that would shock Super Bowl viewers, and to accurately promote it as such.[82]

Under current federal law, the maximum fine the FCC can assess against each licensee for a decency violation is $27,500. In this particular case, the FCC concluded that Viacom (the corporate owner of both CBS and MTV) was ultimately responsible for the broadcast. Since Viacom owns twenty television station licenses, the FCC order proposed to fine Viacom $550,000. The commission concluded that the affiliates of Viacom/CBS did not participate in the planning of the broadcast and could not have anticipated the on-air nudity, so it declined to assess any fine against them. However, it urged the network's affiliates to implement technology that would enable them independently to delay and delete any inappropriate material from the network.

Four of the five commissioners—Republicans Michael Powell, Kevin Martin, and Kathleen Abernathy, as well as Democrat Michael Copps—agreed with the final decision, but not with wholehearted enthusiasm. In a separate statement, Copps argued that the affiliates should not be excused simply because they did not produce the indecent content. He also said that the commission should have focused on the entire halftime show, rather than simply on the exposure of Jackson's breast.

In his appended remarks, Commissioner Martin agreed with Copps that the entire show should have been the subject of the commission's investigation. He also reiterated his long-standing belief that affiliates should be allowed to reject network programming to which they object on decency grounds. While that may be a relevant issue in the context of taped programs, it is difficult to imagine that any local affiliate would have declined to broadcast a four-hour, high-profile, live event, particularly one of the magnitude of the Super Bowl.

The most strenuous objection to the commission's decision, ironically, came from Democratic commissioner Jonathan Adelstein, who warned that the FCC was "responding to a 'wardrobe malfunction' with a regulatory malfunction." He also agreed with Martin that some long-term solution was needed to give local affiliates greater control over the content they receive from the national networks. But his primary concern was the amount of the fine (an issue that Copps raised as well).

"After all the bold talk," Adelstein wrote, "it's a slap on the wrist that can be paid with just 7½ seconds of Super Bowl ad time. The $550,000 fine measures up to only about a dollar per complaint for the more than 542,000 complaints that flooded into the FCC after the broadcast."

In terms of the financial impact on Viacom, Adelstein's point is well taken. Each thirty-second advertisement during the 2004 Super Bowl sold for approximately $2.25 million, or $75,000 per second. And even without the revenues from the advertisements, Viacom wouldn't have any trouble covering the proposed fine. In 2003 alone, Viacom had revenues of $26.6 *billion* and profits of $1.42 billion.[83] Thus, the proposed fine constituted less than four one-hundredths of Viacom's 2003 profits.

Commissioner Adelstein has a legitimate concern regarding the ineffectiveness of the fines issued by the FCC; that is the main reason that some members of Congress want to increase them significantly. But the reality is that even a tenfold increase in indecency fines would be a pittance compared to the revenues generated by shows that most religious conservatives find indecent. In truth, FCC fines would have to be raised to simply obscene levels before they would make a significant and lasting difference in the level of salaciousness on television and radio.

As much as some religious conservatives might like that to happen, Congress is unlikely to raise indecency fines enough to make a difference. The loftiest reason, of course, is that people generally value the First Amendment and the concept of free speech. As the post-Jackson/Timberlake polls indicated, most Americans were reluctant to have an unelected, five-person federal commission overreact to a minor transgression. Vastly increasing indecency fines would only exacerbate the FCC's ability to chill broadcast speech, particularly against the smaller, more marginal stations least able to afford them.

But the more pragmatic barrier to the religious conservative social agenda is that it runs counter to so much of popular taste and, by extension, to the economic interests of some of the country's most influential (and campaign-generous) corporations. As Frank Rich points out, banishing indecency is not possible "in a market economy where red and blue [state] customers are united in their infatuation of 'Desperate Housewives.'" [84] Once in Washington, most politicians quickly learn that while passion may flow from the pulpit and popular support from the middle of the electorate, campaign contributions flow most heavily from the nation's boardrooms.

Chapter Nine

Ask Not for Whom the Wedding Bells Toll

A Love That Now Dares Speak Its Name

Homosexuality—sexual relationships between members of the same gender—is a well-documented practice in human relationships that has crossed boundaries of culture and time. Discussion of its existence, however, has been less than widespread. In Western European culture, this omission can chiefly be traced to the apparent prohibitions against homosexuality contained in the Old Testament, most notably in the books Leviticus and Deuteronomy. Both Christianity and the religion from which it emerged, Judaism, viewed same-sex relations as a crime against God and used the prohibition against homosexuality to distinguish their cultures from the more hedonistic and pagan practices of Greece and Rome.[1]

The specific act of sodomy, originally a religious offense, became a crime against the state in England during the reign of Henry VIII, when chancellor of the exchequer Thomas Cromwell helped guide the Buggery Act through parliament in 1533. Under the law, anyone who was convicted of the so-called crime against nature was hanged. Through England's colonization of North America, similar prohibitions were incorporated into the laws of the American colonies and, eventually, each of the fifty states.[2] Today, the legal prohibitions against physical relations between members of the same sex are steadily disappearing, but they are still condemned by most major branches of Christianity.

Despite the millennia of attempted censorship and theological prohibition, an increasingly frank and open discussion of homosexuality has occurred during the last century (albeit in fits and starts). That conversation, carried on

Oscar Wilde, ca. 1882. (Library of Congress)

in the language and images of mass media and culture, has reflected society's steadily changing attitudes toward homosexuality. More than any other single event, the prosecution of author Oscar Wilde (1854–1900) marked the starting point for the dramatic change.

The man in the dock at London's Old Bailey in the summer of 1895 was one of Ireland's, indeed, one of Europe's great playwrights, a man whose revolutionary fashion sense and irrepressible wit had made him one of the first true international celebrities. His writings had earned him at the age of twenty-eight a lecture tour of the United States, and his two most famous plays, *An Ideal Husband* and *The Importance of Being Earnest*, were playing to rave reviews in London's theater district. And yet, there sat the forty-year-old Wilde, on trial under England's 1885 Criminal Law Amendment Act for alleged "acts of gross indecency with other male persons."

Although married and the father of two sons, there was little question that Wilde was attracted to younger men. Among his many romantic conquests was Lord Alfred Douglas (1870–1945), the son of John Sholto Douglas (1844–1900), the ninth Marquis of Queensbury (best known for the boxing rules that still bear his name). In 1895, four years after his son and Wilde first began their relationship, the increasingly angry marquis left a calling card for Wilde at one his clubs. On the back, he wrote: "For Oscar Wilde posing as a Somdomite [*sic*]." Against the advice of his friends, who urged him to let the matter drop, Wilde pressed charges against the marquis for criminal libel.

The trial, however, went badly for Wilde. Defense counsel for the marquis hired investigators who turned up numerous liaisons between Wilde and various young men. When Wilde testified under oath that the marquis had no grounds to call him a sodomite, the marquis used that information to impeach his credibility. The information collected by the investigators was so unequivocal and damning that the prosecutor for the Crown advised Wilde to drop his complaint against the marquis, which he did. A short time later, however, Wilde himself was arrested and brought to trial.

Wilde offered no further denials of his lifestyle or his relationships. Instead, he presented a passionate defense of male love that is captured in this exchange with the Crown prosecutor, C. F. Gill:

Gill: What is the "Love that dares not speak its name?"

Wilde: "The Love that dares not speak its name" in this century is such a great affection of an elder for a younger man as there was between David and Jonathan, such as Plato made the very basis of his philosophy, and such as you find in the sonnets of Michelangelo and Shakespeare. It is that deep spiritual affection that is as pure as it is perfect. It dictates and pervades great works of art, like those of Shakespeare and Michelangelo,

and those two letters of mine, such as they are. It is in this century misunderstood, so much misunderstood that it may be described as the
"Love that dares not speak its name," and on account of it I am placed
where I am now. It is beautiful, it is fine, it is the noblest form of affection. There is nothing unnatural about it. It is intellectual, and it repeatedly exists between an elder and a younger man, when the elder man has
intellect, and the younger man has all the joy, hope and glamour of life
before him. That it should be so, the world does not understand. The
world mocks at it, and sometimes puts one in the pillory for it.[3]

It was no accident that the erudite Wilde, in defending "the love that
dares not speak its name," made reference first to the biblical story of David,
slayer of Goliath, and Jonathan, son of Saul, the first king of Israel. By doing
so, Wilde purposely invoked a long-simmering theological debate about the
nature of that relationship, which some have characterized (with unwitting
irony) as merely platonic, and others have interpreted as sexual in nature.

Given the challenges of properly interpreting both the original texts and
the meaning of the relationships described, there is no definitive answer as to
whether one of the Bible's great heroes, David, was being physically seduced
when Jonathan "stripped himself of the robe that was upon him, and gave it to
David, and his garments, even to his sword, and to his bow, and to his girdle."[4]
Clearly, Wilde hoped to suggest that whatever the nature of his own relationship with younger men, it was of a kind endorsed by the Bible.

The ploy was unsuccessful. As the evidence mounted against Wilde, public
opinion turned strongly against him, and his name was even pulled from the
bills and advertisements of the theaters that were running his plays.[5] During
the course of the trial, one commentator made a bold prediction that Wilde's
artistic reputation would be permanently ruined: "One thing is certain, however, that no matter what may be the outcome of the case, whether Wilde goes
free or is sent to prison, the death-knell of Wildeism has been rung and the
corpse is prepared for burial. The prurient plays of Wilde and the cognate productions, 'The Second Mrs. Tanqueray' and 'The Notorious Mrs. Ebbsmith,'
which are now called 'Pinerotic,' are doomed and there is a strong reaction
toward a healthier stage representation, while the current decadent literature
will also get a setback."[6]

The trial ultimately proved far more destructive to Wilde's person than to
the reputation of his plays, now routinely performed even in small-town middle
schools. His erudite defense of spiritual love did little to sway the jury, which
after two hours of deliberation returned a verdict of guilty on several charges
of "gross indecency." One news correspondent reported that "[w]hen the sentence was pronounced, Wilde appeared to be stunned." The playwright was

promptly sentenced to two years of hard labor (fortunately for Wilde, the penalty of death by hanging had been removed from the law some years earlier).[7] By the time of his release, his health was ruined, and he died just three years later, deeply impoverished, an exile from his homeland, and almost entirely alone.

It would be a stretch to argue that Wilde's trial resulted in the widespread discussion of homosexuality overnight. The word "homosexual" itself was not used in the coverage of the trial, at least not in two of the leading newspapers of the United States; in fact, the word "homosexual" did not appear in the *Washington Post* until 1907 (in the context of charges of "debauchery practiced by some of the highest men in the [German] empire")[8] and did not appear in the *New York Times* until 1914 (when British writer George Bernard Shaw used the term in a lengthy article about World War I).[9] Nonetheless, in myriad ways, the coded descriptions of the issues in the Wilde trial helped introduce much of the public to a lifestyle until then little discussed and less understood.

THE LOVE BEGINS TO SPEAK IN WHISPERS

It was not until the publication of scientist Alfred Kinsey's *Sexual Behavior in the Human Male* (better known as the Kinsey Report) in November 1947 that the issue of homosexuality was first widely and openly discussed in the United States, in large part because of Kinsey's controversial findings regarding homosexual behavior in the American male. Among other discoveries about sexual practices (all of which, interestingly, were front-page news), Kinsey and his researchers found that 20 percent of the youngest unmarried men had engaged in homosexual behavior at some time, a figure that rose to 40 percent by the age of forty.[10] He also concluded that 4 percent of American males were exclusively homosexual over the course of their lives.[11] (More recent surveys put the percentage of adult males identifying themselves as homosexual at just under 3 percent, and half that rate for adult females.)[12]

The Kinsey Report came under a variety of attacks both scientific and social, but the idea of bringing scientific method to the study of human sexuality (a revolutionary concept in and of itself) struck a chord with the public. The Kinsey Report spent weeks on bestseller lists across the country, and, in response to questions by pollster George Gallup, Americans approved of the release of the report by a margin of five to one. Gallup reported that the typical response from respondents was that "[p]eople should be informed about sex; the subject has been hidden too long."[13]

But while the Kinsey Report may have introduced much of the American public to the term and perhaps even the very concept of homosexuality, it did little to promote its greater acceptance. To the contrary, Kinsey's conclusion that a certain percentage of American men were homosexual helped fuel an aggressive campaign by the federal government to purge so-called sexual perverts from government jobs. This campaign was aided by the contemporaneous and well-publicized efforts of Senator Joseph McCarthy (1908–1957) (R-WI) to rid the State Department in particular and the federal government in general of communists.

The "McCarthy Era" began on February 9, 1950, when McCarthy gave a speech to the Republican Women's Club of Wheeling, West Virginia, in which he alleged that there were fifty-seven "known Communists" working for the US State Department. In a letter to President Harry S. Truman (1884–1972), McCarthy demanded that he investigate the matter and assist congressional committees in doing the same. "Failure on your part," McCarthy wrote, "will label the Democratic party as being the bed-fellow of international communism."[14]

Within weeks of McCarthy's charges, homosexuals were added to the list of State Department security risks: Republican national chairman Guy George Gabrielson (1891–1976) sent a letter to party workers supporting the effort to clean up the State Department:

> Perhaps as dangerous as the actual Communists are the sexual perverts who have infiltrated our Government in recent years. The State Department has confessed that it has had to fire ninety-one of these. It is the talk of Washington and of the Washington correspondents corp.
>
> The country would be more aroused over this tragic angle of the situation if it were not for the difficulties of the newspapers and radio commentators in adequately presenting the facts, while respecting the decency of their American audiences.[15]

There is no little irony in a complaint by a Republican national chairman, particularly in 1950, that newspapers were not discussing homosexuality in sufficiently factual terms; in any case, he could hardly have complained about the coverage of the government's efforts to identify and fire gays over the next three years. That spring, a subcommittee of the Senate Appropriations Committee met with a representative of the Washington, DC, vice squad, who suggested that as many as 3,750 "perverts" worked for the government, with 200 or 300 employed by the State Department.[16]

The Senate authorized the expenditure of $10,000 to determine the extent of the problem.[17] At the end of the six-month investigation in December 1950, a Senate panel concluded that "sexual perverts" were a security risk and called for federal agencies to institute stricter screening methods to keep them out of the government. "The lack of emotional stability which is found in most sex perverts, and the weakness of their moral fiber," the report concluded, "makes them susceptible to the blandishments of foreign espionage agents."[18] In the spring of 1952, the State Department reported to the House Appropriations Committee that it had fired 126 homosexuals, out of a total workforce of nearly 30,000 people.[19] A year later, the State Department said that it had increased its firing of homosexuals to one every three days.[20]

By the middle of the 1950s, the active campaign against gays in the government had largely petered out, and over the next decade there was relatively little discussion of homosexuality in American mainstream media. What little discussion did occur in public rarely moved past the most basic stereotypes: a 1960 front-page article about New York's infamous Forty-second Street, for instance, talked about the rise in homosexual activity in general but a decline in the number of "'flagrant' deviates—those who wear make-up, a feminine hair-do, and walk with a 'swish.'"[21] (And that was from the *New York Times*!)

Gay men and women, of course, had not stopped their personal pursuit of unnamable love. Widespread and vigorous discussion of civil rights in the 1960s provided them with a clear model for gay rights activism. In the years following passage of the 1964 Civil Rights Act, the American Civil Liberties Union was litigating to remove homosexuality as a bar to government employment, and, further, a variety of groups had joined forces under the umbrella of ECHO, the East Coast Homophile Organizations, to promote greater rights and acceptance. The barriers facing ECHO were painfully apparent in the fall of 1964, when the group was denied a meeting space by four Washington hotels before the Sheraton-Park Hotel agreed to host its conference.[22] Nevertheless, the public's opinion of homosexuality was clearly changing.

The following spring, the *Washington Post* ran a lengthy, five-part series that discussed homosexuality in depth. Reporter Jean M. White's first sentence, accurately enough, read, "This series of articles would not have been written five years ago."

"Now," she added, "there is a growing awareness and concern about the problem of homosexuality—brought about in part by a more open and liberal attitude toward sex in general. . . . The conspiracy of silence of the past nurtured myths, misconceptions, false stereotypes and feelings of disgust and revulsion. They still cloud any discussion of homosexuality. But more and more, recognition has come of a need to reappraise our laws—and our attitudes."[23] Over the next five days, White reviewed several aspects of homosexual culture in detail, including its prevalence, the role of homosexuals in society, the scientific understanding of homosexuality, the legal issues, and the movement's growing militancy. Unquestionably, White's study of homosexuality was one of the first thorough and balanced examinations to be published by a mainstream news outlet.

Interestingly, the shift in public perception was matched by a change in the self-image of homosexuals themselves. A 1964 report by the Committee on Public Health of the New York Academy of Medicine found that members of the gay community were rejecting long-standing feelings of defensiveness and instead "would have it believed that homosexuality is not just an acceptable way of life but rather, a desirable, noble, preferable way of life. For one thing, they claim that it is the perfect answer to the problem of population explosion."[24]

OF MILITANCY AND MONEY: THE GAY RIGHTS MOVEMENT FINDS ITS VOICE

Over the course of the 1960s, as the public conversation about homosexuality steadily expanded, the long-hidden gay community rapidly became both a social and an economic force. In a lengthy 1967 article in the *New York Times*, Webster Schott detailed some of the changes taking place: "[Homosexuality] builds circulation for mass magazines. It furnishes topics for symposia. It provokes liberal clergymen to new definitions of love. It serves as fodder for the crazy button and poster industries. It provides TV talkathons with guests, funds research projects and excites intellectuals." Schott also described a new but quickly growing phenomenon: gay tourism. "The traveling homosexual," Schott said, "can even buy a directory of gay saloons so he is never lacking in fun places to go."[25]

Few things more thoroughly illustrated the growing openness about homosexuality in American culture than the production and release of *Midnight Cowboy*, the only X-rated film ever to win the Oscar for Best Picture (1969). (Just two years later, the film was resubmitted to the ratings board of the Motion Picture Association of America and the unchanged film was given an R rating, which it retains today.) The film, starring Jon Voight and Dustin Hoffman, is the story of a young Texan named Joe Buck (Voight) who travels to New York with plans to become a gigolo for a clientele of rich East Coast women. His plans fall through, and with his cash running out, he starts turning tricks as a so-called midnight cowboy on West Forty-second Street. The film earned its X rating for its nudity, its frank depiction of heterosexual and homosexual prostitution, and the simulated fellatio that Voight's character receives in a movie theater. In addition to being an artistic success, the film was also a financial hit, earning nearly $45 million on an estimated shooting budget of $3.6 million.[26]

"It's not a movie for the ages," *New York Times* reviewer Vincent Canby

(1924–2000) wrote, "but having seen it, you won't ever again feel detached as you walk down West 42d Street, avoiding the eyes of the drifters, stepping around the little islands of hustlers, and closing your nostrils to the smell of rancid griddles."[27]

Much to its dismay, the ability of the American public to ignore the growing gay rights movement was about to vanish as well. Just two miles south of the once seedy side streets of Times Square was the Stonewall Inn, on Christopher Street in the heart of Greenwich Village.[28] In the early morning of June 28, 1969, the New York Police Department raided the inn—a well-known gathering spot for the area's gay community—to investigate reports that the unlicensed club was illegally serving alcohol. The two hundred or so people ejected from the Stonewall milled around outside, and tempers started to flare. With startling rapidity, the crowd turned on the handful of police officers who had shown up to raid the bar, and the air was filled with a variety of projectiles, ranging from the vaguely humorous (curlers and lipstick tubes) to the potentially lethal (coins, bricks, and bottles). When the beleaguered officers retreated into the Stonewall, calling for reinforcements, crowd members pulled up a parking meter and tried to use it as a battering ram to break down the door of the inn. Thirteen people were arrested and four officers were injured.[29]

In the wee hours of the following evening, an even larger crowd gathered outside the Stonewall, and the police department sent in its tactical patrol force to break up the demonstration. The crowd, estimated at four hundred people, was pushed out of Sheridan Square by the marching lines of police officers. They responded by lobbing bottles and scrambling through side streets to regroup behind the police lines. It took nearly two hours for the police to restore order.[30]

The battle at Stonewall Inn quickly became a rallying cry for gays, the motivational equivalent of the battle over a rude bridge in Concord, Massachusetts, or Rosa Parks's (1913–2005) quiet but firm refusal to give up her seat. On the first anniversary of the confrontation, thousands of gay men and women from around the country traveled to New York for a "gay-in" in Central Park's Sheep Meadow. (The use of the term "gay" to refer to homosexuals had been in use in the gay community since at least 1955 but was just beginning to see widespread use in the media.)[31] Estimates of the crowd size ranged wildly from one thousand to twenty thousand. According to Martin Robins, political affairs director for the newly formed Gay Activists Alliance, the real significance lay not in the number of people attending but the fact that gays were gathering at all: "We've never had a demonstration like this. It serves notice on every politician in the state and nation that homosexuals are not going to hide any more. We're becoming militant, and we won't be harassed and degraded any more."[32]

The following summer, on the second anniversary of the Stonewall riot, the gathering at Sheep Meadow was preceded by the first "Gay Pride" parade. The march, organized by the Christopher Street Liberation Day Committee, attracted an estimated five thousand marchers.[33] By 1977, "[w]aving placards and chanting rallying cries, a vast sea of homosexual men and women marched up Fifth Avenue under bobbing banners of liberation in what many called the largest homosexual rights demonstration ever held in New York City." According to one observer, "tens of thousands" marched from Greenwich Village to Central Park; similarly huge marches took place in major cities across the United States, including "San Francisco, Miami, Los Angeles, Chicago, Atlanta, Kansas City, Seattle, and Providence."[34] Just two years later, on the tenth anniversary of the Stonewall riots, the crowd for the gay pride parade in New York was estimated at nearly one hundred thousand. The 1979 parade was also memorable for the fact that for the first time, a softball team representing the city's gay community defeated a team representing the New York Police Department. The annual game had been started in 1973 to help foster better relations between the two groups.[35]

The surge of activism in 1977 that spilled well beyond the narrow streets of Greenwich Village can be attributed almost entirely to one person: Anita Bryant, whose successful campaign to overturn the antidiscrimination ordinance adopted in Miami-Dade County taught the gay rights movement as much about political power and the value of fund-raising as the IRS crackdown on religious schools taught the growing evangelical movement. (A year after the Bryant campaign in Florida, a Carter administration proposal to deny tax-exempt status to all-white religious schools outraged and politicized evangelicals.) The battle over the nondiscrimination ordinance in Miami was a profound turning point for both movements: religious conservatives realized for the first time just how far the gay rights movement had come, and gay activists understood how easily some of their gains could be reversed.

But another significant factor was about to enter the equation: the growing economic influence of the gay community. The reports of the steadily swelling crowds at the annual gay pride parades were attracting the notice not only of politicians, religious conservatives, and the media, but, even more significantly, of advertisers. Increasingly, there was awareness that the size of the gay community (and its disposable income) represented an important untapped market.

The initial forays of national advertisers into the gay market occurred in small, typically free publications distributed exclusively to the gay community. In January 1980, not long after Ronald Reagan was sworn in as president, a profile of the *Blade*, a biweekly newspaper distributed to the capital's gay community, reported that the paper was increasingly successful in attracting advertisements from both local merchants and national advertisers. Richard Ray, who advertised his National Car Rental fleet in the *Blade*, offered a succinct analysis: "It's a market that cannot be ignored. A bunch of 'em got money. It's pretty stupid not to advertise to them." Others clearly agreed: the year before, gay publications had even been given their own category in the *Standard Rate and Data of Consumer Publications*—the resource that ad agencies consult when they are planning their media purchases.[36]

Ironically, the struggling economy that had helped usher Reagan into office was also helping promote a greater acceptance of gays. As one Capitol Hill business observed, "They are people with a cause, just like any other group. In hard economic times, the more markets you tap, the better off you are."[37] The same was proving true in the housing market, although with somewhat more mixed results. Changes in the antidiscrimination provisions of the federal lending laws opened up more financing possibilities for gay and lesbian buyers, but discrimination by sellers and potential neighbors continued to be a factor. Amusingly, the gay community found some of its most enthusiastic support among real estate brokers. As one saleswoman put it: "[Gays] buy some of the most interesting homes. The men have a special eye for home improvement. They are not burdened by family expenses and so put a lot more money into remodeling. The end result is usually marvelous. When it comes to resale we all know the 'gay' house is going to be snapped up fast."[38]

As the economic influence of the gay community continued to rise, another subtle but significant cultural shift occurred—the content of advertisements and, in many cases, the very products being advertised were increasingly influenced by the purchasing choices of the gay community. Even in the economically troubled times of the early 1980s, the upper end of the gay demographic was being described by retailers and advertisers as "recession-proof." Advertisers still shied away from using gay spokespersons in their ads—tennis star Billie Jean King, for instance, was dropped from numerous endorsements after admitting in 1981 to a lesbian affair—but they were far less shy about creating sexually ambiguous ads—"gay window advertising"—that could appeal to gay and straight audiences on different levels.[39]

Despite the victory of Ronald Reagan in 1980 and the growing influence of the Moral Majority, the conversation about homosexuality in America had been permanently changed. In the American economy, belonging to a clearly defined and sizable marketing niche may not constitute full social acceptance, but it is certainly a step in that direction. The combination of the movement's own political power and its economic importance helped broaden public understanding of homosexuality and promoted greater—if still incomplete—acceptance of gays and gay lifestyles. The timing of these developments could not have been better, as the gay community (and the nation as a whole) was about to face a profound healthcare crisis with a government reluctant to speak its name.

C. Everett Koop: Speaking Truth to Power about AIDS

When President Reagan nominated C. Everett Koop in 1981 to serve as his surgeon general, Capitol Hill's first objection was that he was too old. The law at the time required surgeon generals to be younger than sixty-four and, at the time of his nomination, Koop was sixty-four and a half. Thanks to some legislative legerdemain by Senator Jesse Helms, that barrier was removed by an amendment to a budget bill. But few on either side of the aisle were fooled. The real objection to Koop serving as surgeon general was his long-standing opposition to abortion, some forms of birth control, and homosexuality. Of particular concern to many was a speech that Koop gave in 1979 at the commencement of the Philadelphia College of Osteopathic Medicine, in which Koop predicted a grim future in which the practice of abortion leads inexorably to "government persecution of religion, the slaughter of defective newborn babies, and court-ordered euthanasia for the senile, the sick and the elderly."[40] The reservations over Koop's views stretched the confirmation process out over six months, but on November 17, 1981, the Senate finally confirmed him to serve as surgeon general.

Unbeknownst to anyone involved in the Koop confirmation battle, the definitive health crisis of Koop's term was beginning that summer. On June 18, 1981, the US Centers for Disease Control and Prevention (CDC) in Atlanta reported that a cluster of five men in Los Angeles suffered from *Pneumocystis carinii* pneumonia.[41] The CDC initially labeled the disease Gay-Related Immune Deficiency (GRID), but as awareness grew that the disease could affect nonhomosexuals as well, it was renamed Acquired Immunodeficiency Syndrome (AIDS) in 1982.

For some religious conservative leaders, the fact that the disease was initially identified in gay men was divine ratification of everything they had been saying about homosexuality. As one anonymous conservative pollster cynically remarked to Fred Barnes of the *New Republic*, "It justifies their prejudices against homosexuals, and it gets Africans, too. If it would only strike the Soviets, it'd be perfect."[42]

The most outspoken and vehement religious conservative leader was the Reverend Jerry Falwell, then at the height of his political and cultural influence as head of the Moral Majority. He declared at a press conference just two years into the epidemic that AIDS was God's way of "spanking" the United States. He claimed that the Reagan administration had failed to take stern measures to prevent the spread of the disease (such as closing all bathhouses and banning gays from donating blood) out of political considerations: "If the Reagan administration does not put its full weight against this, what is now a gay plague in this country, I feel that a year from now, President Ronald Reagan will be blamed for allowing this awful disease to break out among the innocent American public."[43] The AIDS crisis remained a reliable fund-raiser for Falwell. A typical appeal, mailed four years later, requested donations to fund a television special revealing how "homosexuals and the pro-homosexual have joined together with the liberal, gay-influenced media to cover up the facts concerning AIDS."[44]

The antipathy of religious conservatives toward the gay community played a significant role in muting the government's verbal response to the new disease. Unwilling to antagonize his core supporters, President Reagan did not make a public reference to the disease until a White House press conference in September 1985. By that time—more than four years into the epidemic—nearly seven thousand Americans had died of the disease, and thousands more were infected. Many suspected that Reagan's willingness to finally begin talking about the disease stemmed from the AIDS-related death that summer of his friend, actor Rock Hudson (1925–1985).

The news that Hudson was gay came as a shock to many people. An active participant in the studio contract system of the 1940s and 1950s, Hudson was keenly aware of the delicate economics of fame and actively participated in schemes to hide his homosexuality behind a well-honed façade of virile heterosexuality. The most extreme step in the campaign occurred on November 5, 1955, when the studio arranged a hasty wedding between Hudson and his agent's secretary, Phyllis Gates (1925–2006). The marriage, inevitably unhappy from the start, lasted less than three years.[45]

Actress Mamie Van Doren, who went on studio-sponsored dates with Hudson, said his sexual orientation was an open secret in the film community. "[W]e all knew Rock was gay, but it never made any difference to us," she said. "Universal invested a lot of money in Rock, and it was important for his image to remain that of a lady-killer."[46]

A few years later, when the Hollywood scandal sheet *Confidential* threatened to run an exposé of Hudson's secret life as a gay man, Universal purportedly paid the paper to spike the story and offered up instead the information that another of its actors, George Nader (1921–2002), was gay. Nader had cultivated a persona of brawny masculinity in a series of largely forgettable Western and military films, and the disclosure of his homosexuality largely ended his Hollywood career.[47] Nader was a longtime partner of Hudson's personal secretary, Mark Miller, and despite Universal's actions, the three remained close friends throughout Hudson's life. When Hudson died, he left the bulk of his $27 million estate to Miller and Nader.[48]

When President Reagan called Hudson, who lay ill in a Paris hospital, the federal government had already invested $200 million in researching the new disease. But Hudson's death that fall, with its mix of celebrity and secrets kept even during *Pillow Talk*, catapulted AIDS to the front page of the nation's newspapers and magazines. In successive weeks in August 1985, *Time* ran articles headlining AIDS as a "spreading scourge" and a "growing threat." Under attack from the Left for not devoting enough resources to research the disease and from the Right for not doing enough to contain its spread (suggestions included screening everyone in the country for AIDS, shutting down bathhouses across the nation, making it a felony for the AIDS high-risk group to donate blood, and even the quarantining of gay males),[49] President Reagan asked Surgeon General Koop in February 1986 to prepare a comprehensive report on the disease.

If either the president or religious conservatives expected the surgeon general, an evangelical Christian himself, to sternly lecture the gay community on promiscuity and endorse some of the more draconian antihomosexual measures being suggested, they were no doubt sorely disappointed. On October 22, 1986, Koop issued a remarkably unambiguous and evenhanded report on the disease, a thirty-six-page booklet that included explicit information on the sexual practices that make the transmission of AIDS more likely and a detailed summary of the toll that the disease was taking on the nation. He also took to task the people who were using the disease as a chance to bash the gay community. "It is time," Koop wrote, "to put self-defeating attitudes aside and recognize that we are fighting a disease—not people."[50]

Noting that the number of Americans dead from the disease had doubled to just under fifteen thousand from the summer before, Koop laid out his most controversial suggestion: that children receive detailed sex education in the home and in school "at the lowest grade possible." In practical terms, Koop said, that meant that adults should start educating children about sex whenever they begin to ask questions about the subject, which generally occurs around third grade. The goal, Koop said, is to have children grow up "knowing the behaviors to avoid to protect themselves from exposure to the AIDS virus."[51]

Liberals, medical researchers, and gay activists were surprised and delighted with the thoroughness and tone of the surgeon general's report. Senator Ted Kennedy (D-MA) and Rep. Henry Waxman (D-CA) publicly apologized for their opposition to his nomination and applauded his courage. At the

Third International Conference on AIDS in June 1987, Koop received a standing ovation from six thousand doctors. Within a year, twenty million copies of the AIDS report were in print.[52]

On the Right, the reviews were scathing. Following the release of the report, conservative maven Phyllis Schlafly pressured eleven Republicans—including 1988 presidential candidates Bob Dole and Jack Kemp—to withdraw their sponsorship of a May 1987 gala for Koop and skip the event altogether. The dinner was picketed by protesters demanding Koop's dismissal, leading the beleaguered surgeon general to thank members of the audience for choosing to attend: "There has never been a time in my life when I wanted or appreciated such a show of friendship."[53]

The response from within the administration was no friendlier. Secretary of Education William Bennett urged Koop to endorse the teaching of abstinence in schools, and Reagan's domestic policy adviser, Gary Bauer, asked Koop to stop recommending the use of condoms to people having sex outside a monogamous relationship. In both cases, Koop refused.[54] The exchanges clearly took a toll on Koop's view of his former political supporters: "Do I have the respect I had for the conservatives two years ago? Of course I don't. Will I ever again? Never. Do I think Henry Waxman is fair? Yes. There are a lot of compensations now. There were none in 1981. I had a very small constituency, but I didn't gain any friends anyplace. Now every time I get attacked from the right, I get friends on the left and in the middle."[55]

It would be interesting to poll religious conservatives on the question of which of Reagan's high-profile appointments was most disappointing: Sandra Day O'Connor, Anthony Kennedy, or C. Everett Koop. In terms of longevity and the gravity of their decisions, Supreme Court justices obviously trump a surgeon general. But at a critical juncture in the nation's healthcare history, the country was fortunate to have a surgeon general capable of putting aside his own feelings and courageously speaking medical truth to the political power of religious conservatives. In doing so, he permanently shifted the focus of the debate on AIDS from the punitive to the educational. An intelligent man, Koop could have had no illusions about how his report would be received by religious conservatives, but he was clearly committed to providing the public with the best information available about AIDS.

"I feel you can never separate your faith from yourself," he said. "On the other hand, I am the surgeon general, not the chaplain of the public health service."[56]

Don't Ask, Don't Tell . . . But Sign Up

When president-elect Bill Clinton prepared to take office in January 1993, he had a list of promises he intended to keep and a list of political debts to pay. Near the top of both lists was his promise to the nation's gay and lesbian community to end discrimination in the military, an idea he had first publicly floated at a speech at Harvard's Kennedy School of Government. It was the kind of big idea, big policy initiative that appealed to the wonkish Clinton: forty-eight years of discrimination and inequality could be eliminated virtually overnight. It was a noble goal, but one that quickly withered in the harsh light of political reality.

Even before he had a chance to put his humidor on the desk in the Oval Office, President Clinton found himself in a political no-man's-land between two deeply entrenched adversaries. On the one hand, members of the gay and lesbian community were increasingly concerned (and furious) that Clinton might back away from his promise to issue an executive order lifting the ban. On the other hand, of course, were religious and social conservatives, along with virtually the entire command structure of the US military. It was abundantly clear that the president-elect's relationship with the Joint Chiefs—already tenuous because of Clinton's Vietnam war deferments—might quickly become completely unworkable.

On Veteran's Day 1992, Clinton gave his first policy speech after being elected president, and he used the occasion to lay out his positions on various military issues. After the speech, he held a press conference, and reporters asked if he intended to follow through on his oft-repeated campaign promise to allow homosexuals to serve in the military. The new president said that he did: "My position is that we need everybody in America that has got a contribution to make, that's willing to obey the law and work hard and play by the rules."[57] President-elect Clinton then added: "What I want to do is come up with an appropriate response that will focus sharply on the fact that we do have people who are homosexuals who served our country with distinction, who were never kicked out of the military. . . . [T]he issue ought to be conduct—has anybody done anything which would disqualify them, whether it's Tailhook scandal or something else."[58]

The reaction from military leaders and the rank-and-file was rapid and uniformly negative. The following day, General Colin Powell, then the chairman of the Joint Chiefs of Staff, made it absolutely clear that he and the other leaders of the US armed services had no enthusiasm for Clinton's proposal: "The military leaders in the armed forces of the United States—the Joint Chiefs of Staff and the senior commanders—continue to believe strongly that the presence of homosexuals within the armed forces would be prejudicial to good order and discipline. And we continue to hold that view."[59]

Although General Powell's remarks were firm and rather uncompromising, they were more disciplined and less openly threatening than some conservative members of Congress. During the debate over the issue, for instance, Senator Jesse Helms (R-NC) told a television interviewer that "Mr. Clinton better watch out if he comes down here. He'd better have a bodyguard." (After the Secret Service had a few words with the senator about the propriety of threatening a US president, Senator Helms issued a rather grudging apology.)[60] But Helms was merely adding his voice to a chorus of opposition from religious conservatives: the Reverend Lou Sheldon declared that "[a]s Bush wanted to be the educational president, Clinton desires to be the homosexual president with his homosexual activities,"[61] and Operation Rescue founder Randall Terry said that "Clinton has done us a great favor. This is going to help us mobilize people to take action for the next four years."[62]

Some religious and conservative leaders wasted little time using the controversy over gays in the military to boost their political and organizational fortunes. Oliver North, who founded a group called the Freedom Alliance in 1990, sent out tens of thousands of letters in early 1993 to solicit funds for a national campaign against gays in the military. And Jerry Falwell set up a 900-number that he advertised on his television show, *The Old Time Gospel Hour*. Callers paid as much as a $1.95 per minute to listen to a petition against gays in the military and other gay initiatives, and to have their name added to the petition. Falwell told National Public Radio that he had received over one hundred thousand calls after promoting the 900- number on three successive Sundays. The "gays in the military" issue was a fund-raising boost for a variety of other conservative groups as well.[63]

The overarching irony is that there was no question that gays were already serving in the military in 1992 and had probably been doing so since Valley Forge. In fact, the Colonial Army's first inspector general, the Prussian Baron Frederick William von Steuben (1730–1794), joined the revolutionary forces to avoid prosecution by German ecclesiastical authorities for his homosexuality. Von Steuben played an enormously important role in molding the thirteen state militias into an army at Valley Forge; later, his drill books were used by the US Army for thirty-five years, and his idea for a military academy formed the basis of West Point.[64]

In the decade between 1982 and 1992 alone, the military had discharged over fifteen thousand gays from the armed services. Still, in a standing army of 1.8 million soldiers, no one had any illusions about the fact that there were probably tens of thousands of gays still in the military. During the height of the debate, the *New York Times* reported in December 1992 that "in an effort to help [gay service members] deal with the hostility they face, an underground network of gay military groups, as well as a string of bars and clubs, has sprung up to lend support and provide contacts to homosexuals at bases around the country." The relationship between technology and privacy was underscored by the fact that one of the channels for the informal network was the growing number of computer bulletin boards, which service members could use to exchange phone numbers and arrange meetings.[65]

Clinton's push to permit gays to serve openly in the military found stiff opposition on Capitol Hill as well. Legislative leaders in both parties, particularly in the Senate, warned Clinton that his initiative was threatening other aspects of his agenda, and threatened to adopt legislation that would turn the Pentagon's policy of banning gay soldiers into a formal statute. At the end of January 1993, Clinton agreed to delay his plan for lifting the ban on service in the military by gays to give the Defense Department the opportunity to draft an executive order on the practice. The ensuing negotiations proved difficult for the new president, particularly given the reluctance of some of his own party members—such as Senator Sam Nunn, a conservative Democrat from Georgia—to support him. In the midst of the controversy, there were some surprises: the conservative Republican senator Alfonse D'Amato, for instance, flatly declared, "I support allowing gays in the military. It's that simple."[66] Even more startling to conservatives was the outspoken support for Clinton by the iconic Senator Barry Goldwater, who said, "I don't care if a soldier is straight, as long as he can shoot straight." Comments like that, along with the eighty-five-year-old senator's support for abortion rights and an antidiscrimination ordinance for gays in Phoenix, had some conservatives furiously calling radio talk shows and demanding the removal of Goldwater's name from various Arizona buildings.[67]

In the end, however, Clinton was forced to accept a policy well short of his plan to simply erase the ban following his inauguration. On July 18, 1993, he announced what has become known as the "Don't Ask, Don't Tell" policy, under which gays can serve in the military as long as they don't "aggressively declare their sexual orientation or engage in homosexual conduct." The military was also barred from formally inquiring about the sexual orientation of enlisted personnel or new recruits.[68]

Much like religious conservatives twelve years earlier, the gay and lesbian community was deeply disappointed by what they saw as their president's failure to follow through on a campaign promise to an important constituency. Nonetheless, the extensive public debate over the role of gays in the military did as much, if not more, to advance the overall discussion of gay rights than would have been accomplished by the issuance of a single executive order.

The issue of gays in the military took an odd twist a few years later under an avowedly conservative president, when a controversy arose in 2005 over the procedure for granting credentials to White House correspondents. Access to the White House press room is controlled by the president's staff, which hands out two different types of passes: a permanent "hard" pass, for journalists who previously have been issued credentials by the Standing Committee of Correspondents that governs the issuance of press passes on Capitol Hill, and a "daily" pass, which journalists must request each day they want to attend a briefing or press conference. Not surprisingly, it is much easier to get a daily pass than a hard pass, but until early 2005, no one really appreciated just how much easier.

On January 26, 2005, during one of President Bush's rare press conferences,[69] he called on a journalist named Jeff Gannon, who began by claiming that "Senate Democratic leaders have painted a very bleak picture of the U.S. economy," and then asked, "how are you going to work with people who seem to have divorced themselves from reality?"[70] Although it didn't get nearly as much attention as Gannon's "divorced from reality" charge, his follow-up question was just as much a softball inquiry, giving the president the opportunity to explain what effect criticisms of the Iraq war "have on the morale of our troops and on the confidence of the Iraqi people that what you're trying to do over there is going to succeed."[71]

The fact that President Bush called on a virtually unknown reporter and skipped over so many other more experienced (and only slightly less docile) journalists raised a number of eyebrows. Two days later, Media Matters for America reported that Gannon, who had criticized some of his White House press corps colleagues for working off Democratic talking points, had made extensive use of talking points from the Republican National Committee on his conservative radio talk show, as well as in his dispatches for Talon News, a right-wing news Web site.[72]

The Gannon story quickly floated into the "blogosphere"—the rant-filled layer of the Internet still largely populated by overly wordy online diarists and underemployed conspiracists, but increasingly also stocked with dogged researchers and insightful analysts of all political stripes. Helping to get the story out was Media Matters senior fellow Duncan Black, better known among Web denizens as Atrios, the writer of the blog Eschaton. Later on the twenty-eighth, he reported that according to his sources in the White House, "Jeff Gannon" was in fact a pseudonym, and that "Gannon's" real name was James D. "JD" Guckert.[73] Questions were quickly raised about why the White House, which is ostensibly concerned about homeland security, would allow someone access to a presidential news conference under an assumed name.

The most likely answer to that question was outlined in an analysis published on February 2 by Media Matters, in which it became clear that for much of 2004, the three most important words in White House spokesman Scott McClellan's vocabulary were "Go ahead, Jeff." Whenever the questioning from the rest of the press corps threatened to get even slightly unpleasant, McClellan would point to Gannon, say, "Go ahead, Jeff," and Gannon would divert the conversation to a safer topic for President Bush and the administration, usually with a partisan sideswipe along the way.[74] The journal *Editor & Publisher* disclosed that Gannon had been denied a hard pass to the Press Room because of Talon News's lack of journalistic trappings and its connection to GOPUSA.com, a conservative political Web site run by Texas Republican activist Bobby Eberle (of no discernable relation to Paula Jones fund-raiser Bruce Eberle).[75]

Over at DailyKos, one of the Web's leading political blogs, the Gannon/ Guckert story was keeping a number of bloggers busy. It didn't take them long to uncover the fact that one of Gannon's personal Web sites, JeffGannon.com, was registered by a company called Bedrock Corporation, and that Bedrock was also the registered agent for a number of other Web sites, including Hot-MilitaryStud.com, MilitaryEscorts.com, and MilitaryEscortsM4M.com, which reportedly offered male escort services at a rate of $200 per hour or $1,200 per weekend.[76] Further digging produced a photo on America Online of a man resembling Gannon, posing on a couch in his underwear, with a user name "JDG." Copies of the same photo were found on several male escort Web sites, including MeetLocalMen.com and WorkingBoys.net.[77]

As the mainstream media began to show increasing interest in the story, Gannon posted a brief message to his Web site on February 9, announcing his resignation from Talon News:

Jeff Gannon
A Voice of the New Media
The voice goes silent

Because of the attention being paid to me I find it is no longer possible to effectively be a reporter for Talon News. In consideration of the welfare of me and my family I have decided to return to private life.

Thank you to all those who supported me.

Within twenty-four hours, the stories that Gannon had submitted to Talon News, a number of which covered topics relating to homosexuality (including a defense of the proposed ban on gay marriage), were quickly pulled from the Talon Web site.[78]

The manner of Gannon's departure from Talon News gave conservative columnists like Ann Coulter the opportunity to slam liberal bloggers for hounding the poor scribe out of the White House Press Room and from his job not because he used a false name (she listed a number of journalists who use names other than those their parents gave them), but in reality because he may be gay and "may have run" a gay escort service a few years earlier. The whole situation left Coulter sarcastically confused: "Are we supposed to like gay people now, or hate them?" she wondered.[79]

The fact that liberal bloggers effectively "outed" Gannon unfortunately clouded a story that should have received longer-lasting attention. Yes, it is amusing that the antipornography, antigay Bush administration may have been relying on a gay male escort with nude online photos to help take the edge off its press conferences. And, yes, that does raise questions about the thoroughness of the White House vetting process for credentials. But a far more interesting issue—and one that was entirely untouched by either the blogs or the mainstream media—is the fact that many of the gay escort sites created by Gannon were for men currently or formerly in the military. That, more than anything else, probably greased the skids for Gannon's departure from Talon News, since neither the Bush administration nor the Texas Republican Party had any particular desire to be seen endorsing homosexuality in the armed services.

THE GAY COMMUNITY SAYS, "I DO"

If there is one issue that infuriates religious conservatives even more than the idea of gays serving in the military, it is the idea of gay marriage. At the forefront of the opposition has been former presidential candidate Gary Bauer, who has been quoted as equating "homosexual marriage" with "[t]he total destruction of marriage, family, and ultimately society as we know it today."[80]

Even before the burst of gay activism following the Stonewall riots, members of the gay community were talking about the possibility of marrying. "Several homosexuals I talked to recently," wrote New York Times journalist Webster Schott in 1967, "spoke seriously of the homosexual's desire for binding, legal homosexual marriage." Drew Shafer, the head of a Kansas City–based gay activist group called the Phoenix Society for Individual Freedom, put the issue in starkly human terms: "Homosexuality isn't only for the young. One thing the homosexual doesn't want is to grow old alone. You need someone who cares, someone to talk to when you're low. You can't do that staring at the walls of a bachelor apartment."[81]

The legal battle for same-sex marriage dates from 1970, when a Minnesota resident, Jack Baker, sued the clerk of Hennepin County for a license to marry his lover, L. Michael McConnell. He lost his suit in the state courts, and the US Supreme Court refused to hear his case, but in the interim the couple received a marriage license from the city of Minkata in Blue Earth County. The two were married by a United Methodist minister on September 3, 1971, and thirty-four years later, are still married.[82]

The impetus to seek the legal protection of marriage was given a strong if tragic boost by the onset of the AIDS epidemic. As it devastated the nation's homosexual population, the disease threw into stark relief the legal disparities between heterosexual and homosexual couples when it came to issues like bed-side visitations, decisions regarding medical treatment, burial arrangements, and the transfer of property. When Drew Shafer was being transferred to a Kansas City Hospital in the last stages of AIDS, his longtime partner Mickey Ray-Pleger had to threaten legal action simply to ride in the ambulance with him. It was not an atypical story; many other gay men were forcibly prevented from being with their partners as they died.

For years, gay couples had employed stopgap measures, including "con-tracts, wills, and powers of attorney to provide legal protection for themselves and their partners."[83] But such measures failed to provide gay partners with the full range of marital benefits contemplated by state and federal law, and the AIDS epidemic drove home the message that the unorthodox legal nature of the relationship was a tenuous alternative. The push for legal recognition of gay relationships took on new urgency.

There was a brief flurry of excitement in May 1993, when the Hawaii Supreme Court ruled that the state had to show a compelling state interest in barring gay marriage. Writing for the majority, Justice Steven H. Levinson declared that "marriage is a basic civil right" and concluded that as it stood, the Hawaiian ban on same-sex marriages "denies same-sex couples access to the marital status and its concomitant rights and benefits."[84] A year later, however, the Hawaiian legislature passed a bill specifically banning same-sex marriages.[85]

The possibility that a state might authorize same-sex marriages raised the specter that other states might be forced to give "full faith and credit" to the union under Article 4 of the Constitution. That possibility galvanized religious conserv-atives, who spearheaded efforts in at least nineteen states to formally deny any recognition of same-sex marriages authorized in other states. In discussing the idea of same-sex marriage, Jay A. Sekulow, chief counsel for Pat Robertson's American Center for Law and Justice, said that "[i]t strikes at the very core of who we are as a people. Marriage defined as a man and a woman has been around for more than 6,000 years, and has served most cultures very well."[86]

Fearing that individual state action would not be enough, conservatives pushed for the passage of a Defense of Marriage Act, a bill that denies any federal benefits to the members of a same-sex marriage. The bill was sent to the president's desk by the Republican-controlled Congress just six weeks before the 1996 election, presenting Clinton with a classic political dilemma: reject the bill and risk alienating a potentially wide swath of the electorate, or disappoint a key constituency once again. Clinton chose to sign the bill, albeit in a midnight flurry of bill signings out of sight of the press or television cameras.[87]

Fortunately, the Defense of Marriage Act has not significantly slowed the steady march toward legal recognition of gay relationships. The significant breakthrough came on December 20, 1999, when the Vermont Supreme Court ruled unanimously that under the Vermont state constitution, "same-sex couples should have access to all benefits, including medical insurance, hospital visitation and spousal support now given freely to those who marry."[88] The court left it up to the legislature to determine how best to provide those benefits, thereby touching off a bitter four-month battle over whether to recognize gay marriage outright or create some parallel system. In the end, the legislature passed a bill providing for civil unions for same-sex couples, and Governor Howard Dean signed the bill into law on April 26, 2000. (Despite the historic significance of the bill, Dean signed it with little fanfare in his office that afternoon, thereby denying opponents any photos of the occasion for use in political ads in the upcoming statewide election.)

The debate over the adoption of civil unions in Vermont was ferocious and often vicious. In a relatively rare phenomenon for the small state, demonstrators even flew in from out of state. Prominent among them was Randall Terry, who set up an office in the state capital, Montpelier, and frequently demonstrated outside the State House during the chilly Vermont winter. Despite issuing what many people considered to be threats against various supporters of the civil union legislation, Terry eventually shut down his office and left the state after civil unions became law.

A more far-reaching decision was handed down by the Massachusetts Supreme Judicial Court in February 2004, in which the court said that only full marriage, and not civil unions, would satisfy the requirements of the state constitution. After legislators held a state constitution convention in an unsuccessful effort to overturn the court, Massachusetts became the first state to formally issue marriage licenses to gay couples.

In a statement released after the court's ruling, President George W. Bush declared that "[m]arriage is a sacred institution between a man and a woman. If activist judges insist on re-defining marriage by court order, the only alternative will be the constitutional process. We must do what is legally necessary to defend the sanctity of marriage."[89]

In his statement, Bush was alluding to the Federal Marriage Amendment, a proposed constitutional amendment that would define marriage throughout the United States as the union of one man and one woman. Floating the idea prior to his run for a second term was remarkably similar to President Reagan's renewed interest in the school prayer amendment in early 1984. Not only is the Federal Marriage Amendment one of the top priorities of religious conservatives—one of President Bush's core support groups—but it helped underscore the fact that his opponent, Senator John Kerry, hails from Massachusetts. The difficult combination of events in 2005—a bogged-down war in Iraq, a stuttering economy, and the devastating Hurricane Katrina—reshuffled the White House's priorities and left Bush with little time, energy, or political capital to push the religious conservative agenda. Nonetheless, with the midterm elections looming in the fall, critically low approval ratings, and growing rumblings from religious conservatives (Richard Viguerie, among others, wrote an op-ed piece calling for a fall boycott of Republican candidates), he could not afford to ignore his base altogether. In June 2006 the president publicly campaigned for the Federal Marriage Amendment and Senator Frist brought it up for debate on the Senate floor. Although religious conservatives welcomed the increased attention, the amendment's minute chance of passage and the president's somewhat lukewarm enthusiasm for the project left them questioning once again the commitment of their erstwhile Republican allies.

In the meantime, the social and economic forces that promote the idea of gay marriage continue to gather force. This front of the decency wars is obviously far from over, but its overall trajectory is unlikely to differ from the many that have come before it. As states like Vermont, Massachusetts, and, most recently, Connecticut demonstrate through practical experience that legal recognition of gay relationships is not destructive to more traditional pairings (and enjoy the economic benefits of additional tourism and wedding industry revenues), the objections to same-sex marriage will steadily fade. Much as when the churches of New England opened their voting rolls to merchants who had experienced greater economic success than religious awakening, economics and familiarity are helping the country to appreciate (or at least tolerate) a love so long unspoken.

Chapter Ten

At Play in the Laboratories of the Lord

Sacrificing Scientific Truth on the Altar of Ideology

> Now it is such a bizarrely improbable coincidence that anything so mind-boggling useful [as the Babel fish] could have evolved purely by chance that some thinkers have chosen to see it as a final and clinching proof of the *non*-existence of God.
>
> The argument goes something like this: "I refuse to prove that I exist," says God, "for proof denies faith, and without faith, I am nothing."
>
> "But," says Man, "the Babel fish is a dead giveaway, isn't it? It could not have evolved by chance. It proves you exist, and so therefore, by your own argument, you don't. QED."
>
> "Oh dear," says God. "I hadn't thought of that," and promptly vanishes in a puff of logic.
>
> —Douglas Adams, 1980[1]

There is something quintessentially American about the fact that one of the country's most significant legal trials was launched largely as a publicity stunt. In 1925 the Tennessee legislature passed the Butler Act, which made it a misdemeanor to teach the theory of evolution in public schools: "[I]t shall be unlawful for any teacher in any of the Universities, Normals and all other public schools of the State which are supported in whole or in part by the public school funds of the State, to teach any theory that denies the story of the Divine Creation of man as taught in the Bible, and to teach instead that man has descended from a lower order of animals."[2]

Clarence Darrow, ca. 1922. (Library of Congress)

Not long after the passage of the Butler Act, the American Civil Liberties Union (ACLU) announced that it would provide financial support for the defense of any teacher willing to violate the law and test its constitutionality.

Smartly recognizing that a trial over the respective merits of evolution and biblical creation would be a media sensation, some savvy (and arguably cynical) members of the business community in Dayton, Tennessee, persuaded the high school football coach, John T. Scopes (1900–1970), to serve as the test case for the new law. The Scopes trial, as it quickly became known, was not only a clash of the two most popular ideas in Western culture regarding the origin of human life—it also brought together two of the century's great legal figures, William Jennings Bryan (1860–1925) and Clarence Darrow (1857–1938).

Bryan, an attorney who was first nominated to run for president in 1896 by the Democrats at the remarkably young age of thirty-six (and twice more in 1900 and 1908), was nearing the end of his life when the prosecution of John Scopes began. It was a prosecution in which Bryan had a vested interest: a life-long devout Christian fundamentalist, Bryan spent his latter years fighting the growing acceptance of Charles Darwin's theory of evolution. He traveled the country addressing state legislatures, urging them to prohibit the teaching of evolution. Following his persuasive visits, several did. Bryan also supported the passage of an amendment to the US Constitution that would have barred the teaching of evolution in any public school in the country.

The Tennessee legislature was not among those that Bryan directly addressed, but in 1924 he gave a lecture in Nashville titled "Is the Bible True?" A copy of his speech later made its way into the hands of Rep. John Washington Butler (1875–1952), a man already concerned that the teaching of evolution was a threat to the state's children. To help counter what he perceived as an attack on parental and biblical authority, Butler sponsored the law that bore his name. When news of the Scopes trial first broke, Bryan volunteered to serve on the team of lawyers prosecuting the case.

Offering his services to help defend the twenty-four-year-old teacher was the equally prestigious Clarence Darrow, who was then at the height of his own distinguished legal career. Just one year earlier, Darrow had defended the infamous pair Nathan Leopold (1904–1971) and Richard Loeb (1905–1936) in their murder trial for the death of fourteen-year-old Bobby Franks (1909–1924). The two confessed to murdering Franks largely for the thrill of trying to commit the perfect crime (although given the speed with which they were apprehended, both their planning and execution clearly fell short of perfect). In a somewhat surprising legal move, Darrow persuaded Leopold and Loeb to plead guilty rather than not guilty by reason of insanity. That gave Darrow—a dedicated capital punishment foe—the opportunity to argue directly to the trial judge for life imprisonment for his clients rather than the gallows. Darrow proceeded to deliver what is widely regarded as the finest speech of his long career and succeeded in keeping his infamous clients from hanging.

The Scopes trial attracted Darrow not merely because of its high profile—although Darrow was notoriously fond of a good headline—but also because of his confirmed agnosticism. For Darrow, the efforts by religious conservatives and fundamentalists to block the teaching of evolution was a slap in the face to human intelligence and progress. As the imposing attorney stood and surveyed the carnival-like atmosphere in Dayton not long before the trial began, he grandly declared that "Scopes isn't on trial; civilization is on trial." The implication, needless to say, was that Darrow intended to be civilization's savior.

It was a role that over the course of the eight-day trial Darrow undertook with glee. His defense of Scopes culminated in the cross-examination of Bryan, whom Darrow called to the stand to testify as a self-proclaimed expert on matters biblical. To accommodate the overflowing crowd eager to watch the confrontation, Judge John T. Raulston (1868–1956) moved the court outside. Over the course of a long and particularly hot summer's day, Darrow relentlessly grilled Bryan on the literal truth of biblical events, ranging from Jonah and the whale to the Great Flood to Adam and Eve's expulsion from paradise. By the time dusk was falling, an exhausted Bryan was willing to concede that not everything in the Bible should be read as literal truth, but reiterated his belief that Darrow's primary goals were to slur the Bible and mock Christianity. When the court adjourned for the evening, Judge Raulston excused Bryan from the witness chair, declared his testimony irrelevant to the trial, and ordered it entirely stricken from the record.

The following day, Scopes entered a guilty plea at the suggestion of Darrow, who hoped to have the Butler Act overturned on appeal. Judge Raulston assessed a fine of $100 against Scopes (which Bryan graciously offered to pay), and the case went up on appeal to the Tennessee Supreme Court. Much to Darrow's chagrin, the court upheld the constitutionality of the Butler Act but vacated Scopes's guilty plea on technical grounds.[3]

The media coverage of the trial was everything for which Darrow could have wished. Each day, hundreds of reporters (including the well-known and savagely sardonic *Baltimore Sun* scribe H. L. Mencken [1880–1956]) filled papers around the world with long, detailed stories. Adding to the circuslike atmosphere, the Scopes trial had the distinction of being the first to be broadcast by radio. Thanks in large part to Darrow's relentless cross-examination of Bryant (it may have been stricken from the court record but not from public consumption), biblical literalists, religious fundamentalists, and even Southerners in general were depicted with varying degrees of scorn and ridicule.

It would be another generation before the Butler Act was removed from the Tennessee statutes and the teaching of creationism declared unconstitutional, but Darrow and the ACLU largely succeeded in their ultimate goal of slowing and even stopping the anti-evolution movement (an outcome aided by the untimely death of Bryan just five days after the end of the Scopes trial). Indeed, the media coverage was sufficiently hostile and mocking to persuade the majority of fundamentalists that active participation in the political realm was simply too damaging to religious values and their sense of community. It was an attitude that did not change for half a century.

THE STEALTH DEITY: TRYING TO SNEAK GOD
BACK INTO THE CLASSROOM

By the mid-1970s, the generation of fundamentalists scarred by the biting arguments of Darrow and the sardonic coverage by Mencken had largely gone to meet their maker. Religious conservatives and fundamentalists now once again stepped off the sidewalk, this time to prevent attacks on their schools from the Internal Revenue Service and to prevent gays from defending themselves from discrimination. When both efforts proved highly successful (at least in the short term), religious conservatives reached the not terribly surprising conclusion that perhaps politics and religion could and should mix.

Among the leading concerns for religious conservatives was the steadily diminishing role of religion in the public schools. In a pair of decisions in the early 1960s, the Warren Court declared that both the practice of reading the Bible before the start of the school day and teacher-led prayers violated the First Amendment prohibition against the state establishment of a religion.[4] Later that same decade, the Warren Court also rejected state bans on teaching evolution (*Epperson v. Arkansas*)[5] on the same general principle; it was a violation of the Establishment Clause, the Court said, to require teachers to conform their instruction to the views of any particular religion. (The Establishment Clause is the portion of the First Amendment that reads: "Congress shall make no law respecting an establishment of religion.")

With the election of Ronald Reagan as president in 1980, religious conservatives began envisioning a day when the Court's decisions on school prayer and evolution would be overturned, either legislatively or judicially. As with so much else of the religious conservative agenda, however, not much happened on the school prayer front until early 1984, when President Reagan began looking for ways to reenergize the religious conservative wing of his coalition in anticipation of the fall election.

With the help of the White House, conservative Republicans drafted a proposed amendment to the US Constitution to authorize voluntary prayer in public schools: "Nothing in this Constitution shall be construed to prohibit individual or group prayer in public schools or other public institutions. No person shall be required by the United States or by any state to participate in prayer. Neither the United States nor any state shall compose the words of any prayer to be said in public schools."[6]

On March 5, 1984, under intense scrutiny from the media and interest groups on both sides of the issue, the US Senate began debating the bill containing the amendment. Outside the Capitol, fundamentalists staged an all-night rally led by the cheers of college students. "Kids want to pray!" they shouted. "Why can't they pray?"[7]

The following day, President Reagan spoke in favor of the amendment at a meeting of the National Association of Evangelicals: "I firmly believe," he said, "that the loving God who has blessed our land and made us good and caring people should never have been expelled from America's classrooms."[8]

Two weeks later, the school prayer amendment came up for a vote. Despite the presence of hundreds of evangelicals outside the Senate praying for passage, and despite President Reagan's lobbying on behalf of the measure, it fell eleven votes short (56–44) of the two-thirds majority needed for the Senate to pass a constitutional amendment. The fight against the prayer amendment was led in large part by Senator Lowell Weicker (R-CT), who ended the debate by asking, "[w]hy forfeit our birthright of religious liberty for a mess of speculative, political pottage?"[9]

President Reagan said that he was "deeply disappointed" by the Senate's vote and promised that if he was reelected in the fall, he would push for Congress to reconsider the amendment the following year; the issue, however, never again reached the floor of either the Senate or the House. Other Republicans were even angrier. Senator Jesse Helms (R-NC) said that he would continue his attempt to pass legislation that would strip the federal courts of jurisdiction over cases involving "school prayer, abortion, and busing."

"[T]here is more than one way to skin a cat," Senator Helms said during the debate, "and there is more than one way for Congress to provide a check on arrogant Supreme Court Justices who routinely distort the Constitution to suit their own notions of public policy."[10]

The voting patterns on the school prayer amendment helped underscore the growing regional divisions across the United States. In New England, just one senator, New Hampshire's Gordon Humphrey (a Republican) voted in favor of the amendment. In the South, every Democrat (except Arkansas's Dale Bumpers) voted yes. And, perhaps most interestingly, among those voting no was the senior senator from Arizona, Barry Goldwater.

The failure of the constitutional amendment did little to mute the debate over school prayer during the 1984 election. In August, Congress passed the Equal Access Act, which provided that any public school that accepts federal aid and allows nonreligious groups (like the debate club) to meet on school property must allow voluntary religious groups to do so as well. That same week, Republican representatives tried to pass a bill that would have barred all federal funds to any public school that prohibited spoken prayer "by individuals on a voluntary basis." That provision was defeated, but the House did approve a measure supporting the concept of silent prayer.[11]

The real uproar came in late August, when President Reagan attended an "ecumenical prayer breakfast" during the Republican National Convention in Dallas, Texas. During his speech to the seventeen thousand Christian laymen and church leaders in attendance, President Reagan chastised the opponents of the school prayer amendment.

"Isn't the real truth that they are intolerant of religion?" he asked. "They refuse to tolerate its importance in our lives."[12]

Four days later, former vice president and current presidential candidate Walter Mondale was also in Dallas, attending a campaign fund-raiser. Responding directly to President Reagan's remarks, he spoke at length about the importance of religious pluralism and tolerance in American society. "In America," he said, "faith is personal and honest and uncorrupted by political interference. May it always be that way."

Religious conservatives tried to portray the 1984 election as an endorsement of Reagan's view that "religion and politics are necessarily related," particularly when the extremely lopsided results rolled in on election night: the final Electoral College tally was an absolutely brutal 525–13. But despite Reagan's historic victory, religious conservatives continued to lose ground on the issue of religion in the public schools.

The following spring, the Supreme Court heard oral arguments in the case of *Wallace v. Jaffree*,[13] in which an Alabama father challenged the constitutionality of a 1982 state law that authorized the state's public schools to lead spoken prayers and/or permit a daily moment of silence "for meditation or voluntary prayer." There was little question that the spoken prayer provision would be struck down, since it directly contravened the Supreme Court's 1962 decision in *Engel v. Vitale* that barred teacher-led prayers. However, the state's provision for a "moment of silence" was a much closer question.

In a decision issued in June 1985, six of the Court's nine justices concluded that Alabama's "moment of silence" was actually an "endorsement and promotion of prayer," and was therefore unconstitutional. Part of the reason for the Court's decision was trial court testimony by the bill's sponsor, state senator Donald Holmes, in which he admitted that he had no other reason for drafting the bill than to promote prayer in Alabama's public schools.[14] That purpose, Justice John Paul Stevens wrote, violated "the established principal that the government must pursue a course of complete neutrality toward religion."

However, a glimmer of hope was left for religious conservatives. If one sifted through the various concurrences and dissents, there was some suggestion that a majority of the Court would support a properly motivated moment of silence. And, in fact, in 2001 the high court let stand (silently and without comment) a Fourth Circuit ruling in *Brown v. Gilmore* that upheld the constitutionality of a Virginia law that required a moment of silence in public school classrooms.[15] The Supreme Court's decision has largely settled the matter; although conservative Republicans have steadfastly proposed a school prayer amendment in every session of Congress since 1984, the bills have languished untended in various congressional committees.

Senator Helms made good on his legislative threat by introducing the Voluntary School Prayer Act in 1985, the year following the defeat of the school prayer amendment. The bill, as he had promised, was designed to bar federal courts from hearing any lawsuits involving prayer in the schools. The Voluntary School Prayer Act received little support in Congress, however, and despite being repeatedly introduced by Senator Helms in later years never made it past the Senate Judiciary Committee. Years later, Helms's legislation briefly resurfaced during the 2005 confirmation hearings of Judge John Roberts to replace United States Chief Justice William Rehnquist (1924–2005). Some news outlets reported that while working as an assistant attorney general for the Justice Department, Roberts had supported the Helms bill. As it turned out, while Roberts did prepare a memo arguing that the bill was not an unconstitutional interference by Congress in the federal courts, he also concluded that it was "bad policy" and should be opposed by the Justice Department. Ultimately, however, the Justice Department rejected Roberts's legal analysis and opposed the bill as unconstitutional.[16]

THE EVOLVING DEBATE: FROM CREATIONISM TO INTELLIGENT DESIGN

The Scopes trial may have slowed the effort to teach creationism in the schools, but it did not wipe it out entirely. Thanks to some slick repackaging, the battle over what children should be taught about the origin of the human species (and the planet in general) is still being waged in a series of debates across the country. So far, at least, no figures with the towering stature of Darrow or Bryan have emerged to cross rhetorical swords, and there have been no massive media events to match the Dayton trial. As much as anything else, that low-profile approach reflects the more sophisticated political strategy being employed today by supporters of neocreationism.

Well before the Supreme Court struck down state bans on the teaching of evolution, a movement arose that argued that scientific evidence could be adduced to support the biblical account of the Creation in Genesis. Much of the modern impetus for the movement came from the publication of *The Genesis Flood* in 1961. Written by John C. Whitcomb and Henry M. Morris, the book details the geological evidence that the authors believe is proof of the Great Flood (Gen. 6–9) and the proposition that God created the earth and everything on it approximately six thousand years ago. (By contrast, scientists at the US Department of the Interior estimate the age of the earth as between 4.4 and 4.6 *billion* years old.)[17] Over time, adherents of young earth creationism, or creation science (as this view became known), extended their arguments from geology to other areas of scientific inquiry, including biology and astronomy.

Anticipating the Supreme Court's rejection of bans on the teaching of evolution (which occurred in the 1968 decision *Epperson v. Arkansas*),[18] some state legislatures and local school boards began incorporating creation science into their public school curricula as either a replacement for, or at least an equal partner with, evolution. No state went quite as far, however, as Louisiana, which in 1982 passed the Balanced Treatment for Creation-Science and Evolution-Science in Public School Instruction Act.[19]

The constitutionality of the law was challenged by a coalition of Louisiana parents, teachers, and religious leaders, and eventually reached the US Supreme Court under the heading *Edwards v. Aguillard*. Writing for a 7–2 majority in June 1987, Justice William Brennan (1906–1997) noted, as in *Gilmore*, that the intent of the act's legislative sponsor was to restrict what is taught in the public schools. During his trial court testimony, state senator Bill Keith conceded, "My preference would be that neither [creationism nor evolution] be taught."[20]

Noting that the Louisiana act also gave preferential treatment to teachers of creation science (including additional pedagogical resources and statutory protection from discrimination), Brennan wrote, "we agree with the Court of Appeals' conclusion that the Act does not serve to protect academic freedom, but has the distinctly different purpose of discrediting 'evolution by counterbalancing its teaching at every turn with the teaching of creationism.'"[21] After reviewing additional legislative history, Justice Brennan concluded that because "[t]he preeminent purpose of the Louisiana Legislature was clearly to advance the religious viewpoint that a supernatural being created humankind . . . , the Act endorses religion in violation of the First Amendment."[22]

The point of the First Amendment, of course, and even the Establishment Clause, is not to suppress debate or to prevent all challenges to evolution. As the Court said in its conclusion, "We do not imply that a legislature could never require that scientific critiques of prevailing scientific theories be taught. . . . [T]eaching a variety of *scientific* theories about the origins of humankind to schoolchildren might be validly done with the clear secular intent of enhancing the effectiveness of science instruction."[23]

Given the fact that, thirty years earlier, Justice Brennan also wrote the infamous *Roth* decision (which stated in part that something must be "utterly without redeeming social importance" before being found obscene), the language in *Aguillard* raises a similar question of whether a critique of evolution must be utterly without religious motivation in order to be constitutionally permissible. Brennan's phrasing may have been necessary chamber orchestration to secure his majority (including Reagan appointee Justice Sandra Day O'Connor), but it unquestionably has prolonged the battle over the presence of creationism in the public schools.

To be fair, that's not entirely Brennan's fault. If there is any lesson that religious conservatives took away from the Scopes trial and other court battles over the years, it is the awareness that packaging and labeling make all the difference. In 1989 the Texas-based Foundation for Thought and Ethics published *Of Pandas and People*, a "science" textbook designed specifically to answer Justice Brennan's objections regarding the Louisiana statute in *Aguillard*. Without specifically discussing biblical concepts, the book rejects the evidence of evolution and substitutes instead the concept of "intelligent design."

The central precept of intelligent design is the idea of "irreducible complexity," an argument that the structure of life and its myriad components are so intricate and well formed that they could not have arisen through mere chance. *Of Pandas and People* puts it this way: "Because of the high level of improbability that cells could be generated by the random mixing of chemicals, some scientists believe that the first cells were created from the design of some outside, intelligent force."[24] Biochemist Michael Behe, professor at Lehigh University and one of the leading proponents of intelligent design, points to organs like the human eye and the flagellum that propels bacteria as examples of things so complex and inherently functional that the only reasonable conclusion is that the organs are "a purposeful arrangement of parts."[25] Proponents steadfastly deny that intelligent design is based on any one specific "Prime Arranger," saying that is a matter of individual belief, but when asked virtually all give the nod to the Judeo-Christian God.

Not surprisingly, the intelligent design proposal has given rise to a competing theory: "incompetent design." Don Wise, professor emeritus of geosciences at the University of Massachusetts, Amherst, makes the argument that there is ample evidence of stupidity in the design of our bodies.

No self-respecting engineering student would make the kinds of dumb mistakes that are built into us.

All of our pelvises slope forward for convenient knuckle-dragging, like all the other great apes. And the only reason you stand erect is because of this incredible sharp bend at the base of your spine, which is either evolution's way of modifying something or else it's just a design that would flunk a first-year engineering student.[26]

A decade after *Of Pandas and People* was published, two conservative Roman Catholics—Domino's Pizza founder Thomas Monaghan and former Michigan prosecutor Richard Thompson—founded the Thomas More Law Center (TMLC) in Ann Arbor, Michigan. On its Web site, the organization describes itself as "a not-for-profit public interest law firm dedicated to the defense and promotion of the religious freedom of Christians, time-honored family values, and the sanctity of human life. Our purpose is to be the sword and shield for people of faith, providing legal representation without charge to defend and protect Christians and their religious beliefs in the public square."[27]

Among the cases on which the TMLC has worked are battles over nativity displays, a lawsuit against Ann Arbor for offering benefits to same-sex partners, and, most controversially, the defense of the Web site "The Nuremberg Files," which posted mock "Wanted" posters of doctors who perform abortions (and then drew bright red slashes across the posters of two murdered doctors).[28]

For the better part of a decade, lawyers for the TMLC traveled around the country speaking to local school boards, looking for a community that would be willing to introduce intelligent design as an alternative to evolution. The TMLC representatives warned boards that they would inevitably be sued, but promised that the TMLC would provide a defense at no charge. A number of districts turned down the offer, but in Dover, Pennsylvania, the board (headed by chairman Bowie Kuhn, the former baseball commissioner) agreed to become the first school district to formally introduce intelligent design into its science curriculum.[29] The predicted lawsuit quickly materialized when eleven parents (with the assistance of the ACLU) filed suit against Dover in federal court, alleging that the introduction of intelligent design was an effort to teach religion in the schools.[30]

A significant part of the political/public relations strategy pursued by intelligent design advocates is to persuade districts to "teach the controversy." President Bush caused a stir in August 2005 when he endorsed the idea of teaching both evolution and intelligent design, "so people can understand what the debate is about." But the vast preponderance of scientists disagree that there even is a debate.[31] In a lengthy article in the *Guardian*, Professors Richard Dawkins (Public Understanding of Science, Oxford) and Jerry Coyne (Ecology and Evolution, University of Chicago) firmly rejected the idea of intelligent design as a competing theory with evolution: "If ID really were a scientific theory, positive evidence for it, gathered through research, would fill peer-reviewed scientific journals. This doesn't happen. It isn't that editors refuse to publish ID research. There simply isn't any ID research to publish. Its advocates bypass normal scientific due process by appealing directly to the non-scientific public and—with great shrewdness—to the government officials they elect."[32]

Out of concern that a federal lawsuit—and an adverse decision—might threaten the "teach the controversy" approach, the Discovery Institute, the Seattle-based organization that is the leading advocate for intelligent design, actually opposed the law center's strategy from the start. "We thought it was a bad idea," senior fellow John G. West said, "because we oppose any effort to require students to learn about intelligent design because we feel that it politicizes what should be a scientific debate." Nonetheless, one of the school board's leading witnesses in defense of intelligent design was Michael Behe, who is also a fellow at the institute.

The debate over Dover's support for intelligent design took a sharp political twist on Tuesday, November 8, 2005, when all eight of the Dover school board members up for reelection were voted out of office. The clearest loser was Alan Bonsell, the board member leading the push to include intelligent design in the curriculum; during the course of the federal trial, testimony was given that Bonsell had originally sought to have creationism given equal time with evolution in the district's science courses.[33]

The bad news for intelligent design supporters continued on December 20, 2005, when US District Judge John E. Jones III ruled that it was unconstitutional for Dover to require the inclusion of intelligent design in its biology curriculum. He concluded that several board members lied about their motivations in adopting the new curriculum, and wrote that "[t]he citizens of Dover were poorly served by the members of the Board who voted for the ID policy."[34] Interestingly, Judge Jones was nominated to serve in the US District Court in February 2002 by President George W. Bush.

The election results are unlikely to stop the debate over intelligent design in Dover or other hot spots around the country (most notably Kansas, where the State Board of Education has been waffling back and forth on the intelligent design issue over a period of years). However, the results do reduce the likelihood that the Dover school board will pursue an appeal of Judge Jones's decision. Although the connection was more tenuous, the removal of the pro–intelligent design board members was also being viewed as a reflection of President Bush's low popularity ratings and concern over the direction the country was headed.

In the wake of the Dover election results, Rev. Pat Robertson warned the town not to be surprised if it suffered divine retribution: "I'd like to say to the good citizens of Dover: if there is a disaster in your area, don't turn to God, you just rejected Him from your city. And don't wonder why He hasn't helped you when problems begin, if they begin. I'm not saying they will, but if they do, just remember, you just voted God out of your city. And if that's the case, don't ask for His help because he might not be there."[35]

SEX EDUCATION: THE HIGH COST OF "JUST SAY NOTHING"

A more familiar and prosaic type of creationism has caused problems in the schools as well: teen and even preteen sexuality. Long before Surgeon General Koop issued his strong recommendation for early and comprehensive sex education, educators and parents had reached general agreement on the need to include some basic information about sex in public school curricula. As far back as 1930, nearly 50 percent of the public schools taught sex education. Thanks to societal attitudes and a lack of basic research, the results were somewhat erratic. Alfred Kinsey's decision to investigate the sexual behavior of the human male was sparked in large part by the myriad and often frighteningly naive questions about sex that he was asked by his Indiana University students.[36] Over the years, support for the general concept of sex education has continued to grow, and the subject is taught today in roughly 90 percent of all public middle schools and high schools.[37]

Not everyone is supportive, of course. Among other organizations, Phyllis Schlafly's Eagle Forum has been a longtime opponent of sexual education programs in the schools. During the debate in 1986 over the need for increased sex education following the rise of AIDS, Schlafly reiterated her belief that such instruction is simply harmful: "Teachers are authority figures, and when they discuss contraception, they are giving students permission to engage in sexual intercourse. Schools should concentrate on teaching traditional courses that will help students gain admission to college or a job, rather than psychological courses like sex education."[38] Schlafly's comments conveniently overlooked the fact that at the time a million teenagers per year were getting pregnant, and the twin burdens of pregnancy and a new child made the prospect of successfully attending college highly remote.

The opposition of groups like the Eagle Forum did not succeed in stopping sex education, but it has significantly affected the nature of what is federally funded (and therefore taught) in the public schools. In 1981, at the start of the Reagan administration, Congress passed the Adolescent Family Life Act (AFLA), which was designed to prevent teen pregnancy by teaching abstinence and promoting chastity. The law provided about $10 million per year to myriad private groups, about one-fourth of which had religious ties. Groups providing "family planning services, abortion or abortion counseling or referral" were and are ineligible for funds, and all applicants are required to explain how they would involve religious groups in their abstinence programs.

These restrictions not only tied the hands of progressive and pragmatic educators, they also encouraged breaches of the firewall between church and state—one AFLA-funded group asked teenage girls "to pretend Jesus was their date."[39] The ACLU sued to have the program declared unconstitutional, but in the summer of 1988 the Supreme Court issued a 5–4 ruling upholding AFLA, saying that the program has "a valid secular purpose, does not have the primary effect of advancing religion, and does not create an excessive entanglement of church and state."[40]

The push for federally funded abstinence grew stronger in 1996 when Congress passed and President Clinton signed the Personal Responsibility and Work Opportunity Reconciliation Act. Included in the welfare reform package was a provision (Section 510[b] of Title V) authorizing the expenditure of $250 million over five years (to be matched by $200 million in state spending) on programs "promoting sexual abstinence outside of marriage as the only acceptable standard of behavior for young people." Any state programs that accept federal funds under Section 510(b) were and are forbidden from discussing contraceptives, apart from offering information about their failure rates.

The program has the strong support of President Bush, who in his 2004 State of the Union address called for a doubling of the funding for the "abstinence-only" approach. The Sexuality Information and Education Council of the United States (SIECUS) pointed out that, as of 2004, total federal and state spending on the chastity approach to sex education is approaching $1 billion, despite no clear evidence that "abstinence-only" is reducing teen sexual activity.[41] A report on the effectiveness of the "abstinence-only" funding was due in 2004, but Congress extended the "abstinence-only" program without requiring the analysis of the first five-year cycle of funding.[42]

What preliminary evidence is available on the effectiveness of the abstinence-only approach is not encouraging. Only ten states have conducted any review at all of teen sexual attitudes in abstinence-only programs. In general, the survey results show that a few programs have succeeded in improving the attitude of teens toward abstinence in the short term but have done little to promote long-term attitudinal shifts. More important, none of the surveys measured any significant change in the actual sexual behavior of teens.[43]

Even more worrisome are the results of a recent report by Rep. Henry Waxman (R-CA), which showed that eleven of thirteen abstinence-only programs supported by federal money were providing teens with medically inaccurate information.[44] "This report," Waxman wrote, "finds that over two-thirds of abstinence-only programs funded by the largest federal abstinence initiative are using curricula with multiple scientific and medical inaccuracies. These curricula contain misinformation about condoms, abortion and basic scientific facts. They also blur religion and science and present gender stereotypes as fact."[45]

Most important, these programs simply don't work. Even teens who actively pledge to abstain (as opposed to simply attending "abstinence-only" classes) have a hard time keeping their hands off each other or themselves. An April 2005 study published in the *Journal of Adolescent Health* concluded that 88 percent of teens who pledged chastity prior to marriage broke the pledge and engaged in some form of sexual activity (including masturbation). Some aspects of the report were questioned—specifically, the conclusion that chastity pledgers were up to six times more likely to have oral sex and four times more likely to have anal sex (on the theory that only vaginal sex violates the vow of chastity).[46] Still, there was no serious disagreement that when it comes to teens, promises of abstention from sexual activity often end up taking a backseat to teenage hormones.

The real-world consequences of the misinformation or lack of information provided by abstinence-only programs are tragic. The one thing that the federally funded programs are effective in doing is reducing the use of condoms, which helps explain in part the more than eight hundred thousand children born to teenage mothers in the United States each year. It also helps to explain the country's more than nine million cases of sexually transmitted diseases (STDs) in the fifteen- to twenty-four-year age group (the United States has one of the highest rates of teen STDs among industrialized nations) and the fact that half of all new HIV infections occur among people under the age of twenty-five.[47] It is difficult to reconcile the stark human consequences of the failed abstinence-only programs with the "culture of life" so fervently touted by religious conservatives.

Concern over the effectiveness of the abstinence-only approach is leading some states to turn down federal sex education money in order to have the freedom to offer more comprehensive information about sex and contraception. California rejected the money from the start, and Pennsylvania turned it down beginning in 2004. In the fall of 2005, Maine became the third state to opt out, choosing to forgo approximately $160,000 in federal sex education subsidies. Maine recently passed a state law requiring comprehensive, age-appropriate sex education, and the increasingly strict federal regulations would have conflicted with Maine's own law. Administration of the federal abstinence-only program was recently shifted to a new agency, the Administration for Children and Families, which is pushing states accepting federal money to tell teens only that sex outside of marriage is unacceptable and that couples should refrain from sex until they are economically self-sufficient.[48]

In contrast to the federally acceptable programs, Maine's comprehensive approach to sex education has been tremendously effective. Using a combined approach of encouraging abstinence and teaching about contraception, Maine has cut its teen pregnancy rate in half over the last two decades. Dr. Dora Anne Mills, the Maine public health director, said that if Maine continued to accept federal abstinence funds, it would put state officials "in a position of having to turn our backs on proven programs that we have been using for quite a while, versus accepting these (new) standards that we think may actually be harmful to our children."[49]

OF PANDERING AND PEOPLE: THE RIGHT TO DIE WITH DIGNITY

It is unquestionably true that religious beliefs have a role to play in the sexual education of children; they can provide teens with valuable moral and emotional guidelines for the transition to adulthood. But faith and doctrine alone are insufficient alternatives to actual knowledge (and, in the case of teen sex, condoms). The conflict between religious doctrine and public policy is sharpest when the beginning of life is at issue (sex, contraception, and abortion), but the end of life, sadly, can be a political flash point as well.

In February 1990, a Florida woman named Terri Schiavo (1963–2005) lapsed into a persistent vegetative state following cardiac arrest. Utterly without her consent or active participation, Terri Schiavo was transformed over the next fifteen years from a private tragedy to a political cause that warped the relationship between federal and state government, threatened the critical independence of the judiciary, and made a mockery of traditional conservative respect for precedent, separation of powers, and the rule of law. More than anything else, Schiavo's case demonstrated the abject fear with which many Republicans, from the White House on down, viewed the religious conservative wing of their own party, as a steadily unpopular war and sluggish economy made Christian evangelicals a valuable political ally once again.

The lengthy judicial process surrounding the end of Schiavo's life seemed to reach a conclusion in October 2003, when the last appeal by Schiavo's parents, Robert and Mary Schindler, was rejected by Florida Sixth Circuit Court judge George Greer. Pursuant to Judge Greer's order, Schiavo's feeding tube was removed on October 15. In the following days, both Governor Jeb Bush (the younger brother of President George W. Bush and a potential presidential contender) and the Florida legislature came under tremendous pressure from religious conservative groups. Picketers carrying signs accusing Governor Bush of murder marched in front of Schiavo's hospice, e-mails flooded the inboxes of legislators, and "[o]n Christian radio, talk-show hosts implored listeners to hold Bush and state legislators responsible if Schiavo did not survive."[50] Six days later, the Florida legislature passed "Terri's Law," an extraordinary bill that gave Governor Bush the authority to order the resumption of feeding and hydration, which he did.[51]

At the forefront of the effort to prolong Schiavo's life was longtime antiabortion activist Randall Terry. A constant presence at the side of the Schindlers in 2003, Terry applauded the adoption of Terri's Law: "Finally," he said, "a governor and legislature had the courage to stand up to judicial despots because of an overwhelming call by the public."[52]

Terri's husband, Michael Schiavo, found his constitutional challenge to Terri's Law opposed on behalf of the Schindlers by the American Center for Law and Justice (ACLJ), a religious advocacy group founded to help counter the American Civil Liberties Union (which in fact was assisting Schiavo in his challenge). Jay Sekulow, chief counsel for the ACLJ, suggested that Terri's Law simply gave Governor Bush powers analogous to his ability to pardon the life of someone on death row.[53] A year later, however, the Florida Supreme Court unanimously ruled that Terri's Law was an unconstitutional violation of the separation of powers under the state's constitution. In a sternly worded decision, Florida chief justice Barbara J. Pariente said that "[i]t is without question an invasion of the authority of the judicial branch for the Legislature to pass a law that allows the executive branch to interfere with the final judicial determination in a case. That is precisely what occurred here and for that reason the act is unconstitutional."[54]

Yet even more remarkable legislative intervention was about to occur. Shortly after the announcement was made by Judge Greer that once again Michael Schiavo could legally remove his wife's feeding tube, congressional Republicans began work on "A Bill to Provide for the Relief of the Parents of Theresa Marie Schiavo." This brief piece of legislation was designed to remove jurisdiction of the Schiavo case from Florida courts and transfer it directly to federal court. Consideration of the bill was complicated by the fact that Congress had already recessed for Easter, but Republican leaders called legislators back to Washington to debate and pass the legislation.

Perhaps the most remarkable aspect of the debate over the legislation was the willingness of numerous legislators to offer their own assessments of Terri Schiavo's condition, notwithstanding the fact that few of them had any medical training and none had actually examined her. The assessments were based on a videotape made by Bob and Mary Schindler, Terri Schiavo's parents, which the couple used to help generate support for their ongoing legal battle. The videotape, which Michael Schiavo's attorney said was made years earlier in violation of a court's visitation order, appeared to show Terri Schiavo responding to outside stimuli and following suggestions to open and shut her eyes.[55] As others pointed out, however, the most widespread clips from the Schindler tape—purporting to show Terri smiling at her mother or tracking the movement of a balloon—were contradicted by the images contained on far longer tapes made at the request of Judge Greer in 2002, consisting of little more than the Florida woman's unfocused and unchanging stare.[56]

Nonetheless, despite the dubious provenance of the Schindler video and the overwhelming weight of fifteen years of medical examinations, members of Congress did not hesitate to offer their own diagnoses. The two most notable opinions were rendered by House Republican majority leader Tom DeLay and Senate majority leader (and physician) Bill Frist.

"Terri Schiavo is not brain dead," Representative DeLay said. "She talks and she laughs and she expresses happiness and discomfort."[57] DeLay blamed Terri Schiavo's inability to speak on the fact that "she's not been afforded any speech therapy—none!"[58]

Frist spoke repeatedly on the floor of the Senate in support of the legislation. During the course of his initial remarks, he raised extensive questions about the accuracy of Schiavo's diagnosis: "Persistent vegetative state, which is what the court has ruled, I say that I question it, and I question it based on a review of the video footage which I spent an hour or so looking at last night in my office here in the Capitol. And that footage, to me, depicted something very different than persistent vegetative state." Frist then opened a medical textbook, *Harrison's Principles of Internal Medicine* (sixteenth edition), and began comparing its definition of "persistent vegetative state" to what he had seen on the videotape:

> This "unresponsive state in which the eyelids are open"—I quote that only because on the video footage, which is the actual exam by the neurologist, when the neurologist said, "Look up," there is no question in the video that she actually looks up. That would not be an "unresponsive state in which the eyelids are open." . . .
>
> And then, let me just comment, because it says: "absent responses to visual stimuli." Once again, in the video footage—which you can actually see on the Web site[59] today—she certainly seems to respond to visual stimuli that the neurologist puts forth.[60]

In his opening remarks on Saturday, March 19, as the Senate prepared to pass the Schiavo bill, Senator Frist proudly announced that "the Congress has been working nonstop over the last three days to do its part to uphold human dignity and affirm the culture of life."[61] With passage of the Schiavo bill seemingly assured, President George W. Bush abruptly decided to interrupt an Easter vacation on his Crawford, Texas, ranch and fly back to Washington so he could sign the legislation at the White House. Bush's decision to fly to Washington to sign the bill was remarkable for a number of different reasons: the cost of using Air Force One when the legislation could have been flown to Texas far more cheaply; the fact that Bush, notoriously reluctant to interrupt his time in Crawford, cut short a vacation for the first time in his presidency; and the fact that Bush, equally well known for his early bedtimes, left instructions for his staff to wake him when Congress sent over to the White House the final version of the Schiavo legislation (he finally signed the bill at around 1:11 AM).[62]

Despite protestations to the contrary by White House spokesperson Scott McClellan, no one had any illusions that these unusual steps were taken in order to send a strong message to Bush's religious conservative supporters. Richard Cizik, vice president of government affairs for the National Association of Evangelicals, acknowledged as much: "Look, this is a symbolic move, for sure. It's [Bush's] willingness to interrupt his vacation to make a statement. And not just make a statement, because we're not playing games here, but to make a difference, too."[63] An anonymous memo of Republican "talking points" underscored the potential political payoffs:

- This is an important moral issue and the pro-life base will be excited that the Senate is debating this important issue.
- This is a great political issue, because Senator Nelson of Florida has already refused to become a cosponsor and this is a tough issue for Democrats.[64]

But Republicans themselves were hardly unanimous in supporting the Schiavo bill. For economic conservatives in particular, the intervention in the Schiavo case violated their quasi-libertarian views on limited government and long-standing defense of state's rights. Former representative Bob Barr (R-GA), for instance, argued that Congress had overstepped its bounds: "To simply say that the 'culture of life,' or whatever you call it means we don't have to pay attention to the principles of federalism or separation of powers is certainly not a conservative viewpoint." Senator John Warner (R-VA) agreed: "I believe it is unwise for the Congress to take from the state of Florida its constitutional responsibility to resolve the issues in this case."[65]

It quickly became apparent that the Republican leadership had badly misread the mood of the American people. In the week following Congress's action, a CBS poll found that 82 percent of Americans—and a surprising 68 percent of evangelical Christians—thought that Congress acted inappropriately by intervening in the Terri Schiavo case.[66]

The release of Terri Schiavo's autopsy results on June 15, 2005, under-scored the difficulty of making an effective diagnosis on the basis of videotapes. The most significant finding was that approximately half of Schiavo's brain had atrophied following her original collapse in 1990, leaving her blind and per-manently unaware of her surroundings. Dr. John Thogmartin, medical exam-iner for Pinellas County, Florida, stated at a press conference that "[t]his damage was irreversible, and no amount of therapy or treatment would have regenerated the massive loss of neurons." He said that his examination revealed no evidence of any mistreatment of Schiavo, and added that he was unable to determine what it was that caused the original heart failure that led to her vegetative state.[67]

As Dr. Joseph Fins, an internist and director of ethics at New York Presby-terian Hospital/Weill Cornell Medical Center, pointed out to National Public Radio: "We all should be cautious about talking about patients we've never examined, and diagnosis by long distance is problematic. And I think that the doctors in Congress who were making diagnosis were dealing with the body politic and not with a particular patient."[68]

Two days after Terri Schiavo died, Senator Frist appeared on NBC's *Today* show and strenuously denied ever making a diagnosis: "I never, never, on the floor of the Senate, made a diagnosis, nor would I ever do that." Later that same day, during an appearance on ABC's *Good Morning America*, Frist essen-tially conceded that the additional tests he called for in his Senate speech would not have made any difference. "She had devastating brain damage," Frist said, "and with that, the chapter's closed."[69]

What If the Blastocyst You Save Is Gay?

Few chapters in Washington, however, are ever fully closed. During the very last stages of Terri Schiavo's saga, the complicated strands of faith and public policy brought the debate back once again to the beginning of life. A wealthy California businessman, Robert Herring, offered Michael Schiavo $1 million in exchange for giving up his guardianship rights over his wife, in part because Herring believed that emerging embryonic stem cell treatments might provide a cure for Terri. Michael Schiavo, who had been accused of seeking an end to Terri's life support for financial gain, declined the offer.[70]

There was a certain irony to Herring's offer. Throughout much of the legal wrangling over Terri Schiavo, her parents received legal and financial support from Operation Rescue, the vehemently antiabortion group founded by Randall Terry. While Operation Rescue undoubtedly welcomed Herring's financial offer to Michael Schiavo, the group undoubtedly was less enthusiastic about his pro-fessed motives. Operation Rescue equates embryonic stem cell research with abortion and strenuously opposes it. Moreover, as abortion opponents fre-quently argue, one of the risks of touting the promise of the new technique is that such promotion can raise false hopes and expectations among patients and their loved ones. As a matter of medical fact, given the results of her autopsy, even the most advanced stem cell research would not have healed Schiavo.[71]

As a source of medical treatment and potential cures for some of human-ity's most troubling illnesses, however, stem cell research does in fact offer some amazing possibilities. The potential benefits arise from the fact that a stem cell is a cell that has not yet committed to a particular role or function, a state that medical researchers describe as "undifferentiated." Researchers believe that, with the right encouragement, stem cells can be persuaded to grow into various categories of specialized cells that can then be used to treat specific medical conditions and diseases. In a relatively crude form, this process has been used for thirty years to treat leukemia and lymphoma patients. Prior to a patient's chemotherapy (which destroys blood cells), the patient's own stem cells are removed from bone marrow and then reinjected once the chemotherapy is completed. Once back in the patient's bone marrow, the stem cells resume the production of red and white blood cells.

Because of the versatility of stem cells, the range of potential treatments seems almost endless. Researchers suggest that under favorable circumstances stem cells could help cure a wide variety of diseases (cancer, Parkinson's, dia-betes, etc.), reverse the effects of Alzheimer's, regenerate nerves, restore sight, repair heart attack damage, regrow missing teeth, and even cure baldness. Thanks to its potential benefits, stem cell research has attracted some particu-larly high-profile supporters, including, most notably, actor Christopher Reeve (1952–2004). After he was paralyzed from the neck down in a 1995 horseback-riding accident, Reeve spent the last nine years of his life campaigning tirelessly for increased federal funding for stem cell research and expressing an inspiring optimism that he would walk again. Even former first lady Nancy Reagan began supporting stem cell research after President Reagan was diagnosed with Alzheimer's disease. Their son, Ron Reagan, was invited to give a speech at the Democratic National Convention in Boston in July 2004 (a month after his father's death). He used the opportunity to chide his father's former party for its opposition to stem cell research.

"It does not follow that the theology of a few should be allowed to forestall the health and well-being of the many," Reagan said. "And how can we affirm life if we abandon those whose own lives are so desperately at risk?"[72]

Reagan's reference to "the theology of a few" was intended to underscore the fact that the bulk of the opposition to stem cell research—and certainly the most fervent opposition—comes from religious conservatives. Over the last ten years, advances in medical science have transformed a somewhat obscure but fascinating area of research into a proverbial third rail for Republican politicians, or at least those that are concerned about the future electoral and financial support of religious conservatives.

Religious conservatives do not object to stem cell research per se—nobody seriously opposes curing cancer—but they have grave concerns about how the research is conducted. Scientists first identified the existence of stem cells in adults, most notably in blood marrow, which gave rise to the transplant treatments that have been so beneficial in cases of cancer and leukemia. Adult or somatic stem cells can be extracted from a variety of tissues in both adults and children. In 1998, however, researchers at Johns Hopkins University and the University of Wisconsin, using private funds provided by the Geron Corporation, developed techniques for extracting stem cells from blastocysts, the term given to an embryo when it is between roughly fifty and one hundred and fifty cells in size (a stage that typically occurs about five days after conception). Unfortunately, the process of extracting so-called embryonic stem cells destroys the blastocyst. Since it is an article of faith with many if not most religious conservatives that life begins with conception, they view the destruction of a blastocyst as the moral equivalent of murder.

Researchers would probably be just as happy to avoid the controversy were it not for the fact that not all stem cells are created equal. Like ancient Gaul, they are divided into three parts: *totipotent* stem cells, which can grow into any type of cell; *pluripotent* stem cells, which can develop into any type of cell except totipotent; and *multipotent* stem cells, which typically can develop only into cells of a related nature (i.e., a multipotent stem cell taken from bone marrow can form into blood-related cells but not something altogether different, like a hair or retina cell). Currently, the only source of totipotent stem cells are blastocysts. Somatic (or adult) stem cells, in addition to their other limitations,[73] are merely multipotent, and researchers have not succeeded yet in finding somatic stem cell types that correspond to all of the various types of tissue they hope to cultivate.

Given their sheer versatility, it is the totipotent embryonic stem cells that cause the most excitement and offer the most hope of wide-ranging cures. But even before it was known that stem cells could be extracted from blastocysts, Congress had taken steps to limit all types of embryonic research. In 1995 Rep. Jay Dickey (R-AR) introduced an amendment to prevent the Department of Health and Human Services (HHS) from financing the use of embryos for research, and the so-called Dickey Amendment has been attached as a rider to the HHS budget each year since. Once researchers announced their ability to extract embryonic stem cells, the Clinton administration began working on regulations that would have permitted federal funding for further research, but the regulations were frozen by Bush when he took office in January 2001. Eight months later, President Bush announced that federal funds would be made available, but only for programs using the approximately sixty lines of embryonic stem cells already in existence as of August 11, 2001, "where the life and death decision has already been made."

"Leading scientists tell me," President Bush went on, "[that] research on these 60 lines has great promise that could lead to breakthrough therapies and cures. This allows us to explore the promise and potential of stem cell research without crossing a fundamental moral line, by providing taxpayer funding that would sanction or encourage further destruction of human embryos that have at least the potential for life."[74]

At the time, commentators credited the new president with arriving at a Solomonic resolution to the embryonic stem cell research dilemma: in theory, the existing cell lines would be sufficient to allow research to go forward without further antagonizing his antiabortion supporters. But in the intervening four years it has become clear that the existing embryonic stem cell lines are not sufficient to support effective research. Some of the cell lines are clearly not viable (effectively reducing the available number down to the low twenties), others are subject to institutional-use restrictions, and others are available but too expensive for widespread use. And, in early 2005, researchers discovered that all of the existing embryonic stem cell lines have picked up a foreign molecule, most likely from the animal tissue used to propagate the stem cells. The presence of the foreign molecule eliminates the possibility that any cells derived from the existing embryonic stem cell lines can be transplanted into humans, since the human immune system will attack and destroy the new cells.[75]

Private efforts to develop fresh lines of embryonic stem cells are under way at various locations around the country. Harvard University, for instance, has plans to found the Stem Cell Institute to support researcher David Melton's efforts to create his own "open source" stem cell lines that will be freely available to qualified researchers.[76] And a number of other countries (particularly South Korea, the United Kingdom, and China), having reached a different answer on the question of life and death with respect to blastocysts, are making tremendous strides in this area of research.

After a lengthy and emotional debate, the US House of Representatives voted on May 23, 2005, to provide federal funding for embryonic stem cell research using embryos slated for destruction by fertility clinics (H.R. 810, the Stem Cell Research Enhancement Act of 2005). On the floor of the House, abortion opponents invoked the sanctity of life in all its stages, while research proponents spoke passionately about sick and dying friends, family members, and constituents who might benefit from embryonic stem cell research. In the end, 50 Republicans joined the 188 Democrats who voted in favor, while 14 Democrats and 180 Republicans voted against the bill. Although the House vote was an unusual defeat for President Bush in what has generally been a well-disciplined and even tractable Congress (at least until the fall of 2005), the legislation did not pass by a large enough margin to overcome a presidential veto.

At a carefully timed meeting that same day with a group of "snowflake babies" (children born from unused fertility clinic embryos), President Bush promised that he would in fact veto any legislation authorizing embryonic stem cell research: "The children here today," he said, "remind us that there is no such thing as a spare embryo."[77]

Over in the Senate, an identical bill (S. 471) had been introduced on February 28, 2005, by Senator Arlen Specter (R-PA), a notoriously moderate Republican who has frequently clashed with religious conservatives. However, given the opposition of both the Bush administration and the Republican congressional leadership—including Senate majority leader Frist—the bill had little prospect of emerging from the Senate Committee on Health, Education, Labor, and Pensions, to which it had been referred.

American presidential campaigns do not have an official starting date, but in each election cycle there is always an event or two that makes it clear that the next race is actually under way. Typically, these moments occur while politicians are undergoing the process of "centrification"—the usually awkward and often painful search for policy positions that will persuade voters that the politician in question is not the whacked-out liberal or hidebound conservative he or she has always appeared to be.

By the end of 2005, Senator Hillary Clinton (D-NY) already had several such moments to her credit: her attempt to carve out a middle ground on abortion, her unwillingness to call for a timetable for withdrawal of troops from Iraq, her cozying up to former antagonist (and potential 2008 opponent) Newt Gingrich, and her outspoken criticism of violent video games. But for sheer drama and actual impact on a potential campaign, nothing matched the decision by Senate majority leader Bill Frist (R-TN) to reverse his long-standing opposition to legislation that would loosen federal prohibitions on embryonic stem cell research.[78] In a lengthy speech on the floor of the Senate, Frist tried to explain the shift in his position:

> Embryonic stem cells have specific properties that make them uniquely powerful and deserving of special attention in the realm of medical science. These special properties explain why scientists and physicians feel so strongly about support of embryonic as well as adult stem cell research. . . .

While human embryonic stem cell research is still at a very early stage, the limitations put in place in 2001 will, over time, slow our ability to bring potential new treatments for certain diseases. Therefore, I believe the President's policy should be modified. We should expand federal funding—and thus NIH oversight—and current guidelines governing stem cell research, carefully and thoughtfully staying within ethical bounds.[79]

Frist's announcement, not surprisingly, deeply angered religious conservatives. The Reverend Patrick J. Mahoney, director of the Christian Defense Coalition, said, "Senator Frist cannot have it both ways. He cannot be pro-life and pro-embryonic stem cell funding. Nor can he turn around and expect widespread endorsement from the pro-life community if he should decide to run for president in 2008."[80] Another group, the Florida-based Center for Reclaiming America, ran a series of radio television advertisements in Iowa denouncing Frist as a "flip-flopper."[81] The Iowa caucuses are the traditional first step in selecting the presidential nominees, and with Frist already widely viewed as a likely Republican candidate, the ads could be described as one of the first political salvos for the 2008 race.

Although Frist's shift obviously dismayed religious conservatives, his objective clearly was to appeal to more moderate voters. The potential fallout among antiabortion voters will be tightly contained if the White House vetoes any expansion of embryonic stem cell research and Congress fails to override the veto. To some extent, Frist may have been relying on that scenario when he announced his change of position. (It is also worth pointing out that despite the majority leader's newly announced support, six months later the bill still had not emerged from committee.)

On the other hand, of course, if public opinion—already running strongly in favor of embryonic stem cell research—helps persuade the House and Senate to override an increasingly unpopular president, then Frist through his leadership on this issue will have taken a major step toward successful centrification.

A desk lamp featuring *The Greek Slave* by Vermont sculptor
Hyram Powers. The lamp was purchased by the Friends of the
Vermont State House as part of the building's ongoing renovation.
(Copyright © Jordan S. Douglas 2005)

Conclusion

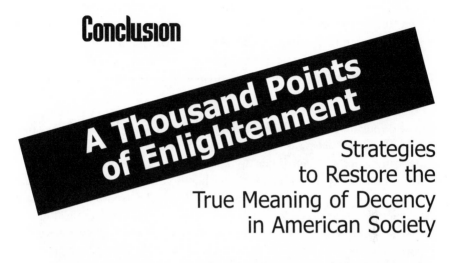

A Thousand Points of Enlightenment

Strategies
to Restore the
True Meaning of Decency
in American Society

> It is not skeptics or explorers but fanatics and ideologues who
> menace decency and progress. No agnostic ever burned
> anyone at the stake or tortured a pagan, a heretic, or an
> unbeliever.
>
> —Daniel J. Boorstin, 1989[1]

Throughout 2004, the residents of the small state of Vermont watched the raging cultural wars in the rest of the country with a certain detached bemusement. Despite recent progress in wiring the state for cable television and the Internet, a feeling persists in much of Vermont that cultural changes don't arrive quite as quickly as in some other states. Many movies, for instance, arrive weeks after they open in more cosmopolitan areas (if they arrive at all), and fashions have been known to bypass the state altogether. The state's long winters and generally rural setting also encourage a live-and-let-live attitude. It is no accident that the state is better known as the birthplace of the taciturn Calvin Coolidge (1872–1933)—the twenty-ninth president of the United States—than of the charismatic evangelical Joseph Smith (1805–1844)—the founder of the Church of Jesus Christ of Latter-day Saints (more widely known as the Mormon Church). "Silent Cal," as he was known, certainly had his own firm views on living a moral life but was in no particular hurry to try to impose those views on others.

It surprised many Vermonters, then, when the aftershocks of the

Jackson/Timberlake incident were felt in the Green Mountains. In 2004 the Friends of the Vermont State House raised $2,500 to purchase a desk lamp as part of the restoration of the Vermont governor's ceremonial office in the State House in Montpelier. The lamp is a reproduction of a famous sculpture called *The Greek Slave*, which was first carved circa 1839 in Florence, Italy, by Vermont native Hiram Powers (1805–1873).[2]

The history of Powers's statue neatly encapsulates many of the themes presented throughout this book. According to the Friends of the Vermont Statehouse, *The Greek Slave* was "one of the first non-Biblical naked females by an American sculptor."[3] According to Powers's own description: "[*The Greek Slave*] is of a young girl—nude, with her hands bound and in such a position to conceal a portion of the figure, thereby rendering the exposure of the nakedness less exceptionable to our American fastidiousness. The feet will also be bound to a fixture and the face turned to one side, and downwards with an expression of modesty and Christian resignation. That she is Christian will be inferred by a cross, suspended by a chain around her neck and hanging or resting on her bosom. I said a young girl, but the form will express puberty."[4]

In addition to positioning the maiden's hand in front of her pelvis, Powers tried to preempt possible objections to the statue's nudity by evoking one of the major political and religious conflicts of the period: the treatment of Christians by the Turks during the Greek revolution in the 1820s. The struggle by the Greeks to end Turkey's occupation of their country had captured the hearts of Europeans. Hundreds, including the poet Lord Byron (1788–1824), traveled to Greece to fight for the revolution, and Powers's *The Greek Slave* became a popular icon of the struggle for freedom in the birthplace of democracy. Powers said that his sculpture was intended to represent a Christian Greek woman, the only member of her family to survive an attack by the Turks. She is shown, Powers said, awaiting sale in a Turkish slave market:[5] "It is a difficult thing to find a subject of modern times whose history and peculiarities will justify entire nudity, but where the subject and its history make this necessary, it may be looked upon with less reserve than it could be if the exposure were intentional on the part of the artist. . . . The 'Slave' is compelled to stand naked to be judged of in the market—this is an historical fact. Few such subjects, however, can be found."[6]

Despite Powers's obvious concern about the reaction to the statue's nudity, his choice of theme proved to be both commercially savvy and socially acceptable. Even before he finished *The Greek Slave*, he sold the statue to a wealthy British officer named John Grant for £300. Upon its arrival in England, *The Greek Slave* proved so popular that Powers was eventually commissioned to make five additional copies of the statue.

With the assistance of his friend and Cincinnati artist Miner Kellogg

(1814–1889), Powers arranged to have two copies of *The Greek Slave* tour the United States from 1847 to 1849, and reportedly, over one hundred thousand people paid to see it. Among them, according to the Smithsonian National Portrait Gallery, was President James K. Polk (1795–1849), who at the time was sitting for a portrait by Kellogg.[7] The statue traveled throughout the eastern United States, including Powers's home state of Vermont. *The Greek Slave* arrived in Burlington for an exhibit timed to coincide with the graduation ceremonies of the University of Vermont, and then was put on display in Powers's hometown of Woodstock. Attendance was sparse, a friend reportedly wrote to Powers, because the statue had the misfortune to arrive in the rural community at the height of haying season.[8]

During its travels, the statue did generate some controversy for its frank depiction of the female form; in some venues, for instance, men and women were only allowed to view *The Greek Slave* separately. But for many American religious leaders, the figure's "unwilling nakedness signified the purest form of Ideal, the triumph of Christian virtue over sin." Far from forbidding their flocks to view the statue, they urged them to see it and to contemplate the sculptor's message.[9] *The Greek Slave* particularly resonated with American abolitionists, who later adopted it as a symbol for their antislavery movement.[10]

Among the thousands of people who saw *The Greek Slave* during its American tour was William Wilson Corcoran (1798–1888), a Washington, DC, banker who made a fortune selling US government bonds in London to help finance the Mexican War. He purchased a copy of *The Greek Slave* in 1851 for $5,000 and installed the statue in the west wing gallery of his house. Much later, in 1874, Corcoran donated his extensive art collection—including his copy of *The Greek Slave*—to the Washington gallery that still bears his name.[11]

An even larger number of people had the chance to view a copy of *The Greek Slave* in 1851 at the Great Exhibition in the Crystal Palace in England. The statue was given pride of place in the center of the "American Department," the wing of the exhibition hall devoted to the industry of the United States. One contemporary illustrator depicted the statue on a pedestal, around which was hung a circular drape that could be opened or closed.[12] Reportedly, the drapes were drawn shut and *The Greek Slave* was hidden from view when the exceedingly proper Queen Victoria (1819–1901) opened the exhibition and toured the displays in May 1851.[13] It is remarkable that a similar fate would befall the US Justice Department's *Spirit of Justice* more than one hundred and fifty years later.

Powers was not the only one to realize the economic potential of emotionally compelling and morally acceptable nudity. In 1849 a small reproduction of the statue was created by Copeland, a British manufacturer of decorative pottery, using a newly developed unglazed porcelain.[14] Best known today as "Parian ware," the porcelain developed by Copeland and other manufacturers was "a whitish biscuit ceramic product containing feldspar, kaolin, and flint (often with smaller amounts of other base ingredients) that in finished form mimics the appearance of marble."[15] The formula for Parian ware quickly crossed the Atlantic and was first manufactured by the United States Pottery Company in Bennington, Vermont, between 1849 and 1858. According to the *New York Times*, the company also imported a British potter to assist in the preparation of reproductions of Powers's work, but the company's "execution was characteristically American, and the Bennington Greek Slave is a folk artist's version of the original."[16] Throughout the end of the nineteenth century, thousands of reproductions of Powers's nude statue were sold for display or for use as lamps in middle-class Victorian drawing rooms in Europe and America.

When the Friends of the Vermont State House announced in the fall of 2004 that they were donating a "Greek Slave" lamp for the governor's ceremonial office, there was no suggestion that a copy of the Powers statue had ever been in the room before. Nonetheless, the figure was consistent with the period of the office (the State House was entirely rebuilt after a fire in 1857) and was a natural selection, given the sculptor's Vermont origins. The Friends hired Milwaukee gaslight restorer Frank Boesel to wire the lamp into the chandelier above the governor's desk, reflecting the nineteenth-century practice of running gas table lamps off larger gasoliers suspended from the ceiling.[17]

Shortly after the lamp was installed, however, the Friends were surprised to learn that Vermont's Republican governor, Jim Douglas, had asked State House curator David Schutz to move the lamp to a different location. The governor's spokesperson, Joe Gibbs, said that the main reason for the move was to protect the lamp from the crowds of legislators and journalists that sometimes gather in the office during the legislative session. However, he added that "[i]t may, frankly, be awkward to explain why there is a nude Greek slave on the governor's desk to a third-grader."[18] Gibbs was referring to the fact that the State House is a popular destination for tours during the school year.

Vermonters reacted to the governor's request with a combination of amusement and disdain. Local writer Chris Bohjalian said that removing the statue was entirely the wrong idea: "You want a third grader to pay attention? Show him a naked statute!"[19] The most outraged response, not surprisingly, came from Polly Billings, one of the leaders of the Friends group: "This is such an affront to the art community in Vermont and the Friends of the Statehouse. We have put hundreds of thousands of dollars into the restoration of Vermont's most important building. And for the descendants [of Hiram Powers], what must they feel when the governor attacks one of their ancestor's most magnificent pieces of art?"[20] Billings went on to point out that *The Greek Slave* offered a valuable history lesson for Vermont students: "[Governor Douglas] was worried about the effect on school children? What better way to teach them about our [Vermont] Constitution, which outlaws slavery? This speaks to Vermont history, abolition and the horror of slavery."[21]

Even the Corcoran Gallery of Art in Washington, DC, still remembered for its 1989 capitulation to Jesse Helms and other religious conservatives over a planned exhibit of Robert Mapplethorpe's nude photos, spoke up in defense of *The Greek Slave*. David C. Levy, the current director of the Corcoran, sent Douglas a letter pointing out that the gallery owns one of the few full-size copies of the statue and added: "The female human form has long been revered and celebrated as an important source of artistic inspiration. Attempts to censor, remove or destroy works of art reflecting this reverence have always, in the light of history, been regarded as misguided and unfortunate."[22]

By the middle of the week, Governor Douglas was clearly getting tired of the sniping over the issue. He insisted that he was only concerned about the lamp's safety, and not the figure's nudity. "I wouldn't care if that statue were wearing a sweater and turtleneck. [The desk] is not an appropriate place for a lamp. . . . It's not a place that lends itself to have historical artifacts."[23]

When the Vermont legislative session opened on January 5, 2005, *The Greek Slave* had been carefully relocated by curator Schutz to the Cedar Creek Room, a large space in the west wing of the State House that commemorates the participation of Vermonters in the 1864 Battle of Cedar Creek in Virginia's Shenandoah Valley. In the early summer, after the legislature departed, the lamp was reinstalled on the governor's ceremonial desk. Largely overlooked in the midst of the "Greek Slave" lamp uproar was the fact that she was not the first but the *fifth* copy of the Powers statue in the State House—for nearly one hundred and fifty years, the Vermont House of Representatives has met beneath a gasolier decorated with four small copies of *The Greek Slave*.[24]

THE DECENCY WARS IN 2005: CONTINUED SKIRMISHES BUT FEW DECISIVE BATTLES

Although 2004—Frank Rich's "Year of Living Indecently"—ended with a mostly bemused discussion of the proper place (literally) of a nude statue in Vermont's State House, the New Year did not usher in a cease-fire in the battle over decency in American society. Religious conservatives certainly had little reason to call for one: More than anything else, the Jackson/Timberlake incident was a publicity bonanza for conservative organizations and their leaders.

The sheer outrageousness of the 2004 halftime show and its startling conclusion made it easier for religious conservatives to press their claim that America's culture was spiraling out of control. Almost instantly, the event became social shorthand for a country more Caligulan than Calvinist.

The most direct consequence of the Super Bowl nudity was the $550,000 fine assessed by the Federal Communications Commission against Viacom in September 2004. But the incident had other consequences that, while more difficult to measure, flowed no less directly from that February night. The 2004 Super Bowl occurred in the middle of the presidential primaries, and, almost overnight, "moral values" became one of the driving issues of the campaign. Thanks to the FCC's spate of indecency fines issued throughout the year, the primary focus was on media decency, but that wasn't the only issue. Religious conservatives were also campaigning in eleven states to pass constitutional amendments defining "marriage" solely as a union between a man and a woman. When President Bush was reelected and all eleven ballot items were passed, analysts quickly trumpeted "moral values" as one of the deciding factors in the election. Initial readings of the exit polls seemed to confirm that conclusion: over one-fifth of voters chose "moral values" as their top issue in the election, and three-quarters of those voters also cast their ballot for Bush. In a separate indicator of Bush's strength among religious conservatives, 78 percent of voters who described themselves as "born-again" voted to reelect the president.[25]

The reports of Bush's strength among Christian voters had religious conservative leaders beaming. Tony Perkins, president of the Family Research Council (the organization once headed by Gary Bauer), issued a statement that read in part: "We are optimistic given the significant increase in faith-driven participation in the moral future of our great nation. We are confident that we can win the culture war."[26] By far, the most effusive was Rev. Jerry Falwell, who wrote in an e-mail to his supporters shortly after the 2004 election: "After more than 25 years since I formed the Moral Majority and began mobilizing evangelicals to participate in the political process, I actually realized the fruit of my labors nationwide as Macel [Falwell's wife] and I watched the election returns into the early hours of Wednesday. I could not hold back the tears of joy. Hour by hour, we observed a 'slam dunk' as the Church of Jesus Christ made the difference in initiating the return of this nation to moral sanity and the Judeo-Christian ethic."[27]

But several religious leaders made it clear that victory was not enough: they expected a reelected President Bush and a strengthened Republican Congress to deliver results. "There has to be a payoff for the [religious conservative] voters," Richard Viguerie said. "There has to be a payoff for the troops of people who have worked so hard for these victories."[28] James Dobson, founder of Focus on the Family, said that if Republicans failed to move forward on the religious conservative agenda, "[t]hey will pay a price for it in four years." D. James Kennedy, head of the massive Coral Ridge Ministries in Fort Lauderdale, Florida, voiced similar sentiments: "Now that values voters have delivered for George Bush, he must deliver for their values."[29]

Among the issues on which religious conservatives expected to see progress, according to CBS's Bill Plante, were reliably conservative appointments to the Supreme Court and lower federal courts, the overturning of *Roe v. Wade*, legislative limitations on the right to abortion, a constitutional amendment outlawing same-sex marriages (similar to those passed by eleven states in November), and additional restrictions on stem cell research.[30] President Bush announced his intention to push for legislation authorizing a broader range of faith-based programs to receive federal funds to provide social services, and some congressional Republicans talked enthusiastically about resurrecting Senator Jesse Helms's proposal for stripping federal courts of their jurisdiction over certain types of cases. In 2004 the House of Representatives actually passed legislation that would have limited the ability of federal courts to hear challenges to the Defense of Marriage Act, as well as challenges to the use of the phrase "under God" in the Pledge of Allegiance. The proposals were not seriously considered by the Senate, but religious conservatives hoped the 2004 election would provide new momentum for the idea of eliminating federal court involvement in church-state issues.[31]

January 2005 seemed to auger the start of a great second term for religious conservatives. In a front-page interview with the *Washington Times*, President Bush reiterated the importance of faith in his life and in his presidency. "I don't see how you can be president," Bush said, "at least from my perspective, how you can be president, without a relationship with the Lord."[32] The president's inaugural speech on January 20 was one of the most religious in American history, beginning with his declaration that "every man and woman on this earth has rights, and dignity, and matchless value, because they bear the image of the Maker of heaven and earth."[33] The following morning, eighty-six-year-old Rev. Billy Graham—credited with helping Bush to embrace religious faith during his struggle with drinking—solemnly thanked God for the president's reelection: "We believe that in Your providence, You've granted a second term of office to our president, George W. Bush, and our vice president, Richard Cheney. Their next four years are hidden from us, but they are not hidden from You."[34]

Religious conservatives were reveling not just in symbolism but in the exercise of actual political power. When Senator Arlen Specter (R-PA) warned President Bush in a postelection press conference that he should not nominate judges intent on overturning *Roe v. Wade*, religious conservatives nearly torpedoed Specter's expected election as chair of the Senate Judiciary Committee. At the urging of James Dobson, Jerry Falwell, and other religious conservative leaders, thousands of people called and e-mailed Congress. Specter himself was called on the carpet in a closed-door meeting with Gary Bauer, Paul Weyrich, and Tony Perkins, and promised to ensure that any Bush nominee would receive "a fair vote."[35]

The herding and roping of Senator Specter was coordinated in large part by a quietly organized and even more quietly run collaborative of religious conservative organizations known as the Arlington Group. Named for the Virginia city in which it was formed, the Arlington Group was the brainchild of the Reverend Donald Wildmon, head of the American Family Association. The group, formed in mid-2003, originally brought together twenty-one different groups and now counts the leaders of nearly seventy conservative religious groups among its membership. The Arlington Group's initial purpose was to fight the forces of secularism in general, but it quickly shifted its focus following two court decisions in 2003: one by the United States Supreme Court overturning a Texas law banning sodomy and one by the Massachusetts Supreme Judicial Court declaring that same-sex couples have a right to marry. The Arlington Group formed a new organization called the Marriage Amendment Project and immediately made it clear that they expected President Bush to push strongly to amend the US Constitution to define "marriage" as the union of one man and one woman.[36]

President Bush omitted the idea from his second-term inaugural speech, however, and when Senate Republicans, led by Senator Bill Frist, announced their top ten legislative priorities for 2005, there was no mention of a "Defense of Marriage" amendment. In fact, only one of the Senate's ten agenda items—a proposal for various tax credits to help support families—appeared to be aimed at religious conservatives. Most of the remaining items were ripped straight from the economic conservative playbook: the restructuring of Social Security, tax simplification, class action lawsuit reform, jobs-and-growth tax relief, and American energy independence (i.e., Alaskan wildlife refuge drilling).[37]

Religious conservatives had been down this road before (1980, 1984, 1988, 2000) and they were not amused. "If Republicans do what they've done in the past," James Dobson said, "which is to say 'thanks so much for putting us in power; now we don't want to talk to you anymore,' they will pay a serious price in four or maybe two years."[38] The Arlington Group sent off a letter to Bush political adviser Karl Rove warning that a lack of enthusiastic support for the marriage amendment would make it "impossible for us to unite our movement on an issue such as Social Security privatization where there are already deep misgivings."[39]

Once again, however, religious conservative groups—the Arlington Group included—were guilty of misreading the temperament of the American public and, more important, the temperament of the people elected by them. It is true that a majority of religious conservatives did vote for Republicans, including Bush, and that in many cases the number of evangelical votes was greater than the margin of victory. This gives religious conservatives the ability to argue—as they do vociferously—that without their support, Republicans would not have been so successful. However, religious conservatives consistently overlook the fact that most Republican candidates receive the majority of their votes from people who are either not evangelical Christians or who are motivated by economic issues more than social ones. Religious conservatives also overlook the fact that few politicians (particularly those running for reelection) are willing to risk alienating significant portions of the electorate by advocating (let alone legislating) the more extreme elements of the religious conservative agenda.

Religious conservatives have seen some success for all their work on behalf of Bush. They applaud most of his judicial nominations, particularly for the less well-publicized seats lower down in the federal judiciary, his support of a ban on certain types of late-term abortions, the law allowing doctors and nurses in federally funded hospitals to refuse to perform abortions, and his decision to prohibit the development of additional lines of stem cells for research.[40]

But even President Bush, himself a born-again Christian and unquestionably the most thoroughly sympathetic president to the concerns of religious conservatives, has simply not pushed their agenda with the enthusiasm for which the Christian Right bargained. Much of that has to do with missteps of the president's own taking: if the "Mission Accomplished" banner so cockily draped on the island of the USS *Abraham Lincoln* in May 2003 had reflected reality, Bush would have had some real political capital to spend on behalf of his religious conservative supporters. When he did grandiosely claim an influx of political chits (in the aftermath of a wafer-thin, three-percentage-point victory in November 2004), it was clear that neither he nor his advisers felt they had any to spare for the Christian Right. Once again, it was the neocons and the econocons who had first dibs at the public policy buffet.

AND HERE WE GO AGAIN . . . A BRIEF MUSICAL INTERLUDE

Super Bowl XL was played on February 5, 2006, at Ford Field in Detroit, Michigan. The game was broadcast by ABC, and the halftime show was sponsored by the telecommunications company Sprint. In a press release issued on November 29, 2005, Sprint and the NFL announced that the main act for the halftime show would be the Rolling Stones. The quotes included in the press release sounded strangely familiar:

> From the Rolling Stones: "We are thrilled to perform for millions of fans at one of the most exciting and highly anticipated sporting events of the year."
>
> From Steve Bornstein, NFL executive vice president of media and president and chief executive officer of the NFL Network: "We are excited to welcome one of the greatest rock n' roll bands in history to the Super Bowl. As we celebrate the 40th anniversary of the Super Bowl this season, it is fitting we work with The Rolling Stones whose music has thrilled audiences around the world for years."[41]

The executive producer for the Rolling Stones halftime show was Don Mischer, who also produced the 2005 halftime show with former Beatle Paul McCartney. Mischer had one other halftime production to his credit: Super Bowl XXVII in 1993, which featured the moon-walking, crotch-grabbing Michael Jackson.

The choice of the Rolling Stones is clearly Year 2 in the campaign to feature near senior citizens in an effort to avoid repeats of the Jackson/Timberlake fiasco. But their age notwithstanding, having the Rolling Stones follow on the heels of Year 1's selection—the graying but still puppyish Paul McCartney—is more than a little ironic. In the mid-1960s, the Beatles and the Rolling Stones were the two cultural poles of the rock world. At one end were the Beatles, still wearing suits and ties, mop-top haircuts, and slightly goofy grins, and at the other, the Rolling Stones, with nary a suit to be seen, perpetual snarls, and steadily growing reports of drug use and abuse. The difference between the two groups was neatly summed up by Gered Mankowitz, the Stones' semiofficial photographer at the time: "The difference in image between the Beatles and the Stones [in the mid-1960s] was that the Beatles looked like they wanted to hold your hand, while the Stones looked like they wanted to ravish your sister."[42] Put in terms of another cultural battle that was taking place at about the same time, the Rolling Stones were *Penthouse* to the Beatles's *Playboy*.

Forty(!) years later, the Stones, the original bad boys of rock-'n'-roll, were headlining the 2006 Sprint Super Bowl halftime show. It was doubtful that there would be an actual wardrobe malfunction (other than skin-tight leather pants on sixty-year-old men), but as the group pounded out a master mix of its well-known standards—perhaps "Brown Sugar," "Honky Tonk Woman," "Let's Spend the Night Together," or even "Mother's Little Helper"?—it was difficult to see what progress religious conservatives have made in this aspect of the decency wars. If the Rolling Stones can be selected just two years after the national uproar over Jackson and Timberlake, then religious conservatives should have no illusions about their ability to impose a narrow and enduring view of decency on the national culture. Not surprisingly, the Stones have a song for that too: "(I Can't Get No) Satisfaction."

SOME STRATEGIES FOR PROMOTING THE TRUE MEANING OF DECENCY

It is tempting to advise those concerned about the political and social impact of religious conservatives to simply sit back and relax while the Republicans engage in ideological fratricide. A perfect example of this advice in action was the scrum over the selection of a replacement for retiring Supreme Court justice Sandra Day O'Connor. President Bush's choice, White House counsel Harriet Miers, was deemed insufficiently trustworthy by religious conservatives on the issue of abortion rights, and the ensuing outcry by Christian leaders over her credentials forced her withdrawal. It was a victory for religious conservatives, but characteristically Pyrrhic. The very act of demonstrating the full extent of their political clout with the current administration lessened their ability to accomplish other items on their agenda. Miers's withdrawal underscored the weakened nature of the Bush presidency, it raised concerns about the extent of the Christian Right's influence in the administration, and it served as a backbone restorative for many legislators generally opposed to the religious conservative agenda but previously unwilling to dig in their heels.

The genteel Vermont dustup in December 2004 over Hiram Powers's nude statue, however, illustrates why a wait-and-chuckle approach is perilous. Even though Governor Douglas's request to move *The Greek Slave* may have been for the statue's own good, it perfectly underscored the way in which the decency wars have warped public discourse and the formation of public policy in the United States. Even a joking suggestion that it would be difficult to explain the nudity of a historically important statue like *The Greek Slave* to a third-grader underscores the damage the religious conservative campaign for "decency" has inflicted on this country.

Over the course of its history, this country has made impressive strides in tolerance and acceptance; in many significant ways, America is far more "decent" than it was a century or even a half century ago—legal segregation has been abolished, the treatment of gays is generally better, women have moved steadily toward equal rights, the disabled are treated with more dignity, and so on. Although progress in all these areas is erratic, there is relatively little reason to believe, in the aggregate, that those gains will be reversed.

But there are still plenty of campaigns, both local and national, being waged in "His" name and in the name of decency, and the potential harm to this country in specific areas is still profound. Religious conservatives continue to command political and media attention that is disproportionate to their actual influence, and, for that reason alone, the decency wars will persist. Active opposition to intolerance and regressive policies is a start, but to really keep the country moving in the right direct, there is a need for more proactive steps.

1. Broaden the Discussion of "Decency"

The most critical shift that must take place is to broaden the definition of "decency" in American discourse. For far too long, the discussion of "decency" or "moral values" has been dominated by censorious concerns about what people read, what they watch, what they listen to, or even what they say. Within individual homes, in the ongoing negotiations between partners, or between parents and children, those are certainly legitimate questions.

The debate over decency at a national or state level, however, should be about how the citizens of this country treat each other and how this nation behaves in the global community. The examples are too numerous to list, but a brief sampling makes the point. How is it decent for the United States to kill at least thirty thousand Iraqi civilians in a war launched under false pretenses? What legitimate claim is there for decency in strenuously defending the ability to torture prisoners, operate secret prisons in allied territory, deny counsel to prisoners, and subcontract the interrogation of unidentified suspects to regimes even less fettered by the rule of law? Can the definition of "decency" be so massaged as to include this country's almost complete rejection of international efforts to rein in global warming?

The nation's recent domestic policies offer few compelling examples of decency. Where is the decency in the fact that the United States is the only industrialized nation that does not provide healthcare to all its citizens (15 percent of the population—45 million—are uncovered)?[43] What was decent about the treatment of the poor and other helpless victims in the aftermath of Hurricane Katrina, or, for that matter, on almost any other day in this country? Is it more decent to honestly discuss sex, abstinence, and contraception—and hand out disease- and baby-preventing condoms—or to inevitably add to the number of abortions, unwed mothers, or AIDS victims? And let's not overlook the need for a decent level of social and educational support for children in low-income families. Failing the adoption of such measures, the Christian Right's vaunted "culture of life" is really little more than a "culture of conception."

The efforts of religious conservatives to frame elections in terms of "decency" is understandable. This country has long prided itself as both reasonable and decent in its handling of both foreign and domestic affairs. But the Left has allowed religious conservatives to accomplish a form of ideological bait-and-switch by limiting the definition of "decency" largely to sexually related issues, while promoting what amounts to Christian Darwinism at home and abroad: God helps those who help themselves. Both economists and neo-conservatives have found this an easy theology to accept.

The issue of decency is bigger than Janet Jackson's breast or Justin Timberlake's boorishness. Campaigns in this country should be about decency, but the critical issue is not, ultimately, who is sleeping with whom or what body parts might be visible; the central question should always be whether this nation is treating its own citizens with basic human compassion and is a moral participant in the world community. Those are decency wars worth fighting.

2. Make Public Education Our Next Major Intellectual Project

More than forty years ago, President John F. Kennedy announced the formation of Project Apollo: "I believe that this nation should commit itself to achieving the goal, before this decade is out, of landing a man on the Moon and returning him safely to the Earth. No single space project in this period will be more impressive to mankind, or more important in the long-range exploration of space; and none will be so difficult or expensive to accomplish."[44]

President Kennedy was inspired in part by the sheer romance of putting a human on the moon and in part by the anticipated scientific benefits from the intense investment in space flight. But the overarching motivation (literally) was a small satellite named *Sputnik* (Russian for "fellow traveler"), which the Soviet Union had launched on October 4, 1957. Falling behind in the space race was a tremendous blow to the United States, and it led to an investment in education and scientific research that rivaled the atomic bomb–building Manhattan Project twenty-five years earlier.

On January 14, 2004, President Bush tried to capture some of the Kennedy magic[45] by announcing plans for the United States to establish a permanent facility on the moon and send a manned spacecraft to Mars by 2020. It is a bold plan, but one unlikely to escape Earth orbit for myriad reasons. Money is, of course, the major issue: in an era of skyrocketing deficits, staggering tax cuts, and spiraling Iraq war costs, there is no widespread support for the kind of expenditures required to put someone on Mars.

But there is a more corrosive problem that is not receiving enough attention. Back in the 1960s, the nation's educational system—from elementary through graduate school—was the equal or superior to every other country in the world. When President Kennedy turned to the nation's education and scientific institutions to staff his Apollo Project, the human resources were available. There's still no shortage of bright people in this country, but the level of competition around the world has exploded over the last forty years. Two-thirds of Japan's college graduates have degrees in science, technology, engineering, and math; the US rate is half that. Asia and Europe also graduate more students with advanced degrees in those fields than the United States.[46] By some estimates, China may be graduating *one million* engineers each year, with India not far behind; the United States, by contrast, graduates an estimated seventy-five thousand engineers per year.[47]

When it comes to math and science, China, India, and Japan may be the United States' most challenging competitors, but they are not the only ones. On a standardized test of "real world" math and science skills administered in 2003, US high school students ranked twenty-fourth out of twenty-nine nations, behind even the Netherlands, Iceland, and Luxembourg.[48] Other tests have shown similar results.

These are the kinds of statistics that throw the debate over intelligent design into stark relief. An ongoing debate over whether students should be taught that the earth is a few thousand years old or the scientifically accepted 4.5 billion years old does not convey the kind of can-do attitude that made it possible for astronaut Alan B. Shepard to practice his golf swing in the ultimate sand trap. It conveys the message that ideology is more important than fact. There is no reason why President Bush's suggestion to "teach the controversy" cannot be honored, but this should be done in a political science or comparative religion class, where the controversy belongs. In the scientific forum, it is not "controversy"; it is a distraction that interferes with our ability to give our children a world-class scientific education.

The primary reason to improve American scientific and mathematic education is to help the country remain competitive in the world economy, a challenge daunting enough, given some of the global disparities in population and resources. But if the United States truly does want to travel to Mars in the next generation, then it absolutely must do one of two things: (1) rebuild its scientific farm team through a comprehensive and rigorous revitalization of math, science, and engineering education; or (2) greatly expand the number of Chinese language classes being taught, so that our astronauts will be able to read the instruction manuals for the hydroponics labs when they eventually get there.

3. Help Foster a True Marketplace of Ideas

Given the complexity of the United States communication infrastructure, it makes sense to have a national body—such as the Federal Communications

Commission—that is charged with supervising the development and implementation of new technologies and the equitable use of existing communication resources. Congress has repeatedly struggled to understand new technologies as they were developed, ranging from the radio to the Internet, and the FCC has the experience and the staff to generally keep pace. The commission plays a vitally important role in relieving Congress of the daunting task of understanding communication minutiae.

The time has come, however, to strip the FCC of one chore: the determination of whether to penalize broadcasters for the transmission of indecency or obscenity. Part of the reason is philosophical: this is a nation founded in large part on certain unalienable rights, among them liberty and the pursuit of happiness. Both principles find expression in the First Amendment, which declares that "Congress [or its commission] shall make no law . . . abridging the freedom of speech, or of the press." If it makes people happy to listen to Howard Stern or Rush Limbaugh, why should the government impinge on their liberty to do so? Particularly disturbing is the fact that the FCC only rules in retrospect; broadcasters can be punished for what they aired, often months or years earlier, but are never told what they *can't* broadcast. Stations are left to divine decency boundaries from the entrails of previous commission decisions. That alone is reason enough to get the FCC out of the decency business.

But the main reason to strip the FCC of its ability to assess fines for broadcast indecency is that, as a practical matter, broadcasting is becoming to a large extent obsolete. The premise has always been that the FCC can fine indecent broadcasts because they are widely available and freely accessible by children, who must be protected. But increasingly, people choose to pay for the signals they receive: 84 percent of US homes with television sets receive advertising-supported cable television services.[49] Radio has lagged somewhat behind for want of a system that could travel with the listener, but now two satellite-based systems are vying to offer consumers high-quality national radio signals for a fee. The justification for FCC indecency supervision is steadily dropping.

Until the era of broadcast vanishes entirely, Congress should take one interim step to minimize FCC action in this area. Currently, a complaint by a single viewer is enough to trigger an investigation, which in turn can result in a possible fine or even the loss of a broadcast license. That leaves the determination of indecency in the hands of as few as four people: the complainant and three of the five commissioners. In a nation of three hundred million–plus residents, that is a staggering and totally unwarranted level of power. If the FCC is going to retain the authority to punish indecent broadcasts, then a requirement should be adopted that the FCC must receive complaints from some reasonable percentage of the audience of any given show before initiating an investigation. Twenty percent would be reasonable, but even if Congress set the bar as low as 10 percent, the FCC could not have opened an investigation of the Jackson/Timberlake incident until it received approximately 9.5 million complaints (it actually received around 500,000).

The other valuable step that Congress could take to ameliorate the decency wars is to require cable companies to offer channels on an à la carte basis. Right now, consumers are forced to purchase different "tiers" of channels that are bundled together. The cable companies argue that the bundles are collectively cheaper than individual channels would be and that they enable the cable companies to help nurture smaller channels that otherwise wouldn't have a large enough viewership to justify the cost of cable distribution. The cable companies have received support from a surprising quarter: religious broadcasters like Pat Robertson and Jerry Falwell, who are concerned that the à la carte approach would both reduce their viewership and make it easier to count how small it actually is compared to those of other programs.[50] As matters currently stand, religious broadcasters can claim a number of viewers equal to every subscriber with access to the cable tier in which their channel appears, whether subscribers actually watch or not. If the cable industry ever adopts the à la carte approach, then it will be possible to know exactly how many people have paid to watch a particular religious broadcaster (or any other channel, for that matter).

The head of the Parents Television Council, L. Brent Bozell, argues that the à la carte approach would solve the television indecency problem because consumers would choose not to purchase "salacious" channels like MTV.[51] It is far more likely, however, that just the opposite would happen. Channels like MTV and Comedy Central would thrive, and the worst fears of the religious broadcasters would be realized.

It will be interesting to see how these issues play out at the FCC, given the changes in its membership. Chairman Michael Powell resigned in January 2005, and, after a two-month delay, President Bush nominated Commissioner Kevin Martin to replace him. Over the years, Martin has consistently taken a stricter line on broadcast indecency than did Powell, and religious conservatives were delighted with his appointment. In a statement, Jan LaRue, chief counsel for Concerned Women for America, announced that she had urged CWA members to "flood" the White House with calls in support of Martin. The new chairman also received enthusiastic support from the Parents Television Council and the Family Research Council.[52]

From a decency perspective, however, Martin's tenure as FCC chair got off to a slow start. In all of 2005, the commission did not hand out a single Notice of Apparent Liability, nor did it assess a single fine. Behind the scenes, however, Martin was pushing the major cable companies to make some changes in either their content regulation or channel offerings. Two cable companies, Comcast Corporation and Time-Warner, were particularly vulnerable to pressure from the FCC chair. The companies have proposed a joint acquisition of the bankrupt Adelphia Cable, and Martin strongly suggested that the purchase could be held up by the FCC without their cooperation on indecency. The cable companies were given three options: create a family-friendly tier, allow à la carte channel selection, or implement content standards. According to one report, most cable channels favored some type of content standards, but two companies refused: Rupert Murdoch's News Corporation, which owns and operates the Fox network and the often-racy cable network FX; and Viacom, which owns a number of edgy networks, including the infamous MTV and Comedy Central.[53]

As a result, cable companies are beginning to roll out so-called family-friendly tiers of cable channels. Time-Warner, not surprisingly, was the first, announcing on December 15, 2005, that consumers will soon be able to order a separate tier of channels for $13 per month that includes the following fifteen channels: the cartoon channel Boomerang, C-SPAN 2 and C-SPAN 3, CNN Headline News, the Science Channel, Discovery Kids, Disney Channel, DIY Network, FIT-TV, Food Network, HGTV, La Familia, Nick Games & Sports, the Weather Channel, and Toon Disney.[54] Other cable companies will come up with their own family-friendly channel lineups.

Even before being implemented, the family-friendly tiers appear to have accomplished their primary purpose: taking the heat off the cable companies on Capitol Hill. Senator Ted Stevens (R-AK) has been putting his own pressure on the cable industry and is planning to have the Senate Commerce Committee (which he chairs) work on the issue of media indecency in 2006. At an informal hearing in early December 2005, however, he suggested that the creation of family-friendly tiers would remove the need for further legislation. That view outraged indecency activists, including Concerned Women for America's Jan LaRue: "Instead of true cable choice, Stevens thinks Americans will be satisfied paying for a family tier with a Jack Valenti-created MPAA rating system that might be fit for the Manson family."[55]

It remains to be seen whether the family-friendly tiers are any more popular or effective than the vaunted v-chip, the electronic filter built into each TV that is designed to work with program ratings to assist parents in regulating what their children watch. What is immediately clear, however, is that Chairman Martin is already demonstrating a willingness to use the FCC's expansive regulatory power to help congressional conservatives impose a particular view of decency on media companies. It would be one thing to use the power of the FCC to create an environment in which each consumer (and each family) can make their own decision about the content they wish to view. Instead, the specter of legislation and/or bureaucratic intransigence is being used to compel cable companies to offer up a predigested selection of channels aimed at satisfying the "decency" concerns of a relatively small number of people. That is a complete misuse of governmental authority and one that runs counter to the most basic principles of the First Amendment.

4. Promote Personal and Parental Responsibility

A compelling argument can be made that the Internet is helping to preserve a free press, and the same may well prove true for other types of speech as well. Cable companies do not want to offer subscribers the ability to select individual channels (fearing the segmentation of the audience and corresponding drop in ad revenues), but soon they may not have a choice. Increasingly, consumers are demonstrating their strong interest in accessing specific content on demand. Unless they respond to this interest, cable companies run a serious risk of losing their audience to other distribution channels (most notably, of course, the Internet).

At the forefront of this trend is the music industry, although it is fair to say that they were dragged kicking and screaming to the head of the line. It was only after the record companies understood the full scope of the financial threat posed by file-sharing programs like Napster, LimeWire, and Morpheus that they embraced a business model that allows consumers to download individual music tracks for a reasonable fee. Technology—in the form of the almost irresistible portable mp3 player the iPod—helped, and now, with the release of the video iPod, networks are beginning to sell downloads of individual episodes of their popular television shows.

As more and more content is purchased directly by the consumer from the producer, without any use of public airwaves, the government's interest in regulating that content correspondingly diminishes. Given that so much of the rhetoric of the Reagan Revolution and the Gingrich Uprising emphasized the need for personal responsibility, it is disingenuous for Republicans to argue that the government should constantly monitor broadcasts lest someone be offended. That is particularly true given the amount of information available today to television viewers. It takes some effort to actually be surprised by the "indecent" content of a show like Desperate Housewives (which, as New York Times columnist Frank Rich pointed out, is just as popular in "red" states as it is in "blue").[56]

The same obligation of personal responsibility extends to the supervision of the video choices of children. There is absolutely no question that parenting is an exhausting and challenging phase of life. It is a grave disservice to both children and country, however, to rely on the federal government to protect children through broadcast limitations. Again, enormous information resources are available to assist parents as are increasingly affordable technology options (such as digital video recorders) to filter what children watch. No parentally implemented system will be perfect (particularly as children get older), and monitoring video consumption is time consuming. But ceding that authority and responsibility to the government is politically dangerous and simply sets a bad example for children about the relative roles of government and its citizens.

5. Give Aid and Comfort to Organizations That Defend the Constitution

When cofounder of the Free Congress Foundation Paul Weyrich began work on the creation of a coalition of conservative thinks tanks and advocacy groups to counter the dominance of liberal groups in the late 1960s and early 1970s, it is doubtful that he could have imagined just how successful those efforts would prove. Over the last thirty years, the interwoven network of conservative organizations, wealthy conservative donors, and religious conservative groups—with their well-honed donation model and indefatigable volunteers—have transformed the political landscape of the country and shifted the debate on most issues significantly to the Right.

The pendulous nature of political debate in the United States is well documented, but as Weyrich convincingly demonstrated, a strong push can speed up the process of shifting the national debate in the opposite direction. It is time—indeed, well past time—for people concerned about individual liberties, the separation of church and state, and the overall constitutional health of this nation and its people to start pushing the conversation in the opposite direction.

Part of the answer lies in individual action: taking personal responsibility for media choices rather than expecting the FCC or Congress to monitor or control media decency, electing representatives dedicated to preservation of individual liberties and a reasonable separation between church and state, monitoring and responding to the legislation proposed at the state and federal levels, and exercising the rights and responsibilities provided by the Constitution and the Bill of Rights.

As important as individual involvement is, however, there is tremendous power in collective action as well. For those looking for ways to leverage their support of the Constitution, there are a wide range of organizations devoted to monitoring and opposing the more extreme efforts of religious conservatives. For decades, for instance, the American Civil Liberties Union (www.aclu.org)

has played a vital role in defending the nation's Bill of Rights. Since the early 1970s, Norman Lear's People for the American Way (www.pfaw.org) has been a powerful voice for the benefits of a pluralistic and progressive nation. And most recently, the twin organizations MoveOn.org Civil Action (devoted to education and lobbying) and MoveOn.org Political Action (a federal political action committee) have demonstrated the compelling power of the Internet for organizing support for progressive policies. A comprehensive list of other liberal advocacy groups can be found at MovingIdeas.org, a project of the American Prospect.

6. *What Would Jesus Deregulate? The Role of Religion in the Formation of Public Policy in a Pluralistic Nation*

One of the major objections to the nomination of Judge Robert Bork to the United States Supreme Court was his fervent embrace of "originalism"—the belief that the interpretation and application of the United States Constitution should be governed by the words used by the Founding Fathers in 1787 and, more specifically, by the meaning of the words at the time the document was drafted. That is a questionable enough theory of interpretation for a document more than two hundred years old, but at least it was written in the language (if not the idiom) that we use today. More important, there is no serious disagreement about what the Founding Fathers actually wrote.

As Clarence Darrow so doggedly pointed out in his cross-examination of William Jennings Bryan in 1925, it is much more difficult to defend the application of "originalism" to a document like the Christian Bible. The text generally in use today was composed over the course of hundreds of years in multiple languages (chiefly Hebrew, Greek, Aramaic, and Latin) by dozens of different authors. There have been over 450 English versions of the Bible alone, with the earliest translations occurring nearly fifteen hundred years ago. There are inconsistencies, omissions, contradictions, and obvious exaggerations scattered throughout the Bible's many books. Even if it were possible to reach consensus on what the actual text of the Bible is and its meaning (no easy task), there is still the basic question of whether every single one of its prohibitions and moral principles—most drafted for a vastly different time and place—are still relevant today.

Only the most fundamental of religious conservatives would try to conform modern-day life to all of the apparent dictates of the Bible. Doing so requires a social contortion that is inherently isolating and, in many particulars, illegal. But efforts to apply the Word of God to specific public policy issues still persist, most notably in the area of homosexuality. As was noted earlier, for instance, there are certainly passages in Leviticus that appear to unequivocally condemn same-sex relationships. For some, that is enough to end the discussion: the act is sin and the actors are sinners. But is the message of the Bible, indeed, of Jesus Christ himself, to be found in millennia-old and debatable text or in the book's broader themes of humility, compassion, and love? A partial answer, at least, was given by the Reverend Jerry Falwell. When Falwell was asked to comment on some volunteer legal work performed by Supreme Court nominee John Roberts for a gay rights group that challenged a Colorado law permitting discrimination in housing against gays, he said: "I may not agree with the lifestyle. And I don't. But that has nothing to do with the civil rights of that part of our constituency." When challenged by MSNBC host Tucker Carlson about his long-standing opposition to special rights for gays, Falwell responded: "Well, housing and employment are not special rights. I think—I think the right to live somewhere and to live where you please or to work where you please, as long as you're not bothering anybody else, is a basic right, not a—not a special right. . . . Civil rights for all Americans, black, white, red, yellow, the rich, poor, young, old, gay, straight, etc., is not a liberal or conservative value. It's an American value that I would think that we pretty much all agree on."[57] It was hardly a ringing endorsement of homosexuality or of a controversial concept like gay marriage, but coming from the old Moral Majority warrior, even a partial recognition of gay rights had jaws dropping across the country.

And therein lies both the strength and the promise of this nation: its inherent pluralism—the promise (albeit sometimes erratically fulfilled) of peaceful coexistence on equal terms. There are many things that are disturbing and destructive about the "decency wars" that have been waged for so long in this country, but none more so than the presumption that the followers of one religion in this nation have the inside track on goodness, and righteousness, and decency, and a mandate from God to impose that religion (or at the very least, its precepts) on everyone else.

The problem with so much of the religious conservative activism over the last thirty-plus years, however, is that its primary goal is to impose the principles of Christianity and, even more specifically, evangelical Christianity, on American culture and politics. The decision of what to believe and which deity to embrace (if any) is an intensely personal decision, one in which government should have little interest and an even smaller role. If religious conservatives ever succeeded in implementing their full political agenda, the net effect would be to turn each individual's citizenship into a contract of adhesion with a Christian God, a compact with little more value than the fine print on the back of a dry-cleaning ticket. Faith and religious values have an important role to play in American society, but not in the formation of its laws or the administration of its government.

Notes

PROLOGUE: SLAVES TO THE RHYTHM: THE NFL, CBS, AND MTV REAP AS THEY SOW

1. Brooks Boliek, "Boob Tube Ploy Raises FCC Ire," *Hollywood Reporter*, February 3, 2004, http://199.249.170.186/thr/article_display.jsp?vnu_content_id= 2081707 (accessed February 3, 2004).

2. Thom Duffy, "Michael Jackson Gets Prime Halftime Slot at Super Bowl," *Billboard*, September 19, 1992.

3. Michael D. Clark, "Super Bowl Is as Much Concert as It Is Football," *Houston Chronicle*, February 3, 2004.

4. Mark Harris, "Beyond the Pale," *Entertainment Weekly*, February 26, 1993.

5. Irv Lichtman, "Michael's Super Halftime Ratings," *Billboard*, February 13, 1993.

6. United Press International, "Super Bowl Ranks Most-Watched Since 1998," February 3, 2004. The National Football League has claimed as many as one billion viewers, but that seems unlikely, given the estimate that the US audience in 2004 topped out at just under ninety million people.

7. Brooke Minton, "Grab the Chips and Dips, It's Game Time," *Oracle*, January 30, 2004; Bruce Horovitz, "Pizza People Prepare Super Bowl Blitz," *USA Today*, January 16, 2004.

8. Sarah Hale Meitner, "Super Bowl Reshapes U.S. Food-Buying Patterns," *Orlando Sentinel*, January 31, 2004; Joan Obra, "Stores Score Big Before Super Bowl," *Fresno Bee*, February 1, 2004.

9. Atkins Nutritionals, Inc., press release, "This Year, Try a Controlled-Carb Super Bowl Sunday," PR Newswire, January 26, 2004.

10. Meitner, "Super Bowl Reshapes U.S. Food-Buying Patterns."

11. Clay Latimer, "Supersized as Cultural Phenomenon, NFL Spectacle Gobbles Up Huge Portion of America's Attention," *Denver Rocky Mountain News*, January 24, 2003.

12. Amy Reiter, "The Wild Evolution of the Super Bowl Halftime Show," Salon .com, January 30, 2004, http://www.salon.com/ent/col/fix/2004/01/30/fri/ (accessed April 23, 2005).

13. Eric Snider, "The Show within a Show," *St. Petersburg Times*, January 23, 1991.

14. "New Kids on the Block," *People Weekly*, July 27, 1992.

15. Richard Corliss, "Kid Power Conquers Hollywood," *Time*, January 7, 1991.

16. Miriam Horn, "Salvaging Saturday Morning Prime Time," *U.S. News & World Report*, March 4, 1991.

17. Bill Carter, "Frito-Lay and Fox Attempt to Outflank the Super Bowl," *New York Times*, January 13, 1992.

18. Ibid.

19. Alan Carter, "'Color' Me Bad," *Entertainment Weekly*, February 14, 1992.

20. Carter, "Frito-Lay and Fox Attempt to Outflank the Super Bowl."

21. A Nielsen rating is an estimate of the size of a show's audience expressed as a percentage of the number of possible televisions tuned to that show. Thus, if there are 100 million television households and 25 million households are tuned to a particular show, the show would have a Nielsen rating of 25.

22. Steve McClellan, "Fox's NFL Bid Drove Up Prices, Drove Out CBS," *Broadcasting & Cable*, January 3, 1994.

23. Ramonica Rice, "MTV at Super Bowl: Fielding a Half Time," CNN.com, January 26, 2001, http://archives.cnn.com/2001/CAREER/trends/01/25/superbowl/ (accessed March 17, 2005).

24. Pamela Davis, "Pop 'n' Rock," *St. Petersburg Times*, January 23, 2001, http://www.sptimes.com/News/012301/SuperBowl2001/Pop_n_Rock_.shtml   (accessed March 17, 2005).

25. Bruce Horovitz, "Super Bowl Accepts No Half-Hearted Effort," USA *Today*, January 26, 2001.

26. National Football League, CBS, and MTV, press release, "The NFL and CBS Look to MTV to Produce the AOL Super Bowl XXXVIII Halftime Show," PR Newswire, December 9, 2003.

27. Press Release, "America Online Sponsors 'The AOL Super Bowl XXXVIII Halftime Show,'" Business Wire, December 9, 2003; Stephen Lynch, "Report: AOL May Ask for Money Back after Halftime Debacle," FoxNews.com, February 3, 2004, http://www.foxnews.com/story/0,2933,110288,00.html (accessed February 3, 2004).

28. Associated Press, "VFW Angry Over Kid Rock Super Bowl Poncho," February 4, 2004, http://www.miami.com/mld/miamiherald/entertainment/7872393.htm (accessed March 23, 2005).

29. Jon Wiederhorn, "Timberlake, Janet Jackson Make Sexy Pair on Justified," MTV.com, September 25, 2002, http://www.mtv.com/news/articles/1457770/20020925/story.jhtml (accessed February 4, 2005).

30. As most people are undoubtedly aware, Tivo is a digital video recording system that allows viewers to record and rewind live action shows. Another, less well-publicized, feature of Tivo is that it allows the company to track, with great specificity, what people watch and rewind to watch again. Company officials were quoted as saying that Jackson's wardrobe malfunction was the "most-replayed moment" in the company's viewership data. "Janet's Breast Makes Net History," BBC, February 5, 2004, http://news.bbc.co.uk/2/hi/technology/3461459.stm (accessed January 31, 2005).

31. "Emerson, Faye," Museum of Broadcast Communications, n.d., http://www .museum.tv/archives/etv/E/htmlE/emersonfaye/emersonfaye.htm (accessed March 9, 2004); Jerome A. Holst, "Nudity–1950s," TVAcres.com, n.d., http://www.tvacres .com/sex_nudity50.htm (accessed February 28, 2004). Most sources point back to one source: Gabe Essoe, *The Book of TV Lists* (Westport, CT: Arlington House, 1981).

32. C. E. Butterfield, "Those Plunging Necklines Worrying Video Studios," *New York Times*, March 19, 1950.

CHAPTER ONE: A NIP IN THE AIR: THE CHILLING EFFECTS OF THE 2004 SUPER BOWL HALFTIME SHOW

1. Seth Sutel, "MTV's Freston: We Got 'Punk'd' by Jackson," MiamiHerald.com, February 3, 2004, http://www.miami.com/mld/miamiherald/entertainment/7864667 .htm (accessed February 3, 2004).

2. Mark Sage, "'Right Breast Stole My Thunder' Says Super Bowl Streaker," News.Scotsman.com, February 3, 2004, http://news.scotsman.com/latest.cfm?id= 2487703 (accessed February 3, 2004).

3. For those interested in viewing photos of what CBS was unwilling to air, it's worth a visit to Robert's Web site: http://www.thestreaker.org.uk/intro.htm. His site has photos and humorous descriptions of his streaks at various political gatherings and major sporting events (including the 2004 Super Bowl).

4. "FCC to Investigate Jackson Breast Exposure Incident," TheDenver Channel .com, February 2, 2004, http://www.thedenverchannel.com/entertainment/2810443/ detail.html (accessed January 31, 2005).

5. Jay Leno, *The Tonight Show*, February 3, 2004.

6. David Letterman, *The Late Show with David Letterman*, February 3, 2004.

7. Jon Stewart, *The Daily Show with Jon Stewart*, February 3, 2004.

8. According to SourceWatch, an ongoing project by the Center for Media and Democracy, the Parents and Grandparents Alliance is (or was) a project of Accuracy in Media, a conservative organization best known for its attacks on mainstream media for its alleged lack of "fairness, balance and accuracy." (The close parallel to the Fox News slogan, "Fair and Balanced," is not a coincidence.) The Parents and Grandparents Alliance operates a Web site under the domain name outragedcitizens.com.

9. Dave Montgomery, "Halftime Escapade Produces Backlash," *Fort Worth Star Telegram*, February 8, 2004.

10. Shaheem Reid and Robert Mancini, "Janet, Justin, MTV Apologize for Super Bowl Flash," MTV.com, February 1, 2004, http://www.mtv.com/news/articles/1484738/02012004/jackson_janet.jhtml (accessed January 29, 2005).

11. "CBS Statement on Super Bowl Halftime Incident," February 2, 2004, http://www.viacom.com/press.tin?ixPressRelease=80254178 (accessed February 1, 2005).

12. Brooks Boliek, "Boob Tube Ploy Raises FCC Ire," Hollywood Reporter.com, February 3, 2004 (accessed February 3, 2004).

13. "Janet's 'Super' Exposure," Access Hollywood.com, February 2, 2004, http://www.accesshollywood.com/news/2811088/detail.html (accessed March 16, 2005).

14. Reid and Mancini, "Janet, Justin, MTV Apologize for Super Bowl Flash."

15. Ibid.

16. "Janet Jackson Reveals What She Meant to Show," WSB-TV.com, February 3, 2004, http://www.wsbtv.com/entertainment/2813550/detail.html (accessed January 31, 2005). For survey vote totals, click on the "Results" link in the "Survey" sidebar.

17. Steve Appleford, "Janet, Justin Sued by Viewer," RollingStone.com, February 6, 2004, http://www.rollingstone.com/news/story/_/id/5937157?rnd=1107491165773&has-player=true&version=6.0.12.1040 (accessed February 3, 2005).

18. AP Worldstream, "Lawyer Loses Lawsuit over Janet Jackson's Halftime Super Bowl Show," May 27, 2004.

19. Associated Press, "Poll: Janet's Revelation No Crime," CBSNews.com, February 21, 2004, http://www.cbsnews.com/stories/2004/02/02/entertainment/main597184.shtml (accessed February 1, 2005); "Poll: Jackson's Act Marked 'New Low,'" *Houston Chronicle*, February 9, 2004.

20. Federal Communications Commission press release, "FCC Chairman Powell Calls Super Bowl Halftime Show a 'Classless, Crass, Deplorable Stunt.' Opens Investigation," February 2, 2004.

21. Boliek, "Boob Tube Ploy Raises FCC Ire."

22. Appleford, "Janet, Justin Sued by Viewer."

23. Neil Roland, "CBS Fined $550,000 by FCC for Indecency at Super Bowl," Bloomberg, September 22, 2004, http://quote.bloomberg.com/apps/news?pid=10000103&sid=aFDKHWEAIFK4&refer=us (accessed September 23, 2004).

24. "Janet Jackson Takes Responsibility for Breast-baring," CNN.com, February 4, 2004, http://edition.cnn.com/2004/SHOWBIZ/TV/02/04/jackson.apology.ap/index.html (accessed February 4, 2005).

25. "Apology Enough After Janet Stunt?" CBSNews.com, February 3, 2004, http://www.cbsnews.com/stories/2004/02/03/entertainment/main597813.shtml (accessed February 1, 2005).

26. Ibid.

27. The phrase "weapon of mass distraction," remarkably, has been around since at least 1996, when M*A*S*H creator Larry Gelbart used it as a title for an HBO movie. Following the intense use of the phrase "weapons of mass destruction" since 2002, the pun has been rapidly gaining popularity. See, e.g., the Word Spy, "weapon of mass distraction," n.d., http://www.wordspy.com/words/weaponofmassdistraction.asp (accessed December 2, 2005).

28. Federal Communications Commission, *In re 1998 Biennial Regulatory Review*, MM docket no. 98–35, May 26, 2000.

29. "Freeing the Airwaves," *Time*, August 6, 1984 (accessed June 10, 2005, in online library Highbeam.com).

30. Federal Communications Commission, *In re 1998 Biennial Regulatory Review*.

31. James Gattuso, "The Myth of Media Concentration: Why the FCC's Media Ownership Rules Are Unnecessary," Heritage Foundation, May 29, 2003, http://www.heritage.org/Research/InternetandTechnology/wm284.cfm (accessed June 10, 2005).

32. *Telecommunications Act of 1996*, Public Law 104-104, 110, Stat. 56, codified throughout Title 47 at *US Code* 47, § 202.

33. Four of the five seats on the Federal Communications Commission are divided evenly between Republicans and Democrats, and when one of them becomes vacant, the president is required to nominate a commissioner from the same party as the departing member. When a vacancy occurs in the chairmanship, the president can appoint someone from whatever party he chooses (although the appointee is typically from the same party as the president).

34. Federal Communications Commission, *In re 1998 Biennial Regulatory Review*.

35. *Time Warner Entertainment Co. v. United States*, 211 F.3d 1313 (DC Cir. 2000).

36. *Fox Television Stations, Inc., v. Federal Communications Commission*, 280 F.3d 1027 (DC Cir. 2002).

37. Federal Communications Commission, "Notice of Proposed Rule Making," FCC 02-249, September 12, 2002, pp. 3–4.

38. Frank James, "Review of Media Ownership Limits May Cause Ownership Concentration, Critics Say," *Chicago Tribune*, September 13, 2002 (accessed June 22, 2005, in online library Highbeam.com).

39. Ibid.

40. Bill McConnell, "Powell Grants Dereg Hearing in Richmond," *Broadcasting & Cable*, December 9, 2002 (accessed June 22, 2005, in online library Highbeam.com).

41. Bill McConnell, "Major Cap Relief? Don't Bet on It," *Broadcasting & Cable*, April 7, 2003 (accessed June 22, 2005, in online library Highbeam.com).

42. Alicia Mundy, "Where on Earth Is Kevin Martin," *Cable World*, July 8, 2002 (accessed June 22, 2005, in online library Highbeam.com).

43. Bill McConnell, "Et tu, Kevin?" *Broadcasting & Cable*, February 24, 2003 (accessed June 22, 2005, in online library Highbeam.com).

44. Federal Communications Commission, *In re 2002 Biennial Regulatory Review*.

45. John Nichols, "Media Giants Get Slapped," *Nation*, July 23, 2003.

46. Bill McConnell, "Passage of 39% Cap No Sure Thing," *Broadcasting & Cable*, December 15, 2003 (accessed July 19, 2005, in online library Highbeam.com). However, as McConnell points out, all the legislation did was relieve the FCC of its obligation under the 1996 Telecommunications Act to review the audience cap regulation every two years. It is not clear that it forbids the FCC from revisiting the issue at the request of a petitioner or even *sua sponte*.

47. Associated Press, "Congressional Leaders Compromise on Media-Ownership Rules," November 26, 2003.

48. "Court Blocks FCC Media Regs," Wired.com, September 3, 2003, http://www .wired.com/news/business/0,1367,60286,00.html?tw=wn_story_related (accessed March 22, 2005).

49. This follows the far better-known Eleventh Commandment, i.e., "A Republican shall not speak ill of other Republicans."

50. Jeff Jarvis, "F*cked by the F*CC," *Nation*, May 17, 2004, http://www.the nation.com/doc.mhtml?i=20040517&s=jarvis (accessed July 4, 2005).

51. Eric Boehlert, "The Media Borg's Man in Washington," Salon.com, August 6, 2001, http://dir.salon.com/tech/feature/2001/08/06/powell/index.html (accessed June 10, 2005).

52. Bill McConnell, "Powell in Perspective," *Broadcasting & Cable*, May 21, 2001 (accessed on June 7, 2005, in online library Highbeam.com).

53. "FCC Censors Back Off," *Denver Rocky Mountain News*, January 20, 2002.

54. Krysten Crawford, "Breasts, Butts, Backs . . . Oh My!" CNN/Money.com, December 16, 2004, http://money.cnn.com/2004/12/16/news/fortune500/yir04_ indecency/index.htm (accessed December 17, 2004).

55. Heather Fleming Phillips, "Observers Say FCC Chairman Powell Is Isolated Due to Political Missteps," *San Jose Mercury News*, August 4, 2003.

56. Federal Communications Commission, *In the Matter of Infinity Broadcasting Operations*, EB-02-IH-0685 (October 2, 2003).

57. Press release, "Morality in Media Congratulates FCC for $375,000 Indecency Fine against Infinity Broadcasting for Airing 'Opie & Anthony Show,'" US Newswire, October 3, 2003.

58. Frank Rich, "Après Janet, a Deluge," *New York Times*, March 21, 2004, http:// www.nytimes.com/2004/03/21/arts/21RICH.html (accessed March 22, 2004).

59. *In the Matter of Complaints against Various Broadcast Licensees Regarding Their Airing of the "Golden Globe Awards" Program*, Memorandum Opinion and Order, October 3, 2003, paras. 5–6.

60. "PTC Demands Response from FCC Commissioners Over F-Word Decision," Parents Television Council press release, October 21, 2003, http://www.parentstv.org/ ptc/publications/release/2003/1021.asp (accessed March 15, 2005).

61. Frank Ahrens, "TV Raciness Embroils FCC in (deleted) Obscenity Flap," *Houston Chronicle*, December 14, 2005.

62. Remarks by Rep. Jo Ann Davis (R-VA), *Congressional Record*, November 20, 2003, p. H11857.

63. H. Res. 482, 108th Cong., sess. 2, December 8, 2003.

64. Gene Weingarten, "Word Games," *Washington Post*, February 29, 2004, http:// www.washingtonpost.com/ac2/wp-dyn?pagename=article&contentId=A3432-2004 Feb24&notFound=true (accessed March 15, 2005).

65. H.R. 3687, 108th Cong.s, sess. 2, December 8, 2003. Among Ose's other legislative proposals was a bill that would have added President Reagan to the Mount Rushmore monument.

66. Weingarten, "Word Games." Not surprisingly, Weingarten's column sparked

an enthusiastic round of discussion in the grammarian blogosphere about exactly how it was that Bono used the word "fucking."

67. S. Res. 283, 108th Cong., sess. 2, December 9, 2003.

68. "The Buzz—Spike Says Jackson Hit 'New Low,'" *Daily News* (Los Angeles), February 5, 2004 (accessed June 20, 2005, in online library Highbeam.com).

69. "Timberlake's Family Offended by Breast-Baring Halftime," WSBVT.com, February 5, 2004, http://www.wsbtv.com/entertainment/2820088/detail.html (accessed January 31, 2005).

70. JC Chasez, press release, "Statement from JC Chasez Regarding the NFL Pro Bowl," February 5, 2004.

71. Tirdad Derakhshani, "Names in the News," Knight Ridder/Tribune News Service, February 6, 2004 (accessed June 20, 2005, in online library Highbeam.com).

72. "NBC Cuts Shot of Exposed Breast from 'ER,'" Zap2It.com, February 5, 2004, http://tv.zap2it.com/tveditorial/tve_main/1,1002,271%7C86173%7C1%7C,00.html (access March 15, 2005).

73. "TNT to Use Delay at NBA All-Star Fetes," AP Online, February 14, 2004 (accessed April 24, 2005, in online library Highbeam.com).

74. "Beyonce Performs at NBA All-Star," AP Online, February 16, 2004 (accessed December 3, 2005, in online library Highbeam.com).

75. Drew MacKenzie, "Grammys Give Janet the Boot," *Mirror* (London), February 6, 2004 (accessed March 31, 2005, in online library Highbeam.com).

76. Josh Grossberg, "Grammys: Janet, Justin In; Luther Out," Eonline.com, February 3, 2004, http://www.eonline.com/News/Items/0,1,13416,00.html (accessed February 3, 2004).

77. Gail Shister, "CBS Hopes to Have Video Delay in Place for Grammys," *Philadelphia Inquirer*, February 3, 2004.

78. "MTV Super Bowl Weekend," February 2, 2004, http://www.mtv.com/onair/super_bowl/2004/ (accessed January 29, 2005).

79. Sutel, "MTV's Freston: We Got 'Punk'd' by Jackson." If Jackson and Timberlake did intentionally pull a prank on MTV, there's a certain rough justice to the stunt, since the description of the show *Punk'd* on MTV's Web site makes no bones about its malicious intent: "Master prankster Ashton Kutcher punks celebs down to earth . . . and sometimes, he even gets 'em crying. The reality show with a straight razor's edge makes superstars suffer for your viewing pleasure." See MTV.com, http://www.mtv.com/onair/punkd/ (accessed February 2, 2005). Interestingly, Timberlake himself was a target of *Punk'd* in early 2003; the show nearly reduced him to tears by claiming that his house would be auctioned to pay back taxes. Jessica Callan, Eva Simpson, and Niki Waldegrave, "3 a.m.: Just a Bad Joke," *Mirror* (London), March 19, 2003 (accessed December 3, 2005, in online library Highbeam.com).

80. Richard Huff and Bill Hutchinson, "Janet's Act Axed from Grammys," *New York Daily News*, February 4, 2004 (accessed March 22, 2005, in online library Highbeam.com).

81. "Timberlake's Family Offended by Breast-Baring Halftime"; "Timberlake: Family Offended by Super Bowl," Associated Press, February 4, 2004.

82. Sadly, Luther Vandross never fully recovered from his 2003 stroke and died on July 1, 2005, at the age of fifty-four.

83. Steve Gorman, "Janet Jackson to Be a Grammy No-Show," Reuters, February 4, 2004, http://entertainment.myway.com/article/id/138644|entertainment|02-04-2004::19:32|reuters.html (accessed March 16, 2005).

84. "Janet Jackson Issues Video Apology for Super Bowl Incident," MTV.com, February 4, 2004, http://www.mtv.com/news/articles/1484801/20040204/story.jhtml (accessed January 29, 2005).

85. "Report: Jackson Asked Not to Present at Grammys," WSBTV.com, February 4, 2004, http://www.wsbtv.com/entertainment/2819234/detail.html (accessed January 31, 2005).

86. MacKenzie, "Grammys Give Janet the Boot."

87. Kaye Grogan, "Rock Stars Still Testing Indecency Buttons," OpinionEditorials.com, March 9, 2004, http://www.opinioneditorials.com/freedomwriters/grogan_20040309.html (accessed March 15, 2004).

88. The Broadcast Indecency Act of 2004, H.R. 3717, *Hearings before the Subcommittee on Telecommunications and Internet of the Committee on Energy and Commerce, House of Representatives*, 108th Cong., 2d sess., February 11 and 26, 2004.

89. CBS, press release, "CBS Statement Regarding Janet Jackson and Justin Timberlake's Participation in 'The 46th Annual Grammy Awards,'" February 8, 2004.

90. Reuters, "Justin Timberlake Accepts Grammy with an Apology," Boston.com, February 8, 2004, http://www.boston.com/ae/music/articles/2004/02/09/justin_timberlake_accepts_grammy_with_an_apology/ (accessed March 16, 2005).

CHAPTER TWO: FROM HENRY VIII TO THE FCC: TRACING THE ORIGINS OF AMERICAN EFFORTS TO LEGISLATE DECENCY

1. John Winthrop, *A Modell of Christian Charity*, 1630. The text of Winthrop's sermon is available on a number of Web sites, including the Hanover Historical Texts Project, http://history.hanover.edu/texts/winthmod.html (accessed December 3, 2005).

2. Throughout the remainder of her life, Catherine staunchly refused to acknowledge the archbishop's declaration.

3. Mary Tudor, daughter of Henry VIII and Catherine of Aragon, is often confused with Mary Stuart, better known as "Mary, Queen of Scots." Margaret, sister of Henry VIII, married James IV of Scotland. Margaret was the mother of James V and grandmother of Mary Stuart. Although Mary, Queen of Scots was sixteen years older than Henry VIII's daughter, Elizabeth I, they were political contemporaries and rivals for the throne of England. Mary Stuart was executed in 1587 after eighteen years imprisonment in England.

4. Edwin S. Gaustad and Leigh E. Schmidt, *The Religious History of America*, rev. ed. (San Francisco: HarperSanFrancisco, 2002), p. 49.

5. Ibid., pp. 50–51.

6. Winthrop, *A Modell of Christian Charity*.

7. A. James Reichley, *Religion in American Public Life* (Washington, DC: Brookings Institution, 1985), p. 56.

8. Ibid., pp. 56–57.

9. It should be noted, however, that in the fall of 1692, Increase Mather spoke out against the use of spectral evidence in witch trials. Such evidence was soon banned by Massachusetts governor William Phipps, which had the practical effect of ending the trials. In addition to the people who were executed, a number of others accused of witchcraft died during imprisonment.

10. Reichley, *Religion in American Public Life*, pp. 59–61.

11. *State of Oregon v. Maynard*, 168 Oreg. App. 118, 5 P.3d 1142 (Oreg. Ct. App. 2000). See also Helen Lefkowitz Horowitz, *Rereading Sex* (New York: Vintage Books, 2002), p. 41; Walter Kendrick, *The Secret Museum* (New York: Viking, 1987), p. 127; and *Paris Adult Theatre I v. Slaton*, 413 US 49 (1973) (Brennan, dissenting).

12. Reichley, *Religion in American Public Life*, p. 69.

13. Ibid., p. 74.

14. Gaustad and Schmidt, *The Religious History of America*, pp. 123–32.

15. Barbara M. Cross, ed., *The Autobiography of Lyman Beecher*, vol. 1 (Cambridge, MA: Belknap, 1961), pp. 252–53.

16. Gaustad and Schmidt, *The Religious History of America*, pp. 140–42.

17. Horowitz, *Rereading Sex*, p. 49.

18. "Who Was George Williams?" Young Men's Christian Association, n.d., http://www.ymca.net/about/cont/georgew.htm (accessed December 20, 2004).

19. *Uncle Jonathan*, "Walks In and Around London," 1895, 3d ed., reproduced from the Web site for the John Johnson Collection Exhibition, Bodleian Library, University of Oxford, 2001, http://www.victorianlondon.org/buildings/crystalpalace.htm (accessed December 4, 2005).

20. When the first international conference for the YMCA was held in 1854 in Paris, there were a reported 397 Ys in 7 different nations, with more than 30,000 members. "A Brief History of the YMCA Movement," Young Men's Christian Association, n.d., http://www.ymca.net/about/cont/history.htm (accessed March 17, 2004).

21. Horowitz, *Rereading Sex*, pp. 301–302.

22. Ibid., p. 300. Jesup had been named for one of the company's owners, Morris Ketchum, who was a friend of his father.

23. Ibid., pp. 308–309.

24. Thomas P. Lowry, MD, *The Story the Soldiers Wouldn't Tell: Sex in the Civil War* (Mechanicsburg, PA: Stackpole, 1994), p. 55.

25. Ibid., p. 54.

26. Frederick S. Lane, *Obscene Profits* (New York: Routledge, 2000), p. 44.

27. Act of March 3, 1865, chap. 89, 89 Stat. 507.

28. Horowitz, *Rereading Sex*, pp. 359–64.

29. J. C. Furnas, *The Life and Times of the Late Demon Rum* (New York: Putnam, 1965), p. 167.

30. Reichley, *Religion in American Public Life*, p. 216.

31. See Charles Gallaudet Trumbull, *Anthony Comstock, Fighter* (New York: Fleming H. Revell, 1913).

32. Horowitz, *Rereading Sex*, pp. 317–18.

33. Ibid., pp. 367–68.

34. Robert Bremer, ed., introduction to Anthony Comstock, *Traps for the Young*, repr. (Cambridge, MA: Belknap Press of Harvard University, 1967), p. x.

35. "A Raid Upon Dealers in Obscene Merchandise," *New York Times*, March 16, 1872, p. 3.

36. There is some disagreement about the cause of Haynes's death. Horowitz simply states that he died. Horowitz, *Rereading Sex*, p. 371. However, Comstock biographers Heywood Broun and Margaret Leech say that he committed suicide. Heywood Broun and Margaret Leech, *Anthony Comstock: Roundsman of the Lord* (New York: Albert and Charles Boni, 1927), p. 84.

37. Trumbull, *Anthony Comstock, Fighter*, pp. 64–65.

38. Ibid., pp. 65–66.

39. Bremer, ed., introduction to Comstock, *Traps for the Young*, p. xi.

40. Broun and Leech, *Anthony Comstock*, pp. 128–29; Trumbull, *Anthony Comstock, Fighter*, p. 83.

41. Justice Strong's willingness to aid in the drafting of legislation that might one day come before him on the Court was almost certainly improper but not overly surprising. Justice Strong was a deeply religious man and an active participant in the National Reform Association, the principal aim of which was to amend the US Constitution "to indicate that this is a Christian nation." Coincidentally, at the same time that Comstock was lobbying for his antiobscenity legislation, the National Reform Association successfully sponsored The Coinage Act, giving the Secretary of the Treasury the authority to put the phrase "In God We Trust" on US coins.

42. Colfax was one of the central figures in the Crédit Mobilier scandal, and his association with the construction company cost him renomination as vice president for a second term with Ulysses S. Grant.

43. Trumbull, *Anthony Comstock, Fighter*, pp. 85–86; *Senate Journal*, 42d Cong., 3d sess., February 11, 1873, 319; S. 1572, 42d Cong. (1872).

44. Ibid.

45. Anthony Comstock published a book by that title in 1883. See Comstock, *Traps for the Young* (New York: Funk & Wagnalls, 1883).

46. Marshall Brain, "How Stuff Works: The Simplest Radio," HowStuffWorks .com, n.d., http://electronics.howstuffworks.com/radio1.htm (accessed April 9, 2005).

47. "W. A. O. A.," *Modern Electronics*, January 1910, p. 471, as reproduced in Thomas H. White, "Pioneering Amateurs (1900–1917)," http://earlyradiohistory.us/ sec012.htm, n.d. (accessed April 10, 2005).

48. H. Gernsback, "Wireless and the Amateur: A Retrospect," in *Modern Electrics*, February 1913, pp. 1143–44, as reproduced in White, "Pioneering Amateurs (1900–1917)," http://earlyradiohistory.us/1913retr.htm, n.d. (accessed April 11, 2005).

49. It's worth pointing out, of course, that it has only been relatively recently that

practical use could be made of the frequencies at the higher end of the spectrum, which require correspondingly higher levels of power to generate. In the earliest days of radio, at the turn of the twentieth century, the physical limitations of both power sources and transmission equipment restricted operators to the low end of the radio frequency spectrum.

50. White, "Building the Broadcast Band," United States Early Radio History, February 12, 2004, http://earlyradiohistory.us/buildbcb.htm (accessed April 9, 2005).

51. "Regulation of Wireless," in *Electrical World*, March 3, 1906, pp. 437–38, as reproduced in White, United States Early Radio History, http://earlyradiohistory.us/1906reg.htm (accessed on March 15, 2005).

52. The requirement that ships carry wireless was a direct response to the heroic role wireless operator Jack Binns played during the collision of the White Star liner *Republic* and the SS *Florida* off Nantucket the year before. With the *Republic* slowly sinking beneath him, Binns stayed at his post for hours, helping to guide rescue ships to the collision site. It was arguably the first tragedy covered by the media in "real time" and it made Binns a national hero.

53. White, "Building the Broadcast Band."

54. "President Moves to Stop Mob Rule of Wireless," *New York Herald*, April 17, 1912, as reproduced in White, United States Early Radio History, http://earlyradiohistory.us/1912mob.htm (accessed April 11, 2005).

55. Major Butt was in fact one of the more than fifteen hundred passengers and crew who perished in the *Titanic* disaster.

56. Ibid.

57. White, "Building the Broadcast Band."

58. *Congressional Record*, 1927, 3027.

59. "Politicians Seeking Credit for Radio Legislation," *New York Times*, January 10, 1926.

60. "Coolidge Opposes More Commissions," *New York Times*, April 28, 1926.

61. Radio Act of 1927, Public Law 623, sect. 12, 69th Cong., 1st sess., February 23, 1927.

62. "President Signs the Radio Control Bill; Will Name Board of Five to Regulate Air," *New York Times*, February 24, 1927.

63. "The Freedom of the Air," *New York Times*, April 29, 1927.

CHAPTER THREE: RELIGIOUS BOYCOTTS AND CORPORATE SELF-CENSORSHIP: PRIVATE EFFORTS TO CLEANSE AMERICAN CULTURE

1. James M. Skinner, *The Cross and the Cinema: The Legion of Decency and the National Catholic Office for Motion Pictures, 1933–1970* (Westport, CT: Praeger, 1993), p. 37. There are multiple versions of the pledge; this is the most comprehensive listing of objections and promises.

2. "Fair rent" was a rent that took into account good times and bad; "fixity of

tenure" meant that a tenant could not be evicted from his land so long as he paid the rent; and "free sale" referred to the obligation of the landlord to compensate the tenant for any improvements the tenant made on the property if he was evicted or if the land was sold.

3. Among the complaints raised by the colonists in the Declaration of Independence was the fact that King George III had assented to various "Acts of pretended Legislation," including "cutting off our Trade with all parts of the world."

4. In 1975 Xerox ran a highly successful ad campaign about a monk who secretly used Xerox equipment to make five hundred copies of an illuminated manuscript—the campaign's slogan, read as the clever Brother Dominick piously raised his eyes heavenward, was "It's a Miracle." (In one of the funnier bits of cross-cultural irony, the Christian monk was played by Jewish comedian Jack Eagle, already famous for his years of stand-up in the Borscht Belt. Masha Leon, *Forward*, July 14, 1995.)

5. The city is located in the middle of the nation's largest appellation, Rheinhessen, and each year, half a million sipping, swirling, slurping, and spitting tourists visit Mainz to attend the annual late-August Mainz Wine Market, held outdoors in the city's Rosengarten and Stadtpark.

6. Marshall McLuhan, *The Gutenberg Galaxy: The Making of Typographic Man* (Toronto: University of Toronto Press, 1962), p. 207.

7. Philip Meggs, *A History of Graphic Design*, 2d ed. (New York: Van Nostrand Reinhold, 1991), p. 73.

8. "The Index Indexed," *Time*, April 29, 1966, p. 74.

9. *United States v. Roth*, 354 US 476 (1957).

10. "Wilde's Books Taken from Libraries," *New York Times*, April 10, 1895.

11. "Oscar Wilde's Books Withdrawn," *Washington Post*, April 10, 1895.

12. Eugene P. Metour, "More 'American Comstockery,'" *New York Times*, February 9, 1906.

13. E. P. C., "Quite So!" *New York Times*, February 17, 1906.

14. Upton Sinclair, "The Boycott on 'The Jungle,'" *New York Times*, May 18, 1906.

15. "Asks Decent Book Pledge," *New York Times*, October 2, 1939, p. 12.

16. "'Censorship' Laid to Church Group," *New York Times*, May 6, 1957, p. 22.

17. "Court Order Curbs Detroit Book Ban," *New York Times*, May 15, 1957, p. 70.

18. "War on Smut Begun by a Citizen's Group," *New York Times*, February 26, 1959, p. 33.

19. "Crime Laid to Reading Fare," *New York Times*, September 28, 1959, p. 34.

20. "Obscene Material Becoming Bolder, Opponent Contends," *New York Times*, October 23, 1965, p. 33.

21. For the curious, the novel (long since in the public domain) is available in full at a number of Web sites. A paperback version is also available from Random House.

22. H. Hyde Montgomery, *A History of Pornography* (New York: Farrar, Straus and Giroux, 1964), p. 99.

23. *Memoirs v. Massachusetts*, 383 US 413, 418 (1967), *citing Roth v. United States*, 354 US 476 (1957).

24. *Massachusetts v. Memoirs*, 349 Mass. 69, 73, 206 N.E.2d 403, 406 (1965).

25. *Memoirs v. Massachusetts*, 383 US 413, 419 (1966).

26. *Redrup v. State of New York*, 386 US 767 (1967).

27. "The Index Indexed."

28. Skinner, *The Cross and the Cinema*, p. 1.

29. The film was banned by the New York City police, and a local judge ruled that filmmaker John B. Doris's purpose was "to degrade marriage and its sacred confidences." *Orange Blossoms* was destroyed and lives on only in the description of its content by the court. Edward de Grazia and Roger K. Newman, *Banned Films: Movies, Censors, and the First Amendment* (New York: R. K. Bowker, 1982), pp. 9–10.

30. Tim Dirks, "1900s," The Greatest Films, n.d., http://www.filmsite.org/milestones1900s.html (accessed November 12, 2005).

31. Skinner, *The Cross and the Cinema*, p. 2.

32. "Picture Shows All Put Out of Business," *New York Times*, December 25, 1908.

33. Frank Walsh, *Sin and Censorship: The Catholic Church and the Motion Picture Industry* (New Haven: Yale University Press, 1996), p. 7.

34. *Mutual Film Corp. v. Ohio Indus'l Comm.*, 236 US 230, 244-45 (1915).

35. "Mayor Makes War on Sunday Vaudeville," *New York Times*, December 29, 1908.

36. "The Nation-wide Wave of Moving Pictures," *New York Times*, January 3, 1909.

37. That puts Chaplain just below the ranks of today's highest-paid actors—including Tom Cruise, George Clooney, Nicholas Cage, and Leonardo DiCaprio—each of whom can command $20 million per picture. (The financial calculation is courtesy of the Federal Reserve Bank of Minneapolis, http://minneapolisfed.org/research/data/us/calc/). Chaplin also unwittingly helped usher in the era of the public's fascination with the private lives of movie stars. He was married four times (each time to significantly younger women), divorced contentiously three times, and fathered ten children. He was, as old-time reporters like to say, "good copy."

38. "Movie Men Form a Board of Trade," *New York Times*, September 10, 1915.

39. "Brady Heads Picture Body," *New York Times*, August 17, 1916.

40. "Film Censorship Hearings Begun," *New York Times*, January 14, 1916.

41. "Federal Movie Bill Ready," *New York Times*, May 8, 1916.

42. Richard S. Randall, *Censorship of the Movies: The Social and Political Control of a Mass Medium* (Madison: University of Wisconsin Press, 1968), p. 15; Skinner, *The Cross and the Cinema*, p. 5.

43. "Arbuckle Acquitted in One-Minute Verdict; One of His Films to Be Released Immediately," *New York Times*, April 13, 1922, p. 1.

44. Randall, *Censorship of the Movies*, p. 15.

45. Walsh, *Sin and Censorship*, pp. 26–28.

46. De Grazia and Newman, *Banned Films*, p. 28.

47. "Puritanic Village Planned by Movies," *New York Times*, February 1, 1922.

48. "Committee Shelves Movie Censorship," *New York Times*, May 5, 1926.

49. "Presbyterians Ask for 'Clean Movies,'" *New York Times*, May 24, 1922.

50. Gregory D. Black, *The Catholic Crusade against the Movies, 1940–1975* (Cambridge: Cambridge University Press), p. 9. With the US population estimated at 110,049,000 by the US Census Bureau, that means that 1 out of every 3 people was going to the movies each week.

51. Ibid., pp. 9–10.

52. De Grazia and Newman, *Banned Films*, p. 31.

53. Ibid., p. 33.

54. Dirks, "Sexual or Erotic Films," Filmsite.org, n.d., http://www.filmsite.org/sexualfilms.html (accessed August 10, 2005).

55. Prior to 1948, the studios owned extensive chains of movie theaters. On May 3, 1948, the US Supreme Court ruled in *U.S. v. Paramount Pictures, Inc.*, 334 US 131 (1948) that the movie producers were in violation of antitrust laws, in part because of their vertical ownership of movie production, distribution, and theaters.

56. De Grazia and Newman, *Banned Films*, p. 35.

57. Ibid., p. 33.

58. Ibid., p. 41–42. According to Gregory Black, the language used by Cicognani in his speech was drafted for him by Martin Quigley. See Black, *The Catholic Crusade against the Movies*, p. 21.

59. De Grazia and Newman, *Banned Films*, pp. 42–43.

60. Walsh, *Sin and Censorship*, p. 102.

61. Ibid., pp. 116–17.

62. For the first hundred years or so of European settlement in America, the founding religion in each colony (especially the Massachusetts Bay Colony) exercised tight control over virtually every form of entertainment.

63. See Black, *The Catholic Crusade against the Movies*, p. 28.

64. "Butler Broadcast on Exploit Cut Off," *New York Times*, April 26, 1931.

65. "Celler Condemns Radio Censorship," *New York Times*, March 24, 1927.

66. "Representative Says Stations Should Be More Liberal in Censoring Talks," *New York Times*, May 29, 1927.

67. "Amos 'n' Andy Do Not Doubt 100,000 Listeners Are Right," *New York Times*, November 24, 1929.

68. "Song Censorship for Radio Begun," *New York Times*, August 15, 1934.

69. "Radio Heads Laud Song Censorship," *New York Times*, August 16, 1934.

70. "Radio 'Love' Held Vital to Profits," *New York Times*, March 16, 1940. Soap companies sponsored the "love dramas" because they were broadcast at a time during the day when housewives were the predominant audience; as a result, the dramas over time became known "soap operas."

71. In addition to his myriad entertainment accomplishments, Cantor was a founder of the March of Dimes and the first president of the Screen Actors Guild.

72. "Cantor Censored in Televised Act," *New York Times*, May 27, 1944.

73. Sidney Lohman, "News of TV and Radio," *New York Times*, June 27, 1954.

74. "Beatles Manager Here to Quell Storm over Remark on Jesus," *New York Times*, August 6, 1966.

75. "Beatles Manager Here to Quell Storm over Remark on Jesus." Not every religious leader disagreed with Lennon: the Reverend Richard Pritchard, head of the Westminster Presbyterian Church in Madison, Wisconsin, said that "[t]here is much validity in what Lennon said. To many people today, the golf course is also more popular than Jesus Christ."

CHAPTER FOUR: "A SOLDIER IN GOD'S ARMY": ANITA BRYANT, JERRY FALWELL, AND THE RISE OF EVANGELICAL POLITICS

1. Despite the fact that it aired just once, *Daisy Girl* is widely considered to be the most famous political ad of all time. The advertisement is available for viewing on the Public Broadcasting Service Web site. "The :30 Second Candidate," http://www.pbs.org/30secondcandidate/timeline/years/1964b.html.

2. During the campaign, a group of psychiatrists tried to turn the mocking slogan into an actual diagnosis that Goldwater was deranged. Goldwater sued for libel and won. Michael J. Gerson and Mike Tharp, "Mr. Right," *U.S. News & World Report*, June 8, 1998.

3. Richard Lucayo, "Where's the Party?" *Time*, August 19, 1996.

4. William A. Rusher, "So Long, Barry," *National Review*, December 31, 1986.

5. Bart Barnes, "Barry Goldwater, GOP Hero, Dies," *Washington Post*, May 30, 1988.

6. Ronald Reagan, "Rendezvous with Destiny," address on behalf of Senator Barry Goldwater, Republican candidate for President, October 27, 1964, http://www.reaganfoundation.org/reagan/speeches/rendezvous.asp (accessed August 12, 2005).

7. Milton Bracker, "Yale Survey Finds No Red Influence or Threats to Academic Freedom," *New York Times*, February 18, 1952.

8. William F. Buckley and L. Brent Bozell, *McCarthy and His Enemies: The Record and Its Meaning* (New Rochelle, NY: Arlington House, 1954), p. 335.

9. "Buckley Starting Weekly Review," *New York Times*, October 14, 1955.

10. Nurith C. Aizenman, "The Man Behind the Curtain," *Washington Monthly*, July 1, 1997.

11. David Grann, "Robespierre of the Right: What I Ate at the Revolution," *New Republic*, October 27, 1997.

12. Rich Lowry, "How the Right Rose," *National Review*, December 11, 1995.

13. Paul M. Weyrich, "Trent Lott: Freed from the Constraints of Leadership," EnterStageRight.com, June 2, 2003, http://www.enterstageright.com/archive/articles/0603/0603lott.htm (accessed August 12, 2005).

14. Grann, "Robespierre of the Right."

15. Steven Rattner, "A Think Tank for Conservatives," *New York Times*, March 23, 1975.

16. Aizenman, "The Man Behind the Curtain."

17. Weyrich, "The Most Important Legacy of Joe Coors," EnterStageRight.com,

March 24, 2003, http://www.enterstageright.com/archive/articles/0303/0303coors.htm (accessed August 12, 2005).

18. Lowry, "How the Right Rose."

19. David Brock, *Blinded by the Right* (New York: Three Rivers, 2003), pp. 79–80.

20. Matthew Miller and Peter Newcomb, "The 400 Richest Americans," *Forbes*, September 22, 2005, http://www.forbes.com/400richest/ (accessed October 27, 2005). Although Scaife's fortune remained unchanged from the year before, his ranking dipped nearly 50 places, from a tie for 234 to a tie for 283. David Armstrong and Peter Newcomb, "The 400 Richest Americans," *Forbes*, September 24, 2004, http://www.forbes.com/2004/09/22/rl04land.html (accessed September 15, 2005).

21. Robert G. Kaiser and Ira Chinoy, "Scaife: Funding Father of the Right," *Washington Post*, May 2, 1999.

22. Aizenman, "The Man Behind the Curtain."

23. "A.D.A. Sees 'Pernicious' Threat from U.S. Rightist Organizations," *New York Times*, May 22, 1978.

24. John Wicklein, "Evangelist Asks Push on U.S. Reds," *New York Times*, August 6, 1961.

25. "Right-Wing Group Loses Tax Status," *New York Times*, November 17, 1964, p. 22.

26. Donald Janson, "A Rightist Plans Test of Tax Laws," *New York Times*, August 9, 1965, p. 48.

27. Janson, "Christian Crusade, Prospering Despite Tax Exemption Loss, Breaks Ground for College," *New York Times*, August 4, 1969.

28. "Justices Bar Hargis Tax Plea; Religious Groups Fear Impact," *New York Times*, October 14, 1973.

29. John Lubell, "In Affluent, Conservative Tulsa, Okla., Revivalist Religion Is Big Business," *New York Times*, November 22, 1970.

30. Jimmy Carter, "The Playboy Interview," *Playboy*, November 1976.

31. 347 US 483 (1954).

32. Lawrence J. McAndrews, "The Politics of Principle: Richard Nixon and School Desegregation," *Journal of Negro History*, June 22, 1968.

33. Eileen Shanahan, "Schools in South May Avoid Taxes," *New York Times*, August 3, 1967.

34. John Herbers, "South's New White Schools May Face a U.S. Tax Move," *New York Times*, January 7, 1970.

35. Fred P. Graham, "Federal Judges Rule Out Benefit for Segregated Private 'Academies,'" *New York Times*, January 14, 1970.

36. Eileen Shanahan, "Church Schools Get Racial Order," *New York Times*, May 23, 1975.

37. "Senate Votes to Block I.R.S. on School Bias Penalties," *New York Times*, September 7, 1979.

38. Stuart Taylor Jr., "Tax Exemption Ruling: An Old Question Still Lingers," *New York Times*, June 14, 1983.

39. Dave Anderson, "America's Party," *Cigar Aficianado Online*, January/February

2002, http://www.cigarinsider.com/Cigar/CA_Archives/CA_Show_Article/0,2322 ,1051,00.html (accessed June 24, 2005).

40. Martin King, "Another New Day Dawns for Oklahoma's Anita Bryant," BaptistMessenger.com, August 16, 2001, http://www.baptistmessenger.com/Issue/ 010816/7.html (accessed May 23, 2005).

41. Johnson's burial site shared a name with the Stonewall Inn, a bar in New York City where four years earlier, gays had rebelled at perceived police harassment. The battle at the Stonewall Inn is widely considered to mark the start of gay rights activism, which helped spur the move for antidiscrimination ordinances across the country, including Miami-Dade County.

42. Thomas C. Tobin, "Bankruptcy, Ill Will Plague Bryant," *St. Petersburg Times*, April 28, 2002.

43. "Bias against Homosexuals Is Outlawed in Miami," *New York Times*, January 19, 1977.

44. B. Drummond Ayres Jr., "Miami Debate over Rights of Homosexuals Directs Wide Attention to a National Issue," *New York Times*, May 10, 1977.

45. "Bias against Homosexuals Is Outlawed in Miami."

46. Ayres, "Miami Debate over Rights of Homosexuals Directs Wide Attention to a National Issue."

47. Ibid.

48. B. Drummond Ayres Jr., "Miami Acts Tuesday on Homosexual Law," *New York Times*, June 5, 1977, p. 22.

49. B. Drummond Ayres Jr., "Miami Votes 2–1 to Repeal Law Barring Bias against Homosexuals," *New York Times*, June 8, 1977, p. 1.

50. "Notes on People: Miss Bryant Gets Pie in Face," *New York Times*, October 15, 1977.

51. George Vecsey, "Secular Bookings Off, Anita Bryant Sings at Revivals," *New York Times*, February 21, 1978.

52. Ed Dobson and Cal Thomas, *Blinded by Might* (Grand Rapids, MI: Zondervan Publishing House, 1999), p. 14.

53. Jerry Falwell, *Listen America!* (New York: Bantam-Doubleday, 1981), p. 25.

54. Ruth Murray Brown, *For a "Christian America": A History of the Religious Right* (Amherst, NY: Prometheus Books, 2002), p. 156.

55. George Vecsey, "Militant Television Preachers Try to Weld Fundamentalist Christians' Political Power," *New York Times*, January 21, 1980; Wallace Turner, "Group of Evangelical Protestants Takes Over the G.O.P. in Alaska," *New York Times*, June 9, 1980.

56. Vecsey, "Militant Television Preachers Try to Weld Fundamentalist Christians' Political Power."

57. Turner, "Group of Evangelical Protestants Takes Over the G.O.P. in Alaska."

58. John Herbers, "Ultraconservative Evangelicals a Surging New Force in Politics," *New York Times*, August 17, 1980.

59. Jerry Falwell, "Recruitment Begins for First Million," Moral Majority Coalition, n.d., http://www.faithandvalues.us/article_recruitment.htm (accessed July 15, 2005).

60. Jack Gould, "Pastore's Plan to Preview Shows Alarms Network," *New York Times*, March 17, 1969.

61. Jack Gould, "Perils of Pastore," *New York Times*, March 23, 1969, p. D23.

62. Les Brown, "TV Sex and Violence: New Move Highlights Problems," *New York Times*, November 28, 1974.

63. "F.C.C. Asks House to Aid in Rulings," *New York Times*, February 21, 1975.

64. Leslie Jackson Turner, "But the Republic Stood: Program Producers' Perceived Pivotal Moments in Network Television Broadcast Standards of the 1970s," *Journal of Broadcasting & Electronic Media*, January 1, 2000, quoting Brett White, personal communication, January 31, 1996.

65. Turner, "But the Republic Stood."

66. Richard Levine, "Counting Heads: TV Demographics," *Alicia Patterson Foundation Reporter* 1, no. 3 (1977).

67. Ibid.

68. Walt Belcher, "Say Good Evening, Charlie, and See How the Angels Earned Their Wings," *Tampa Tribune*, March 8, 2004.

69. Beth Harris, "The True Story of TV's 'Charlie's Angels,'" *Cincinnati Post*, March 8, 2004.

70. "The Man with the Golden Gut," *Time*, September 5, 1977.

71. Michael Schneider, "That '70s Showcase Leaves Lasting Legacy," *Variety*, April 28, 2003.

72. Turner, "But the Republic Stood."

73. Joseph Lelyveld, "Off Color," *New York Times*, November 6, 1977.

CHAPTER FIVE: LOSING THE DECENCY WARS, ONE LIVING ROOM AT A TIME: A DECADE OF DEREGULATION, CABLE, PHONES, AND COMPUTERS

1. Kenneth A. Briggs, "Dispute on Religion Raised by Campaign," *New York Times*, November 9, 1980.

2. Joseph F. Sullivan, "Falwell Warns Jersey Liberals at Capitol Rally," *New York Times*, November 1, 1980.

3. David S. Broder, "The Social Agenda Could Spoil the Party," *Washington Post*, November 23, 1980.

4. Albert R. Hunt, "Reagan and 'Depth,'" *Wall Street Journal*, November 3, 1980.

5. Hedrick Smith, "Reagan Loyalists Are Wondering about Their Champion's Loyalty," *New York Times*, November 20, 1980.

6. Smith, "Managers, Not Ideologues," *New York Times*, December 12, 1980.

7. "Prayer Left Unanswered; the Senate Rejects a Constitutional Amendment," *Time*, April 2, 1984.

8. John McLaughlin, "Social-agenda Headaches," *National Review*, August 23, 1985.

9. David Corn, "The Backstabbers," *Nation*, March 7, 1987.

10. Laura Sessions Stepp, "Astrology Reports Disturb Some Evangelical Leaders," *Washington Post*, May 5, 1988. See, e.g., Deuteronomy 4:19 ("And lest thou lift up thine eyes unto heaven, and when thou seest the sun, and the moon, and the stars, even all the host of heaven, shouldest be driven to worship them, and serve them, which the LORD thy God hath divided unto all nations under the whole heaven.")

11. Quoted in William Martin, "How Reagan Wowed Evangelicals," ChristianityToday.com, June 22, 2004, http://www.christianitytoday.com/ct/2004/125/21.0.html (accessed June 13, 2005).

12. During the 1964 campaign, Goldwater was overheard saying, "Let's lob a nuclear bomb into the men's room at the Kremlin." Twenty years later, speaking into what he thought was a dead mike, President Reagan jokingly said, "My fellow Americans, I am pleased to tell you that I have signed legislation to outlaw Russia forever. We begin bombing in five minutes."

13. Bruce Hahn, "Speak Out, Cable TV Customers: You Deserve More Choices," *Roanoke Times*, July 12, 2005, http://www.roanoke.com/editorials/commentary%5C27251.html (accessed July 14, 2005).

14. "U.S. Households with Cable Television, 1977–2000," *World Almanac and Book of Facts 2002*, Primedia Reference, Inc., 2002 (accessed on July 14, 2005, in online library Highbeam.com).

15. Richard Setlowe, "Many Strands Grew Together to Build Cable," *Variety*, November 3, 1997.

16. "Poor Reception; Warner Curtails QUBE," *Time*, January 30, 1984 (accessed on July 13, 2005, in the online library Highbeam.com).

17. Andrew L. Yarrow, "Cable TV Moves to the Music," *New York Times*, July 4, 1982.

18. Setlowe, "Many Strands Grew Together to Build Cable."

19. Glenn Garvin, "MTV Brought More Than Music to Television," *Miami Herald*, August 28, 2004 (accessed on July 13, 2005, in the online library Highbeam.com).

20. Setlowe, "Many Strands Grew Together to Build Cable."

21. Stewart Powell, "What Entertainers Are Doing to Your Kids," *U.S. News & World Report*, October 28, 1985 (accessed on July 14, 2005, in the online library Highbeam.com).

22. Eric Pace, "An Advertising Boom Comes to Cable Television," *New York Times*, March 23, 1982.

23. Ed Levine, "TV Rocks with Music," *New York Times*, May 8, 1983.

24. Peter Kerr, "Music Video's Uncertain Payoff," *New York Times*, July 29, 1984.

25. "The Music Dies for Turner," *Broadcasting*, December 3, 1984.

26. Terence Moran, "Sounds of Sex, Why Daddy Took the T-Bird Away," *New Republic*, August 12, 1985.

27. Jon Pareles, "Debate Spurs Hearings on Rating Rock Lyrics," *New York Times*, September 18, 1985. It is not clear from contemporary news reports who did the analysis of rock lyrics and arrived at the 8 percent figure.

28. Moran, "Sounds of Sex."

29. Stephen Holden, "Recordings Will Carry Advisory about Lyrics," *New York Times*, August 9, 1985.

30. Eric Levin, "Lay off Them Blue Suede Shoes," *People Weekly*, November 4, 1985.

31. Jay Cocks, "Rock Is a Four-Letter Word," *Time*, September 30, 1985.

32. Jon Pareles, "Should Rock Lyrics Be Sanitized?" *New York Times*, October 13, 1985.

33. Holden, "Recordings Will Carry Advisory about Lyrics."

34. Cocks, "Rock Is a Four-Letter Word."

35. Eric D. Nuzum, *Parental Advisory: Music Censorship in America* (New York: Perennial, 2001).

36. Irving Molotsky, "Hearing on Rock Lyrics," *New York Times*, September 20, 1985.

37. Ibid.

38. *Record Labeling: Contents of Music and the Lyrics of Records, Hearing before the Committee on Commerce, Science, and Transportation*, United States Senate, 99th Cong., 1st sess., September 19, 1985, p. 60.

39. Pareles, "Debate Spurs Hearings on Rating Rock Lyrics."

40. Molotsky, "Hearing on Rock Lyrics."

41. "Parents and Pols Take Up a Battle against Lyrics That Hurt," *People Weekly*, April 16, 1990.

42. "Fr. Morton A. Hill, SJ," Morality in Media, n.d., http://www.moralityinmedia .org/index.htm?aboutUs/hillbiog.htm (accessed March 15, 2004).

43. Ibid.

44. 413 US 15 (1973). In *Miller*, the Supreme Court revisited the obscenity standard established in *Roth* and *Memoirs*. The Court ruled that in order for a work to be found obscene: (1) the average person, applying contemporary community standards, must find that the work, taken as a whole, appeals to the prurient interest; (2) the work must depict or describe, in a patently offensive way, "sexual conduct" as that term is specifically defined by applicable state law; and (3) the work, taken as a whole, must lack serious literary, artistic, political, or scientific value. The most significant change by the Court was the elimination of the requirement that the work be "utterly without redeeming social importance."

45. Philip Shenon, "Meese Names Panel to Study How to Control Pornography," *New York Times*, May 21, 1985.

46. Moran, "Sounds of Sex."

47. Francis X. Clines, "A Tale of Two Views of Erotica," *New York Times*, September 15, 1985; Carole S. Vance, "Porn in the U.S.A.," *Nation*, August 2, 1986.

48. "Meese Commission Letter Presses Stores to Drop Adult Mags," *Supermarket News*, April 21, 1986.

49. Matthew L. Wald, "'Adult' Magazines Lose Sales as 8,000 Stores Forbid Them," *New York Times*, June 16, 1986.

50. Shenon, "Playboy and Booksellers Suing Pornography Panel," *New York Times*, May 20, 1986.

51. Shenon, "Sturm und Drang und Pornography," *New York Times*, April 15, 1986.

52. "Chill Factor," *Time*, June 23, 1986.

53. Robert Pear, "Playboy and Justice Dept. Trying to Settle Lawsuit," *New York Times*, November 8, 1986.

54. Robert Pear, "Panel Calls on Citizens to Wage National Assault on Pornography," *New York Times*, July 10, 1986.

55. Edwin McDowell, "Some Say Meese Report Rates an 'X,'" *New York Times*, October 21, 1986.

56. "Excerpts from Final Report of Attorney General's Panel on Pornography," *New York Times*, July 10, 1986.

57. Margie Bonnett Sellinger, "The Shame of America," *People Weekly*, June 30, 1986.

58. Vance, "Porn in the U.S.A."

59. Katherine Bishop, "Justice Dept. Team Leading Broad Effort on Obscenity," *New York Times*, August 22, 1987.

60. Marjorie Hyer, "O'Connor Choice Draws Bouquets and Brickbats," *Washington Post*, July 17, 1981.

61. Bill Peterson, "Reagan Choice for Court Decried by Conservatives but Acclaimed by Liberals," *Washington Post*, July 8, 1981.

62. Stuart Taylor Jr., "A Multifaceted Conservative," *New York Times*, July 2, 1987.

63. Ibid.

64. Lou Cannon and Edward Walsh, "Reagan Nominates Appeals Judge Bork to Supreme Court," *Washington Post*, July 2, 1987.

65. Particularly egregious was the publishing of a list of Bork's personal video rentals, an action so outrageous that it inspired Congress to adopt the Video Privacy Protection Act the following year.

66. Lou Cannon, "Ginsburg Nomination May Trigger New Fight," *Washington Post*, October 30, 1987.

67. Al Kamen and Ruth Marcus, "Drug-Use Admission Created a 'Clamor,' Embarrassed Reagan," *Washington Post*, November 8, 1987.

68. Lou Cannon and Ruth Marcus, "Judge Kennedy Likely Nominee," *Washington Post*, November 9, 1987.

69. Kamen and Marcus, "Drug-Use Admission Created a 'Clamor.'"

70. Al Kamen, "Kennedy: No 'Fixed View' on Abortion," *Washington Post*, December 15, 1987.

71. "Self-Service TV," *Time*, April 22, 1966, p. 81.

72. Lee Smith, "Sony Battles Back," *Fortune*, April 15, 1985.

73. In 1984 the US Supreme Court ruled in favor of Sony. Just two years later, the sale of videocassettes surpassed the domestic box office ticket sales.

74. Tony Schwartz, "The TV Pornography Boom," *New York Times*, September 13, 1981.

75. Robert Lindsey, "Sex Films Find Big Market in Home Video," *New York Times*, April 5, 1979.

76. Richard Zoglin, "VCRs: Coming on Strong," *Time*, December 24, 1984.

77. Schwartz, "The TV Pornography Boom."

78. "The Big Switch: 1980s," *People Weekly*, June 22, 1989.

79. *Sable Communications v. Federal Communications Commission*, 492 US 115, 117–18 (1989).

80. Richard Lacayo, "Reach Out and Touch Someone," *Time*, December 21, 1987.

81. Mark Kernes, "Gloria Leonard: I'm Still Standing," *Adult Video News*, July 1999, http://www.adultvideonews.com/archives/199907/inner/iv0799_2.html (accessed August 13, 2005).

82. Joseph L. Galloway, "Crackdown on Pornography—a No-Win Battle," *U.S. News & World Report*, June 4, 1984.

83. *Sable Communications v. Federal Communications Commission*, 492 US 115, 120 (1989).

84. "Get off the Telephone," *Time*, August 1, 1988.

85. 492 US 115 (1989).

86. 429 US at 126. Three members of the Court—Justice William Brennan, Justice Thurgood Marshall, and Justice John Paul Stevens—said that they would have declared the ban on "obscene" speech between consenting adults unconstitutional as well.

87. See "indecent," Merriam-Webster Online Dictionary, http://www.m-w.com/.

88. There are widespread rumors on the Internet that the movie acronym "W.O.P.R." was a pun on the actual name of NORAD's main computer, BURGR. However, there is nothing approaching a credible source for that connection.

89. Patrick Kampert, "A Low-Key Pioneer Sparked Dawn of Modern Computing," *Chicago Tribune*, February 14, 2003.

90. "The Origin of Computer Bulletin Boards," Freeware Hall of Fame, n.d., http://www.freewarehof.org/ward.html (accessed March 2, 1998).

91. Twenty-one years later, computer users can buy a 57.6 kbs modem (roughly 192 times faster) for less than $50.

92. Jack Rickard, "Home-Grown BB$," *Wired*, 1997.

93. "There's an X-Rated Side to Home Computers, Parents Warned," *Los Angeles Times*, December 25, 1987.

94. Rickard, "Home-Grown BB$."

CHAPTER SIX: THE POST-REAGAN HANGOVER: A FOUR-YEAR REARGUARD ACTION AGAINST CULTURAL INDECENCY

1. "Bush, Koop Chide Religious Right on Rigid Stands," *New York Times*, February 7, 1987, quoting an address by Vice President Bush to the annual gathering of the National Religious Broadcasters.

2. William Bole, "Presidential Elections Showed a Deep Rift between Jews and Evangelical Christians," *Washington Post*, November 11, 1984.

3. Ari L. Goldman, "O'Connor Denies Plan to Excommunicate Anyone," *New York Times*, June 18, 1990.

4. Robert D. McFadden, "Archbishop Calls Ferraro Mistaken on Abortion Rule," *New York Times*, September 10, 1984.

5. Lou Cannon, "A Lot of New Hampshire Fever Going Around These Days," *Washington Post*, January 13, 1980.

6. Adam Clymer, "Optimistic Bush 'Fired Up,' Feels Drive 'Is Moving,'" *New York Times*, November 23, 1979.

7. T. R. Reid, "Reagan Is Favored by Anti-Abortionists," *Washington Post*, April 12, 1980.

8. Clymer, "Optimistic Bush 'Fired Up.'"

9. Dudley Clendinen, "'Christian New Right's' Rush to Power," *New York Times*, August 18, 1980.

10. Hedrick Smith, "Reagan Wins Nomination and Chooses Bush," *New York Times*, July 17, 1980.

11. Martin Tolchin, "Conservatives First Recoil, Then Line Up behind Bush," *New York Times*, July 18, 1980.

12. "Groups of Religious Conservatives Won't Control Reagan, Bush Says," *New York Times*, November 11, 1980.

13. Thomas B. Edsall, "Onward, GOP Christians, Marching to '88," *Washington Post*, June 30, 1985.

14. Followers of this charismatic branch of Protestant Christianity believe that an individual's commitment to Jesus Christ is confirmed by baptism in the Holy Spirit, typically accomplished by a "laying on of hands by believers who already have been Spirit-filled." Richard N. Ostling, "Power, Glory—and Politics; Right-Wing Preachers Dominate the Dial," *Time*, February 17, 1986.

15. Thomas B. Edsall, "TV Preacher Eyes GOP Nomination," *Washington Post*, August 19, 1985.

16. Ibid.

17. David Shribman, "Michigan Results Expose Weakness of Robertson and Other Republican Presidential Contenders," *Wall Street Journal*, August 7, 1986.

18. Fellow Nixon scribe William Safire once said that no story could be written about Buchanan without using the word "combative," which offers some insight into how Buchanan was viewed by the media. William Safire, "Buchanan's Win Wish," *New York Times*, January 19, 1987.

19. Patrick J. Buchanan, "No One Gave the Order to Abandon Reagan's Ship," *Washington Post*, December 8, 1986.

20. Wayne King, "Choice of Quayle Met by Sighs of Relief on the Party's Right," *New York Times*, August 17, 1988.

21. Safire, "Buchanan's Win Wish."

22. Dorothy Gast, "Falwell Says His Clout Undiminished," *Washington Post*, December 20, 1985.

23. Thomas B. Edsall, "'Moral Majority' Name Changed to Boost Image," *Washington Post*, January 4, 1986.

24. Ibid.

25. George Esper, "Revenue Shortfalls Force TV Ministers to Fine-Tune," *Washington Post*, July 12, 1986.

26. Ironically, Swaggart himself was defrocked by the Assemblies of God denomination after being caught hiring hookers in New Orleans in 1988.

27. Joyce Wadler, "Breaking Faith, Two TV Idols Fall," *People Weekly*, May 18, 1987.

28. Laura Stepp, "Falwell Quitting as Moral Majority Chief," *Washington Post*, November 4, 1987.

29. The sentence was overturned on appeal by the US Court of Appeals for the Fourth Circuit; upon remand to the District Court, Bakker was sentenced to eight years in prison and was released in 1993 after serving five years (with time off for good behavior).

30. Rich Lowry, "How the Right Rose," *National Review*, December 11, 1995.

31. Reed originally made the statement during an interview published by the *Norfolk Virginian Pilot* on November 9, 1991. The remark has been widely cited online; see, e.g., Sidney Blumenthal, "Fall of the Rovean Empire?" Salon.com, October 6, 2005, http://www.salon.com/opinion/blumenthal/2005/10/06/rovean_empire/index.html?sid =1398400 (accessed October 8, 2005).

32. Leslie Kaufman, "Life Beyond God," *New York Times Magazine*, October 16, 1994, p. 50.

33. "American Family Association," Southern Poverty Law Center, n.d., http:// www.splcenter.org/intel/intelreport/article.jsp?pid=869 (accessed May 25, 2005).

34. Tom Shales, "The Rebellion of the 'Fed Ups,'" *Washington Post*, May 17, 1978.

35. Joel Swerdlow, "The Great American Crusade in Televisionland: Moral Majority's Offensive against 'Offensive' TV," June 7, 1981, *Washington Post*, p. K1.

36. Ibid.

37. Ibid.

38. Tom Shales, "Television Boycott Dropped," *Washington Post*, June 30, 1981.

39. John Carmody, "The TV Column," *Washington Post*, January 29, 1982.

40. John Carmody, "The TV Column," *Washington Post*, March 5, 1982.

41. Philip Shenon, "The Boycott against RCA-NBC," *New York Times*, November 21, 1982.

42. Paula Span, "The Mother Who Took on Trash TV," *New York Times*, October 10, 1989.

43. "A Mother Is Heard as Sponsors Abandon a TV Hit," *New York Times*, March 2, 1989.

44. Span, "The Mother Who Took on Trash TV."

45. "Too Bawdy at the Bundys," *Time*, March 13, 1989.

46. Bill Carter, "TV Sponsors Heed Viewers Who Find Shows Too Racy," *New York Times*, April 23, 1989.

47. "A Shock to 'Shock' TV," *Washington Post*, May 8, 1989.

48. Span, "The Mother Who Took on Trash TV."

49. Dusty Saunders, "Fox to End Raunch-athon with Bundys," *Rocky Mountain News*, April 23, 1997.

50. In a bit of news that should warm the hearts of American cultural imperialists everywhere, the original scripts for *Married* are being used now by the Caracal Network in Colombia to produce a South American version of the show, called *Casados . . . con Hijos*. The show's director, Andres Marroquin, summarized the show's potential appeal for Colombians: "This is what happens after 17 years of marriage," he said. "They have this aggressive, acidic way of treating one another: I can't live without you or with you. They treat each other badly, but it's something that people can understand here." Steven Dudley, "America's Dysfunctional Bundys Live On in Colombian TV Show," Knight Ridder/Tribune News Service, October 9, 2004.

51. A. J. Jacobs, "Head of the Crass: How 'Married . . . with Children' broke ground for TV's White-Trash Heap," *Entertainment Weekly*, November 25, 1994.

52. William H. Honan, "Congressional Anger Threatens Arts Endowment Budget," *New York Times*, June 20, 1989.

53. *Congressional Record*, May 18, 1989, p. S5594.

54. Elizabeth Kastor, "Funding Art That Offends," *New York Times*, June 7, 1989.

55. Ibid.

56. Elizabeth Kastor, "Gays, Artists to Protest at Corcoran," *New York Times*, June 16, 1989.

57. Elizabeth Kastor, "Corcoran Cancels Photo Exhibit," *New York Times*, June 13, 1989.

58. Elizabeth Kastor, "Corcoran Decision Provokes Outcry," *New York Times*, June 14, 1989.

59. Ibid.

60. Roxanne Roberts, "900 Protest Corcoran Cancellation," *New York Times*, July 1, 1989.

61. Elizabeth Kastor, "WPA Show Attracts Thousands," *New York Times*, July 26, 1989.

62. Elizabeth Kastor, "House Trims NEA Budget as Reprimand," *New York Times*, July 13, 1989.

63. Elizabeth Kastor, "NEA Grant Ban Proposed," *Washington Post*, July 25, 1989.

64. The proposal was similar to the one that Helms attached to an education funding bill in 1988 to block "obscene or indecent communication" by telephone. The "indecent" portion of the so-called Helms Amendment was ultimately overturned as unconstitutional by the US Supreme Court in *Sable Communications, Inc., v. FCC*, 492 US 115 (1989).

65. Anthony Lewis, "Summer of the Booboisie," *New York Times*, August 10, 1989.

66. William H. Honan, "House Shuns Bill on 'Obscene' Art," *New York Times*, September 14, 1989.

67. Kara Swisher, "Helm's 'Indecent' Sampler," *Washington Post*, August 8, 1989.

68. Isabel Wilkerson, "Trouble Right Here in Cincinnati: Furor Over Mapplethorpe Exhibit," *New York Times*, March 29, 1990.

69. Isabel Wilkerson, "Cincinnati Gallery Indicted in Mapplethorpe Furor," *New York Times*, April 8, 1990.

70. Ibid.

71. Isabel Wilkerson, "Judge Bars Action against Exhibition," *New York Times*, April 9, 1990.

72. Fox Butterfield, "Disputed Art Show Opens Peacefully," *New York Times*, August 2, 1990.

73. Isabel Wilkerson, "Test Case for Obscenity Standards Begins Today in Ohio Courtroom," *New York Times*, September 24, 1990.

74. "Obscenity Jurors to View 5 Photos," *New York Times*, September 7, 1990.

75. Isabel Wilkerson, "Clashes at Obscenity Trial on What an Eye Really Sees," *New York Times*, October 3, 1990.

76. Isabel Wilkerson, "Witness in Obscenity Trial Calls Explicit Photographs 'Destructive,'" *New York Times*, October 5, 1990.

77. Isabel Wilkerson, "Cincinnati Jury Acquits Museum in Mapplethorpe Obscenity Case," *New York Times*, October 6, 1990.

78. Barbara Gamarekian, "Arts Nominee Speaks Out against Helms Amendment," *New York Times*, September 23, 1989.

79. Barbara Gamarekian, "White House Opposes Restrictions on Arts Grants," *New York Times*, March 22, 1990.

80. Ibid.

81. Michael Oreskes, "Bush Position on Art Group Evokes Protest from the Right," *New York Times*, March 23, 1990.

82. "Arts Grants' Anti-Obscenity Clause Ruled Unconstitutional by Judge," *New York Times*, January 10, 1991, discussing *Bella Lewitsky Dance Foundation v. Frohnmayer*, 754 F. Supp. 774 (C.D. Calif. 1991).

83. Vincent Canby, "Review/Film: 'Poison,' Three Stories Inspired by Jean Genet," *New York Times*, April 5, 1991; David Johnston, "Stormy Days and Sleepless Nights for 'Lightning Rod' at Arts Agency," *New York Times*, May 3, 1991.

84. Robin Toner, "Buchanan at 40%," *New York Times*, February 19, 1992.

85. William H. Honan, "Head of Endowment for the Arts Is Forced from His Post by Bush," *New York Times*.

86. William H. Honan, "Arts Figures Fear for the Endowment after Frohnmayer," *New York Times*, February 24, 1992.

87. "Mr. Bush's Artless Surrender," *New York Times*, February 26, 1992.

88. Patrick J. Buchanan, "1992 Republican National Convention Speech," Buchanan.org, August 17, 1992, http://www.buchanan.org/pa-92-0817-rnc.html (accessed October 26, 2005).

CHAPTER SEVEN: THE ORAL MAJORITY:
ON TALK RADIO, THE ISSUE OF DECENCY GETS PERSONAL

1. Rush Limbaugh, *The Rush Limbaugh Show*, February 6, 1997, as transcribed by William Ross, "Everything I Know I Learned from Talk Radio," http://www.seanet .com/~billr/talktop.htm (accessed October 27, 2005).

2. "'High Fidelity' Broadcasters Seek Channels," *Washington Post*, March 19, 1940.

3. Alfred R. Zipser, "Frequency Is High in FM Radio Sales," *New York Times*, November 15, 1959; John Burgess, "A New Day Dawns for AM Radio Stations," *Washington Post*, February 28, 1988.

4. "FM Radio Has to Change Its Tune," *Business Week*, September 24, 1966, p. 173.

5. Ibid.

6. John Burgess, "A New Day Dawns for AM Radio Stations," *Washington Post*, February 28, 1988.

7. Ibid.

8. Irvin Molotsky, "FCC Gets Advice on New AM Stations," *New York Times*, March 25, 1985.

9. Reginald Stuart, "FCC in Plan to Bring More Listeners to AM," *New York Times*, April 4, 1986.

10. *Great Lakes Broadcasting Co.*, 3 F.R.C. Ann. Rep. 32, 33 (1929), *rev'd on other grounds*, 59 App.D.C. 197, 37 F.2d 993, *cert. dismissed*, 281 US 706 (1930).

11. "FCC Decree Bars Bias on the Radio," *New York Times*, January 18, 1941.

12. *Red Lion Broadcasting Co. v. FCC*, 395 US 367 (1969).

13. Thomas W. Hazlett and David W. Sosa, "Chilling the Internet? Lessons from the FCC Regulation of Radio Broadcasting," Cato Policy Analysis no. 270, Cato Institute, March 19, 1997, http://www.cato.org/pubs/pas/pa-270.html (accessed September 4, 2005).

14. *Red Lion Broadcasting Co. v. FCC* (emphasis supplied), *quoting Associated Press v. United States*, 326 US 1 (1945).

15. Fred W. Friendly, "What's Fair on the Air?" *New York Times*, March 30, 1975. The article was excerpted from a book Friendly was writing for Random House. At the time he published the article, Friendly was serving as the Edward R. Murrow Professor of Journalism at the Columbia Graduate School of Journalism.

16. Ibid.

17. Ibid.

18. Ibid.

19. Hazlett and Sosa, "Chilling the Internet?"

20. Clemens P. Work, "A Look at FCC's Fowler: Apostle of the Free Market," *U.S. News & World Report*, May 13, 1985.

21. *Telecommunications Research & Action v. FCC*, 801 F.2d 501 (DC Cir. 1986).

22. Kenneth B. Noble, "Reagan Vetoes Measure to Affirm Fairness Policy for Broadcasters," *New York Times*, June 21, 1987.

23. Robert D. Hershey Jr., "FCC Votes Down Fairness Doctrine in a 4–0 Decision," *New York Times*, August 5, 1987.

24. Jeffrey Yorke, "Tea but No Sympathy," *Washington Post*, February 14, 1989.

25. E. J. Dionne, "Waves on Airwaves: Power to the People?" *New York Times*, February 15, 1989.

26. Lewis Grossberger, "The Rush Hours," *New York Times Sunday Magazine*, December 16, 1990, p. 58.

27. Stefan Kanfer, "Can This Guy Be Serious?" *New York Times*, October 1, 1992.

28. Mark Goodman, "Rush Limbaugh," *People Weekly*, October 19, 1992.

29. Grossberger, "The Rush Hours"; Daniel S. Levy, "A Man. A Legend. A What?" *Time*, September 23, 1991.

30. Lawrence Laurent, "Pyne Runs Roman Circus," *Washington Post*, April 18, 1967.

31. Bill Lambrecht, "Radio Activity in a Big Rush, Voters Take Their Anger from the Airwaves to Ballot Box, Boosting GOP Fortunes," *St. Louis Post-Dispatch*, November 13, 1994.

32. Peter Viles, "Talk Explodes in National Syndication," *Broadcasting & Cable*, May 17, 1993.

33. Elizabeth Kolbert, "The People Are Heard, at Least Those Who Call Talk Radio," *New York Times*, January 29, 1993, p. A12.

34. Amy Bernstein, "Show Time in the Rush Room," *U.S. News & World Report*, August 16, 1993.

35. Mitchell Fink, "No Rushing Rush," *People Weekly*, July 12, 1993.

36. Peter Viles, "Hosts, Callers Trash Clinton on Talk Radio," *Broadcasting & Cable*, July 12, 1993.

37. Morgan Stewart, "Pump Up the Volume," *Campaigns & Elections*, October 1, 1993.

38. "Radio Talk Shows Becoming Very Influential in Congress," *National Public Radio*, October 26, 1993.

39. Paul Kurtz, "The 'Culture Wars' Intensify," *Free Inquiry*, December 22, 1994.

40. Lambrecht, "Radio Activity in a Big Rush."

41. Tim Poor, "Keeping the Faith: Christian Conservatives Showed Their Growing Role," *St. Louis Post-Dispatch*, November 13, 1994.

42. "Rightward, Christian Soldiers," *Christian Century*, November 23, 1994.

43. "School Prayer on GOP Docket," *Christian Century*, December 7, 1994.

44. Major Garrett, "Prayerful GOP Looks for Legal Loophole," *Insight on the News*, May 8, 1995.

45. "A 'Contract with the Family,'" *Christian Century*, May 24, 1995.

46. John Carmody, "Court of Appeals versus the FCC," *Washington Post*, January 19, 1976.

47. Tim Weiner, "Oliver North on the Airwaves: Definitely Not Modulated," *New York Times*, March 17, 1995.

48. John Tierney, "A San Francisco Talk Show Takes Right-Wing Radio to a New Dimension," *New York Times*, February 14, 1995. Savage trademarked the phrase "compassionate conservative" in 1998 and actually threatened to sue George W. Bush over his use of it in the 2000 campaign. David Gilson, "Michael Savage's Long, Strange Trip," Salon.com, March 5, 2003, http://www.salon.com/news/feature/2003/03/05/savage/ (accessed November 6, 2005).

49. Jeff Cohen and Norman Solomon, "Bennett's Hypocritical Pose," *Capital Times*, November 6, 1995.

50. Erik Eckholm, "From Right, a Rain of Anti-Clinton Salvos," *New York Times*, June 26, 1994.

51. "Scandalous Charges in a Falwell Video," *Christian Century*, June 1, 1994.

52. "Media Attacks on President Clinton Harmful to Society," National Public Radio, July 7, 1994, quoting *Bill and Hillary's Clinton's Circle of Power*. According to various reports, Larry Nichols was an employee at the Arkansas Development Finance Authority under Clinton, and was fired. He filed suit against Clinton and other state officials, but his lawsuits were dismissed by both state and federal courts.

53. David Bowermaster, "Whatever It Is, Bill Clinton Likely Did It," *U.S. News & World Report*, August 8, 1994.

54. George C. Church, "The Clinton Hater's Video Library," *Time*, August 1, 1994.

55. Douglas Jehl, "Clinton Calls Show to Assail Press, Falwell and Limbaugh," *New York Times*, June 25, 1994.

56. "Media Attacks on President Clinton Harmful to Society."

57. Jehl, "Clinton Calls Show to Assail Press."

58. "San Francisco Station Ousts a Blunt Host," *New York Times*, February 17, 1995.

59. David Stout, "Some Rightist Shows Pulled, and Debate Erupts," *New York Times*, April 30, 1995.

60. Todd S. Purdum, "Shifting Debate to the Political Climate, Clinton Condemns 'Promotors of Paranoia,'" *New York Times*, April 25, 1999.

61. Stephen Labaton and Jeff Garth, "Reports of Visit Despite Limits of Access," *New York Times*, January 27, 1998.

62. Francis X. Clines, "First Lady Attributes Inquiry to 'Right-Wing Conspiracy,'" *New York Times*, January 28, 1998.

63. David Brock, "Living with the Clintons," *American Spectator*, December 1993. Brock later apologized for and repudiated his role in the Whitewater/Troopergate controversies in his book *Blinded by the Right: The Conscience of an Ex-Conservative* (New York: Crown, 2002).

64. Ira Chinoy and Robert G. Kaiser, "Decades of Contribution to Conservatism," *Washington Post*, May 2, 1999.

65. Stephen Labaton, "Suit Accuses President of Advance," *New York Times*, May 7, 1994.

66. Marci McDonald, "A Case of Hijacking: How the Conservatives Made the Paula Jones Lawsuit Their Own," *U.S. News & World Report*, April 13, 1998.

67. Don van Natta Jr. and Jill Abramson, "Quietly, a Team of Lawyers Kept Paula Jones's Case Alive," *New York Times*.

68. McDonald, "A Case of Hijacking."

69. Ironically, Coulter was born in New Canaan, Connecticut, the same town in which nineteenth-century moralist Anthony Comstock was born.

70. Gene Lyons, "Hunting the President," *Washington Monthly*, March 1, 2000.

71. David Daley, "Ann Coulter: Light's All Shining on Her," *Hartford Courant*, June 25, 1999.

72. Michael Isikoff, *Uncovering Clinton: A Reporter's Story* (New York: Crown, 1998), p. 183.

73. "2 Leave Case That Accuses the President," *New York Times*, September 10, 1997.

74. Neil A. Lewis, "Jones's Lawyer Likes Underdog Role," *New York Times*, March 1, 1998.

75. Lewis, "Group behind Paula Jones Gains Critics as Well as Fame," *New York Times*, January 18, 1998.

76. Frank J. Murray, "Jones Almost Fired Rutherford Group," *Washington Times*, April 26, 1998.

77. Frank J. Murray, "Spinning for Paula Jones," *Washington Times*, July 19, 1997.

78. William Gaines and David Jackson, "Jones, Not Her Lawyers, Gains from Legal Fund," *St. Louis Dispatch*, February 27, 1998.

79. "Paula Jones' Lawyers Get Lion's Share of $850,000 Settlement," CNN.com, March 5, 1999, http://www.cnn.com/ALLPOLITICS/stories/1999/03/05/jones.fees/ (accessed November 11, 2005).

80. Maureen Dowd, "Murder of an Anatomy," *New York Times*, October 18, 1997.

81. Michael Hedges, "Conservative Radio Spot Seeks Victims of Clinton," *Denver Rocky Mountain News*, November 13, 1997.

82. Michael Isikoff, "A Twist in Jones *v.* Clinton: Her Lawyers Subpoena Another Woman," *Newsweek*, August 11, 1997.

83. Evan Thomas, "Clinton and the Intern," *Newsweek*, February 2, 1998.

84. Tim Weiner and Jill Abramson, "In the Case against Clinton, Some Links to Conservatives," *New York Times*, January 28, 1998.

85. Peter Baker, "Linda Tripp Briefed Jones Team on Tapes," *Washington Post*, February 14, 1998.

86. Melinda Henneberger, "Conservative Talk Radio Finding Cause for Revelry," *New York Times*, January 29, 1998.

87. Ibid.

88. Marc Fisher, "On Radio, Scandal Talk Is Free and Unfettered," *Washington Post*, February 19, 1998. As of December 2005, Billy Bush is a coanchor for *Access Hollywood*.

89. Ibid.

CHAPTER EIGHT: NOW IS THE YEAR OF OUR DISSED CONTENT: WHY THE FCC REENLISTED IN THE WAR ON INDECENCY

1. Bill Stewart, "Alt Hierarchy History," LivingInternet.com, 1996–2005, http://www.livinginternet.com/u/ui_alt.htm (accessed November 16, 2005).

2. "Information Back Alleys," *New York Times*, January 3, 1995, citing data compiled by Brian Reid, Internet technology manager, Digital Equipment Corp.

3. Gary Chapman, "Net Gain," *New Republic*, July 31, 1995, p. 10.

4. Robert H'obbes' Zakon, "Hobbes' Internet Timeline v.8.1—Growth," last updated August 28, 2005, http://www.zakon.org/robert/internet/timeline/#Growth

(accessed November 14, 2005). The estimated number of Web sites as of August 2005 is 70,392,567.

5. John Simons, "The Web's Dirty Secret: Sex Sites May Make Lots of Money, but Their Popularity May Soon Taper Off," *U.S. News & World Report*, August 19, 1996.

6. Anthony Flint, "Skin Trade Spreading across the US," *Boston Globe*, December 1, 1996.

7. Philip Elmer-Dewitt, "Censoring Cyberspace: Carnegie Mellon's Attempt to Ban Sex from Its Campus Computer Networks Sends a Chill along the Info Highway," *Time*, November 21, 1994, p. 102.

8. Edmund L. Andrews, "Smut Ban Backed for Computer Net," *New York Times*, March 24, 1995.

9. Christopher Stern, "New Law of the Land," *Broadcasting & Cable*, February 5, 1996.

10. Edmund L. Andrews, "Senate Supports Severe Penalties on Computer Smut," *New York Times*, June 15, 1995.

11. *Congressional Record*, June 14, 1995, S8330.

12. Andrews, "Senate Supports Severe Penalties on Computer Smut."

13. "Issues and Controversies: Internet Regulation," Facts on File News Service, September 15, 1995, http://www.facts.com/cd/i00034.htm (accessed July 28, 2000).

14. Andrews, "Senate Supports Severe Penalties on Computer Smut."

15. Chapman, "Net Gain."

16. Frank Rich, "Newt to the Rescue," *New York Times*, July 1, 1995.

17. Internet Freedom and Family Empowerment Act, 104th Cong., 1st sess., H.R. 1978 IH, June 30, 1995.

18. Elmer-DeWitt, "On a Screen Near You—Cyberporn," *Time*, July 3, 1995.

19. Elmer-DeWitt, "Fire Storm on the Computer Nets: A New Study of Cyberporn, First Reported in a *Time* Cover Story, Sparks Controversy," *Time*, July 24, 1995, p. 57.

20. Ibid.

21. "How *Time* Fed the Internet Porn Panic," *Harper's Magazine*, September 1995.

22. Senator Charles Grassley (R-IA), *Congressional Record*, June 26, 1995, p. S9017.

23. *Telecommunications Act of 1996*, Conference Report 104-458, 104th Cong., 2d sess., January 31, 1996, p. 189.

24. Ibid.

25. *FCC v. Pacifica Foundation*, 438 US 726 (1978).

26. *Sable Communications v. FCC*, 492 US 115 (1989).

27. *American Civil Liberties Union v. Reno*, Adjudication on Motions for Preliminary Injunction, C.A. no. 96-963 (E.D. Pa., June 11, 1986).

28. *Reno v. American Civil Liberties Union*, 521 US 844 (1997) (internal quotations, citations, and ellipses omitted).

29. Ted Bridis, "Congress Moves Ahead on Bills Restricting Internet," Associated Press, October 8, 1998.

30. *Referral to the United States House of Representatives pursuant to Title 28, United*

States Code, sect. 595(c). Submitted by Office of the Independent Counsel, September 9, 1998, http://icreport.loc.gov/icreport/ (accessed November 17, 2005).

31. Prior to receiving the Lewinsky tapes from Linda Tripp in January 1998, Starr had spent roughly $30 million on his failed Whitewater investigation. He spent approximately $10 million more investigating the truthfulness of President Clinton's statements regarding his relationship with Lewinsky.

32. David Streitfeld, "Publishers Balk at Lewinsky Book Deal," *Washington Post*, September 17, 1998.

33. Edwin McDowell, "Some Say Meese Report Rates an 'X,'" *New York Times*, October 21, 1986.

34. Marjorie Connelly, "Clinton Holds Mostly Steady in the Polls," *New York Times*, September 23, 1998.

35. Amy Harmon, "Tangled Web Tangles Up the World Wide Web," *New York Times*, September 12, 1998.

36. NetPartners Internet Solutions, Inc., press release, "Internet Broadcasts of Starr Report Costs [*sic*] Businesses Over $450 Million in Lost Employee Productivity," Business Wire, October 2, 1998. For an extensive discussion of the role of the Internet in the workplace, as well as efforts to control usage, see Frederick S. Lane, *The Naked Employee: How Technology Is Compromising Workplace Privacy* (New York: Amacom, 2003).

37. Jeri Clausing, "New Internet Decency Bill Clears Hurdle in House," *New York Times*, September 24, 1988.

38. "U.S. Lawmakers Rush to Curb Internet Smut," Reuters, October 17, 1998.

39. Jeri Clausing, "Controversial Internet Proposal Is Attached to Budget Bill," *New York Times*, October 15, 1988.

40. Muriel Dobbin, "GOP Promises Right Wing It Will Try Harder," *Denver Rocky Mountain News*, May 9, 1988.

41. Bob Kolaskey, "Have We Been Down This Road Before?" IntellectualCapital.com, September 24, 1998.

42. Ralph Z. Hallow, "Ashcroft Breaks GOP's Silence," *Washington Times*, January 31, 1998.

43. David Johnston and Neil A. Lewis, "Religious Right Made Big Push to Put Ashcroft in Justice Dept.," *New York Times*, January 7, 2001.

44. David Goldstein, "Faith Is at the Fore as Ashcroft Faces Attorney General Confirmation Hearing," Knight Ridder/Tribune News Service, January 14, 2001.

45. Johnston and Lewis, "Religious Right Made Big Push to Put Ashcroft in Justice Dept."

46. Joseph L. Conn, "God, Guns, and the GOP," *Church & State*, November 1, 1998.

47. Conn, "Election '98 After Shock," *Church & State*, December 1, 1988.

48. Michael Rust, "Social Disease in the GOP?" *Insight on the News*, March 22, 1999.

49. "Can He Save the Republicans," *U.S. News & World Report*, November 16, 1998.

50. Ibid.

51. Greg Pierce, "Inside Politics: Recipe for Disaster," *Washington Times*, December 3, 1998.

52. Ron Fournier, "Political Notebook: Bradley May Run," Associated Press, December 2, 1998.

53. "Conservative Champion Gary Bauer Comes out of the Shadows," Knight Ridder/Tribune News Service, February 1, 1999.

54. John B. Judis, "The Mouse That Roars," *New Republic*, August 3, 1987.

55. Ryan Lizza, "What Was Gary Bauer Thinking," *New Republic*, March 20, 2000.

56. Ralph Z. Hallow, "McCain Admits His Own Remarks Hurt Campaign," *Washington Times*, March 3, 2000.

57. Lizza, "What Was Gary Bauer Thinking."

58. Timothy Egen, "Wall Street Meets Pornography," *New York Times*, October 23, 2000.

59. John Acola, "XXX-rated e-commerce," *Denver Rocky Mountain News*, May 21, 2000.

60. Egen, "Wall Street Meets Pornography."

61. Johnston and Lewis, "Religious Right Made Big Push to Put Ashcroft in Justice Dept."

62. Ibid.

63. Alison Mitchell and Robin Toner, "Lott and Conservatives Rallying Behind Ashcroft for Justice Post," *New York Times*, January 11, 2001.

64. Alison Mitchell, "Senate Confirms Ashcroft as Attorney General, 58–42, Closing a Five-Week Battle," *New York Times*, February 2, 2001.

65. Nicholas Confessore, "Porn and Politics in a Digital Age," PBS.org, February 7, 2002, http://www.pbs.org/wgbh/pages/frontline/shows/porn/special/politics.html (accessed May 21, 2002).

66. Leon Satterfield, "Naked Justice from Attorney General's Office," The Truth, Mainly, March 4, 2002, http://thetruthmainly.tripod.com/2002/20020304.html (accessed November 18, 2005).

67. Maureen Dowd, "Cover-ups Take a Turn for the Literal," *Atlanta Journal and Constitution*, January 31, 2002.

68. Calvin Woodward, "Uncovered Statues Remain in D.C.," Associated Press, March 1, 2002.

69. Dowd, "Cover-ups Take a Turn for the Literal."

70. Barry M. Horstman, "The Naked Truth: Exposed," *Cincinnati Post*, March 9, 2002.

71. Paul Singer, "Justice Officials Fall Short in Targeting Porn, Conservatives Say," *Chicago Tribune*, August 22, 2003.

72. Wayne Slater, "Conservative Political Base Key to Bush Re-Election," *Dallas Morning News*, January 7, 2004.

73. Mark Kernes, "Bruce Taylor Back in DOJ Saddle," *Adult Video News*, February 3, 2004, http://www.avn.com/index.php?Primary_Navigation=Articles&Action=View_Article&Content_ID=72798 (accessed May 24, 2004).

74. Neil Munro, "Testing Porn's Protection," *National Journal*, April 10, 2004.

75. Frank James, "FCC Chairman Michael Powell Seeks Obscenity Crackdown," *Chicago Tribune*, January 14, 2004.

76. Rep. Fred Upton (R-MI), Capitol Hill press release, January 14, 2000.

77. One of the most common complaints heard about the FCC's handling of indecency complaints is the length of time between complaint and decision. Fifteen to eighteen months is about average, which helps put the Jackson investigation (seven months) in perspective.

78. Federal Communications Commission, Notice of Apparent Liability for Forfeiture, File No. EB-02-IH-0786, January 27, 2004, paras. 2 and 3, n. 9.

79. As of this writing, Viacom is scheduled to split into two corporations—Viacom and CBS Corporation—at the end of 2005.

80. "Infinity Broadcasting Company," Hoovers.com, n.d., http://www.hoovers.com/infinity-broadcasting/—ID_58372—/free-co-factsheet.xhtml (accessed November 18, 2005).

81. Federal Communications Commission, Notice of Apparent Liability for Forfeiture, File No. EB-04-IH-0011, September 22, 2004, paras. 12–15.

82. Ibid., para. 23.

83. "CBS Fined $550,000 by FCC for Indecency at Super Bowl," Bloomberg, September 22, 2004.

84. Frank Rich, "The Year of Living Indecently," *New York Times*, February 6, 2005.

CHAPTER NINE: ASK NOT FOR WHOM THE WEDDING BELLS TOLL: A LOVE THAT NOW DARES SPEAK ITS NAME

1. Two thousand years later, the views of both Christianity and Judaism toward homosexuality are much more nuanced. Both religions have subdivided into myriad strains of belief, some of which no longer view homosexuality as immoral (such as the Union of American Hebrew Congregations, for instance, Unitarian Universalism, or the Friends General Conference [a branch of the Quakers]).

2. In fact, one of the first executions under English law in the New World was for the crime of buggery, which at the time could refer to either homosexual acts or bestiality. According to William Bradford, longtime governor of Plimoth Plantation, a sixteen- or seventeen-year-old named Thomas Granger was hanged for buggery of "a mare, a cow, two goats, five sheep, two calves, and a turkey." Relying on the admonition of Leviticus 20:15, "[a]nd if a man lie with a beast, he shall surely be put to death; and ye shall slay the beast," the animals were hanged in front of Granger and buried in a pit. Granger himself was then hanged. William Bradford, *Of Plimoth Plantation 1620–1647*. For an interesting commentary by a distant relative of Granger, see Susanne "Sam" Behling, "Thomas Granger," Sam's Genealogy, 1997, http://homepages.rootsweb.com/~sam/tgranger.html (accessed November 24, 2005).

3. Douglas O. Linder, "Testimony of Oscar Wilde," Famous World Trials, 2005, http://www.law.umkc.edu/faculty/projects/ftrials/wilde/Crimwilde.html (accessed December 8, 2005).

4. 1 Sam. 18:4.

5. "Oscar Wilde Imprisoned," *New York Times*, April 6, 1895.

6. "Oscar Wilde on Trial," *Washington Post*, April 7, 1895. The term "Pinerotic" is a reference to Arthur Wing Pinero, British playwright and contemporary of Wilde who wrote the two plays listed in the excerpt.

7. "Oscar Wilde Is a Convict," *New York Times*, May 26, 1895.

8. "Berlin Scandal Inquiry," *Washington Post*, June 14, 1907.

9. George Bernard Shaw, "'Common Sense about the War,'" *New York Times*, November 22, 1914. It should be pointed out that he did not use it in a positive sense; he expressed the hope that the "March of Democracy" would consign "the forty tolerated homosexual brothels of Berlin" to "the dustbin."

10. "Survey Finds 50% of Men in U.S. Guilty of Sex Crimes," *Washington Post*, November 19, 1947.

11. Jean M. White, "Those Others: A Report on Homosexuality," *Washington Post*, January 1, 1965.

12. Amicus Brief of the Human Rights Campaign et al., *Lawrence v. Texas*, No. 02-102 (US Supreme Court, January 16, 2003), p. 34 n. 42, citing National Health and Social Life Survey, as summarized in Edward O. Laumann et al., *The Social Organization of Sex: Sexual Practices in the United States* (Chicago: University of Chicago Press, 1994).

13. George Gallup, "Kinsey Survey of Sex Habits Is Widely Approved by Public," *Washington Post*, February 21, 1948.

14. "M'Carthy Insists Truman Ousts Reds," *New York Times*, February 12, 1950.

15. "Perverts Called Government Peril," *New York Times*, April 19, 1950.

16. William S. White, "Inquiry by Senate on Perverts Asked," *New York Times*, May 20, 1950.

17. "$10,000 Voted to Investigate Perversion in U.S. Agencies," *Washington Post*, June 8, 1950.

18. "Federal Vigilance on Perverts Asked," *New York Times*, December 16, 1950.

19. "State Dept. Reports It Fired 126 Sex Perverts in 14 Months," *Washington Post*, March 26, 1952.

20. Milton Magruder, "State Dept. Firing Sex Deviates," *Washington Post*, March 27, 1953.

21. Milton Bracker, "Life on 42nd St. a Study in Decay," *New York Times*, March 14, 1960.

22. Jean M. White, "Homophile Groups Argue Civil Liberties," *Washington Post*, October 11, 1964.

23. White, "Those Others: A Report on Homosexuality."

24. Robert Trumbull, "Homosexuals Proud of Deviancy, Medical Academy Study Finds," May 19, 1964, *New York Times*, p. 1.

25. Webster Schott, "Civil Rights and the Homosexual," *New York Times*, November 12, 1967.

26. "Business Data for Midnight Cowboy (1969)," IMDB.com, n.d., http://www.imdb.com/title/tt0064665/business (accessed November 25, 2005).

27. Vincent Canby, "Film: Midnight Cowboy," *New York Times*, May 26, 1969.

28. The original Stonewall Inn is no longer in existence, although a similarly named bar now operates where the 1969 business once stood.

29. "4 Policemen Hurt in 'Village' Raid," *New York Times*, June 29, 1969; Jerry Lisker, "Homo Nest Raided, Queen Bees Are Stinging Mad," *New York Daily News*, July 6, 1969.

30. "Police Again Rout 'Village' Youths," *New York Times*, June 30, 1969.

31. Cecil Adams, "How Did 'Gay' Come to Mean 'Homosexual'?" Straight Dope, January 1, 1986, http://www.straightdope.com/classics/a2_271b.html (accessed December 8, 2005).

32. Lacey Fosburgh, "Thousands of Homosexuals Hold a Protest in Central Park," *New York Times*, June 29, 1970.

33. Paul L. Montgomery, "5,000 Homosexuals March to Central Park for a Rally," *New York Times*, June 28, 1971.

34. "Homosexuals March for Equal Rights," *New York Times*, June 27, 1977.

35. "Homosexuals' Parade Marks 10th Year of Rights Drive," *New York Times*, June 25, 1979.

36. Thomas Morgan, "Loaded with Ads, Newspaper for Homosexuals Flourishes," *Washington Post*, June 22, 1980.

37. Ibid.

38. Andree Brooks, "Homosexuals Find It Easier to Buy Homes in Suburbs," *New York Times*, June 18, 1978.

39. Stuart Elliott, "Advertising: Homosexual Imagery Is Spreading from Print Campaigns to General-Interest TV Programming," *New York Times*, June 30, 1997. This is a technique still in use. One particularly effective example occurred in 1997, when Arnold Communications in Boston created an ad for the Volkswagen Golf that featured two young men driving around town, picking up and then abandoning a musty old chair. Volkswagen received a large number of calls from viewers asking if the two young men were more than just friends (a conclusion encouraged by the fact that the ad debuted during the episode of *Ellen* in which Ellen Degeneres's character reveals that she is gay). A bemused Volkswagen denied any hidden message.

40. Susan Okie, "Health Official Sees Abortion Leading to Euthanasia," *Washington Post*, May 9, 1981.

41. The disease was subsequently renamed *Pneumocystis jiroveci* pneumonia.

42. Fred Barnes, "The Politics of AIDS," *New Republic*, November 4, 1985.

43. Sue Cross, "Jerry Falwell Calls AIDS a 'Gay Plague,'" *Washington Post*, July 6, 1983.

44. Michael Doan, "Jerry Falwell's Anti-AIDS Dollar Drive," *U.S. News & World Report*, May, 4, 1987.

45. Jeff Yarbrough, "Rock Hudson: On Camera and Off," *People Weekly*, August 12, 1985.

46. Ibid.

47. Tom Vallance, "Obituary: George Nader," *Independent* (London), February 8, 2002. Nader did, however, go on to play the character of FBI agent Jerry Cotton in a series of successful German films.

48. Scot Haller, "A Lawsuit over Rock's Estate Exposes Scandal—and Asserts a Lover's Right to Know," *People Weekly*, November 25, 1985.

49. Barnes, "The Politics of AIDS."

50. Christine Russell, "AIDS Report Calls for Sex Education," *Washington Post*, October 23, 1986.

51. Ibid.

52. Sandra G. Boodman, "Caution: the Surgeon General of the United States Can Be Hazardous to Your Complacency," *Washington Post Magazine*, November 15, 1987, p. 18.

53. Richard Stengal, "Testing Dilemma: Washington Prepares a Controversial New Policy to Fight AIDS," *Time*, June 8, 1987.

54. Boodman, "Caution: the Surgeon General of the United States Can Be Hazardous to Your Complacency."

55. Ibid.

56. Ibid.

57. Thomas L. Friedman, "Clinton to Open Military's Ranks to Homosexuals," *New York Times*, November 12, 1992.

58. "Excerpts from President-Elect's News Conference in Arkansas," *New York Times*, November 13, 1992. The "Tailhook scandal" refers to claims of sexual harassment that allegedly occurred at the thirty-fifth annual meeting of the Tailhook Association in Las Vegas, Nevada, in September 1991. The group is a nonprofit, fraternal organization committed to the advancement of the interests of sea-based aviation.

59. John H. Cushman Jr., "Top Military Officers Object to Lifting Homosexual Ban," *New York Times*, November 14, 1992.

60. Peter Martin, "Jesse Helms to Retire from US Senate," World Socialist Web site, August 31, 2001, http://www.wsws.org/articles/2001/aug2001/helm-a31.shtml (accessed August 30, 2005).

61. Neal Conan, "Military Gay Ban Issue Draws Conservative Christians," National Public Radio, February 11, 1993.

62. Peter Applebome, "Gay Issue Mobilizes Conservatives against Clinton," *New York Times*, February 1, 1993.

63. Conan, "Military Gay Ban Issue Draws Conservative Christians."

64. Randy Shilts, "What's Fair in Love and War?" *Newsweek*, February 1, 1993.

65. Eric Schmitt, "Military's Gay Subculture: Off Limits but Flourishing," *New York Times*, December 1, 1992.

66. Gwen Ifill, "Clinton Accepts Delay in Lifting Military Gay Ban," *New York Times*, January 30, 1993.

67. Timothy Egan, "Goldwater Defending Clinton; Conservatives Feel Faint," *New York Times*, March 24, 1994.

68. Eric Schmitt, "Partial Step on Gay Ban," *New York Times*, July 18, 1993.

69. During his first term, President George W. Bush held just seventeen solo press conferences, far fewer than his father (eighty-four), Carter (fifty-nine), Clinton (forty-four), and even Reagan (twenty-seven). Mark Jurkowitz, "Communication or Manip-

ulation?" *Boston Globe*, March 7, 2005, http://www.boston.com/ae/books/articles/2005/03/07/communication_or_manipulation/ (accessed September 2, 2005).

70. "President Holds Press Conference," Office of the Press Secretary, White House, January 26, 2005, http://www.whitehouse.gov/news/releases/2005/01/20050126-3.html (accessed September 2, 2005).

71. Ibid.

72. Media Matters for America, press release, "Gannongate: Media Matters for America Uncovers White House Reporter Copying GOP Documents," US Newswire, January 28, 2005.

73. Byron York, "Gannongate: The Weird Story of a Non-Scandal," *National Review*, March 14, 2005.

74. Media Matters for America, "'Go Ahead, Jeff,'" MediaMatters.org, February 2, 2005, http://mediamatters.org/items/200502020014 (accessed September 2, 2005).

75. Joe Strupp, "White House Correspondents Criticize Alleged 'Softball Thrower'—and Jeff Gannon Fires Back," *Editor & Publisher*, February 2, 2004; Media Matters for America, "Gannongate."

76. As of November 26, 2005, "HotMilitaryStud.com" now redirects to a hard-core sex site titled "AWOL Marines." "MilitaryEscorts.com" and "MilitaryEscorts M4M" now redirect to a gay dating site, "OutPersonals.com."

77. Mary Ann Akers, "Gannon Fodder," *Roll Call*, February 16, 2005.

78. Eric Boehlert, "Fake News, Fake Reporter," Salon.com, February 10, 2005, http://www.salon.com/news/feature/2005/02/10/gannon_affair/index.html (accessed September 2, 2005).

79. Ann Coulter, "Republicans, Bloggers and Gays, Oh My!" TownHall.com, February 24, 2005.

80. Bill Ervolino, "Gay Weddings' Best Man: George W. Bush," *Bergen County (NJ) Record*, February 25, 2004.

81. Schott, "Civil Rights and the Homosexual."

82. Tim Campbell, "Gay Marriage—the Early Years," *Pulse of the Twin Cities*, April 8, 2005, http://pulsetc.com/article.php?sid=1015 (accessed November 27, 2005).

83. George Dullea, "Homosexual Couples Find a Quiet Pride," *New York Times*, December 10, 1984.

84. Jeffrey Schmalz, "In Hawaii, Step towards Legalized Gay Marriage," *New York Times*, May 7, 1993.

85. "New Hawaiian Law Bans Gay Marriage," *New York Times*, June 24, 1994.

86. David W. Dunlap, "Fearing a Toehold for Gay Marriage, Conservatives Rush to Bar the Door," *New York Times*, March 6, 1996.

87. Todd S. Purdum, "Gay Rights Groups Attack Clinton on Midnight Signing," *New York Times*, September 22, 1996.

88. Tamara Lush, "Court Orders Equal Benefits, Stops Short of Gay Marriage," *Burlington Free Press*, December 21, 1999.

89. Rose Arce, "Massachusetts Court Upholds Same-Sex Marriage," CNN.com, February 6, 2004, http://www.cnn.com/2004/LAW/02/04/gay.marriage/ (accessed November 27, 2004).

CHAPTER TEN: AT PLAY IN THE LABORATORIES OF THE LORD: SACRIFICING SCIENTIFIC TRUTH ON THE ALTAR OF IDEOLOGY

1. Douglas Adams, *The Hitchhiker's Guide to the Galaxy* (New York: Ballantine, 1980), p. 59. Adams, who died of a heart attack at the relatively young age of forty-nine, was a self-described "radical atheist."

2. Tenn. H.B. 185 (1925).

3. At the time, Tennessee criminal court judges were not authorized to assess fines above $50, as Judge Raulston had done.

4. *Abington Township v. Schempp*, 364 US 298 (1960); *Engel v. Vitale*, 370 US 421 (1962).

5. 393 US 97 (1968).

6. Martin Tolchin, "11 Short of Passing," *New York Times*, March 21, 1984.

7. "When Politics Mixes with Prayer," *U.S. News & World Report*, March 19, 1984.

8. George J. Church, "Mixing Politics with Prayer; Uncle Sam Jumps into the Church-State Debate," *Time*, March 19, 1984.

9. Tolchin, "11 Short of Passing."

10. Ibid.

11. "Equal Access: Congress and Student Piety," *Time*, August 6, 1984.

12. William R. Doerner, "Setting Out to Whomp 'em: The Republicans Sound the Battle Cry as They Renominate Reagan and Bush," *Time*, September 3, 1984.

13. 472 US 38 (1985).

14. Michael S. Serrill, "Uproar over Silence; the Court Stirs Again the School-Prayer Debate," *Time*, June 17, 1985.

15. Brooke A. Masters, "Va. Minute of Silence Survives Test in High Court," *Washington Post*, October 30, 2001.

16. Bill Sammon, "Prayer Bills 'Bad Policy,' Roberts Wrote in '85 Memo," *Washington Times*, July 28, 2005.

17. United States Department of the Interior, Branch of Isotope Geology, "The Age of the Earth," n.d., http://www2.nature.nps.gov/geology/usgsnps/gtime/ageofearth .pdf (accessed December 8, 2005).

18. 393 US 97.

19. La. Rev. Stat. Ann. sects. 17:286.1–17:286.7 (West 1982).

20. *Edwards v. Aguillard*, 482 US 578, 587 (1987).

21. *Edwards v. Aguillard*, quoting *Aguillard v. Edwards*, 765 F.2d 1251, 1257 (5th Cir. 1985).

22. *Edwards v. Aguillard*, 482 US at 578, 591, 593.

23. *Id.*, at 578, 593–594 (emphasis supplied).

24. Michelle Goldberg, "The New Monkey Trial," Salon.com, January 10, 2005, http://www.salon.com/news/feature/2005/01/10/evolution/ (accessed January 10, 2005).

25. Laurie Goodstein, "Expert Witness Sees Evidence in Nature for Intelligent Design," *New York Times*, October 18, 2005.

26. Maggie Wittlin, "The Other I.D.," SeedMagazine.com, November 15, 2005, http://www.seedmagazine.com/news/2005/11/the_other_id.php (accessed December 8, 2005).

27. Thomas More Law Center, "About Us," ThomasMore.org/about.html, n.d. (accessed November 29, 2005).

28. Goodstein, "In Intelligent Design Case, a Cause in Search of a Lawsuit," *New York Times*, November 4, 2005.

29. Ibid.

30. Robert Siegel and Michele Norris, "ACLU Files Lawsuit to Challenge Pennsylvania School District's Decision to Require Teaching of Intelligent Design," National Public Radio, December 14, 2004.

31. To underscore the point, the National Center for Science Education launched Project Steve (named in honor of famed biologist Stephen Jay Gould). The aim of the semiserious project is to list all the scientists named Steve (including variants like Stephen or Stephanie) who support the theory of evolution and reject the teaching of "creationist pseudoscience." As of December 2005, 677 scientists had signed on to Project Steve. As the Web site points out, since less than 1 percent of all scientists are named Steve, that implies that tens of thousands of scientists support the general theory of evolution. See National Center for Science Education, "NCSE Project Steve," http://www.ncseweb.org/resources/articles/3541_project_steve_2_16_2003.asp (accessed December 8, 2005).

32. Professors Richard Dawkins and Jerry Coyne, "One Side Can Be Wrong," *Guardian*, September 1, 2005.

33. Goodstein, "The 2005 Elections: School Board; Evolution Slate Outpolls Rivals," *New York Times*, November 9, 2005.

34. "Judge Bars 'Intelligent Design' from Pa. Classes," Associated Press, December 20, 2005.

35. Alan Elsner, "Televangelist Robertson Warns Town of God's Wrath," Yahoo.com, November 10, 2005, http://news.yahoo.com/s/nm/20051110/ts_nm/religion_robertson_dc (accessed November 10, 2005).

36. Howard A. Rusk, "Concerning Man's Basic Drive," *New York Times*, January 4, 1948.

37. Scott Simon, "Profile: History of Sex Education in American Public Schools," National Public Radio, February 7, 2004.

38. Sharon Johnson, "School Sex Education Enters a New Phase," *New York Times*, January 9, 1986.

39. Ruth Marcus, "Funding for Religious Groups to Promote Chastity Upheld," *Washington Post*, June 30, 1988.

40. Ibid.

41. Sexuality Information and Education Council of the US, press release, "President Proposes Doubling Unproven Abstinence-Only-Until-Marriage Funding Programs in State of the Union," US Newswire, January 21, 2004.

42. Debra Hauser, MPH, "Five Years of Abstinence-Only-Until-Marriage Education: Assessing the Impact," Advocates for Youth, n.d., http://www.advocateforyouth.org/publications/stateevaluations/ (accessed November 29, 2005).

43. Ibid.

44. Brian H. Kehrl, "States Abstain from Federal Sex Money," Kansas City infoZine, November 30, 2005, http://www.infozine.com/news/stories/op/storiesView/sid/11666/ (accessed November 30, 2005).

45. Rep. Henry A. Waxman, "The Content of Federally Funded Abstinence-Only Education Programs," US House of Representatives, Committee on Government Reform, Minority Staff, Special Investigations Division, December 2004, p. 26.

46. Betsy Querna, "Sex Matters: Virginity Study Bashed," *U.S. News & World Report*, June 17, 2005, http://www.usnews.com/usnews/health/articles/050617/1sex matters.htm (accessed June 19, 2005).

47. Martin L. Haines, "Abstinence-Only Programs Tell Half-truths about Sex," *Asbury Park Press*, November 9, 2005, http://www.app.com/apps/pbcs.dll/article ?AID=/20051109/OPINION/511090391/1030/POLITICS (accessed November 30, 2005).

48. Kehrl, "States Abstain from Federal Sex Money."

49. Ibid.

50. Abby Goodnough, "Taking Heart in Florida," *International Herald Tribune*, October 25, 2003.

51. Mitch Stacy, "Fla. Gov. Orders Comatose Woman Be Fed," *Associated Press*, October 22, 2003.

52. Goodnough, "Taking Heart in Florida."

53. "ACLJ Asking Florida Court to Permit Intervention of Terri Schindler," *Business Wire*, October 30, 2003.

54. David Sommer, "State's High Court Tosses Out Terri's Law," *Tampa Tribune*, September 24, 2004.

55. Sommer, "Schiavo's Parents Are Still Banned from Visiting Their Daughter Alone," *Tampa Tribune*, May 18, 2004.

56. Brad Smith, "Schiavo Videotapes Offer Powerful but Misleading Evidence," *Tampa Tribune*, March 20, 2005.

57. "Bush Signs Controversial Bill to Save Brain-Damaged Woman," *Agence France Presse English*, March 21, 2005.

58. Shailagh Murray and Mike Allen, "Schiavo Case Tests Priorities of GOP," *Washington Post*, March 26, 2005.

59. The Web site to which Senator Frist referred was TerrisFight.org, a site set up and maintained by the Terri Schindler-Schiavo Foundation, a volunteer organization working to support Bob and Mary Schindler.

60. Senator William Frist, *Congressional Record*, March 17, 2005, p. S3091.

61. Frist, *Congressional Record*, March 19, 2005, p. S3095.

62. "Profile: Consequences of the Terry Schiavo Case for Congress and the White House," National Public Radio, March 25, 2005.

63. Elisabeth Bumiller, "The Schiavo Case: The President," *New York Times*, March 21, 2005.

64. The uniform denials of authorship by congressional Republicans led some conservative bloggers to argue that the "talking points" memo was a Democrat-created

fake; however, Senator Mel Martinez (R-FL) disclosed that it had been written by an aide in his office, who was subsequently fired. See "Florida Republican Confirms Authenticity of GOP Talking Points, Obtained by ABC News," ABCNews.go.com, April 7, 2005, http://abcnews.go.com/Politics/Schiavo/story?id=600937 (accessed November 28, 2005).

65. Jesse J. Holland, "Bush Role in Schiavo Case Bothers 'Right,'" AP Online, March 23, 2005.

66. Murray and Allen, "Schiavo Case Tests Priorities of GOP."

67. Melissa Block and Robert Siegel, "Analysis: Terri Schiavo's Autopsy Report Released," *National Republic Radio*, June 15, 2005.

68. Ibid.

69. Charles Babington, "Frist Defends Remarks on Schiavo Case," *Washington Post*, June 17, 2005.

70. Alex Chadwick, "Interview: Robert Herring Discusses Offer of $1 million to Terri Schiavo's Husband to Transfer Legal Right to Decide His Wife's Medical Issues to Her Parents," National Public Radio, March 18, 2005. One newspaper, the *London Independent*, reported that the amount was actually $10 million, but most other sources reported the lower figure.

71. Block and Siegel, "Analysis: Terri Schiavo's Autopsy Report Released."

72. Beth Fouhy, "Ron Reagan Backs Stem Cell Research," Associated Press, July 28, 2004.

73. It can be very difficult to isolate somatic stem cells, since they often occur in very small quantities in a given type of tissue. Researchers have some questions about how vigorously somatic stem cells will replicate and many contain DNA abnormalities reflecting the age and lifestyle of the person from whom they are harvested.

74. "Text of the Announcement by President Bush on Federal Funding for Embryonic Stem Cell Research," *Transplant News*, August 17, 2001.

75. Mark Henderson, "Stem Cells Found to Be Contaminated," *London Times*, January 24, 2005.

76. William J. Cromie, "Melton Derives New Stem Cell Lines," *Harvard University Gazette*, March 4, 2004.

77. Ron Hutcheson, "Defying Bush, House Votes to Expand Stem-Cell Research," Knight-Ridder/Tribune News Service, May 24, 2005.

78. "Frist Breaks with Bush on Stem Cell Research," MSNBC.com, July 29, 2005, http://www.msnbc.msn.com/id/8750167/ (accessed December 9, 2005).

79. Senator William Frist, 109th Congress, 1st sess., *Congressional Record*, July 29, 2005, S9323.

80. "Frist Breaks with Bush on Stem Cell Research."

81. Steven Ertelt, "Pro-Life Group Blasts Bill Frist on Stem Cell Research in Iowa Ads," LifeNews.com, August 26, 2005, http://www.lifenews.com/bio1117.html (accessed August 26, 2005).

CONCLUSION: A THOUSAND POINTS OF ENLIGHTENMENT: STRATEGIES TO RESTORE THE TRUE MEANING OF DECENCY IN AMERICAN SOCIETY

1. Daniel J. Boorstin, "The Amateur Spirit," 1989, in *Living Philosophies: The Reflections of Some Eminent Men and Women of Our Time* (New York: Doubleday, 1990).

2. "Powers's Greek Slave," *New York Times*, November 14, 1913. Powers moved to Florence at the age of thirty-two, and lived there the remainder of his life.

3. The Friends of the Vermont Statehouse, "Politically Incorrect?" *Proceedings*, Spring 2005, p. 1, http://www.vtstatehouse.org/2005-02.pdf (accessed December 10, 2005).

4. Daniel Martin Reynolds, "Hiram Powers and His Ideal Sculpture" (PhD diss., Columbia University, 1975), pp. 137–38, quoting correspondence from Hiram Powers to Colonel John Preston, January 7, 1841. In the final execution, Powers changed the design slightly: the young woman is unadorned, and the cross symbolizing Christianity hangs from the post to which she is shackled, along with a locket symbolizing love and fidelity.

5. Mark Bushnell, "The Nude Slave Created a Stir from the Start," *Rutland Times-Argus*, January 9, 2005.

6. George MacAdam, "Diana Looks at a Changed World," *New York Times Sunday Magazine*, April 26, 1925, p. SM8. It is worth pointing out that the article, which details the history of nudity in New York statuary, is also accompanied by photographs of several nude female statues (including *The Greek Slave*).

7. See Portraits of the Presidents, "James K. Polk," National Portrait Gallery, n.d., http://www.npg.si.edu/exh/travpres/polks.htm (accessed December 11, 2005).

8. Bushnell, "The Nude Slave Created a Stir from the Start."

9. Robert Hughes, *American Visions: The Epic History of Art in America* (New York: Alfred A. Knopf, 1997), p. 218.

10. Wilson Ring, "Sculptor Celebrated with Bicentennial," *Burlington Free Press*, July 29, 2005.

11. Sarah Booth Conroy, "A Scandalous Precedent," *Washington Post*, June 18, 1989.

12. See the Great Exhibition of the Industry of All Nations, 1851, "The Displays," Kenneth Spencer Research Library, University of Kansas, n.d., http://spencer.lib.ku.edu/exhibits/greatexhibition/displays.htm (accessed December 11, 2005).

13. Conroy, "A Scandalous Precedent."

14. Marvin D. Schwartz, "Antiques: Spiritual Nudes in the Parlor," *New York Times*, March 23, 1968.

15. David Hewett, "A Major Pottery Tempest the Museum's Parian Teapot," *Maine Antiques Digest*, June 1998. "Parian" was the brand name given to the bisque by Minton, another English pottery company. See Schwartz, "Antiques: Spiritual Nudes in the Parlor."

16. Schwartz, "Antiques: Spiritual Nudes in the Parlor." Schwartz identifies the Bennington company as the "American Pottery Company," but that was a successor

company established in Peoria, Illinois, by the founder of the United States Pottery Company, Charles W. Fenton. See "Pottery Worth Having in Peoria," *Antiques and the Arts*, February 10, 2004, http://www.antiquesandthearts.com/GH-2004-02-10-14-27 -07p1.htm (accessed December 11, 2005).

17. The Friends of the Vermont Statehouse, "Gaslight!" *Proceedings*, Fall 2004, pp. 1, 4, http://www.vtstatehouse.org/2004-09.pdf (accessed December 11, 2005).

18. Wilson Ring, "Nude Statue to Be Shelved in Vt. Legislative Session," Boston .com, December 12, 2004, http://www.boston.com/news/local/vermont/articles/2004/12/ 12/nude_statue_to_be_shelved_in_vt_legislative_session/ (accessed December 13, 2004).

19. Chris Bohjalina, "Face It: Great Statues Like to Be Naked," *Burlington Free Press*, December 26, 2004.

20. Wilson Ring, "Group Rallies to Save 'The Greek Slave,'" *Burlington Free Press*, December 14, 2004.

21. Ibid. The "Constitution" to which Billings was referring is not the US Constitution, which *does not* explicitly outlaw slavery but instead the Vermont Constitution, which does do so. Adopted in 1777, the Vermont Constitution was the first to flatly declare that "all persons are born equally free and independent" and that no person "born in this country, or brought from over sea," should be legally required "to serve any person as a servant, slave or apprentice." See Vermont Constitution, Chapter 1, Article 1.

22. Richard Leiby, "In Vermont, Statue May Be More Than Governor Can Bare," *Washington Post*, December 19, 2004.

23. Wilson Ring, "Douglas Insists He Doesn't Object to Nude, but It Must Go," Boston.com, December 15, 2004, http://www.boston.com/news/local/vermont/articles/ 2004/12/15/douglas_insists_he_doesnt_object_to_nude_but_it_must_go/ (accessed December 15, 2004).

24. The Friends of the Vermont Statehouse, "Politically Incorrect?"

25. Matt Stearns and Charles Homans, "Social Conservatives Turn Out in Force to Fuel Bush, GOP Victories," Knight Ridder Washington Bureau, November 3, 2004.

26. Arnold Hamilton, "Focus on Moral Values Drove Bush's Victory," *Dallas Morning News*, November 3, 2004.

27. Rob Boston, "The Religious Right and Election 2004: Religious Right Leaders Exaggerate Their Role at the Polls in a Bid to Win More Power in Washington, D.C.," *Church & State*, December 1, 2004.

28. Dan Rather and Bill Plante, "Religious Right Expects Payback," *CBS Evening News*, November 4, 2004.

29. Boston, "The Religious Right and Election 2004."

30. Rather and Plante, "Religious Right Expects Payback."

31. Boston, "Faith-Based Frenzy: Religious Right Wish List for Congress Includes Church Funding, Court Stripping, a Federal Marriage Amendment and More," *Church & State*, January 1, 2005.

32. James G. Lakely, "President Outlines Role of His Faith," *Washington Times*, January 12, 2005.

33. President George W. Bush, Inaugural Speech, January 20, 2005, http:// www.whitehouse.gov/inaugural/ (accessed December 15, 2005).

34. Bill Sammon, "Prayer Starts Bush's Second Term," *Washington Times*, January 22, 2005.

35. Rob Boston, "Power Play," *Church & State*, January 1, 2005.

36. Russell Shorto, "What's Their Real Problem with Gay Marriage? (It's the Gay Part)," *New York Times*, June 19, 2005.

37. Senator Bill Frist (R-TN), news conference, Washington Transcript Service, January 24, 2005.

38. Elmer Smith, "Religious Right Gets a Dose of Reality," *Philadelphia Daily News*, January 27, 2005.

39. Matthew Cooper, "What Does Bush Owe the Religious Right?" *Time*, February 7, 2005.

40. Ibid.

41. Press release, "The Rolling Stones to Perform during Sprint Super Bowl XL Halftime Show on ABC," Superbowl.com, November 29, 2005, http://www.superbowl.com/features/entertainment/rollingstones (accessed December 12, 2005).

42. Kenneth Wright, "Beatles or Stones? Choose Both," Scotsman.com, February 10, 2004, http://news.scotsman.com/topics.cfm?tid=983&id=159452004 (accessed December 12, 2005).

43. Remigio G. Lacsamana, "Universal Health Care Is Ideal, but Presents Practical Problems," *Daytona Beach News-Journal Online*, December 8, 2005, http://www.news-journalonline.com/NewsJournalOnline/Opinion/Editorials/03OpOPN36120805.htm (accessed December 15, 2005).

44. President John F. Kennedy, Special Message to the Congress on Urgent National Needs, delivered in person before a Joint Session of Congress, May 25, 1961. See John F. Kennedy Library and Museum, http://www.jfklibrary.org/j052561.htm (accessed December 15, 2005).

45. Duke University professor Alex Roland described President Bush's announcement as a classic "Kennedy gambit," routinely practiced by Republican presidents running for reelection. Interestingly, President Bush's father, George H. W. Bush, also called for a manned Mars mission. Press release, "News Tip: Congress Should Regard Bush's Mars Proposal as Political Ploy, Duke Professor Says," January 10, 2004, http://www.dukenews.duke.edu/2004/01/congress_0104.html (accessed December 15, 2005).

46. Kym Reinstadler, "Teachers Urged to Make Science, Math Interesting," *Grand Rapids Press*, December 15, 2005.

47. Charles J. Murray, "America's High-Tech Quandary," *Design News*, December 5, 2005.

48. Lisa Snell, "U.S. Students Flunk Math Again," *School Reform News*, February 1, 2005.

49. "2005 Cable TV Facts," OneTVWorld.com, http://www.onetvworld.org/?module=displaysection&section_id=209&format=html (accessed December 15, 2005).

50. Jube Shiver Jr., "Televangelists on Unusual Side in Indecency Debate," *Los Angeles Times*, November 29, 2005.

51. L. Brent Bozell III, "Viewers Want End to 'Slime,'" *USA Today*, April 28, 2005.

52. Gretchen Gallen, "Kevin Martin Picked to Helm FCC," *Xbiz.com*, March 17, 2005, http://xbiz.com/news_piece.php?id=7955 (accessed May 16, 2005).

53. Andrew Wallenstein, "Family-Friendly Package Vexes Cable Biz," *Hollywood Reporter*, December 18, 2005.

54. "Time Warner Cable Announces Family Tier," Associated Press, December 15, 2005.

55. Concerned Women for America, press release, "CWA: Stevens' Indecency Hearings—A Bridge to Hollywood at Public Expense," December 13, 2005.

56. Frank Rich, "The Year of Living Indecently," *New York Times*, February 6, 2005.

57. Jerry Falwell, *The Situation with Tucker Carlson*, MSNBC, August 5, 2005, http://www.msnbc.msn.com/id/8870977/ (accessed December 15, 2005).

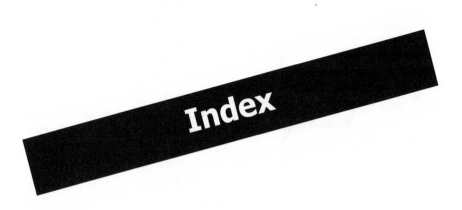

Index

Page numbers followed by * denote pictures.